To my good friend
Arthur, the great. I. Tocain.

Advance Praise for
Lessons From Fallen Civilizations

"In reading Larry Kelley's book, I have found new hope that my country will be liberated and the Persian people freed from the foreign tyranny of Islam."

Roya Teimouri
Human Rights Activist

"In Lessons From Fallen Civilizations Larry Kelley reminds us how important history is in informing and instructing the future. As the book suggests, history is written by the winners. To this point, though it has lost battles, Western Civilization has been winning the war. That may change. As Kelley documents, loss will be catastrophic. That said, Kelley is no defeatist. The book is solidly written, rich in useful detail, and a must read for those who want to keep the writing of history in our hands."

Jack Cashill
Best-selling author of *Deconstructing Obama*

"Western CIV 101 before the imams of political correctness took over our campuses. Larry Kelley's Lessons from Fallen Civilizations is a sweeping tour de force that reminds us that civilization as we know it is a fragile miracle that modern day barbarians could easily sweep away with the help of a complacent polity if we fail to protect and defend it."

Kenneth R. Timmerman
Best-selling author of *Countdown to Crisis: the Coming Nuclear Showdown with Iran*

"In developing his unique list of immutable principles that govern the fall of great Western Civilizations, Kelley makes a compelling contribution in the effort to reverse America's decline. His prescriptions for countering the Islamic threat generally and the Iranian theocracy specifically are dead on. If I were elected President next November, I would order each of my cabinet secretaries to read Lessons From Fallen Civilizations by inauguration day."

Jerome Corsi
Best-selling coauthor of *Unfit for Command*

"The West is at a crossroads. If you want to really understand how other cultures fell, why the United States is at a precipice, who the real threat is to our survival, and what we must do to avoid the fates of Greece, Carthage, and Rome, listen very closely to what Larry Kelley is telling you in Lessons From Fallen Civilizations. Our Founders understood well these messages from history—so should we."

Chris Field
Executive Editor, *The Blaze Magazine*

"America was forged from a different model of government, endowing the individual with personal freedoms and responsibilities. But Americans have failed to pay attention to those immutable laws that either allow nations to thrive or cause empires to crumble. America is under attack, incredibly subject to the same forces and philosophies that have led to the collapse of other once great cultures. Will America survive? Larry Kelley compellingly shows us that history is repeating itself. This time America is in the cross hairs and if we don't act fast, we'll lose."

Sue Farley
Best-selling author of *Trust Are You Kidding?:*
Pitfalls of the Current Trust System Exposed

LESSONS
FROM
FALLEN CIVILIZATIONS
Can a Bankrupt America Survive the Current Islamic Threat?

by
LARRY KELLEY

Hugo House

DISCLAIMER
The purpose of this book is to educate. The author and/or publisher do not guarantee that anyone following these techniques, suggestions, tips, ideas, or strategies will engender success. The author and/or publisher shall have neither liability nor responsibility to anyone with respect to any loss or damage caused, or alleged to be caused, directly or indirectly by the information contained in this book.

Publisher's Cataloging-in-Publication Data

Kelley, Larry.
    Lessons from fallen civilizations : can a bankrupt America survive the current Islamic threat? / Larry Kelley.
        p. cm.
    ISBN: 978-1-936449-09-5
    1. World history. 2. Civilization, Ancient—History.
    3. Terrorism—Religious aspects—Islam. 4. Comparative civilization.   I. Title.
CB251 .K371 2011
909—dc22

                                                                    2011936447

Library of Congress Control Number: 2011936447

ISBN: 978-1-936449-09-5 (hardcover)
        978-1-936449-13-2 (softcover)

Excerpts from *Horse Soldier* Reprinted by permission of International Creative Management, Inc. Copyright © [2012] by {Doug Stanton}

Hugo House Publishers, Ltd.
Englewood, Colorado
Austin, Texas
(877) 700-0616
www.HugoHousePublishers.com

Dedication

To my beloved wife and sons

and

The women of Islam,
murdered by their own relations,
deposited in unmarked graves,
that they be welcomed as saints
by the one true loving God.

Table of Contents

Part Three: Resurgent Militant Islam   259

PREFACE

Like many Americans, I presume, I took the 9/11 attacks personally. Watching fellow American men and women leap from those 100-story burning buildings caused me to begin a decade-long journey to find out why Muslims attacked us and what the underpinnings of their rage were. More specifically, I wanted to find out if, and how, they might destroy us. Ever since then, I have been researching and writing articles on this topic for *Human Events, Townhall Magazine,* and my website (www.larrykelley.com).

In writing this book, I attempt to discover causation in history, more specifically, the subset of causes which contribute to the fall of great civilizations. In that endeavor I emphasize original sources including two men who are credited with having invented the craft of history writing, Herodotus and Thucydides.

Herodotus (484 BC to 20 BC)

Considered in the West to be the father of history, he was a Greek speaker from Ionia, located on today's West Coast of Turkey. One of his primary motives for writing his *Histories* was to record for posterity the events of the Persian Wars, that had begun roughly 40 years before, so that the kleos (Greek word for great deeds) of the men who fought in the wars would not be lost. Herodotus was unique—a first—because he recorded what eye witnesses told him about the events surrounding the Persian invasions of 490 BC and 480 BC. And he also attempted to *explain the causes* of those events. This was utterly new.

What made Herodotus unique to human history writing was that he specifically sought to understand *how* the great war got started, what the spark was that touched it off, and most important to us, the inheritors of Western Civilization, how it was that such a vastly smaller army and navy of Greeks could defeat such an enormously larger Persian empire. He was the first writer in human history to systematically try to discover *why* events occurred. He began a literary tradition of Greek writers who focused on the epic quality of history writing where important events revealed larger human themes, a tradition in which I'm a participant.

Ominously, Herodotus also concluded that, after traveling throughout the Aegean and the Eastern Mediterranean and interviewing vast numbers of eye witnesses, there was an inevitability to war between the East and West. There seemed to him, based on his research, to be a fundamental animus between the cultures. Most important for our time, he also saw that the Greek army won because it was guided by a culture of free men, composed of soldiers who fought for their possessions, their homes, farms, and families. Whereas, the soldiers of the Persians were essentially slaves and fought for nothing.

The body of his work is titled *Histories,* which in ancient Greek meant inquiries. Although we get our word, history, from him, there was no such word in the ancient Greek when Herodotus was alive.

And so I confess to you that it was with this Herodotus-like posture of humility that I embarked on this voyage not knowing all that I would discover.

Thucydides (455 BC to 401 BC)

Thucydides was a contemporary of Herodotus even though he was born a generation later. In the mid-fifth century, the city of Olympia hosted the Panhellenic festivals that we now refer to as the ancient Olympics. These festivals included games such as: chariot races, boxing, and foot races; and also religious rites, theater, and readings of poetry. There were no publishing houses in fifth-century Athens. Herodotus' work was performed, that is read aloud, in small theaters both in the Agora of Athens and at Olympia during the Panhellenic festival and games. It was at Olympia that the boy, Thucydides, was first introduced to Herodotus. It was recorded that he wept when listening to the master read portions of the new literary art form which he called *Histories*.

Thucydides' life work is his account of the great Greek civil war that we today refer to as the Peloponnesian War. Although both historians sought out eyewitnesses to battles and tried to record actual events, Herodotus took license and added mythic flourishes. Thucydides' work is much more sober and, in his view, scientific. Born into a family of means, he was educated by professional sophists and was clearly influenced by Herodotus and by the intellectual explosion that was occurring in *hyper* democratic mid-fifth-century Athens.

Another man who clearly influenced Thucydides was Hippocrates, the founder of modern medicine; a man who founded a discipline where he and his followers observed the course of various diseases and worked out prognoses based on previous studies. Thucydides uses the Hippocratic model to describe a sickness, perhaps better stated, a pathology, in the body politic of Athens that led them to abandon their ideals and to commit atrocities. His record of the Peloponnesian war combines elements of a warning, or better stated, a diagnosis.

In short, what he accomplished was awe inspiring because only one man in Western Civilization had ever considered writing about the *causes* of history, his contemporary Herodotus. Thucydides took that idea and expanded it into the exploration of how human traits govern the laws of history, how they generate recognizable patterns in societal behavior. Considered one of the greatest writers and thinkers of all time, Thucydides moved the approach to history writing immeasurably past the new ground broken by his elder and quite literally invented modern and, he would say, scientific historiography.

His book records twenty years of the Peloponnesian War which lasted from 431 BC to 404 BC. Thucydides believed the war would be the greatest in the long warlike history of the Greek-speaking world. He sought to record the actual events that he actively participated in as an Athenian general, and to teach his readers how huge events demonstrate *fundamental patterns of history*. In some sense, he saw his purpose as issuing a warning. As the ancient alarmist, he judged that the war would be cataclysmic for the Greeks. He died before the end of the war and will be remembered as the first in human history to conclude that future events and patterns of events were bound to repeat, based on the essential nature of men. Thucydides wrote:

> *"It will be enough for me if these words of mine will be judged useful by those who want to understand clearly the events which happened in the past, human nature being what it is, and will at some time and in much the same way, be repeated in the future."* [1]

Some modern historians believe that what he accomplished is still unrivaled, as he combined elements of objective history writing, literature, and tragedy as well as explored the collective human psyche. His life's work was far more than recording events of the great Greek civil war. It was his herculean attempt to isolate and understand the lessons of human history while he also incorporated the most compelling art form of his day, the Greek tragedy. In his history, he portrayed his native Athens as a tragic hero, possessed of both greatness and yet fatal flaws.

Because he also endeavored to make history writing a scientific discipline, Thucydides held that the more closely he observed an event, the more accurate would be his understanding of it. He eschewed the notion that morality played a role in dictating the result of human events or in determining which side would win out in a conflict. Instead he saw, for example, that states will generally opt for self-interest over morality, an observation clearly echoed, some might say stolen, by Winston Churchill 2500 years later when he coined the aphorism, "Countries don't have friends, they have interests."

---

1. Thucydides, *The Peloponnesian War*, trans. Elizabeth Vandiver of Maryland University.

While Thucydides observed and recorded the prosecution of the civil war that would ultimately destroy the Greek Polis, a small sampling of the many societal principles that Thucydides isolated and described for the ages are:

- Weakness invites the domination of the stronger
- Power always seeks to increase itself
- Necessity is the engine of history

Thucydidean Essays and the Great Man Theory

This book is highly influenced by Thucydides in the sense that I operate as a student in the school of the man who, while recording the catastrophic events of the Peloponnesian war, was the first to see that the great war demonstrated patterns of events that future civilizations would repeat based on the laws of human nature.

However, I will concede that there is clearly a symbiosis between great men and the currents of their age. Some historians subscribe to the notion that history is strictly determined by great leaders. Instead, I subscribe to Thucydides' view—that patterns repeat because human nature does not change greatly over time. Great men and women understand and make use of their instinctual knowledge of human nature and the immutable laws of history. Therefore, I believe, what transcends great men century after century, are the patterns of human behavior that Thucydides was amazingly able to see and describe in the mid-fifth century BC.

This book was written to demonstrate that Thucydides was correct in his view that patterns of events are bound to repeat, that they create immutable laws of civilization, due to the nature of men. It was my focus to isolate the subset of those patterns of behavior, those "immutables" that presage the fall of civilizations. Paying homage to Thucydides, Herodotus, as well as some great modern historians like Victor Davis Hanson and Bernard Lewis, I sought to isolate these repeating patterns, from one civilization to the next, one millennium to the next. I looked to isolate, metaphorically as a biologist might dissect the body of a diseased organism, immutable laws that lead repeatedly, time and again, to *civilizational* decline and failure—laws that superimpose themselves on all time and all peoples.

Lessons From Fallen Civilizations

This work, that some may categorize as comparative history, is the product of nearly a decade worth of research. It begins with the Battle of Marathon and ends with the current Middle East Upheaval of 2011.

TIMELINE

PART ONE: Ancient Threats to Western Civilization

The Fall of the Greek Polis
490 BC   The Battle of Marathon
480 BC   The Persian Army crosses the Hellespont into Europe
           The Battle of Thermopylae
           The Battle of Salamis
479 BC   The Greeks destroy Persia's remaining land army
431 BC   The Peloponnesian War begins
430 BC   The Plague of Athens begins
414 BC   The Athenians are defeated in Sicily
413 BC   Sparta makes an alliance with Persia
405 BC   Athens surrenders to the Spartan Alliance
346 BC   Philip II negotiates the Peace of Philocrates
343 BC   Macedon defeats Ancient Greece at Chaeronea

The Fall of Carthage
First Punic War
264 BC   First Punic War (with Rome) begins
256 BC   Rome wins its very first naval battle (off Mylae)
241 BC   Carthage suffers destruction of its fleet and surrenders
238 BC   Rome seizes Corsica and Sardinia

Second Punic War
219 BC   Hannibal begins his march from Spain
218 BC   Hannibal emerges on the Italian side of the Alps
           Hannibal defeats Scipio the Elder at Trebia
217 BC   Hannibal defeats Flaminius at Lake Trasimene
216 BC   Hannibal defeats Paulus and Varro at Cannae
211 BC   Scipio the Younger captures Cartagena, Spain

205 BC Scipio returns to Rome and is elected Consul

Sicily is brought under complete Roman control

204 BC Scipio invades Africa

202 BC Scipio defeats Hannibal at Zama—Carthage surrenders

End of Second Punic War

197 BC Romans defeat Macedon and cede all Greek Mainland

182 BC Hannibal dies by his own hand in Bithynia

Third Punic War

149 BC Rome declares war

146 BC Carthage is destroyed

The Fall of Rome (in the West)

AD 377 Rome allows Fritigern's Goths to cross the Danube River

AD 378 Valens is destroyed by the Goths at Adrianople

AD 383 Gratian (the last effective Emperor) is killed in civil war

AD 395 Theodosius dies and leaves a divided empire

AD 406 The Rhine freezes and thousands of Germans invade

AD 407 Alaric leads an army of Goths into Italy

AD 410 Alaric sacks Rome (first time in 800 years)

AD 451 Aetius commands German armies against the Huns at Chalons

AD 455 Gaiseric's vandals sack Rome

AD 476 Danubian Chieftain, Odoacer, deposes Boy Emperor

Romulus Augustulus

Roman Empire in the West disappears

PART TWO: The Rise of Islam

The Fall of the Christian Middle East

AD 570 The Prophet Muhammad is born

AD 623 Muhammad conducts his first successful raid

AD 630 Mecca falls to Muhammad's army

AD 635 Caesarea falls

AD 643 Egypt and Armenia fall

AD 647 Tunisia falls

AD 669 Constantinople is besieged

AD 711	Islamic conquest of Spain is complete
AD 717	Constantinople is besieged
AD 732	Charles Martel defeats Rahman at Poitiers
AD 840	Sicily falls to Islam
AD 840	Rome is besieged and Papal cemeteries are defiled
AD 1095	Pope Urban II commissions First Crusade
AD 1099	Crusaders capture Jerusalem
AD 1203	Genoese Crusader army sacks Constantinople
AD 1291	Tyre falls to Crusaders
	Rise of Ottomans
AD 1302	Osman, founder of the Ottomans, wins first battle against Byzantium
AD 1326	Osman's son, Orhan, captures Bursa and founds first Ottoman capital
AD 1338	All of Anatolia falls to Ottoman conquest
	Christian rule is expunged from Asia
AD 1453	Constantinople falls to Islam
	Official end of the Roman Empire

The Fall of the Ottomans

AD 1529	First Ottoman siege of Vienna fails
AD 1571	Ottoman Navy is totally destroyed at Lepanto
AD 1676	Sultan Mohammad IV appoints Mustafa Grand Vizier
AD 1683	Mustafa commands army of 500,000 and begins march on Vienna
	Jan III Sobieski defeats Mustafa at Vienna
AD 1684	Austria, Venice, Poland, Tuscany, Malta, Russia declare war on the Ottomans
AD 1689	Russia ejects Ottomans from the Port of Azov
AD 1699	Ottomans sign first peace treaty with Infidels at Carlowitz
AD 1774	Russia ejects Ottomans from the Crimea
AD 1882	Britain ejects Ottomans from Egypt
AD 1918	Ottoman Empire ends at close of World War I

PART THREE: Resurgent Militant Islam

The Rise of Modern Militant Islam

AD 1928   Sheikh Hassan al-Banna founds the Muslim Brotherhood

AD 1949   Al-Banna is assassinated in Egypt; Sayyid Qutb,
           al-Banna's heir apparent, publishes Social Justice in Islam

AD 1950   Qutb arrives in Egypt with plans to overthrow the regime
           and establish a new Caliphate

AD 1954   Nasser is almost assassinated by the Muslim Brothers,
           Qutb is imprisoned

AD 1962   Qutb's terrorist manifesto, *Milestones,* is published
           (Later, greatly influences Osama bin Laden)

AD 1966   Qutb put to death, martyred for Islam

AD 1973   Saudi Arabia funds North American Islamic Trust (NAIT)
           to acquire 300 mosques in the US

AD 1979   The Shah of Iran is deposed, Khomeini founds the first
           modern terrorist state

AD 1985   The Muslim Brotherhood founds International Institute
           of Islamic Thought (IIIT)

AD 1994   Council on American-Islamic Relations (CAIR) is founded

AD 2001   (April) Hamid Zakeri attempts to warn the CIA of coming attacks

AD 2001   (September) Nineteen Muslim terrorists kill almost
           3,000 Americans on American soil

AD 2001   (November) Allied forces expel al Qaeda and Taliban rule
           from Afghanistan

AD 2003   US Invasion of Iraq begins and topples the Hussein regime
           in six weeks

AD 2011   Congressional hearings held on American Muslim radicalization

INTRODUCTION

Immutable Laws That Govern Civilizations

> "On Sunday, October 31, 2004, virtually on the eve of the
> US presidential election, the Majlis, Iran's Parliament, met in Tehran.
> The bill before them would require the government to enrich uranium.
> The session was carried live on national radio. As the assembly
> voted unanimously to enrich uranium, the members of parliament
> took up the chant: Death to America . . . Death to Israel." [1]
>
> JEROME CORSI, *ATOMIC IRAN*

On September 12, 2001, like most Americans, I was riveted to the television networks' coverage of the 9/11 aftermath. It was a day like that of the JFK funeral. Normal programming on all the major networks was suspended and the coverage alternated among desultory shots of the collapsed Trade Center Towers at ground zero, Mayor Rudy Giuliani's press conferences, and fatuous man-on-the-street interviews. One extremely brief interview screamed at me, so much so that I was surprised that a major television network had failed to see the negative reflection upon its own relentless America-is-the-problem sophistry and allowed the damning footage to run.

This segment was a catalogue of various New Yorkers' responses to the attacks. It included a young male student from one of the city's most exclusive, private grammar schools, reserved for gifted children. Out of the mouth of this babe came an oracle for the ages, "Of course, before [the attacks] we all thought that the cops and the military were bad but then after [the attacks] we said—who's going to protect us?"

The genesis of this book comes out of that child's unguarded, uncensored remark and a single line from an essay by the military historian, Victor Davis Hanson. He wrote:

---

1. Jerome Corsi, *Atomic Iran* (Tennessee: WND Books, 2005), 19.

"War is not merely a material struggle, but more often a referendum on the spirit. No nation has ever survived once its citizenry ceased to believe its culture worth saving." [2]

Hanson is reflecting upon the Greeks' defeat at Chironea in 334 BC and their immediate and total capitulation to a far less advanced civilization of Macedon. That capitulation was for him a demonstration of an immutable law—No civilization (no matter how previously heroic), can long endure once its citizenry ceases to passionately believe in its culture and consequently ceases to defend it.

Over the intervening decade, in researching and writing this book, I've come to the conclusion that Hanson is correct—that he is issuing a fear-inspiring message for our times and for this civilization, one made abundantly clear by the unwitting statement from the gifted child from one of New York's privileged families the day after 9/11.

For me, it was an ominous epiphany which caused me to want to uncover the events, decisions, and underlying causes for the failures of past civilizations. First, I wanted to see if Hanson was right. Was it really the loss of love for their culture that caused the magnificent Greek civilization to fall? Second, as I studied other now extinct civilizations, was it a loss of love for one's culture, an immutable timeless factor in the death of many, most, or all failed civilizations? Third, were there other "immutables" and did they repeatedly contribute to the demise of once successful peoples? And fourth, what are the lessons inherent in those immutables, assuming they exist, for us, the citizens of an American civilization at its zenith, and yet at war with worldwide resurgent militant Islam and also embroiled in a period of extreme cultural polarization and a potential financial implosion?

The Saga of Western Civilization

It was not until two days after the attacks, on my drive to work, that I was stunned by a sudden realization—this is the initial phase of World War III. The enormity of the 9/11 events conveyed to me that massive battle lines had been drawn. And what had just begun was nothing less than a tectonic struggle, a fight to the death between barbarity and civilization, and between Islam and Judeo Christendom. Peaceful coexistence, it seemed, was now a dead issue. From this realization I pondered the fact that all great civilizations fail, remembering the immortal lines of Percy Bysse Shelley's "Ozymandias:" [3]

---

2.   Victor Davis Hanson, *War Will be War* (*National Review*, May 6, 2002), 36.

3.   P.B. Shelley, *Ozymandias*.

". . . Two vast and trunkless legs of stone
Stand in the desert . . .
. . . And on the pedestal these words appear:
'My name is Ozymandias, king of kings:
Look on my works, ye Mighty, and despair!'
Nothing beside remains. Round the decay
Of that colossal wreck, boundless and bare
The lone and level sands stretch far away."

If America, like all great civilizations, will one day fail, I began to consider: Might we forestall our eventual demise? Can we assume that we will prevail yet again militarily as we have done in our defining wars against the British, the Axis Powers, and the Soviet Union? Can this country avoid pitfalls that have destroyed all other great civilizations of the past?

On my drive to work a couple days after 9/11, I decided to study a number of now deceased civilizations that were once resident in Europe and the Mediterranean. I wanted to find out what happened as they fell and what the failed policies were that led to their destruction.

> *Newsweek* Magazine Cover
> *December 7, 2009*
> **HOW GREAT POWERS FAIL**
> Steep Debt, Slow Growth,
> and High Spending Kill Empires—
> and America Could Be Next

From that research, as did Thucydides, I began to see repeating patterns of failure in the fall of great civilizations. I produced a list of ten Immutable Laws—laws which govern great civilizations, laws that, when violated, serve to undermine a civilization's ability to repel outside threats and cause it to wither in the face of crises.

Lessons from Fallen Civilizations spans the life of Western Civilization, beginning with its infancy at the Battle of Marathon in 490 BC to the present war, with what I refer to as Resurgent Militant Islam.

In his account of the Peloponnesian War, Thucydides portrayed his home city, Athens, as a tragic hero, possessed of greatness yet tragic flaws. Similarly, Western Civilization is the main character of this work. The story will at times pause at various desperate moments and dramatize, in what I call historic fiction, the epic battles of Marathon, Salamis, Cannae, Poitiers, and Vienna, where the life of Western Civilization is very much in doubt.

The aim of this book is to encourage the reader to consider our good fortune, to marvel that Western Civilization has survived, and to understand that we are its beneficiaries. At the same time, it is written to warn that all that we hold dear can be lost. The benefits bestowed upon us by the survival of Western Christendom have been won by the enormous skill, blood, and treasure of our forbearers. Moreover, as Ronald Reagan warned, "Freedom is never more than one generation away from extinction."

This book exposes, in dramatic detail, moments in time—the battles at Poitiers in AD 632 and at Vienna in 1683, when Islam nearly conquered the West. It makes clear that it is not enough to simply understand the general ways that civilizations fail. It outlines what we must know specifically about Islamic culture, which, for fourteen centuries, has always sought to subjugate Western Christendom. It makes the case that our time to act decisively is short because major elements within Islam are once again gathering strength and bristling for war.

Note to the Reader

In researching this book, I discovered incontrovertible laws that, when violated or ignored, serve to undermine even the most robust civilizations. I found that their properties repeat in the fall of great civilizations and repeat in varying degrees to shape our present.

They are timeless.

Each of the ten immutables are listed with brief examples to demonstrate how these principles govern the survival of great civilizations, first in the distant past and then in the present. Throughout the rest of the book, the immutable that applies will be listed.

Immutable Law #1
No nation has ever survived once its citizenry
ceased to believe its culture worth saving.
(Hanson's Law)[4]

In Professor Hanson's essay, *War Will Be War*, which became the genesis for this book and was the inspiration for this immutable law, he wrote:

> *"Themistocles' Athens beat back hundreds of thousands of Persians; yet little more than a century later Demosthenes addressed an Athens that had become far wealthier—and could not marshal a far larger population to repulse a few thousand Macedonians."*

The professor goes on to allude that the allied armies of less than thirty Greek city-states defeated the Persian Empire, repelling an army ten times their size in 479 BC. Yet one hundred forty years later, after losing only one battle to Philip II of Macedon at Chaeronea, in 338 BC, the same Greek city-states ceded their magnificently innovative culture and its associated freedoms to their new Macedonian overlords. In so doing, the Greeks remained a subjugated people for the next 2,400 years.

In October 2001, American Special Forces troops, mounted on horseback during a pitched battle with the Taliban in Northern Afghanistan, reported seeing enemy fighters running toward them with their hands in the air and, in the next instant, falling forward dead in the dirt. They were native Afghan men who had been shot in the back by their foreign Taliban commanders from Pakistan, Chechnya, and Saudi Arabia. The Taliban had conscripted the Afghans with the threat they would kill their families if they did not join the army. The Afghan farmers, shopkeepers, and teachers who had once welcomed the Taliban as their liberators from the Russians now dreaded them.

---

4.   I also reference this immutable as "Hanson's Law."

Immutable Law #2
In battle, free men almost always defeat slaves.
(Herodotus' Law)

In 450 BC, Herodotus completed his *Histories* of the great war between the Greeks and Persians. (It is from his work that we know the details surrounding the battle of Thermopylae popularized in the film, *500*). Herodotus, considered the first Western historian, attempted to understand how an army and navy of only one hundred thousand Greeks were able to defeat an invading army of one million men.

Herodotus tells us that Pythius, a Greek-speaking subject of the Persian Empire, received an audience with the king. He explained that he had five sons and had sent four of them into the Persian army that was on its way to Greece. Pythius then presented his youngest son to Xerxes and asked if he could keep him. He begged the king to spare his youngest boy from service in the campaign. In a rage, Xerxes had the boy cut in two and each half of the body dumped on either side of the road so that it would send a message to the army as they marched past.

Herodotus spent many years wandering the Mediterranean and recording interviews with soldiers who had fought in the war or who were eye witnesses. He determined why the Greeks defeated the vastly larger army of Persians who were forced to fight and were treated like slaves. The Greeks won the great war because they were free men.

—⁂—

In 2003, some months after the fall of Baghdad, Paul Bremer, the US interim governor of Iraq, wrote an op-ed for the *Wall Street Journal.* He stated that Saddam Hussein's army collapsed in a mater of weeks because his Sunni-dominated regime commanded an army of mostly Shiite conscripts who, seeing the US forces moving toward them, deserted and went home. The Shiites, along with the Kurds, comprised the vast majority in Iraq, and hated the ruling Sunni Baathist regime. Once they believed that the US was finally about to liberate their country, they saw no reason to fight and die for their slave masters who lived in gaudy and heavily armed palaces.

Saddam Hussein's army, when confronted with the Western forces, stripped off their uniforms and ran away. They too were slaves and were unwilling to fight for the butcher of Baghdad.

Immutable Law #3
*Appeasement of a ruthless outside power
always invites aggression.
Treaties made with ruthless despots are
always fruitless and dangerous.*[5]

Prior to the ultimate conquest of the Greek mainland in 338, Greek allies, Thebes and Athens, negotiated the Peace of Philocrates with Philip II of Macedon. This gave him their acquiescence to the capture and enslavement of two small Greek city-states which stood in the way of his invading armies.

The principle wrapped inside the Athenians' Peace of Philocrates has an immutability and colossal significance that cannot be overstated for twenty-first century West. The attempt by a civilization at appeasement of a ruthless enemy committed to its conquest will accomplish the opposite of the appeaser's wishes. It will *always* invite attack. Further, the attempt at appeasement will signal that the time to strike is *now*.

—⚬—

For Athens and its allies, to allow Macedon to absorb two small buffer states without so much as a diplomatic protest was tantamount to Neville Chamberlain's letter to Adolf Hitler. It forfeited the Western Allies' alliance with Czechoslovakia and freed Hitler to absorb a nearly defenseless neighbor without retaliation.

It was tantamount to Bill Clinton's transfer of nuclear weapons technology to China, tantamount to Jimmy Carter and Madeline Albright's gift of uranium-fueled power plants to North Korea.

All are examples of the principle of appeasement, a civilization-threatening tactic.

---

5. This immutable contains a strong corollary to a Thucydides' dictum—Weakness invites domination by the stronger.

Immutable Law #4
If a people cannot avoid continuous internal warfare,
they will have a new order imposed from without.

As the fifth century wore on, leading to the final disappearance of Roman governance in Western Europe, Roman armies continued their long suffering tradition of proclaiming their generals Emperor. While vast portions of Europe and North Africa were being overrun by Germanic invaders, Roman armies continued to fight civil wars headed by challengers to the throne, "usurpers" who would be Emperor. By contrast, the Greek speaking Roman Empire of the East, based in Constantinople, enjoyed an orderly succession of Emperors and managed to survive for nearly a millennium longer than did the West.

—⁂—

Soon after President Obama was inaugurated, while the US was conducting conventional war in two theaters, Iraq and Afghanistan, and countless other clashes by American clandestine services, he directed his Attorney General to open criminal investigations against members of the previous administration. These investigations were aimed at senior officials within the Bush (GW) administration who had been tasked with drawing up the guidelines for the interrogation of captured terrorists. The launch of these investigations did not result in actual civil war. Yet it was unprecedented for an American president to signal, during wartime, that he was prepared to criminalize his domestic political enemies and at the same time offer up a propaganda bonanza to the country's real enemy, resurgent militant Islam.

Immutable Law #5
When a free people, through taxation, is deprived of its ability to acquire wealth and property, collapse is presaged.

Crushing taxation imposed upon the middle and lower class Romans contributed to the loss of the Roman provinces of Gaul, Iberia, and North Africa to the German invaders of the fifth century. In the second and first century BC, the Roman Empire had a great expansion when its armies ultimately gained control of lands from Southern Scotland to the Euphrates River. Each spring, at the beginning of the campaigning season, Roman farmers and merchants patriotically sent their sons to serve in the legions. Most of the soldiers' fathers were men of modest means and loyal citizens, who could pay their taxes with the produce of as few as two days a month.

By the fourth century AD the beleaguered ordinary citizen was ruined by his tax burden, forced to give up most of his produce to the state. Loyalty to the government, composed of wealthy bureaucrats who resided in distant Rome, disappeared. Roman provincials sided with the local German warlord as a method to escape the Roman tax collector.

Today, one in seven Americans is unable to adequately feed his family and is forced to collect food stamps. Due to burdensome regulations and taxation, more and more American private enterprises, from shoe manufacturers to technology call centers, continue to move their operations out of the United States. This has made it more and more difficult for US citizens to find gainful employment within the borders of the world's lone superpower. As it was in the last days of the Western Roman Empire, wealthy bureaucrats are provided risk-free cushy employment and lavish retirements by out-of-work citizens who are losing their homes to foreclosure. If this situation is allowed to persist, patriotism and a willingness to defend the country will surely be replaced by a wide-spread *refusal to defend* the central government.

Immutable Law #6

To hold territory, a state must be populated by those loyal to the central authority. When immigration overwhelms assimilation, the fall is predicted.

In the summer of 376 AD, the Roman Emperor, Valens, agreed to allow a very large tribe of Goths to settle in Thrace. He could not have imagined that this decision would set in motion events which led to the Empire's total defeat at Adrianople and, ultimately, the sack of Rome. It was in Thrace, an Eastern province, where the Goths first settled. After they migrated into Italy and sacked Rome, it was the West that granted this very same band of brigands a homeland in southern Gaul, proving to the barbarian world that rebellion would be rewarded.

In the East, the disastrous policy of settling whole tribes inside imperial borders was abandoned. Moreover, the East never lost its devotion to the realm. The citizens of Constantinople proudly proclaimed themselves Romans until the last day of their empire in 1453. During the second, third, and fourth decades of the fifth century the West continued to admit vast numbers of Germans into the Western Empire under the terms of formal treaties, while they fecklessly allowed Roman localities to be plundered and, ultimately, subjugated by these same new arrivals. Consequently, in large swaths of the West, Romanization and a commensurate loyalty to the central government continued to disintegrate. The result was that often whole Western regiments failed to report for battle while others even defected to the German side.

—⁂—

Today, all across Europe, in Britain, Sweden, the Netherlands, Belgium, and France, there are huge numbers of "no go" zones (over 180 in France alone). These zones are inhabited by unassimilated Muslims where the police will not enter; where sharia courts, not Euro common law, are increasingly the legal authority; and where home-grown terrorists are cultivated and attacks are planned. In 2008, British Intelligence services were following two thousand potential terrorists, two hundred radical Islamic networks, and thirty active terrorist plots.[6]

---

6. *Britain Monitoring 30 Terror Plots*, (*The Australian* (blog) April 13, 2008, http://www.theaustralian.com.au/news/world/m15-boss-reveals-30-terror-plots-against-britain/story-e6frg6so-1111112500593/.

Immutable Law #7
With the loss of fiscal solvency
comes a loss of sovereignty.

After the fall of the Roman Empire of the West in AD 476, the Emperor Justinian came to power in Constantinople, the capital of the still existent Roman Empire of the East. With the help of some able generals, Justinian was able to reclaim portions of North Africa and Italy previously lost to the Germanic invasions. His wars of early sixth century AD devastated the Eastern Roman population with crushing taxation. While Roman armies of the East reclaimed portions of the former Western Empire, they were unable to establish a tax base, and the core Greek-speaking population in Constantinople and Anatolia had no more to give. Justinian's hold on his reclaimed territories was tenuous and short lived. The Romans would never again be a dominant power, instead, a people in decline.

—*m*—

By 2011, under the new president, Barack Obama, the federal budget ballooned to $3.5 trillion dollars with projected revenues of only $2 trillion. Mid-year 2011, US creditors China and Japan began to signal that they had no more desire to invest in our debt. Moreover, American entitlements—Medicare, Medicaid, and Social Security were projected to be equal to the entire revenue collected from taxes. This meant that America would need to borrow or create $1.5 trillion in fiat money before it could pay one soldier's salary or fuel one fighter jet. Spring 2011, the midpoint of Obama's first term in office, polls indicated that 70% of Americans believed that the country was "headed in the wrong direction," a euphemism for decline.

That's right—seven in ten Americans believed that the country was in decline!

Immutable Law #8

Debasing the currency always destabilizes the governing authority.

During the late second century and early third centuries AD several Roman Emperors attempted to inflate the Empire's wealth. They recalled some of the outstanding gold coinage, secretly melted it down, and reissued it with leaden cores. In each case, this tactic was nearly catastrophic. The secret became instantly common knowledge among the Roman citizenry who reacted by refusing to accept the Empire's coinage in exchange for goods and services. This in turn meant that the Emperor could not pay or provision his own armies. Each time the Roman debasement was attempted, all bogus coinage was again recalled and reissued with the lead removed.

―∾―

Since the United States completely abandoned the gold standard in 1971, the buying power of the dollar has plunged by 96 percent. In 1971 an ounce of gold sold for $35. By 2011, an ounce of gold sells for $1,500. Instead of melting our coinage and adding lead, the US debased its currency by issuing trillions of new dollars.

During the Bush (GW) years, 2000-2008, the entire US economy grew in real terms from $10 trillion annually to $14 trillion. This increase was roughly the size of the entire economy of China. Yet, due to trillions of fiat spending and the wholesale debasement of the US economy during the post-Bush years, the International Monetary Fund predicted in 2011 that the size of the Chinese economy will eclipse that of the American economy by 2016.

Immutable Law #9
*When a civilization accepts the propaganda
of its enemy as truth, it has reached the far side
of appeasement and capitulation is nigh.*

In 340 BC the Athenian ambassadors to Macedon, who had negotiated the Peace of Philocrates, returned to Athens and addressed the Assembly. They extolled the virtues and peaceful intentions of the warlord to the north, King Philip II. "He has no intentions of conquering Athens and he will be an important ally in deterring Persia from returning to make war on the Greeks," they said. Only Demosthenes stood to warn the men of Athens that they would one day lose their freedom to Macedon.

Just two years later, in 338 BC at Chironea, twenty thousand Athenians and Thebans were killed by the pikes of the Macedonian phalanxes and by the cavalrymen led by Philip's son, the future Alexander the Great. With that appalling loss of life, all organized resistance to Philip on the Greek mainland of Attica ceased.

—⁜—

In the so-called "Arab Spring," revolutions overthrew Muslim dictators, with many of the newly liberated Muslims bristling for another war with Israel. In May 2011, coordinated attacks on Israel's northern border by Syria and Hezbollah were joined by calls from the new ruling elites in Egypt to bring the whole of the Arab world against Israel. With the chaos reining across the Middle East, the Iranian regime continued to vow to wipe Israel off the map, was emboldened, and gained influence across the region.

While the storm gathered around our only reliable ally in the Middle East, the President of the Free World took the side of the Muslims. They pretended to be outraged by Israel building some new houses in Jerusalem, its ancestral capital of twenty-five hundred years. He failed to observe that no other country in human history, continuously attacked by its surrounding enemies, could survive if it operated its capital city and foreign policy according to the dictates of those same enemies. The fact that our president made the case that Israel, one of America's most important allies, should do so, represented the far side of appeasement.

Immutable Law #10
Declining civilizations will always face superior firepower from ascending civilizations because sovereignty is only temporarily uncontested.

In the First Punic War, during the late 240s BC, the Carthaginians grew weary of the long war with Rome and made the decision to decommission much of their fleet and to release from their employ many of their mercenary sailors. This proved to be an extraordinarily ill-fated decision. They voluntarily ceded to Rome, their mortal enemy, naval superiority and mastery of the seas.

Although it would be another one hundred years before the fall of Carthage, over this period Rome continued to consolidate its naval superiority and mastery of the Western Mediterranean. This would prove decisive in preventing Hannibal from being reprovisioned and resupplied with new weaponry, especially siege equipment. The Carthaginians' decision to cede military control of the seas made them, a naval trading power, vulnerable to Rome. It was a fatefully bad decision which set in motion the events which led to a huge military advantage for Rome and to the ultimate destruction of Carthage.

—⁓—

By 2008, Barack Obama's election year, America had enjoyed air superiority since World War II, and it had been sixty years since a single American soldier had lost his life on the ground due to an attack from the air. During the Bush (GW) presidency, the country had proven that it could build a missile defense system capable of mind-boggling technological precision, capable of "hitting a speeding bullet with a bullet."

Obama stated numerous times during his campaign that he "would not weaponize space" and that he would not deploy a "costly unproven" missile defense system.

Incomprehensibly, in 2009, President Obama cancelled the F-22 Raptor jet fighter, an act which threatened Americans' air superiority. As the eminent military historian, Mark Helprin, apocalyptically put it, "Cancelling the F-22, the most capable fighter plane ever produced, is yet another act in the tragedy of a nation that, bankrupting itself, (is) losing its will to prevail." [7]

---

7.   Mark Helprin, *Why the Air Force Needs the F-22* (*Wall Street Journal*, February 22, 2010), A19.

In Summary—This Book is About Us

This book is a survey of comparative history which begins with the Battle of Marathon in 490 BC and covers the fall of the Greek polis, Carthage, Rome, the Christian Middle East, Byzantium, and the Ottoman Empires. It demonstrates how immutable laws govern the fall of great civilizations and how these can be seen to repeat over time and are at work now.

Above all, it is a story which chronicles some of the decisions, deeds, and heroics of our ancestors which contributed to our enormously successful culture. It draws attention to those decisions we must make and the actions we must take in order to remain a free people.

Western Civilization will be capitalized as it is the central character of this book.

PART ONE
Ancient Threats to Western Civilization

Immutable Laws
Governing the Fall of Civilizations

1   No nation has ever survived once its citizenry ceased to believe its culture worth saving. (Hanson's Law)

2   In battle, free men will almost always defeat slaves. (Herodotus' Law)

3   Appeasement of a ruthless outside power always invites its aggression. Treaties made with ruthless despots are always fruitless and dangerous.

4   If a people cannot avoid continuous internal warfare, it will have a new order imposed from without.

5   When a free people, through taxation, is deprived of its ability to acquire wealth and property, collapse is presaged.

6   To hold territory, a state must be populated by those loyal to the central authority. When immigration overwhelms assimilation, the fall is predicted.

7   With the loss of fiscal solvency comes a loss of sovereignty.

8   Debasing the currency always destabilizes the governing authority.

9   When a civilization accepts the propaganda of its enemy as truth, it has reached the far side of appeasement and capitulation is nigh.

10 Declining civilizations will always face superior firepower from ascending civilizations because sovereignty is only temporarily uncontested.

CHAPTER ONE

The Fall of the Greek Polis

323 BC

We do not emulate the customs of our neighbors;
no, rather than imitating anyone else,
it is more the case that we are an example for others to follow.[1]

PERICLES

As described in the Preface, Herodotus broke new ground as he was the first chronicler of events who attempted to understand causation in history. A generation after the great Persian War, he traveled the Mediterranean interviewing survivors. He attempted to find out how a collection of small, tremendously outnumbered Greek cities defeated the Persians, who had amassed the largest empire up to that point in human history. His conclusion is embodied in:

IMMUTABLE #2
In battle, free men will almost always defeat slaves.
(Herodotus' Law)

Six years before the defeat of the combined armies of Athens and Thebes by the armies of King Philip II and his son, the future Alexander the Great, the Athenians signed a treaty with the Macedonians called the Peace of Philocrates.

Most histories of Greece don't even mention this treaty. Its provisions and signatories remain somewhat obscure. The terms that are known resulted in the final defeat of Athens and Thebes, her only remaining Greek city-state ally, at the Battle of Chaeronea in 338 BC. This defeat resulted in the complete capitulation to Macedon

---

1.   His immortal funeral speech, recorded by Thucydides in the Peloponnesian War.

by the remaining independent city-states of the Greek mainland, the Peloponnesus and the Aegean islands. The treaty was the catalyst for the rapid subjugation of the Greek world centered around the independent polis, a world which, at its height, was composed of 1,500 city-states. That subjugation of the Greek homeland lasted until the conclusion of its war of independence against the Ottomans in 1820, over two millennia later.

History's Most Important Battle

One hundred fifty-two years before the Greeks lost their liberty to Macedon, on a September morning in 490 BC, the Athenians and their allies from the tiny city-state of Plataea changed human history. Many historians consider the battle of Marathon the most influential in human history because it marks the exact beginning of the ascendancy of the West over the East. Additionally, without that battle's outcome in favor of the Greeks, there may not have been a Western Civilization. To give clarity to the cataloguing of events and causes of a peoples' demise, it is useful to take a look at what first made that people flourish.

Because war accelerates history, what allowed the Athenians to lead the Greek world and become the founding fathers of Western Civilization can be attributed to and witnessed in their defeat of the Persian expeditionary force at Marathon. On that battle field, they proved the power of an idea—an idea that still shapes our world today—the strange notion that *the many should rule the few*. Ten thousand Athenians and Plataeans purchased the freedom of 1500 odd Greek-speaking city-states that

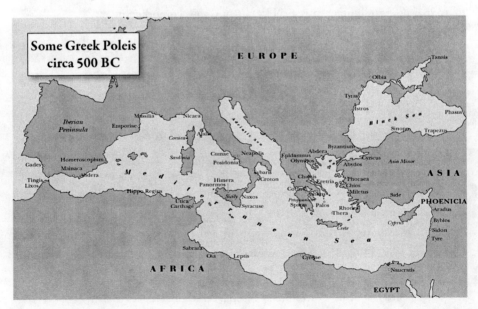

Some Greek Poleis circa 500 BC

were spread across the Mediterranean from Marseilles to the western coast of Turkey. The power and authority of Greek culture, that still drives Western institutions, was birthed on the plain of Marathon that September day in 490 BC.

A few days earlier, Miltiades, the commanding general of the Greek allies, through an undoubtedly brilliant piece of oratory, convinced the newly democratic Athenian assembly that they could defeat the Persians. Moreover, he asked them to leave a small force behind to defend the city and send the bulk of their soldiers to meet the Persians in the field.

Miltiades was an Athenian blue blood from a very wealthy family that, like most of the aristocratic elite, traced their lineage back to a Homeric mythic hero, in his case, to Achilles and ultimately to Hellas. Miltiades truly believed that he was descended from a god. Yet, he was an advocate, like his father, of the radical new idea—democracy. His family owned a large estate in northern Greece, in the province of Thrace, attached to the small city-state Cheronese. In addition to being a citizen of Athens due to his father's birth, his roots were also in Thrace on his mother's side of the family where they were the ruling barons of the Cheronese. Cimon, his father, was a great Athenian statesman, one of the first men to embrace democracy, a reformer, and an archon.

When his father was assassinated twenty years before the battle of Marathon, the fledgling Athenian democracy was temporarily disbanded, and a tyranny was again imposed on Athens as in innumerable ages past. This time it was imposed by the Pisistratus family. The young Miltiades was allowed by the usurpers to escape Athens and travel back to his mother's homeland and become the Prince of Cheronese that was by then an Athenian colony.

Soon after Miltiades assumed the head of his barony, the Persian armies crossed the Dardanelles and for a time even conscripted the men of Cheronese into their army. The Persians had not yet conquered his lands, but like many of the Greek city-states on the Ionian coast, Miltiades and the Cheronese had been brought into the Persian sphere of influence, and this meant military service when the king needed new legions for a campaign near that region.

The Persian king, Darius, then a young man, led an army into Russia in an effort to conquer the Scythians, fierce nomadic warrior/horsemen, the precursors of the Cossacks. On this campaign, Miltiades and some of his fellow vassal Greek commanders from Ionia were left to guard a bridge that the Persians built across the Danube. The main Persian army crossed into the wilds of Russia pursuing the Scythians. Upon receiving word that Darius' army was losing its encounters with its enemy, Miltiades proposed to his Greek cohorts that they break the bridge down, leave the scene, and let Darius perish by hunger or Scythian arrows. His terrified Greek compatriots would not go along with his idea. Through inevitable treachery, word of Miltiades' proposal reached the god/king Darius who vowed to have a special execution for the Athenian when he was brought to him in chains after the destruction of Athens.

While Miltiades was away from Athens ruling the Cheronese, he fathered five sons with his wife, a Thracian princess, and conquered two island states, Imbros and Lemnos, for Athens. During this time, the Athenians revolted and, with the help of the Spartans, in 510 BC drove out Hippias, the tyrant son of Pesistratis. They then appointed Cleisthenes, a popular demagogue, to write a new and even more "democratic" constitution. Having endured a millennium of constant internal warfare among the Athenian oligarchs, suddenly the largest city-state on the mainland of Greece, with 140 indigenous municipalities and villages, had a system of government where every citizen of military age had an equal vote in the affairs of state. For the first time in human history, a strange new system of governance emerged and was set in stone, etched on the walls of the Agora, a system of government where *the many ruled the few*.

The tyrant Hippias and his adherents were able to make their escape from Athens, sail across the Aegean, and land in Ionia at Sardis, the capital city of a Persian satrapy, ruled by Greek puppet governor, Artastaphernes. Hippias convinced the satrap that the newly populist Athenians might be dangerous to Ionian and Persian interests, and that he should be helped by Persia to regain his rightful throne. The nineteenth century English historian Edward Creasy writes, "When the Athenians heard of Hippias' practices, they sent envoys to Sardis to remonstrate with the Persians against taking up the quarrel of the Athenian refugees. But Artastaphernes gave them in reply a menacing command to receive Hippias back again if they looked for safety. The Athenians were resolved not to purchase safety at such a price, and after rejecting the Satrap's terms, they considered that they and the Persians were declared enemies." [2]

And so it was that the exuberant Athenians, with the adoption of this strange new system they were calling *democracy*, almost immediately caused coexistence with the King of Persia impossible. Word spread rapidly around the Greek Aegean. Soon, a number of the Ionian Greek states (on the mainland of today's Turkey) under Persian rule sent requests to the Greek homeland asking for help in their impending revolt against Persia. Freedom and revolution were contagious. Many Greek Ionian states sought independence and democratic rule and were clearly influenced by the lead of Athens.

But only the Greek cities of Athens and Eretria on the Island of Euboea sent men

---

2.   E.S. Creasy, *The Fifteen Decisive Battles of the World: from Marathon to Waterloo* (New York: Dorset Press, 1987), 15

and ships to fight for the liberation of the fellow Greek-speakers inside Ionia. That expedition succeeded only in burning down the capital of Sardis before being driven off by Persian forces. Herodotus, in his *Histories*, writes that their decision was "ill-judged," for it set in motion the epic confrontation between Asia and Europe.

Over the next two years, Darius sent armies and fleets to successfully crush the Ionian rebellion in Turkey, including a large flotilla of Phoenician galleys that was ordered to take Cheronese and capture Miltiades. Fortunately, Miltiades received word before the Persians reached his city and was able to load six boats with as much of his treasure as he had time to collect, and, with his five sons commanding the other boats, fled his homeland forever. Miltiades was vigorously pursued, and one his boats and sons was captured. When he reached Athens, the citizens were in a high state of anxiety. They projected on Miltiades their greatest hopes and fears and immediately elected him one of their ten generals. Faced with an invasion by Persia, for the Athenians, Miltiades was suddenly the *new* Achilles, transcendent from the heroic past, the defender of Athens.

Shortly, word reached Athens that the city of Eretria had fallen to the Persians after seven days of siege. The remaining Eretrians were enslaved in retribution for joining in the attacks in Ionia. From the shores of Attica on the Greek mainland, scouts could look across the narrow channel to the island of Euboea and see smoke from the burning city. They soon learned that the Eretrians, except a few who had committed treachery with the enemy, were being bound as slaves and made ready for shipment back to Persia.

With this news, every able bodied Athenian citizen in the general assembly freely and orderly volunteered to join the muster and put their fate in the hands of ten generals and one War Ruler. Nine thousand men equipped with their gleaming personal armor, men in their twenties, thirties, forties, and fifties, followed the lead of Miltiades and marched out of the gates of Athens toward the plain of Marathon. It's a mystery, and historians can only speculate, what Miltiades said to convince them to leave the defense of the city walls to meet the larger more mechanized enemy in the field.

The next day, when the Athenians completed their march of twenty-six miles, arriving at a ridge above the plain where the Persians were encamped on the waters edge, they could see Euboea and the still smoldering ruins of Eritrea across the channel. Approximately one mile below them, the endless line of Persian galleys, six hundred in all, were beached next to the plain of Marathon.

Miltiades brought an aura of invincibility to the war counsel the night they arrived on the bluffs above Marathon. A number of the generals were still unsure that fighting the Persians on an open battlefield was to their advantage. In the commanders' tent there were nine other generals, including Themistocles, who would command the winning fleet at the naval battle at Salamis ten years later, and Aristides, who led the Athenian troops at the final and decisive battle against the Persians at Plataea.

Herodotus interviewed some of the Marathon veterans and records that, after much discussion, the ten generals voted 5 to 5 to stay and engage the enemy. This left the deciding vote to Callimachus, the designated Polemarch (*War Ruler*), a blue blood, and one of the two archons elected for that year. He, like Miltiades, was a patriot, committed to the new egalitarianism of Athens. Under the rules of the new democracy, the other archon was left to lead the defense of the city.

According to Herodotus, Miltiades turned to him and said, "It now rests on you, Callimachus, either to enslave Athens or, by assuring her freedom, to win yourself an immortality of fame, such as not Hamidius and Aristogiton have acquired fighting here on this very ground; for, never since the Athenians were a people were they in so much danger as they are in at this moment. If they bow the knee to these Medes (the Greek word for Persians), they are to be given up to the tyrant, Hippias; and you know what we then will suffer." [3]

Herodotus records that the vote of the brave War Ruler was gained and the council determined to give battle. As Creasy puts it, ". . . and such was the ascendancy and acknowledged military eminence of Miltiades, that all the other generals gave up their days of command to him, and cheerfully acted under his command." [4]

The Battle of Marathon
(Depicted in Historic Fiction)

Nine thousand free citizen soldiers from Athens and 1,000 soldiers from a tiny polis, Plataea, looked down upon the 26,000 Persians encamped by their ships, beached on the shores beside the plain of Marathon. While the Persians were only an expeditionary force, the Persian Empire commanded the largest army and navy in the world. The men the Greeks saw sleeping on the beach represented the largest empire ever amassed, one that stretched from the Hindu Kush to Egypt and north to Ionia on the eastern shores of the Aegean. In Darius' (the Persian king) time, blended into the Persian realm were northern Indians, the

---

3.   *Herodotus,* Book VI, section 109. To understand what the Greeks would suffer, just a few months earlier, the Persian expedition attacked, conquered and razed Miletos one of the Greek city-states on the west coast of Turkey that had participated in the Ionian revolt. Like the city Eritrea, all the male inhabitants were killed and the women and children sold into slavery.

4.   E.S. Creasy, *Fifteen Decisive Battles of the World*, (Dorsett Press, 1987), 10.

Assyrians, the Syrians, the Babylonians, the Chaldeans, the Phoenicians, the Lydians, the Phrygians, the Parthians, the Medes, Egyptians and Cyrenians, the Greek colonists in Asia Minor (then called Ionia), and the Greek inhabitants of the many islands of the Aegean.[5] Even Thrace in northern Greece had succumbed to Persian rule. There was a feeling among the other Greek city-states that they simply could not stand before the enormous Persia on the field of battle. Only Athens and its tiny ally, Plataea, chose to oppose them.

Themistocles, the younger general, spoke to Miltiades, "General, I assure you, my day to command the army is yours. I submit my men to your authority, gladly."

"Thank you, I did not doubt your loyalty, and for it I am forever grateful. But I have a very different motive for seeking your private counsel."

"What is that, General?"

"How many paces away from the Mede archers would you feel safe, in your armor, on the battlefield?"

Thinking for a moment, Themistocles said, "Ah, 300 paces."

"On the battlefield, as we approach the Medes, could you estimate that distance accurately?"

"Yes, I believe so."

"How can you be sure?"

"Three hundred paces is how far I can throw a javelin, General. I *know* that distance."

"Good. This is my plan . . . "

The next morning, as the sun crept up over the ultra-blue Aegean into a cloudless blue-black sky, all the Greek Hoplites' eyes were focused on Miltiades' tent to see if he would exit in full battle dress, the signal that it would be this day that he would order the attack. When the general-in-command emerged, he was not wearing his greaves or his breastplate—he had decided to wait. Pheidippedes, the greatest runner in the Greek world, was not back from Sparta. Miltiades judged it would take four days to complete the 200 miles roundtrip and that Pheidippedes would arrive some time that day. He wanted to know—would the Spartans be joining the Athenians?

Just as Miltiades had surmised, the great runner arrived at camp at midday to great shouts of applause and anticipation from the Athenian soldiers. Every Greek knew that only a demigod could have run that distance in four days.

5.   E.S. Creasy, *Fifteen Decisive Battles of the World* (Dorsett Press, new edition, 1987), 15.

Again, all eyes were trained on the general's tent. As soon as the meeting adjourned, word spread among the ranks like a chill wind—the Spartans were not coming. A palpable feeling of gloom descended on the men. Didn't the Spartan oligarchs know that the Athenian situation was hopeless?

Later that same day, over the crest of the hills to the west of their camp, marched 1,000 Plataeans, all the military-age men from that tiny neighboring city-state. In following the example of the Athenian democrats, their assembly voted to march to Marathon to join in the struggle for freedom. Although the arrival of the Plataeans only added about 10% in numbers to the host of the Greeks, their arrival and valor boosted the morale of the fighters immeasurably.

The generals agreed that Athena surely had interceded in their behalf.

While he waited to give the order for the battle to commence, Miltiades knew that he and his army had left behind men inside the walls of Athens who were

A Greek Hoplite Warrior was duty-bound to supply his own armour

traitors. The traitors would try to break the Athenian resolve and open the gates to the Persians in hopes of leniency or, in the case of the ringleaders, special privilege in the new Athenian satrapy. Miltiades knew that it was this form of treachery that caused the final destruction of Eretria just across the narrow channel from where he stood. Everyday he waited, it gave the forces of treachery inside Athens another day to sap the resolve and courage of those left behind to defend the city, and for insurrection to take hold, but he decided to wait three days until his predetermined day for chief command would come round in the rotation. Although the generals had given him unbridled command of the army, relinquishing their tribes to him, he was keenly aware that for countless generations, Athens had been mired in endless internal civil wars, where one clan's tribe fought the other clan's army for power, wealth, and supremacy.[6] He waited for his original place in the order of command as a gesture aimed at sealing the loyalty of all the generals, some of whom may have been plotting his

---

6.   The Greek word for these endless civil wars is *stasis*.

overthrow. His stratagem was indicative of his genius for both generalship and self-preservation.

Miltiades' three-day wait to attack was dangerous from the standpoint of allowing the traitors in the city time to plot and send signals to the Persians. He had received reports that there were flickering lights coming off the walls of Athens, directed out to the countryside, messaging the enemy. It allowed him time to study the enemy encamped on the plain below, near their boats at the water's edge. He noticed that each morning the cavalry took a great deal of time bringing their horses off the boats, unhobbling them, saddling them, and preparing the riders for battle. Secondly, the archers were slow in taking their places to be arrayed in formation. He watched them perform these drills each of the mornings while he waited. Given his position on the heights above the plain of Marathon, he could see the Persians very well while they could not see the Greeks at all. His position gave him complete discretion as to when he would give battle.

On the night before Miltiades' day in their rotating system of command, he met with his fellow generals to tell them to prepare for battle in the morning. Before the sun was visible above the horizon, he awoke and walked to the edge of his hilltop camp to look down at the Persians through the dim gathering light. Although he could not account for the riders, he could clearly see that the horses were gone. This presented him with both a problem and perhaps a window of opportunity. He had planned to attack before the Persian cavalry was saddled, and able to race around the Greeks to create a second flank behind them. Miltiades well understood that, in hand-to-hand combat, a soldier must know that his enemy is in front of him. Any fear that he will be attacked from another direction creates a distraction that reduces enormously his ability to fight.

While he was nervously straining to decide what to do about the missing cavalry, he noticed that many of his own soldiers, dressed in full battle gear, were beginning to amass at the edge of the bluff to view the Persians. Miltiades rushed out along the ridge line exhorting his hoplites to move away from the bluff's edge to stay out of view of the Persians below and go back to their units and review their battle plans. Next he ordered runners to fan out to the east, west, and back towards the city to see if any could locate the cavalry. He then sent messengers to his generals, ordering them to keep their troops ready for the assault that would happen as soon as he could determine where the Persian horseman were.

By noon all the runners were back in camp. Not one had sighted the cavalry.

This created a tension in Miltiades that briefly manifested itself in his stomach muscles cramping spasmodically. Taking control of himself with a prayer to Athena, he gave the order to form up and ready for the attack. Almost instantly 11,000 men were in their appointed phalanxes, standing at attention. Each was dressed in 60 pounds of gleaming polished armor, breast plate, greaves, shield with pointed boss, nine-foot pike, short sword, and helmet. What transpired was the most important military engagement in human history and one of the most brilliantly executed.

Each of the generals bore a flag on their pike so, when raised, it would designate the commander and allow him to also signal other commanders during the confusion of the battle. Miltiades looked back over his shoulder to the proud men and boys of Athens. According to the long held custom, the men of each tribe were arrayed together, neighbor fighting by the side of neighbor, friend by friend, brother by brother.

He raised his pike and shouted, "Men of Greece, the world will remember what you will do here today. You must and you will drive the Medes into that ocean!" He said, glancing over his shoulder at the brilliant blue Aegean, "They have never fought men such as you. The gods are watching and they are behind you. You are free men!" And with that, he turned and began running at an even pace down the hill toward the flat portion of the plain. All eleven thousand followed and instead of walking, as was the usual practice of a Greek hoplite phalanx, they also began to run behind their commander.

When Miltiades reached the flat portion of the plain, he slowed to a brisk walking speed. This allowed all the phalanxes to regroup and get back in formation. Once this occurred, the army of hoplites broke into a modulated, manageable run. They began shifting the men who made up the rear of the center outward toward either ends of the line. This lessened the depth and strength of the center while strengthening the far left and right. Herodotus, who traveled to Mesopotamia and interviewed some of the surviving Persians who had seen action that day, reports that they were mesmerized by the relatively small contingent of madmen running toward them, men who had no cavalry and who were clearly rushing toward their own destruction.

Once Themistocles, who was commanding one of the center line phalanxes, reached a place on the field that he judged to be 300 paces from the enemy, just outside the archers' range, he stopped and raised his flag-draped pike. With that, Miltiades and the other generals came to a stop. They each took stock of the enemy 300 paces away. Miltiades allowed the men a few seconds to gather their breath and a little time for some of the older soldiers to get back in their ranks. Next, he lowered his pike toward the enemy and screamed, "Run!"

All 11,000 broke into a full sprint, screaming. The citizen soldiers, many of whom were Olympians, came running while the Persians archers were only able to get off one volley of arrows, nearly all of which flew over the heads of the Greeks. Miltiades' plan for avoiding the Persian arrows worked flawlessly. With a horrific explosion of centrifugal force, the Greeks, with nine-foot pikes pointing forward, crashed into the Persian line. Over a thousand Persian defenders who stood at the front, armed only with wicker shields, were killed instantly by the first impact. The Asian men armed with short scimitars were a mismatch for the highly skilled, athletic Greeks, armed with long iron-tipped pikes.

While the first wave of Greek hoplites was freeing its pikes from the collapsing front line, pikes from the soldiers in the line behind them converged with the next row of Persians. On the outsides of the Athenian line, the far right and far left, where Miltiades had oversized his forces, they began doing battle with the Persian irregulars. These conscripted combatants were a motley assembly from obscure regions, mountain dwellers of Afghanistan to herdsman from Ethiopia, men unable to even understand the Persian language. They quickly began to either collapse in fear or break ranks and run.

Before Miltiades could impale his first Asiatic, he saw that his phalanx was moving forward as resistance was crumbling. Their footing was difficult as they stepped on and over the quivering and appalling dead and dying. The breakdown in resistance gave him the chance to look back along the front to see what was happening. Through the din of battle, he saw that at the center of his line, the Greeks under Themistocles, whose line was only four deep, were engaged in furious hand-to-hand combat with battle-hardened Persian regulars who were arrayed in a ten-deep formation. As best as he could determine, the Greeks on the far opposite flank, commanded by the Platean general Stesilaus and the War General Callimachus, were also routing the enemy. The second phase of Miltiades' plan was working as he hoped. And as he watched, the dreaded thought occurred to him that the Persian cavalry might appear at any moment and attack him from one of his flanks or from behind him.

As the retreating irregulars in front of him were dying or fleeing off the plain into the marshes, it gave Miltiades a chance to again look back to see what was happening to his center line. The Greeks were slowly retreating back up the plain in good order, and with minimal losses, due to their expert swordsmanship. Next he gave the order to his vassals to not pursue the fleeing enemy. Instead, they were to form up again into their phalanx positions, wheel around, face the center, and commence marching toward the area where the Persian regulars had been. As his wing began to move along the bluff above the beached Persian boats, he could see, through the rising dust, the Plataeans and Athenians moving toward him, soon to close the gap. His heart leapt into his throat. The third phase of his plan was working. Over five nights, he and his generals debated whether this phase of his plan could or would work. A number said it would not be possible to keep order, to keep men on the flanks from pursuing the enemy, if they could be forced into a retreat. They argued that when an enemy has confronted a man in mortal combat moments earlier, the overwhelming desire for any soldier is to run that fleeing man down and kill him so that he cannot reform and attack anew.

Given Miltiades' uncanny knowledge of the professionalism of his free citizen soldiers, he had been correct. In the heat of battle, they rose above the impulse to pursue the vanquished Persian irregulars and implemented flawlessly the third phase of his plan. Shortly, the two phalanxes from opposite sides of the field met in the center and sealed off the Persians' path to their ships. Miltiades could see Themistocles and Callimachus had rallied their soldiers on the other end of the plain to higher ground, part of the way up the hill toward their camp. Again he urged his men to run toward the rear of the enemy to save their countrymen. Soon the Persian regulars were in a trap. Being attacked on two sides, the battle turned into a route as hundreds more Persians were surprised and impaled by onrushing Greek pikes. For several hours until dusk, the Persian regulars fought valiantly against the Greek attackers on two sides. With losses mounting, they finally broke ranks and, in an every-man-for-himself fashion, began running toward any opening they could find back toward their ships. The Olympians gave chase.

The final phase of the battle, and most costly for the Greeks, took place on the water's edge while the Persians desperately attempted to free their moorings and set sail. Many of the Greeks chased the Persians onto the boats and fought them there but invariably were outnumbered and many were cut down. Miltiades helplessly watched this phase of the battle as it took on a frenzied ferocity that defied his or any of the Greek generals' ability to direct its actions. In fact the War Ruler, Calimachus, was himself killed trying to board a galley.[7] Some of the Persians had left their campfires burning which gave the

7.   Herodutus tell us that the brother of the great playwright, Aeschylus, also fought that day and died

Greeks the means to torch boats still at anchor, causing many to be easily killed in the shallows, turning the fabled blue Aegean red with hundreds of Persians bobbing lifelessly.

By nightfall, what remained of the Persian fleet and army had loosed their moorings and was safely away from the shore. Although it was dark and he had lost several of his generals, Miltiades judged that they had killed at least ten Persians for each Greek lost. There was no time for rejoicing or even preparing their dead for burial. The battle had lasted six hours. His survivors were struggling against exhaustion.

Yet Miltiades also knew that the Persian fleet would sail south along the coast and likely put in at the Athenian port of Phaleron, a short march of six miles to the city walls. He feared that if Persians got there before he and his victorious army, the Athenian defenders inside Athens might be convinced to open the gates and capitulate. He knew that the banished tyrant, Hippias, had traitors inside the city working to convince the citizens that resistance would be futile. Not knowing if he had survived the battle, Miltiades called for Pheiddipedes, hoping he could perform one more superhuman feat of endurance, and he thanked the gods when he got word from a soldier that the great runner was indeed alive.

Miltiades stood beside one of the Persians' abandoned campfires when the runner-warrior emerged from the darkness still dressed in his battle armor. His breastplate and right dagger arm were still painted in blood. "General, you asked for me. What is it that I can do?"

"Are you wounded, Pheiddipedes?"

"No, General."

"The Medes are sailing to the Phaleron tonight and will march on Athens tomorrow."

"Do they have siege equipment?"

"They don't plan to lay siege. Hippias and the Medes have traitors inside our city. If we are not there, they may convince our families and compatriots to open the gates and will do so by telling them that you and I lay dead in this field."

"I understand, General."

Choking on his words, Miltiades laid his hand on Pheidippedes' shoulder. "One more time, I need you to prove that you are the greatest Olympian and warrior of all time. I need you to go to Athens tonight and tell our countrymen

---

from his hand being severed as he tried to prevent a galley from escaping into deeper water.

what we have done here today and to implore them not to open the gates to the Medes. Can you do it?"

"I can, General."

With difficulty in holding back a flood of emotion, Miltiades said, "I would rather send another man. But this mission is such that I can only send you. There are Medes out there searching for our messengers. You have proven over and over that you will survive against all odds. I pray to Athena that you will do so again, that you will survive so that our countrymen will not be tricked into surrendering and so that *Athens* will survive."

As Miltiades watched the Greek world's most famous citizen-soldier disappear into the darkness, his grief was gradually replaced by a calm that came from knowing that if the Athenians somehow still lost the city to the Persians, at least he made the best decisions he could make. He won the day against an enemy three times the size of his force and he sent a messenger to Athens who, above any other mortal, had the best chance of getting the message through. His calm came from contemplating the heroism of this great warrior and the Olympians he had commanded that day. Miltiades concluded that free men were given a gift by the gods that made them superior to all others.

Shortly after his meeting with Miltiades, Pheidippedes began the twenty-six mile run to the walls of Athens that today is commemorated every four years at the modern Olympics. Over the previous ten days, he had run 200 miles to Sparta and back, fought in the battle at Marathon, and was again running to save his countrymen and their freedom.

Before the hint of dawn, in the blackness of a moonless night, he reached the walls of Athens. Near enough to be heard, he called up to the men stationed on the Athenian embattlements, to the men above the gates, "Rejoice, we've conquered!" He attempted to shout to them a second time but his voice choked and he began coughing blood. The great Olympian warrior then stumbled and fell face down in the dust. His countrymen would forever say that his heroic heart had given its all, and then burst.

In Its Infancy, Human Freedom Survives to Fight Another Day

Owing to the relentless advance of collectivism, it's apparent that too many of us Western moderns take our hard-won freedoms for granted. Rufus Fears, an American classicist, observed that the ancient Greeks were unique in that they invented a strange new system of governance where the many ruled the few, and that *no people untouched by the Greeks ever came up with such an idea.*

The language of ancient Egypt did not even have a word for freedom, so obscure was the concept to our ancient forbearers. The British philosopher, James Mill, saw the battle at Marathon as more vital to the development of English liberty than the battle of Hastings where William the Conqueror won English independence for his island kingdom.

Robin Waterfield writes about the evolution of democracy that gained a standardization in the fifth-century BC among 1,500 Greek-speaking poleis (city-states) spread around the shores of the Mediterranean and Black Sea.

> *"In most states, about a third of the population could afford hoplite arms and armor, so that each state could call on a relatively large fighting force. . . . In a hoplite phalanx, then, the wealthier smallholders and artisans stood shoulder to shoulder with aristocrats. . . . The political consequences were inevitable . . . the Greek middle classes became aware that they were just as important for the defense of their city as the aristocrats, so there was no reason why they should not be equal participants in the political process."* [8]

For centuries, prior to the initial invasion by the Persians and the battle at Marathon, the Greeks lived in fiercely independent city-states and spent much of their time making war on one another. (A cessation of hostilities was convened once every four years at the festival and games in Olympia.) Democracy sprung from the evolution of Greek infantry warfare that relied on a middle-class farmer or merchant who considered it his honor-bound duty to procure his own armor and answer the call to arms when his city went to war. As the importance of the well-disciplined middle-class infantrymen grew, the land-owning aristocrat, who earned his command by virtue of owning enough land to provide for the maintenance of his horse, would retain the authority to command a phalanx.

By the dawn of the fifth century, it was the infantryman whose skill and discipline determined the outcome of the battle. So it was only natural that the men who were so vital to the outcome of their city's wars be given a voice in the battle plans and a voice in civic affairs as well. Scholars see that it is from that distant evolution of the phalanx and hoplite warfare that the Greeks embraced the broad concept we call *democracy*.

The battle at Marathon in 490 BC is so profoundly important to the development

---

8. Robin Waterfield, *Athens: A History, from Ancient Ideal to Modern City*, (New York: Basic Books, 2005), 44.

of human history because it was the first battlefield test of the free, "democratic" man. By the time the Athenians participated in the burning of Sardis four years earlier, evidence suggests that there were many variations of democracy springing up in various Greek poleis around the Aegean, governments run by free citizen soldiers. Some of those clamoring for freedom included the Greek speaking Persian subject cities on the Ionian coast of today's Turkey.

Only eighteen years earlier the Athenians had thrown off the tyrannical rule of the Peisistratus family that ran Athens as its private fiefdom for several generations. Hippias, the Peisistratus heir to the Athenian throne, had been expelled from the city by the original Athenian democrats. European democracy was only a teenager. In fact, Athenian democracy was so young that on the eve of the battle of Marathon, Hippias was still alive and conspiring with the Persians, certain that he would be reinstalled as the new Athenian satrap.

The Persians were resoundingly defeated at Marathon, and they would be back. Ten years later, in 480 BC, Herodotus, the main source for the Greco-Persian wars, tells us that a Persian army of one million men crossed the Hellespont, moved toward the center of Greece, and devoured everything in its path, "drinking small rivers dry." To properly assess the sheer desperation of the Greek's position is to understand that the Persian empire controlled a land mass roughly the size of the United States. Greece was not a country, just a collection of autonomous city-states spread across the Mediterranean, some so small they had only 1,000, military age men.

A generation after the close of Persian wars, in the 450s BC, Herodotus traveled far and wide throughout much of the eastern Mediterranean seeking out and talking to people who had either fought in, or knew people who had fought in, the Persian wars. He is considered the father of history because he sought to learn how such a small army and navy of Greeks could defeat such a larger invading force. He was the first historian to attempt to understand the *causes* of events.

Herodotus tells us that when news of the advance of the Persian army and navy reached their citadels, the Greek mainland was thrown into panic. In the face of this terror, no comprehensive alliance outside of Athens and Sparta could be formed. In fact, the well-armed Thebes, located on the central Grecian mainland directly in the path of the oncoming Persians, "medized" and capitulated without a fight, and without donating a single soldier to the cause of freedom. When the war with the Persians resumed ten years after Marathon, less than thirty Greek cities joined the war for Greek freedom. The rest either stayed neutral, were conscripted by, or sided with the Persians. The Greek allies, who chose to do battle, were led by the Spartans and the Athenians.

The Greek northern mainland has steep mountain ranges running across its entire breadth which create very narrow passes through which an invading army must pass to reach the central portion of Greek heartland. Thermopylae is one such pass. It was there that the King of Sparta, Leonidas, took his personal bodyguard of 300 men, together with 400 renegade Thebans and 700 Thespians, to make a stand. They were joined by several thousand Greek recruits from other allied poleis. Leonidas selected his defensive tactics and position well. At one point, Thermopylae is only fifty feet wide. For three full days, they held off an army at least 20 times their size. As Barry Strauss, author of the brilliant work of scholarship, *The Battle of Salamis,* writes, "Only trained and hardened Spartans could have carried out a maneuver as the Spartans did at Thermopylae: turning and retreating in an orderly way and then, once they had tricked the Persians into charging, changing course in an instantaneous wheel and crushing the enemy."[9]

Through the treason of a Greek named Ephialtes, the Persians were led through an alternative pass and were able to attack Leonidas' forces from the rear. Consequently, all 300 Spartans, including their king, were killed. And the Greeks' performance ranks among the most improbable in all of the history of human warfare. Tales of their heroism galvanized the Greek resistance. Herodotus records one such tale—a scout reported to Leonidas that the approaching Persian archers were so numerous that "they will darken the sky with their arrows." To which one Spartan was said to have replied, "Fine. We'll fight in the shade." Thermopylae, recently commemorated by the Hollywood production *300*, had significance for the Greeks of antiquity somewhat like the Alamo had for 19th century Americans. The men who died at Thermopylae instantly achieved a mythic status.

The same days that the battle of Thermopylae was waged, thirty miles away in the bay of Artemisium off the northern coast of the island of Euboea, the Greek navy, commanded by Themistocles, fought the vastly larger Persian navy. Just as Miltiades commanded the men who saved Athens in 490 BC, only ten years later (480 BC) the charismatic, wily Themistocles led a Greek armada that saved the entire Greek world from Persian domination.

The victory was possible because, during the decade between the battle of Marathon and the second Persian invasion, the Athenians discovered an enormous vein of silver at Laurium. Many in the new assembly of free Athenians argued that the money (mined exclusively by slaves) should be dispersed equally among the

9.   Barry Strauss, *The Battle of Salamis: The Naval Encounter that Saved Western Civilization,* (New York: Simon and Shuster, 2004), 34.

citizen members. But Themistocles, the most charismatic and eloquent politician of that decade, convinced the Athenians that their livelihoods were threatened by their arch rival, Aegina, an island people resident just a few miles from the entrance to the Athenians' port on Phaleron Bay. His initiative, which proposed that the Athenians needed to invest in a navy, was accepted. By the second Persian invasion, the Athenians had produced 200 state-of-the-art triremes, fully staffed, and ready for battle.

While the Spartan, Euribiades, was elected as the commander of all Greek forces, Themistocles was elected commander of the Greek allied navy, based on his foresight. In the Athenian democracy of the fifth century, generals did not receive their commands through military promotions. They were elected by the Assembly of their peers. To be elected general was the most prestigious position in the hyper-democracy of Athens. It was the only office where one could be elected every year, such was their martial ethos.

Strauss records that only fourteen Greek city-states provided ships for the war against Persia which invaded the Greek heartland with the largest military force ever assembled. Themistocles' entire command, moored at Artemisium, was only 333 ships. Opposing the Greeks, was an enormous navy that outnumbered them four to one. The Persians had 1,207 triremes with an additional 120 added from recently acquired *Greek-speaking* allies. What the Greeks and Themistocles did not fully understand was that the Persian fleet was also a "floating tower of Babel" composed of Phoenicians, Egyptians, Greeks, Cypriots, Carians, and Pamphylians. "With all its different languages, communication alone was no small problem." [10]

The beginning of the invasion had been several years in the making. For the entire spring and summer of 480 BC, the Persian navy followed and provisioned the vast Persian army that was personally led by Xerxes, the Persian king. They followed the army across the Hellespont, down through Thrace, and on toward central Greece. Finally, at Artemisium, the opposing navies met. And Themistocles proved the far superior war tactician.

Strauss provides vivid descriptions of life inside the ancient trireme. While the Greek ships were heavier than the average Persian boats, both sides employed vessels that were very similar in design. They were not sailing ships. They were propelled by oarsmen. The new Athenian boats were staffed by 200 men who operated in incredibly tight quarters, 170 oarsmen on three rows below deck. On deck there were ten marines in bronze hoplite armor, four archers, and assorted craftsmen and rowing masters. Each vessel had a captain. The most important individual was

10. Ibid, 17.

the helmsman or pilot, the man on whose quick decisions the lives of the crew depended, once the battle began. The oarsmen on the top row had small windows; the two rows below them had no windows, requiring a kind of superhuman capacity for claustrophobia. As Strauss puts it—because the ship was so dependent on human power, victory depended on training and toughening the men, and moral mattered. The successful captain had to be as much a coach and psychologist as a naval commander. It required extraordinary skill to keep good order with so many men toiling blindly in such close quarters. With tens of thousands of closeted rowers, it required of Themistocles' uncanny powers of leadership to lead such a fleet in battle. Superb planning, innovative flag and auditory signals, skill, training, and discipline were paramount.

At dusk on August 27, 480 BC, Themistocles sent his boats out of the protective bay to challenge the vastly larger Persian armada that was arrayed in the ten-mile-wide bay between the Island of Euboea and the mainland. For three successive days, he led his fleet on hit and run skirmishes designed to reveal the capability of the Persian navy. His tactics were equal parts raid and experiment. He chose evenings to challenge the Persians. He knew the Persians would cease their pursuit once darkness fell because they had no desire to wage war in the dark without a friendly shore nearby. Each evening, the Greeks demonstrated great rowing precision, rowed confidently into the calm, sheltered bay, and formed a tight circle, each boat pointing its imposing ramming prow out toward the enemy. The Persian fleet responded by forming a semicircular

Greek Trireme

line opposing the Greeks. Their Persian ships moved to positions almost touching the Greeks with their foreign language clearly audible.

On that first evening of the three-day battle, Themistocles' primary aim was to test the Persians' ability in performing the all-important maneuver known as diekplous, which in Greek meant "through and out." It entailed that a group of allied ships pour through a hole in the enemy line, using the trireme's main weapon, its iron ram. The object was to initially sheer off the enemy ship's oars, crippling the boat and killing many of the rowers, while at the last moment, rapidly pulling in the ramming ship's own oars. Once a significant portion of the enemy ship's oars were severed, an allied boat would approach the crippled ship and ram it. When ramming an opponent, it was most advantageous to backwater the oars just before impact. This allowed the attacker to sink the opponent ship and avoid being lodged in it. Breaking free of the doomed ship prevented its marines from jumping aboard the attacking ship and inflicting losses in hand-to-hand combat. Enormous skill was necessary to perform these maneuvers. Skill and precision, combined with strength and endurance, determined life and death.

For a brief period, the two opposing fleets conducted a strange pattern of feinting moves to see how the other would respond. The Greeks, a brand new naval power, completed their fleet only two years earlier. So even though the Athenian rowers had practiced, they had never executed commands in battle. Artemisium was the young democracy's first naval engagement. The Greeks rowed toward the unnerved Persians with trumpets blaring and thousands of oarsmen singing their paeans. On a predetermined signal, the Greeks backwatered and formed a very tight circle of the right and left flanks. As the Persians attempted to oppose the well-disciplined Greeks, the soldiers on the decks of the opposing fleets were so close to each other that they made eye contact. An eerie silence descended over the surreal scene. Suddenly, with a predetermined rapport of trumpets, the Greek triremes began to sprint through a small gap that had opened in the Persian formation, shearing off the oars of the luckless Persian ships on both sides of the opening and sinking them, as more Greek craft poured through the ever widening Persian opening. As each additional Greek boat poured through the gap, it enlarged the hole in the Persian line by crippling and sinking its ships.

By the time the Greeks had completed their break-out maneuver, darkness was gathering over the bay. The Athenians rowed back into their harbor at Artemisium without the Persians giving chase. Once ashore, Themistocles was able to determine that virtually all his ships had escaped, while only a few were damaged. Yet they had sunk or captured thirty Persian boats. Over the succeeding two days of engagements, the outcome was much of the same. While the Athenians did lose some boats the following evenings and suffered some damage to others, Themistocles, the brilliant tactician, saw that the Persians, who were not seafaring people, could not match the Greeks' precise maneuvers. More importantly, he saw how their boats could be made to collide with each other and how their enormous numbers could be made to work against them. Based on these observations, the great naval strategist would set a trap for the Persians that would preserve the Western world's young and fragile freedom.

The poet, Pindar memorialized Artemisium in his immortal lines:

> *There the sons of Athens set*
> *The stone that freedom stands on yet.*

On the third night of the battle word spread, amid a thousand Athenian campfires, that Thermopylae had fallen. All the Athenians knew that the only large city-state between the massive Persian land army and their families inside Athens was Thebes. And Thebes had joined the enemy. The Athenians and their allies did not wait for dawn. They said their prayers and that night set sail for their homeland ports. Among the Greek allies, each city-state would now decide if they would attempt to defend themselves against the coming Persian siege or evacuate and flee to other parts of the Mediterranean.

By late August 480 BC, once the Persian land army broke through at Thermopylae, they met no resistance in central Greece. When they approached Athens they found that the city, surrounding farmlands, and port were abandoned except for a few zealots who had barricaded themselves inside the Acropolis. With contempt, the Persians killed the remaining Athenians and burnt the city to the ground.

In advance of the Persian hoard, the city's entire civilian population of men, women, and children packed their belongings and fled south along the shores of the Saronic Gulf. There they crossed the very narrow isthmus which joins the Greek mainland to the Peloponnesus and encamped on the other side. All able-bodied Athenians, hoplites, marines, and sailors prepared for battle, boarded ships, sailed into Ambelaki Bay, and moored next to the island of Salamis. The distance between their moorings and the mainland was less than three kilometers of open sea. The Persians, under Xerxes, were bent on conquering all of Greece, hunting down and destroying the Athenians, killing all the military-age men, and enslaving the women and children— this for the crime of beating them at Marathon.

The Battle of Salamis

Of September 25, 480 BC, Strauss writes, "It was a morning like no other." At one point, the Peloponnesus was separated by just a few hundred yards from Salamis Island. Many Athenian families were on the Island's bluffs, overlooking the Ambelaki Bay where the Greek allies were boarding their boats. The families prayed, sang, and cheered as their beloved husbands, sons, and brothers boarded the boats and made the last preparations for battle. The Greek allies had 368 ships of which 180 were Athenian. Another twenty-three city-states contributed the balance of the Greek armada. In all, sixty-two thousand men made their last preparations for the largest and most consequential naval battle in the history of the ancient world.

As the Greeks rowed into the Saronic Gulf, they began to bear down on the Persians who had been waiting for them since the middle of the night.

Herodotus records that the night before the battle, wily Themistocles sent his slave to tell Xerxes that the Greeks were disunited and some of the fleet were deserting in the middle of the night. The Persian king was tricked into sending his entire fleet of 1,200 boats into the harbor in the middle of the night. There the rowers expended energy to maneuver and stay in formation instead of sleeping. Additionally, the ruse served to make the Persians feel that the Greeks were afraid and desperate, and would be easy prey because they had lost their will to fight. For Themistocles, this brilliant piece of psychological warfare created the greatest of all force multipliers, the element of surprise.

The playwright Aeschylus, who fought at Marathon, Artemisium, and Salamis, wrote *The Persians*, the only surviving play from Greek antiquity that depicts events of the day, rather than the mythic past. Along with Herodotus' *Histories*, it is considered to be a source document for the battle of Salamis. He tells us that the Persian armada was shocked to see that the Greek ships had not attempted to flee or surrender. Instead the Greeks poured out of the Ambelaki and Paloukia Bays, rowing straight toward them in smart formations, gaining speed. They were shocked to hear the oncoming Greeks singing paens, as Strauss puts it, "song-like shouts that were a combination prayer, cheer, and rebel yell."

Themistocles' ruse had worked because it sowed among the enemy what the Greeks believed was a gift from the gods—panic. Moreover, the enormous Persian fleet had been drawn into a very narrow portion of the bay where their lighter, faster boats could not maneuver. They ran afoul of each other, and the heavier Greek boats rammed them at will. Aeschylus' play describes the battle from the point of view of a Persian messenger to Xerxes' mother, Queen Atosa.

And the Greek ships, alert to the chance, encircled ours
And began to ram them. Our ships capsized, and the sea so filled

With wrecks that the water could not be seen.
The beaches and rocks were strewn with corpses, and every ship
Of the Eastern armada rowed away in disorderly flight.

Xerxes watched the battle from a safe bluff overlooking the gulf, then ordered the decapitation of several Phoenician commanders he deemed guilty of malfeasance, and summarily returned with what was left of his fleet to Persia. He left his general, Mardonios, to continue the war for another year.

In 479, the following year, the united armies of Greece wiped out the trapped Persian army on the Greek mainland near the city of Plataea. It was in that year, during the months leading up to and culminating with the battle of Plataea, that the ancient Greek-speaking peoples experienced their first and last Panhellenic unity. For the Greeks, who invented so much including sport, their only experience with panhellenic unity was a truce, a brief cessation in the never ending war among Greek city-states that took the form of the festival and games held in Olympia every four years.

What we refer to today as the "Olympics" was first held in 776 BC and held every four years for a millennium until they were banned by the Christian Roman Emperor Theodosius in AD 393.

It brilliantly fostered a panhellenic Olympic spirit which gave every Greek a deep sense of pride in being Greek. The festival and games in ancient Olympia were a respite from war where Greek athletes, poets, and dignitaries of city-states from Spain to the Black Sea converged on Olympia to compete in the games as peers, not as military rivals.

The year between Salamis and Plataea was new, an extended time when every Greek-speaker from Athens and Sparta, to the residents of the tiniest poleis, was united in the quest to defeat the Persian invader. Sadly, the Greeks would soon be at each other's throats again.

Yet it's important to reflect that, like Marathon, Salamis was a battle that saved an infant Western Civilization and it was a defining moment for the Greek Polis. Because, in defeating a much larger Persian invader, it demonstrated that Greek culture was now ascendant.

IMMUTABLE #10
Declining civilizations will always face
superior firepower from ascending civilizations
because sovereignty is only temporarily uncontested.

It showcased how a strange, new Greek culture that valued the individual above all else, that valued creativity and freedom, was superior to a culture where slavish devotion to the god-king was demanded and ruthlessly enforced. The battle created a new paradigm for warfare. Whereas the Persian arrow men had long been the dominant shock troops used to conquer new realms, they were made impotent by the simple instruments of the Greek fisherman and ferryman, the boat and oar.

As Strauss points out, although ancient sea battles usually began with both sides rowing toward each other in tight formations, they quickly devolved into chaos and individual duals, one ship versus another. The outcome of these duals depended on the character and creativity of the captain, his flexibility and cunning, his ability to size up and anticipate his opponent's next move. The other key player was the pilot who stood on the quarterdeck behind the captain and operated a pair of rudders connected to a tiller. His athleticism needed to match the captain's situational awareness for the vessel to survive the chaos of battle while performing kills.

Eleutheria—Ancient Greek for Freedom

So it was Greek creativity and athletic prowess that defeated the Persian fleet at Salamis. According to Herodotus, who is our primary source for the Persian War, the root cause for the Greek victory over the vastly larger and richer Persian invader was freedom. After the publication of his *Histories* some forty years later, it became widely accepted by Greeks, that it was their eleutheria (ancient Greek for freedom) that made the difference in their unlikely victory over the Persians at Marathon, Salamis, and Plataea. For the Greeks, it was not just a word that simply referred to consensual government, an idea that arose in a number of the late sixth-century Greek city-states for the first time in human history. It embodied a broad set of brand new organizing principles. "It ensured the individual citizen freedom of association, freedom to own property and acquire wealth without fear of confiscation, and freedom from arbitrary punishment and coercion."[11]

Hanson also points out that one hundred years after the Persian wars, when Greece was losing its martial spirit and beginning to rely on mercenaries rather than its own citizen soldiers for its defense, its freedom slipping away, Aristotle understood how important the expanded concept of freedom was to the defense of the Greek poleis.

> *"Infantrymen of the polis think it is a disgraceful thing to run away . . .*
> *professional soldiers, who rely from the outset on superior strength, flee*

---

11. Victor Davis Hanson, *Carnage and Culture: Landmark Battles in the Rise of Western Power*, (New York: Random House, 2001), 50.

as soon as they find out they are outnumbered, fearing death more than dishonor." [12]

The Golden Age of Greece and the Athenian Empire

Modern historians largely agree with Herodotus' conclusion that it was the Athenians, under the leadership of Themistocles, who were the most influential and responsible for the victory of Western freedom over Eastern domination. Yet, like the hero of an ancient Greek tragedy, it was the Athenians, the residents of classical Athens, who were most responsible for the ultimate conquest of Greece by the Macedonians.

For the following two years after the battle of Plataea, from 479 to 477 BC, while Athens rebuilt its city and erected new walls surrounding it, the Greek city-states were uncharacteristically united. With the Athenians and Spartans in the lead, they conducted mopping up operations to destroy Persian strongholds on various islands throughout the Aegean archipelago and inside the Black Sea. They even liberated Greek-speaking city-states on the Turkish coast, then called Ionia. Because the Athenians owned the largest, most dominant navy, these operations were largely theirs. Under the general and successor to Themistocles, Cimon, the Athenians audaciously sent an expedition up the Eurymedon River and destroyed two hundred Persian boats. This in turn, created for the Athenians still greater power and a sense of entitlement. They began to see themselves as the protectors of the Greek people, and, ominously, their overlords.

With this new-found power, the Athenians quickly collected 140 city-states into a *Delian League*. Its purpose was to raise taxes, build ships, recruit men, and manufacture arms so members of the league could stay on a war footing and be ready to repulse the next invasion by Persia that was widely assumed to be soon coming. The League was so named because its treasury was located on the sacred island of Delos where Greek myth had it that Apollo had been born. Initially, the member states joined the league on their own volition and paid their tribute willingly. Most of the league was composed of island or coastal peoples who either paid the league in ships or silver. But the members were beginning to see that the league was rapidly becoming a wholly owned subsidiary of the city of Athens, its maritime empire of the Aegean. Tensions among some of the member states began to build as the decade of the 470s wore on.

In 470, the Island of Naxos was the first member state to go into open rebellion from the League by refusal to pay its tribute that was in newly built ships. Thucydides records that in response to Naxians' revolt, ". . . the Athenians besieged them until they

---

12. Aristotle, *Nicomachean Ethics*, 3.1116b16-23.

surrendered. This was the first state to be enslaved." He goes on to say that even though this enslavement was not common practice, the Athenians enslaved others as well. The Naxian revolt took place less than ten years after the formation of the Delian League. By this time, the Athenians had incorporated nearly 300 states into its league, mostly through coercion or outright force.

In 465 BC, the very wealthy island of Thasos went into revolt because Athens had demanded a share of its commercial profits. Waterfield writes,

> ". . . Athenian commitment to the cause of imperialism was so great,
> they besieged the city for three years until forcing capitulation. This
> military activity had little to do with the Persians and everything to do
> with the ships, timber, and precious metals which Thasos controlled and
> Athens needed."[13]

The Athenians were clearly violating the freedoms and the fierce independence that was so prized and so endemic to the Greek-speaking peoples who occupied poleis throughout the Mediterranean. Athenian rule was becoming increasingly unpopular among both the members of the League and those states who were fearful of being absorbed by it. It was this growing animosity toward the empire that caused Pericles, the greatest statesman of the fifth-century Athenian democracy, to observe, "It may have been wrong to take it. But it is too risky to let it go."[14]

As the league was inexorably transformed from a collection of allies to the subjects of the Athenians, the Spartans worried that Athens was beginning to threaten their sphere of influence. It lay in the Peloponnese, on portions of the Greek mainland outside Attica, and to the east with Greek city-states located in Sicily and on the Italian mainland.

Although the Athenians ruled the seas, the Spartans were a landlocked people. Their boys were raised in communal martial camps and trained from birth to be the best infantrymen in the ancient world. On land, they were superior to a like-size force of Athenians. In 465, they were ready to come to the aid of Thasians and attack Attica, the Athenian heartland. However, that year, a huge earthquake near Sparta precipitated a revolt by their slave population, the Helots. This revolt took two years to quell. The Spartans' difficulties were so great they petitioned other cities, including the Athenians, to send military contingents to put down the rebellion.

Soon after the Athenians arrived, they were asked by the Spartans to leave. It

---

13. Robin Waterfield, *Athens: From Ancient Ideal to Modern City*, (New York: Basic Books, 2004), 77.
14. Thucydides, *The Peloponnesian War*, 2.63.2.

seems the Spartan oligarchs became very uneasy when news reached them that the brash contingent of Athenians admitted into their ranks was openly speaking of freedom and democracy. With the expulsion of their force by the Spartan elites, the Athenians were so outraged that they ostracized their general-in-command, Cimon, for pro-Spartan leanings. With Cimon's ostracism came the ascendancy of Pericles, who became something of a spiritual leader in Athens, a statesman who was elected every year to the rank of general until his death in 431 BC. As Waterfield puts it, "This spelled the end of the anti-Persian alliance." By the close of the 460s, Sparta and Athens had entered a "cold war."

In the cold-war phase of the great Greek civil war, also known as the First Peloponnesian War (460 to 451 BC), battles were sporadic and not costly in terms of blood and treasure. Life inside most Greek citadels, including Sparta and Athens, went on nearly as usual. Most of the battles fought by Athens were against Spartan allies, proxy wars such as Korea and Vietnam were for the US in the 20th century. However, Athens did engage Spartan forces at Tanagra in 457 and was defeated, and with that defeat, they never again entertained a land empire. In 454, Athens dropped all pretexts of operating an alliance of equals and unilaterally transferred the treasury of six thousand talents, a vast war chest, from the island of Delos to Athens.[15]

In 451, Cimon returned from exile and convinced the Assembly to negotiate a five-year truce with Sparta. With that in place, he was given command of an expedition to Cyprus commissioned to attack a Persian fortress and was killed. Like Cimon, Pericles was from a very old and noble family, related to Cleisthenes, the man who produced the constitution of democratic Athens. He was a refined, well-educated general who had proven himself on the battlefield. As a powerful orator he was the unrivaled, most influential citizen of Athens. His primary objective was to reorient the Athenian policies away from preparations for a future war with Persia, in favor of concentrating on what he saw as their true enemy, Sparta.

With vast funds at their disposal, Pericles convinced the Assembly to commission the construction of defensible walls that stretched five miles from the city all the way to the port on the Piraeus. So large was the area inside these walls, that during an invasion it could house the entire population of Attica. Pericles told them that Athens could be provisioned by its vast navy and maritime allies, and could withstand a siege *indefinitely*. Just as Themistocles convinced the Athenians to build a navy a brief time prior to the Persian invasion, Pericles alone was the man who conceived of and executed this grand military strategy.

---

15. A talent of silver was the cost to produce a trireme.

Hostilities resumed between Sparta and its allies, and Athens and its allies. These hostilities continued sporadically until a second, thirty-year truce was negotiated in 446 BC. With the vast treasury housed in Athens, it became the wealthy peace-time capital of an Aegean empire that attracted foreigners who came seeking fame and fortune from all over the Greek world. It instantly became the cultural center and trade emporium of the eastern Mediterranean. Playwrights, poets, sculptors, and artists came looking for benefactors, men such as Polygnotos, the master painter of Thasos, and Herodotus of Halicarnassus, the father of modern history. He read his history of the Persian war aloud to the Athenians who rewarded him with a tidy fortune. Large numbers of Sophists came to teach the young Athenian men. Of these, Socrates, the native son of Athens, became the most important philosopher of the Western world. Anaxagoras of Klazomenai came and developed the scientific method and postulated the composition and origins of the universe.

The fortune seekers arrived by the thousands, merchants and craftsmen of every description. Because Athens was an enormously rich maritime power and the fleet was constantly being expanded and refitted, the city attracted shipwrights and suppliers of tackle and various shipping accoutrements. Athens even hosted the first international banking operations which were instituted to provide bottomry (maritime) loans. Pericles personally invited the wealthy man Cephalus, a highly reputed arms dealer, to relocate some of his manufacturing operations to the Piraeus. All this was occurring in Athens when most northern Europeans were still nomadic hunter/gatherers.

Finally, Pericles, the first citizen of Athens, convinced his countrymen that a portion the city's newly expropriated wealth should be appropriated toward a massive building program. It would begin with security, in the form of the five-mile-long walls connecting it to its port, and end with the complete glorification of its unique culture. He wanted Athenians to regard their city as the leader of the Greek world.

Most Westerners have a vague understanding of the Greco architectural splendor demonstrated by the Athenian buildings on the Acropolis. Rivaled in magnificence were buildings such as the Parthenon and the Propylaia located at the end of five-mile-long walls and at the Athenian port Peiraieus. While nothing remains of them, it staggers the imagination to think of an ancient fifth-century civilization where even a mercantile port facility would be constructed to project the never-before-equaled grandeur of its society.

As the great British historian, Kenneth Clark, observed:

"There have been three or four times in history man has made a leap forward that would have been unthinkable under ordinary

evolutionary conditions. One such time was about the year 3000 BC when quite suddenly civilization appeared, not only in Egypt and Mesopotamia but in the Indus Valley; another was in the late sixth century BC, when there was not only the miracle of Ionia and Greece— philosophy, science, art, poetry, all reaching a point that wasn't reached again for 2000 years." [16]

Tragically, by the beginning of the 430s BC, total, climactic war between the Spartan allies and the Athenian allies became inevitable. In that ensuing great civil war began the destruction of the civilization built around the Greek polis.

The Resumption of the Great Peloponnesian War (431 to 404 BC)

The first phase of the Peloponnesian war, that ended in 446 BC with a thirty-year truce, officially resumed in spring 431 BC with the Spartans' invasion of Attica—the richest Greek city-state of roughly 500,000 people. It was the size of Rhode Island, its capital was Athens, and its inhabitants were citizen Athenian clans, resident aliens, and slaves. Thucydides gives us the most detailed account of the war, first as an Athenian general, and later as an ostracized ancient embedded reporter. His account provides a vivid description of how the emotionally charged irrationality of the Athenian Assembly was the primary cause of the Athenians' defeat, how the war effort was mismanaged by an Assembly of "mob rule."

During the fifth century, in democratic Athens, every full-blooded Athenian citizen who owned enough property and wealth necessary to produce his own battle armor to serve in the infantry, was authorized to vote in the Assembly. It was where every civic issue, small and large, including the conduct of the war, was decided. By the outset of the war, those Athenians *eligible* to speak and vote in the Assembly represented about fifty thousand men. Aliens living in Athens, women, and the approximate one hundred thousand slaves were excluded. The Assembly met on the Pinx, a steeply terraced hill beside the Agora and Acropolis. It accommodated only six thousand men. In fact, the Athenian constitution stipulated that a quorum of six thousand was necessary for the most important votes. As Waterfield points out, many Athenian citizens lived in remote areas of Attica where travel to the city was arduous. Some even lived on the islands of Salamis and Euboea. So, in practice, while all citizens had the *right* to speak and vote, normal attendance in the Assembly was about two thousand.

---

16. Kenneth Clark, *Civilization: A Personal View* (New York: Harper and Row Publishers, 1969), 23.

Few men in the Assembly could command its attention. Without the aid of modern public address systems, it was a rare man who had the oratory skill, charisma, and reputation to control the Assembly and gain sway over the majority (hence our current word, demagogue). Most in attendance merely voiced their opinions through heckling or jeering.

The war resumed because both Athens and Sparta claimed grievances. For Sparta and its allies, Athens built a menacing empire to the east of the Greek mainland, in the Aegean and on the coast of Turkey. It wasn't until Athens intervened in a trade dispute between Corinth and Corcyra (modern day Corfu) on behalf of Corcyra, located on the western Adriatic coast, that the Peloponnesian league became truly alarmed. Powerful Spartan allies Corinth, Magara, and Aegina had lucrative trading partners in Italy and enjoyed unfettered freedom of the seas to the west of Greece. So when they saw Athens forging an alliance in the west with Corfu, this caused them to feel fundamentally threatened.

The mostly oligarchic members of the Peloponnesian league differed from the Athenian Delian League because they were not required to pay tribute by Sparta. It was a coalition of the willing. They saw that since the 450s, the radical governmental ideology of democracy had spread to city-states throughout the Greek world and taken root as far away as the Greek colony of Thurii in southern Italy. As states threw off old oligarchies or tyrannical regimes and adopted democratic forms of governance, Spartan influence upon the Greek world declined while Athenian influence rose. As Hanson puts it, *"The die hard wealthier supporters of Sparta throughout the Aegean must have felt that they were losing influence in their own communities to an upstart underclass."* [17] The Spartans bristled at what they saw as a democratic imperialism. (Ironically this same charge was leveled against the US during the second Iraq war by some of America's enemies and its own political Left.) Thucydides wrote that it was the fear of the Athenian empire felt by Sparta and its allies that was the true cause of the war.

By the 430s, Sparta hated the Athenians for what they were and for what they did. It was a fundamentalist oligarchic state steeped in the prehistoric past and rooted in a culture of hoplite warfare. It was suspicious and envious of the Athenian empire that was based on shipping, commerce, and relentless expansionism.

Waterfield describes Spartan culture as "one of the most bizarre cultures the world had ever seen." The land-locked state located in center of Laconia functioned as one huge military camp and training facility. To avoid overpopulation and a shortage of

---

17. Victor Davis Hanson, *A War Like No Other* (New York: Random House, 2005), 13.

farmland at home, most Greek city-states sent second- and third-born sons off to join new colonies or to found new sister states around the Mediterranean.

Instead, Sparta chose to conquer and enslave its Laconian neighbors. The Spartan state, at its peak, could field no more than 40,000 hoplite warriors, but it ominoursly sat atop a massive volcano of 250,000 rebellious slaves called Helots (captives). It was for this reason, Waterfield points out, that they felt compelled to raise their children to be warriors. Rebellion by the Spartans' massively larger slave population was common and required great military skill to quell.

Male children were taken from their mothers at six or seven years of age to live in barracks until graduation at age 20 and were trained to fight. Homosexuality was common and encouraged under the rational that it would further add to the cohesion and zealotry of the fighting units, lovers defending lovers. Plutarch wrote that their traditions revealed an underlying culture of barbarous cruelty.

> *"The young men's commanders would send those who gave them the impression of being the most intelligent out into the countryside... with nothing more than a dagger. ... By day the young men spread out and found remote spots where they could hide and rest, but at night they came down to the roads and murdered any Helots they caught."* [18]

Despite the Spartans' inferiority to the Athenians in cultural and scientific advancement, their training and ethos made them the best infantrymen in the world. Sparta was virtually the only important Greek city-state able to afford a permanent standing army, due to their vast numbers of slaves. Athens ruled the seas and both sides knew each other's strengths. Thucydides tells us that Pericles had achieved the status of "first citizen." So as the war in 431 BC resumed, Pericles convinced his countrymen that the Athenian forces should not try to fight the Spartans on land. Instead, they should fight a defensive war from inside their massive long walls that protected their city and their port. In this way, he told them, even if Sparta destroyed much of the agriculture of Attica, Athens could be supplied by its captive empire.

The twenty-seven-year Greek civil war began when the Spartan Army invaded Attica in the spring of 431 BC. In advance of the attack, based on Pericles' proscription, the Athenian farmers and rural villagers packed up their families and what few belongings and provisions they could transport by hand or ox cart, and moved inside Athens' protective long walls. The ravenous Peloponnesian invaders cut

---

18. Plutarch, *Lycurgus*, 28.

down the Athenians' abandoned grape vines, harvested or burned the wheat fields, and felled olive trees. The Spartan-led army of sixty-thousand thought they could induce the Athenians to come out of their fortress to defend their sacred soil, as they did at Marathon. This was a tactic that Sparta had employed successfully for centuries. Had Athenians been drawn out of their fortress city and defeated in one afternoon early in the war, they might have lost their empire, but they would have lost far fewer of its citizen soldiers, farms, woman, and children. As in time immemorial, their fellow Greek non-combatants would be left unharmed.

Pericles' great gamble was that Athens was vastly richer than was Sparta. Using its enormous wealth of 6,000 talents (one talent was enough money to build a new 200 seat trireme), its armada of nearly 300 ships, and its empire, it could win a war of attrition against a superior land army. With almost a thousand square miles to cover, small platoons of ravagers were ambushed and easily killed or captured for ransom by the Athenian cavalry eager to settle scores.

That spring, while the Spartan army was in Attica, Pericles sent some of the fleet loaded with heavily armed hoplites to conduct raids on unfortified coastal villages located along the Peloponnesian coast. These raids, conducted against unarmed noncombatants, caused senseless murder to quickly spread.

Ominously, for the first time in Greek history *any* enemy man, woman, slave, or child was fair game for slaughter or enslavement by the Athenians, the Spartans, and the allies of both. This was a new form of terror, random violence which carried with it a level of banality and cowardice. Each side often avoided doing battle with roughly

Ancient Athens with the Acropolis with the Parthenon

equal opposing forces and instead sought out easy targets of unarmed civilians. Tragically over the twenty-seven year war, the Greeks reduced themselves to wicked assassins much like the terrorists of today.

Thucydides writes at the beginning of his histories that, at the outset of the war, he felt compelled to record its impending events. He knew this war would be the most momentous event in the history of the Greek people. In terms of suffering and death, Athenians and much of the Greek world ultimately experienced suffering on a scale that no one could have imagined. The war conscripted every polis—neutrality was not an option. Each city-state felt compelled or was forced to join one alliance or the other. Those which tried to remain out of the war were dealt with savagely. Tragically, the enormous creative power of the entire Greek world would be harnessed with the objective of *killing fellow Greeks*.

The Plague

One year later, May 430 BC, news reached the Athenians that the huge Peloponnesian army was on the move again, headed toward Attica. As the year before, a vast throng of people, roughly 150,000 rural residents of Attica, descended upon Athens: families of wealthy landowners, their slaves, and poor farmers. The city, built to house about 100,000 residents, was unable to provide proper sanitation for the vast numbers of its new temporary inhabitants. As the Peloponnesian invaders came within a day's march from the walls of Athens, they learned that Athenians were dying in huge numbers inside the city. Forward scouts reported seeing many columns of smoke rising from within the long walls—funeral pyres for the cremated dead.

Thucydides, one of the few who contracted the disease and recovered, provides a lurid description. It began with violent heat in the head, followed by burning eyes, severe coughing, vomiting of bile, dry heaves, dysentery, violent spasms, and almost always death.

The historian tells us succinctly that 4,400 hoplite infantrymen, 300 cavalrymen, and "an indeterminable number of common people" died. From these numbers, Hanson extrapolates that a third of Athenian adult soldiers and another 40,000 to 50,000 women, slaves, and children died during the terrible four years it took for the disease to run its course.

Toward the end of the war, an Athenian expeditionary force was entirely wiped out in attempt to conquer Sicily. Even though Sicily was a catastrophic campaign, twice as many Athenians died on the streets of Athens with the plague.

To make matters worse, Pericles, the spiritual leader of Athens, died of the plague in 430 BC. For Thucydides, Pericles' death represented a spiritual death of the Athenian people. What he believed emanated from the plague was a loss of honor and civility for Athens. From this point forward in his narrative of the war, his tone becomes darker and his pessimism borders on despondency over the barbarity of human nature, a theme that surfaced more and more frequently.

For Thucydides, Athens was a tragic hero in a grand drama, a victim of its previous successes and guilty of extreme hubris.[19] Since the close of the Persian War, fifty years earlier, no other Greek city-state had constantly been at war. Hanson writes:

> *"No government was as reckless and dangerous as Athens' Assembly . . . in minutes, it could call for the execution of a man or an entire captured city across the seas on the flimsiest of charges. . . . The philosopher Socrates had doubts about democratic Athens' hubris and megalomania . . . yet he battled bravely in three of Athens' most difficult engagements, Potidaea, Delium, and Amphipolis. . . . Thucydides used the broad message of the war's senselessness to explore his own bleak views about human nature."* [20]

Thucydides illustrates the murderous irrationality of the Athenian Assembly in his account of the campaign in 428 BC, during the third year of the war against Mytilene, the largest city-state on the island of Lesbos.

The Mytilenian oligarchic council voted to secede from the Athenian Empire. Quickly Athens dispatched a fleet to blockade the city. The Assembly decided to make an example of the Mytilenians to discourage rebellion elsewhere in its empire. The siege lasted a whole year—ultimately Mytilene succumbed. The Athenian general in charge of the operation rounded up the city's leaders and sent them to Athens for execution, then waited for the Assembly's decision on what to do with rest of the residents. Word came to execute all the male citizens and enslave all the females and children. On the following day, the Assembly reversed itself and decided to spare the innocent residents of Mytilene, those who were not leaders of the insurrection. An Athenian ship arrived at the fallen city just before the commander could carry out the mass annihilation. Nevertheless, the result was that the Assembly approved the execution of 1,000 of its former allies. As Waterfield puts it, "If the Athenians had occupied the moral high ground, they lost it then."

---

19. A concept developed by the Greeks to signify a broad set of principles, defined succinctly— outrageous arrogance, resulting in acts that would eventually be punished by the gods.

20. Victor Davis Hanson, *A War Like No Other,* (New York: Random House, 2005), 17.

By 416 BC, the war had raged for twelve years and Athens had devolved into an unconscionable killing machine. For the entire duration of the war, the very small island of Melos had resisted being brought into the Athenian Empire. The Assembly decided to launch an attack. Thucydides constructs a dialogue between the Melian leadership and the Athenian envoys. When asked by the Melians what justified their attack, the Athenians replied, "The strong have dominion over the weak." From the Athenians' point of view, the fact that they had the power to conquer Melos gave them the right to do it. War is war.

To preserve its manpower, the Athenians starved Melos into surrendering. This time, all the men of the island were executed, the women and children led off to the slave markets in Athens. Hard to sell elderly were left to die. Because hubris must be punished by the gods, the tragedy of Athens was now moving rapidly to its climax.

The Defeat in Sicily

Before the war with Sparta and its allies began, Pericles told the Athenians in one of his scores of orations before the Assembly that, although it probably had been a mistake for Athens to have acquired its empire, it would be folly to give it up. In this address he somehow envisioned his city's demise and warned his countrymen not to increase the size of the empire further. But they disregarded Pericles' prescient admonition.

On the eve of the Sicilian expedition, word reached the Athenian empire that Sicily to their west had discovered huge new deposits of gold, and there was a small enclave of colonists on the island who wished to align with Athens and its allies.

The Assembly quickly authorized a massive expedition comprised of triremes, cargo ships, and enough troop transports to carry thousands of Hoplite warriors. Its mission, to defeat Spartan military installations on Sicily and bring the island into the Empire. Some Athenian Hawks brazenly predicted that the capture of Sicily would yield enough gold to double their treasury.

The night before the expedition was to set sail, a terrible omen occurred. Someone defaced a number of statues of the god, Hermes, that were placed at various points around the city and on the walls leading down to the Piraeus. This struck fear in many of the Athenians, especially the soldiers and sailors poised to embark.

As rumors swirled, suspicion fell upon the Athenian commander Alcibiades. Although he had proven himself an able general, capable of winning engagements, he was a notorious womanizer and a dilettante. It was fashionable in Athenian society to single such people out for ostracism on the grounds that they might try to seize power and institute a new tyranny. Alcibiades escaped capture and defected to the Spartans.

A feckless general, Nikias, was selected in his stead, a commander who managed to lose all his ground troops and all his ships. While the Athenian armada was moored in the Syracuse harbor, they were surprised by the Spartan allied ships, led by the Corinthians, who blockaded the mouth of the harbor and totally destroyed them, all one hundred and sixty triremes and 40,000 men. Those not killed on the ground were completely cut off from supply. Eventually they surrendered and were sold into slavery. Syracuse was the first naval engagement Athens had lost in a century. With their defeat, the Athenians' belief in their naval supremacy was destroyed.

The Beginning of the End of Athenian Hegemony

By fall 413 BC, Athenian military-age manpower had fallen by a third due to both the plague and Sicilian catastrophe. The Spartans had taken up permanent lodging in Attica and had captured the fortress city of Dekeleia. Their presence liberated the Athenians' slaves who worked the silver mines at Laurion, and in so doing, a vital source of Athenian revenue was eliminated. And yet, with a supply of grain and tribute from their captive maritime empire, Athens would soldier on.

While it had gained the advantage on the ground, Sparta did not have the means to launch a naval attack on Athenian holdings in the Aegean. But Persia was waiting in the wings and was more than willing to fund the Greeks' suicidal civil war. Sparta, for its part, was more than willing to sell out Greek Athenian allies living in Ionia (today's eastern Turkey), while agreeing to recognize the lands as part of the Persian Empire after the conquest of Athens in exchange for the gift of a Persian financed navy. The gods were tightening the noose around Athenians.

Also in 413, Sparta concluded treaties with the Greek's mortal enemy, Persia, and began acquiring massive funds from Persian Satraps in Ionia. In these treaties, the Spartans agreed to allow the Persian Empire to reestablish its sovereignty over the Greek speaking colonies of Ionia, once the Athenians had been defeated. Sadly, as the decade came to a desultory close, Spartan Greeks sold out Ionian Greeks in exchange for future power over other Greek countrymen. These shameless treaties were brokered by Alcibiades, the rakish Athenian general who defected to the Spartans. By this time, he had fathered a child with the wife of one of the Spartan kings who was away on a campaign in Attica. Alcibiades was a reckless Bill Clinton-like figure, willing to risk a dalliance with a Spartan princess, knowing that in doing so, he risked everything in the pursuit of personal conquest. He did so anyway, because he could.

By 411 BC, the Spartans were in command of a Persian-financed fleet staffed by mercenaries. Their mission was to wreak havoc upon the Athenians' Aegean island allies whose tribute supplied the waning Athenian war effort. In the same year, the very wealthy island of Rhodes defected from the Athenian Empire. And, when the city of Abydos, located on the strategic entrance to the Hellespont, was surrounded by a Spartan hoplite land expedition, they defected too. When the Spartans gained control of the entrance to the Black Sea, they began to cut off grain shipments headed to Athens. Relentlessly, piece by piece, Sparta stripped away the Athenians' access to money and food.

Meanwhile the Athenian Assembly was running out of money. The Empire increasingly relied upon donations from the powerful, wealthy families to fund the war effort. These donations increasingly became less and less voluntary. As a result, many of Athens' wealthiest families openly advocated for an end to the war and a peace treaty with Sparta, even if meant an end to democracy. Rule by the many had become too costly for the Athenian landed gentry, most of whom had foreign estates often acquired through propitious marriages.

In 407 BC, the Assembly sent desperate messages to Alcibiades asking that he come back and take over command of the combined Athenian forces. Perhaps because he was homesick, or possibly because he knew that his sexual dalliances inside the Spartan Court made him vulnerable to forces outside his control, he accepted and returned home to much fan fare and adulation. His command lasted less than six months—his luck had run out.

The Spartans and their Persian benefactors sensed that Athens was mortally wounded, and they had no intention of signing a peace treaty that would leave any of the Athenian empire in tact. The tribute-paying Athenian empire was the prize they had given so much blood and treasure to win. By 407 BC, Alcibiades had met his match in Lysandros, the Spartan general whose burning ambition was to strip Athens of its empire and to install himself as the new

© Marie-Lan Nguyen / Wikimedia Commons

The Apollo Belvedere was reputedly Napoleon's most prized possession, looted from the Vatican. It demonstrates the ancient Greeks' reach for divinity, carved at a time when most Europeans were still brutish hunter gatherers.

ruler of the Spartan-dominated Aegean empire. That same year, Persian money enticed Athenian-allied oarsmen to defect to Spartan side for better pay. For the first time, Spartans had parity with Athenians in naval war-making powers.

In late 407 BC, Alcibiades took his fleet to the Ionian port city of Notion, near Ephesus, then departed to search for much needed tribute—food and money for his sailors. With novice commander Antiockhos in charge, Lysandros surprised the fleet still moored in the harbor and was able to wipe it out. When the news reached Athens, the Assembly quickly convened, removed Alcibiades of his command, and sent a young general, Konon, to replace him. It was too late. The remaining city-states allied with Athens on the Ionian coast (today's western Turkey), opened their gates to Persian and Spartan forces, and fell like dominoes. This vast portion of the Greek-speaking world, once the crown jewel of the Athenian empire, was forever stripped away. It was lost to Europe and became part of Asia. Alcibiades was banished to his fortress estate on the Cheronese only to be assassinated by a Persian special-forces unit two years later. So ended the life of a great and daring, some would say, reckless, Athenian.

In 406 BC, the Athenians were reduced to melting down sacred statues cast in gold to fund the building and launching of a new hastily constructed fleet. One-hundred boats were manned by novice sailors, boys and slaves, and commanded by ten newly-elected, untested generals. Yet, in an engagement outside the port of Mytilene, where the better trained and larger Spartan fleet blockaded the hapless Konos, the Athenians won decisively, sinking seventy-five enemy boats while only losing twenty-five.

Suddenly, the long besieged Athenians' hopes were raised. After twenty years of deprivation and massive loss of their sons and fathers, they thought the tide had turned, that the gods were with them, and that they might regain control of the seas. In the Agora, there was even talk of repatriating Ionia. But, for reasons we moderns can only speculate upon today, the Athenians decided to throw it all away.

In the midst of the elation, it was learned that, in the aftermath of the battle, none of the surviving Athenian fleet had been dispatched to troll the battlefield and pick up any of their sailors still alive, clinging to the wreckage of their vessels. This was standard practice. Perhaps the young generals delegated this task to junior officers and, for unknown reasons, it had not happened.

In Athens, it was presumed that many sailors were lost due to the oversight. Enraged, the Assembly sent word that all the ten young generals be recalled and put on trial for treasonous malfeasance. Two were killed in the battle and two escaped into the Grecian badlands, never to be heard from again. Of the six who were brought back for trial, all were found guilty and executed. This act was a manifestation of the public cultural death wish, born from the desperate knowledge among the citizens of Athens that they were losing the war. After the pointless murder of its own novice commanders, as Waterfield puts it, ". . . the end came quickly."

In 405 BC, the Athenian fleet, under a still newer and less able cadre of elected generals, sailed to the Hellespont on a desperate mission to retake the cities there. The Athenians knew it was utterly vital that they free the route through the narrow Hellespont so food shipments could arrive in Athens from their allied grain producers located on the shores of the Black Sea. The fleet put in and beached its ships at Aegospotami. Half the Athenians were dispatched to Sestos, eighteen kilometers down the Hellespont, in the hope of securing food, while the other half foraged locally. Lysandros found the poorly-led Athenians beached and in indefensible disarray. In a devastating surprise attack, all but ten ships were destroyed. Three thousand Athenians were killed. Several hundred others ran away. Grain could no longer be shipped through the Hellespont. Athens had lost nearly all of its allies and offensive capabilities.

On their way to blockade Athens, the victorious Spartan and Persian fleet made stops at Aegean islands where the former Athenian allies threw open their gates to joyous celebrations and hailed Lysander as a liberator and a demigod. The news traveled at incredible speed. In just a week, all of the Athenians' Aegean allies declared themselves free from the Empire. By the end of October, 405 BC, Lysander's 150 ships formed a blockade outside the Athenian port of Peiraieus, while tens of thousands of Spartan allied forces were encamped just outside javelin range of the city's walls. The starving Athenians tearfully clutched their sons and husbands, believing that they would soon face the same fate as the Melians. They believed that the men would be put to death, the women and children sold into slavery. Instead, Lysandros was able to quell the desires for butchery. The Thebans desired clemency, arguing that the Athenians had played such a heroic role in defeating the Persians two generations earlier.

Nevertheless, the terms of the Athenians' surrender included the destruction of its long walls leading to its port, the formal dissolution of its empire on both land and sea, and the installation of pro-Spartan oligarchs, governors which became known as the "Thirty Tyrants."

As the walls were being torn down, Xenophon wrote that the Athenians themselves celebrated amid "The music of pipe girls . . . (the Athenian) people thought that this marked the beginning of freedom for Greece."[21] Instead, it was the beginning of the end of Greek freedom and the beginning of the end of a civilization organized around the fiercely independent city-state, the polis.

---

21. Xenophon, *Hellenica*, Book 2, 23.

Dead Men Walking

At the close of the fifth century (400 BC), every educated Greek, no matter where he lived throughout the Mediterranean, recognized that in their grandparents' day, it was the Athenians who provided the leadership and heroism at Marathon and Salamis, and made the difference between victory and defeat before the Persians. Yet, the Athenians had been decimated and humiliated for their war crimes, leaving the Greek world with a great vacuum of leadership and confidence.

Almost every Athenian statesman who assumed military command had perished in the war. The city's military leadership had literally been shorn away. As Hanson points out, roughly 40,000 military-age men lived in Athens before the outbreak of the war. By the time of their surrender, the number had fallen to 15,000—a loss of 60%. And, due to the plague and hunger, the civilian population had fallen by 100,000 citizens. To put this in context, the US lost 400,000 in World War II, which represents .3 percent in a population of 133 million. Imagine the impact on the American psyche if the country had lost 100 times that figure—44 million. For some of the small city-states, the losses were even worse. Whole populations of young military-age men were killed or executed. The great Greek civil war had been too long and too brutal for the Greeks to remain the confident martial people they were before the war.

For the next sixty-seven years, while the Greek world remained free of outside domination, they again indulged in petty wars among themselves. Due to the enormous toll they exacted upon themselves during the thirty-year long civil war, their nationalism was exhausted. Their fealty to the Greek way of life, since the mythic heroic ages, had always centered around a fiercely independent polis. Greece became what the Western Europeans are today, incapable of rallying its peoples, Athenians, Thebans, Corinthians, Corcyreans, to meet a confident well-armed outside invader. They were incapable of defeating a major existential threat as they had one hundred years earlier. The once fiercely independent Greek city-state was a dead man walking.

Greek Life after the Defeat of the Athenians

After the Athenian surrender, the Spartans continued to be financially supported by the Persians and rapidly earned the enmity of most of their fellow Greek city-states. The occupying government of "Thirty Tyrants" imposed a reign of terror in Athens and murdered hundreds of their opponents, even those suspected of treachery. The Athenians, who largely wished to reinstitute democracy, were able to expel the Spartan thugs fairly quickly, only to find that a group of ten oligarchs and their families were plotting to regain power over the city, power enjoyed one hundred years earlier before the adoption of the democratic constitution written by Clisthenes. The leading democrats called a conference to meet with representatives of the wealthy families. When the delegates of the oligarchs arrived at the appointed meeting place, the democrats murdered all of them. Within the Greek states, a low grade murderous civil war continued without interruption.

In the six decades after the Peloponnesian war, the world of the Greek polis continued to produce awe-inspiring intellectual breakthroughs in the fields of architecture, sculpture (a deification of the human form), theater, medicine, historiography, naval warfare, commerce, banking, philosophy, and scientific inquiry. As part of this intellectual ferment, sophists increasingly argued that service to one's polis and to one's people was not an unquestioned ideal as it had been before the Great War. Many of the sophists, hired by wealthy families as tutors, often moonlighted as free-lance philosophers and were the ancient equivalents of community organizers and agitators, teaching their students to question authority and the status quo. In Athens, Socrates, a common soldier lucky to survive the war, taught that a man's conscience was a better guide to conduct than the demands of the state. As this notion grew dominant, it confirmed that Athens was not going to duplicate its "Periclean" military greatness. From his devoted student Plato, we know that the Assembly condemned Socrates to death for, among other things, the corruption of the young.

In the successive two generations after the death of Socrates, Plato and Aristotle developed an enormous body of work that built upon Greek thought and morals, and quite literally became the pillars of Western philosophy, ethics, and epistemology. As Thomas Noble of Notre Dame University points out, during the post-war years, Greek thinkers and teachers demonstrated in a very sophisticated way that appearances can be deceiving, that the world around us is likely not what it seems. Even more important, through their elaboration of epistemology, they built the scientific method into Western tradition. They made the West unique when they developed a positive doctrine and a large technical methodology for qualifying, analyzing, and questioning data and assumptions. This was an achievement of stunning proportions, even greater than the invention of democracy, because it resulted in the West's ultimate ascendancy—its military and scientific dominion over the East.

Aristotle possessed one of the widest-ranging minds that ever lived. He personally wrote and taught ethics, politics, music, medicine, embryology, astronomy, botany, history, zoology, rhetoric, and poetry. He traveled to Macedon and was hired by Philip II to tutor his young son Alexander, the eventual king of all Greece. And yet, it's worth noting that during the years leading up to the Greeks' subjugation by Macedon, both Plato (427-347 BC) and Aristotle (384-322 BC) concluded that democracy was fatally flawed as the basis for the organization of society. It never occurred to either of them that the fiercely independent, incessantly warlike polis should be abandoned. In fact, Aristotle, whose "academy" studied the constitutions of 150 Greek poleis, concluded that the natural human condition was to live in a polis, that man was a "political animal," that Athens was entirely too big, and that a polis should be no larger than one where "all the adult male population could be summoned by the call of a single crier."

Additionally, both Plato and Aristotle believed that an ideal society should be ruled by a "few of the best." Neither was able to define how their "philosopher kings" would be chosen or why anyone would agree to be their subordinates. Nor did it occur to them that the Greek polis had simply exhausted itself as the primary unit around which their civilization was ordered. While the Greeks fulminated over how to best rule the polis, a whole new paradigm, the first European proto-nation state, was being constructed by Philip II of Macedon, north of the Greek mainland.

On the Greek mainland, in the 370s and 360s BC, the city of Thebes, north of Athens, that had been allied with Sparta, began to establish what some historians call the Theban hegemony. They were able to do so, partly because they lost relatively few men in the civil war and partly because they produced some skilled generals. One of these was Epaminondas who defeated a Spartan invasion force on the Theban territory of Boeotia. At the battle of Leuctra, his Thebans massacred 400 Spartan hoplites. As Waterfield points out, this represented about 40% of the remaining Spartan military age men. The following year, 369 BC, Epaminondas led a Theban invasion into the Spartan homeland, Laconia. There, on Spartan soil, he wiped out the balance of the Spartans' military. Next he freed roughly 200,000 Helots; the men, women, and children who provided the slave labor upon which Spartan society was based, and with that the Spartan hoplite, the greatest infantryman the Greek world ever produced, ceased to exist.

The Theban hegemony was brief. Epaminondas was killed battling a coalition of Athenian allies in 362 BC. Without a leader of equal stature, the Thebans retreated to Boeotia to become a footnote in history. In the 350s, with the Spartans scattered to the winds, with Persia preoccupied, and with several insurrections inside its empire, decimated and war-weary Greeks were confronted with a new and ominous threat looming to the north. The Macedonian king, Philip II, through diplomacy, conquest, and eleven marriages, consolidated his power over all the tribes of Macedon then turned his eyes south to Greece.

Philip II Begins the Destruction of Free Greece
In his relentless, ferocious quest for more power and more territory, Philip II

of Macedon proved over and over that he was a brilliant military strategist. He was equally skilled as a politician, or perhaps more aptly put, a practitioner of the art of political deception. He was like most absolute rulers of history—ruthless and an amoral opportunist. And Philip was also very skillful. For more than a decade, he had pressed southward into Thessaly and east into Thrace, bringing into his growing empire one and then another of the northern Greek poleis, some of which capitulated without a fight. On one occasion, he sent troops to aid in yet another Greek civil war (the Sacred War). They fought alongside the Thesalians for control of the temple to Apollo on Delphi, the spiritual capital of Greece. In this act, he was brilliantly attempting to market himself as a liberator and protector of Greek culture. When he sent a larger troop towards Delphi to take the city and incorporate it into his realm, the Athenians learned of his intent and sent a force to fight him (coincidentally at Thermopylae where the Spartans fought to the last man against the Persian hoards one hundred and fifty years earlier). On this occasion, he elected to retreat, for the moment, in an effort to cultivate his public relations victory and conserve his resources. He would be back.

During the same period, the decade of 350s BC and into the 340s, Philip II continuously allowed diplomats from the important city-states of central Greece, such as Athens and Thebes, to visit his court. His minions engaged the visitors in endless talks, while he waited for his opportunity to strike. The opportunity arose when Athens was weakened with the dissolution of treaties and alliances with several northern neighbors, including Phocis and Alos. While informing the Athenian and Theban ambassadors of his peaceful intentions, he marched on both cities, destroyed their defenses, and brought these buffer states in central Greece into the Macedonian orbit. Thebes and Athens did not protest and even were signatories, in 346 BC, to a treaty with Macedon, the Peace of Philocrates.

In the same way that Adolf Hitler coerced France and England to give up on their alliances with Czechoslovakia, Athens and Thebes acceded to Philip's political treachery and threw two small buffer states, fellow Greeks with whom they were estranged, to the dogs. In this hubristic act of appeasement, allies Thebes and Athens signed the death warrants for many of their countrymen. In so doing, they gave away their last remaining line of defense between them and Macedon, and therefore violated:

IMMUTABLE #9
When a civilization accepts the propaganda of its enemy as truth,
it has reached the far side of appeasement and capitulation is nigh.

With all northern Greece already in Philip's hands, the plains of Attica and Boeotia were wide open to him in 346 BC.

The Battle of Chaeronea (338 BC)

Philip waited patiently as he continued to muster an even larger army, sufficient in size to capitalize on his opportunity. When ready, he marched south and captured Delphi, the spiritual center of Greece. The march continued toward the center of the Greek homeland and he duped Thebes and Athens. The great orator and anti-Macedonian, Demosthenes, later described the panic and chaos that swept the city of Athens when the news of Philip's impending invasion arrived. On the following day when the town crier called for a meeting of the Assembly, the entire city appeared on the Pnyx, the steep hill beside the Agora where the Assembly met. The perception of doom was so widespread that when the crier asked over and over, "Who wishes to speak?" no one volunteered. Athens sent a messenger to Thebes asking it to join them in resisting the Macedonians.

One hundred and fifty years earlier, 30 Greek poleis joined the alliance that stood against the Persians. Now in 338 BC, despite the fact that the Greek world was far more numerous and richer than it had been during the Persian invasion, it was able to muster an army from only *two* cities, Athens and Thebes.

Philip II adopted the Greek hoplite tactics and refined them to produce what would become the awesome Macedonian phalanx. Its basic unit was an extremely dense square, a 256 man formation composed of 16 men across and 16 men deep, each standing in a very tight formation. Along with helmet, breast plate, and shield, each warrior carried an enhanced fifteen foot pike with a counter weight at the butt end that required less strength to hold it in a horizontal, forward thrusting position. The first five rows pointed their pikes forward while the remaining eleven rows of men rested their pikes on the man in front, forming a 45 degree roof that provided a bristling barrier to arrows. Philip II put his entire kingdom on a war footing by endlessly training and drilling his vast army. This resulted in them being able to conduct complicated

Greek Iron Helmet

battlefield maneuvers that were nearly impossible for his enemies to match or counter. His army, now composed of more than 200 phalanx units, was a vast killing machine. Once moving on the field of battle, it was practically unstoppable.

The Macedonians met the Greek allies in a field near the small city of Chaeronea. The commanders were Lysicles of Athens, Theagenes of Thebes, and Philip II and his sixteen year old son, the future Alexander the Great of Macedon. Alexander led an elite core of 2,000 cavalrymen while the other three commanders led infantrymen. Thirty-two thousand Macedonians stood facing 35,000 Greeks, ready to decide the fate of Europe.

Alexander the Great

Our primary source for the battle, historian Diodorus, tells us that the two sides fought bitterly for a large portion of the day when, ultimately, Philip gave the order to his Macedonian infantry to retreat. This was an extraordinarily difficult maneuver for thirty-thousand men in phalanx formation to perform—walk backward and remain in their ranks, while in the white hot heat of battle. Yet, the retreating Macedonians remained in formation while the Athenians, who made up the left flank, sensed an advantage and rushed forward on the attack. The Thebans on the right side, sensing a trap, stayed their ground. This created a gap between the two allied armies.

When the sixteen-year-old Alexander, the future conqueror of Asia, saw this opening, he instantly gave the order to his cavalrymen to charge through it and cut the Greek enemy into two disconnected halves. Just as was the Persians' fate at the Battle of Marathon, the Athenians had to worry about an attack coming at them from their rear. Discipline broke down and the advantage quickly shifted to the Macedonians who established and maintained the flanking maneuver.

Seeing the gap filled by Alexander's cavalry, Philip gave the command to send in ground troops to widen the gap and ordered the main body of his troops to halt their retreat and move forward. Soon the Athenians were caught in a trap where they could not go forward nor retreat. Hundreds of Athenians were killed and thousands laid down their weapons and surrendered. The Thebans, vastly outnumbered, continued to fight and suffered thousands of casualties before surrendering. The battle was over as nightfall descended. Vast numbers of Athenians and Thebans lay dead or dying. Greece was lost. There were no new armies to muster. As was the case at the start of the Peloponnesian war, rural Athenians moved inside the city to take up residence behind its walls, and there was no empire and no navy to supply the city. Resistance was futile. In their usual fashion, the Athenian Assembly tried and executed their general, Lysicles, for the crime of losing the battle at Chaeronea.

Philip offered the Greeks generous terms because he could afford to do so. He returned all prisoners and allowed Thebes and Athens to run their affairs so long as they would agree to his rule. They could govern themselves as long as they knew he had a veto and they did not. In an act of respect, Philip II sent his son on a peace mission to Athens where Alexander ceremonially offered the city the urns holding the cremated remains of their dead.

His first acts as king of all Greece were to impose a general confederacy of all Greek states, the League of Corinth, and to declare war on Persia. Due to incessant war upon itself, the Greek world was subservient to Macedon, the barbarian realm seen for centuries as the half-breed step-child. The world of the Greek polis exhausted its desire to defend itself; by its continual and catastrophic internal warfare, by its inability to unite against its outside foes, by its inability to see itself as nation of people rather than a collection of mortal enemies who spoke the same the language. It would be nearly two and a half millenniums before the Greeks would be an independent, free people again.

IMMUTABLE #4
*If a people cannot avoid continuous internal warfare,
it will have a new order imposed from without.*

MODERN COROLLARIES

A single EMP (electromagnetic pulse) weapon has the potential to destroy the United States. China and the Iranian mullahs are both working on EMP weapons. Iran has repeatedly stated it is "desirable and achievable" to bring about "a world without America," and has tested EMP delivery missiles from platforms on the Caspian Sea. (More regarding Iran's EMP weapon program appears in Chapter 6, pg 269.)

For the twenty-first century West, the principle wrapped inside the Athenians' Peace of Philocrates has an immutability and colossal significance that cannot be overstated. The attempt by a civilization at appeasement of a ruthless enemy committed to its conquest will accomplish the opposite of the appeaser's wishes. It will *always* invite attack. Further, the attempt at appeasement will signal that the time to strike is *now*.

For Athens and its allies, to allow Macedon to absorb two small buffer states without so much as a diplomatic protest, was equivalent to Neville Chamberlain's letter to Adolf Hitler that forfeited the Western Allies' alliance with Czechoslovakia and freed Hitler to absorb a defenseless neighbor without retaliation. It was tantamount to Bill Clinton's transfer of nuclear weapons technology to China, and to Jimmy Carter and Madeline Albright's gift of uranium fueled power plants to North Korea. All are examples of the principle of appeasement, a civilization-threatening tactic.

The endless negotiations, that began during the Bush Administration, aimed at convincing the Iranian regime to halt their nuclear weapons development, continued three years into the Obama administration. Obama's unceasing prostrate pronouncements, iterating his desire for "dialogue," were greeted with scorn and insults by the Mullahs, and rebuffed by the Iranian leadership who would continue to refer to the US as the "Great Satan." His attempts to engage them were simply a continuation of the US and Europeans' feckless negotiations which could potentially amount to America's Treaty of Philocrates.

It's hard to imagine how the American policy toward its most determined enemy, the terrorist-sponsoring Iranian regime, could have been more repudiated. During his campaign, Obama pronounced that his approach to dealing with the Iranian regime versus that of his predecessor, President Bush, would be superior because it would be characterized as one of "engagement." Just as Philip II saw that the Greeks were too demoralized to resist and he took the opportunity to attack them, the Iranians rebuffed Obama's feckless attempts to schedule direct talks. Instead they offered their own set of "preconditions" such as the American abandonment of its only trusted Middle Eastern ally, Israel. They installed thousands of new centrifuges aimed at refining plutonium into weapons-grade material, held phony elections to support their puppet hard-liner president, and brutally put down a rebellion by their people. With all this, Obama's only response was tepid and timid, indicating his hope for a cessation of violence and stability in Iran so that he could get back to the business of appeasing the regime there.

Obama's 2009 Cairo Speech—Appeasement of all Islam

In June 2009, the new President Obama used his historic speech in Cairo to placate 1.2 billion Muslims who, from birth, have been taught that it is their god-given destiny to one day rule the infidel. Additionally, he used the occasion to demoralize Israel. In a speech riddled with historical falsehoods and fabrications, he ascribed a moral equivalence to the annihilation of six million Jews by the Axis Powers in World War II with the treatment of the Palestinians at the hands of the Israelis over the last 50 years.

A more shocking and dangerous juxtaposition could scarcely be imagined when one considers that tiny Israel, our forward ally in the war against radical Islam, is already losing its martial spirit, its will to fight on, because it has shed so much blood and treasure in its struggle to survive. Yet, Obama's humiliation of Israel was self-defeating because it provides American and other western intelligence services with enormous data regarding the designs of radical regimes such as Iran and Syria. It has conducted fearless bombing raids on Arab nuclear reactors in Iraq and Syria and thereby kept nuclear arms out of the hands of America's most dangerous enemies. Such juxtaposition further demoralizes a vitally important ally and it emboldens the "jihadists" by endorsing their propaganda and justifying their cause.

Obama's appeasement came with great cost.

He disheartened a key ally and emboldened our enemies. In denigrating the Iraq war as a "war of choice," he dismayed the troops fighting there and the families of soldiers killed liberating that country. Not finished, he broke the spirt of the families of American soldiers killed in Bosnia, Kosovo, and Afghanistan—recent wars where the US liberated Muslim populations from their repressive regimes. So intent was Obama upon empowering Muslims with a sense of pride, he sought to sublimate himself as a coreligionist leader of the free world, asking them for forgiveness for past western transgressions.

Ominously, President Obama's actions in 2009 on the foreign policy stage greatly damaged national security, because when a civilization adopts the propaganda of its enemy, it occupies the far side of appeasement. Similarly, in conquering Greece, Philip II showed that he understood the following ageless principle of the aggressor.

IMMUTABLE #3
Appeasement of a ruthless outside power always invites its aggression. Treaties made with ruthless despots are always fruitless and dangerous.

Cooling the Planet Trumps American Military Preparedness

As described earlier, during the decade between the battle of Marathon in 490 BC and the invasion of Greece by the Persians in 480 BC, a huge vein of silver was discovered in the Athenian countryside at Laurion. It was Themistocles who convinced the Athenian Assembly to invest in the construction of a navy. In so doing, the Greeks preserved a nascent western civilization and won the battle of Salamis.

In 2009, the Obama administration elevated the passage of an anti-global "Cap and Trade" legislation to one its top priorities. The *purported* objective of this legislation was to limit carbon emissions that resulted from energy exploration, production, and usage—through the implementation of massive taxes on those vital activities.

But by the end of 2009, almost no one, except perhaps former Vice President Al Gore and the Obama administration's climate change advisors, believed that limiting American usage of energy and lessening the resulting carbon-based emissions would have a substantive effect on the planet's climate. Nor did anybody know or propose what ought to be the optimum mean temperature of the planet, or why, over the past decade, the planet seemed to be slipping into a very mild cooling trend.

Yet in June 2009, an anti-global warming "Cap and Trade" bill was proposed by the House of Representatives, the self-appointed body of climate experts. In actuality, the Democrat controlled House's unspoken reason to enact the bill was to provide the government with the means to tax every corporation and every individual for their energy usage. If enacted, the bill would have constituted the largest transfer of wealth ever, creating vast sums of new monies for non-military spending, for nationalized medical care, and for the new climate change bureaucracy, among other distributionist objectives. The Cap and Trade bill would have been the largest assault on private property, privacy, and basic freedoms in American history.

President Obama, in championing his climate-change bill, made it clear he would not follow the example of past leaders such as Themistocles, instead quite the opposite. Perhaps for the first time in history, the leader of a great civilization would actively seek to prevent his own country from extracting its indigenous wealth-producing precious resources, extracting and producing the fuel necessary to power its economy and military, and obtaining the resulting revenues to expand its wealth and pay down its debts. Obama signaled, in the face of a severe recession, that he would seek to *lessen* the exploration and production of energy resources, and *lessen* military strength and intelligence gathering services necessary to counter threats confronting the country all across the globe. In 2009, while almost all other facets of government received promises of unprecedented hundreds of billions of dollars (monies not yet received by the treasury or produced by the economy) the new president cut funds for vital military weapon systems, missile defense, and the world's most advanced fighter jets, the F-22 Raptor.

There is a reverse corollary to the Obama Cap and Trade initiative—that being if Themistocles, despite the growing threat from Persia, convinced the Assembly to *disband* the Athenian ship building programs and ordered the silver mines shut down. Such a decision for the Greeks would have meant that there would have been no battle at Salamis. Instead, the subjugation of their culture, the extinction of their freedoms, and their domination by Persia would have occured. Had they done so, the Greeks would have violated the following immutable principle of civilizational survival.

IMMUTABLE #10
*Declining civilizations will always face
superior firepower from ascending civilizations
because sovereignty is only temporarily uncontested.*

Yet They Threw It All Away

In 406 BC, toward the end of the long and brutal Peloponnesian war off the coast of Mytilene and after many years of military defeats, the Athenians won a decisive naval battle against the Persian-backed Spartans. Yet the Assembly voted to execute the new generals for their failure to rescue survivors. As Waterfield puts it, for the Athenians, "... the end came quickly ... they threw it all away." Shortly thereafter, the Athenians lost the remainder of their fleet at Aegospotami with massive loss of life. They continued to make war on other Greek cities, killing their own Athenian citizens. Quite literally, the cultural capital of the Greek world had descended into a suicide cult.

During his first 100 days in office, President Obama nearly eliminated America's ability to gain information from terrorists captured on the battlefield. Through an executive order, he outlawed waterboarding and other *"enhanced interrogation techniques,"* procedures that did not fit the definition of torture. He recklessly stood by while his Attorney General and congressional leaders impugned the capabilities of American intelligence agencies.

The Democrat controlled Congress of the United States moved to criminalize their Republican predecessors from the Bush administration in the spring of 2009. Whatever for? Democrat party leaders openly informed the press that they intended to prosecute Bush administration officials at the highest levels and prove that they secretly authorized the torture of non-uniformed terrorists captured on the Afghan and Iraqi battlefields. Just as the torture scandal was heating up in the sycophantic press, news leaked out that Nancy Pelosi, the then Speaker of the House, approved of the very same interrogation techniques in oversight meetings conducted shortly after the attacks of 9/11.

As the generals of Mytilene were condemned by the Athenian Assembly in 406 BC, those who controlled the American congress in 2009 threatened to criminalize their political opponents with personal destruction. In so doing, they too threatened to *throw American security all away.*

Incredibly, while this brazen display of cultural suicide played out in the nation's capital in the late Spring of 2009, it was also revealed that a plot to blow up the tallest building west of the Mississippi, the US Bank Tower, was discovered through the use of "advanced interrogation techniques" conducted by the CIA on Khalid Sheikh Mohammed and two other individuals who were key planners in the 9/11 attacks.

During this very same period, Warren Buffett defected from the Obama financial advisory team. Known as the world's most successful investor, he held majority positions in some the world's largest insurance companies, and was a man who knew a great deal about risk. Warren publicly stated, prior to Obama's election, that the probability that the West would sustain a WMD attack some day is 100%. Not if—when.

The night before the battle at Salamis, Themistocles sent his slave and trusted aid to covertly provide the Persians with false information. He posed as a traitor and tricked them into believing that the Greek allies were too afraid to fight and they were planning to flee their positions during the cover of night. Upon his aid's safe return, Themistocles was provided with key intelligence regarding the Persians' strategies and intentions. As a result, he could determine what the Persians would do and could plan accordingly. This brilliant subterfuge drew the Persians into a trap where their greater numbers worked against them and sapped their rowers' strength treading water for many hours before the start of battle.

The Church Committee hearings of the 1970s imposed the "wall" between the CIA and the FBI, prohibiting communication between the two departments. This contributed to the weakening of our intelligence gathering capabilities that ultimately resulted in the 9/11 attacks. In Obama's first 100 days, our intelligence agents working to uncover the next attack, one which may well be catastrophic, must now worry about their own government's propensity to prosecute *them*.

For two and a half millenniums, good intelligence has proved critical in the outcome of important conflicts. Yet as Jed Babbin of *Human Events* has observed, "This war (against radical Islam) is much more dependent on intelligence than any other war before. We are not fighting against mass armies of forces; we're not fighting to retake ground that an enemy has conquered. This is a situation where intelligence is nearly the whole game."

By the beginning of 2012 it had become apparent that President Obama is willing to impugn our intelligence community for an ancillary political gain. He was actually the transnationalist he has always proclaimed to be, with all the confused motivations and loyalties this assertion betrays of an American Commander-in-Chief. He was betting his presidency, and quite possibly, the nation's survival on the perverse narcissistic gamble that he can somehow render inoperable the immutable dictum of the pre-Socratic Greek philosopher, Heraclitus. A dictum as true today as it was in the shadowy mists of our distant past—"war is the father of us all." Our president seems unaware of still another related dictum.

IMMUTABLE #4
*If a people cannot avoid continuous internal warfare,
it will have a new order imposed from without.*

Summary

The night before the battle of Plataea in 479 BC, where the allies would destroy the stranded Persian army left by Xerxes on the Greek mainland and free Europe from Asian invaders, a banquet was held for the Persian high command. It was hosted by the Thebans, who were still supporting Persia at this stage of the war. Herodotus reports that the commanding Persian general Mardonios told his host, Thersander, he knew that he and most of his men camped across the river would be dead the following day. When he was asked, by his Theban host, why he was not attempting to put together a plan to change that outcome, he replied, "My friend, what God has ordained, no man can prevent . . . we continue to take orders from our commander." [22]

Anthony Pagden adds a historic perspective to this moment in *Worlds at War*. In this conversation, Herodotus claims to have heard from a very aged Thersander himself, a description of what it meant to a Persian subject. Here was a Persian general unable to adapt and respond to the conditions on the battlefield, and resigned to death due to his inability to confront the unmitigated authority of his supreme leader. As Pagden puts it, "It was . . . to become an enduring image not only of the Persians but, after them, of the whole of Asia." [23]

In his *Histories*, Herodotus concluded the only way the Greeks defeated vastly larger armies and navies of Persia was because Greek soldiers were free men, not slaves.

The Greeks, a warlike collection of peoples who lived in independent poleis spread around the Mediterranean between 500 and 300 BC, somehow conceived and developed new disciplines which made primal impacts on all future human existence. They invented *isonomia*, equality before the law. The notion that the archon, the most powerful man of the polis, could not imprison the citizen goat herder without the due process of law.

Democracy, the notion that the many should rule the few, was a concept so unique, that no civilization untouched by the Greeks ever conceived of it, let alone implemented it. The Greeks invented international sport and combined it with religious observations and diplomacy. The Olympic Games were held in Olympia for roughly a thousand years from around 700 BC to AD 393 until they were banned

---

22. Herodotus, *Histories*, IX,16.

23. Anthony Pagden, *Worlds at War* (New York: Random House, 2009), 18.

by the Christian Roman Emperor, Theodosius. They invented epistemology, the scientific method, which begat the Roman Empire; the renaissance, the enlightenment, the industrial revolution, and the West's eventual military dominance over the more populous East, a dominance which began at Marathon.

Greek commanders were elected. Two generations after Marathon, in 401 BC, Xenophon, the great adventurer, thinker, and chronicler, was voted to take command of the beleaguered army of ten thousand Greek mercenaries who found themselves trapped far from home, inside the Persian Empire. Upon taking command, he told his men, "If anyone has a better plan to propose, let him do so."

Herodotus

From the time of Miltiades to the conquest of Greece by Macedon, most Greek armies were organized around the notion of democracy and freedom of expression. A man might walk into one battle a common foot soldier, and ride to the next as a general.

A generation after the Greeks expelled the Persians, Herodotus, the father of history, spent twenty years wandering the Mediterranean interviewing those who fought in the Persian wars. He was searching for answers to learn how the vastly outnumbered Greeks defeated the Persians. He surmised that the Greeks' brilliant military superiority was the result of their freedom—that in battle, free men will generally defeat slaves. Yet it was his protégé, Thucydides, the chronicler of the Peloponnesian War, who saw that the Greeks could destroy themselves by turning their brilliant war making prowess inward, upon themselves.

IMMUTABLE #1
*No nation has ever survived once its citizenry
ceased to believe its culture worth saving.
(Hanson's Law)*

CHAPTER TWO

The Fall of Carthage

146 BC

"It's fatal to enter a war without the will to win."
GENERAL DOUGLAS MACARTHUR

On the eve of its first war with Rome, in 264 BC, the Carthaginian Empire was positioned in the Mediterranean world of antiquity in many ways that mirror the US position in the West today. Although Rome controlled much of the Italian peninsula, it was a lesser land-based power with a much smaller agrarian economy. Carthage was the Mediterranean's leading maritime power and an economic powerhouse with interests and trading partners spread as far afield as the Black Sea, the Canaries, the British Isles, and even Scandinavia.

As the US achieved its world power status due to the defeat of the Axis Powers in World War II, the fall of Carthage came at the expense of the Roman ascendancy. Therefore, the fall of Carthage is also the story of the rise of Rome. With its defeat of Carthage, Rome began a rapid acquisition of its overseas empire. Had Rome been defeated by Carthage, the Greco-Roman trajectory of Western Civilization would have been dramatically altered.

Located on a bluff above a magnificent natural harbor on the coast of what is today Tunisia, the City of Carthage was originally settled around the eighth century BC by the Phoenicians, who were enormously intrepid seafarers. Their maritime business interests stretched from their original home around Tyre (in today's Lebanon) to the North Atlantic. They are believed to have developed the first alphabet—symbols which represented sounds, as opposed to pictograms, an invention of comparable importance to the wheel. The Phoenicians, from whom we get the word phonetics, invented the alphabet because they needed an efficient way to keep track of their burgeoning trading accounts.

By 246 BC, Carthage was an old city that the Romans viewed with some reverence, as it figures prominently in Virgil's national epic, *The Aeneid*.

Over the intervening five centuries after its founding, Carthage had become the dominant city of the Western Mediterranean. It had developed its own culture, separate and distinct from greater Phoenicia. It evolved an oligarchic democracy that bestowed untold riches on its wealthiest ruling families. It produced a thriving middle class of citizens which participated in a form of national profit sharing. It developed, along the coast of North Africa, in an area that was more arable than it is today, a system of agriculture that was the best and most productive in the known world. Additionally, Carthage controlled areas of Spain that included very lucrative gold and silver mines. Yet the inhabitants were fairly few in number. Estimates are that, at their zenith, Carthaginians represented only about 500,000 citizens. During wartime, their force multiplier was that they could easily afford a well-paid army and navy composed largely of mercenaries.

Some of the ruling families, such as the Barcids, produced the great generals, Hamilcar and his son Hannibal. They controlled vast revenue streams beyond the wildest dreams of contemporary Romans. "For people like the Barcids, whose family income each year from mining alone was over 300 talents (one ton of silver) . . . cosmopolitan luxury must have been as natural a state of life as it is for present day oil sheikhs." [1]

Most of what is known of the Carthaginians we know from Roman historians— Polybius (200 to 118 BC), Titus Livius known as Livy (59 BC to AD 17), Dionysius of Halicarnassus (60 to after 7 BC), and Cassius Dio (AD 155 or 163/164 to after 229). Virtually everything that the Carthaginians may have written about themselves is lost, submerged in the dust of history.

In the middle of the third century BC, the Carthaginians controlled the Western Mediterranean, Spain, Corsica, Sardinia, Sicily, and the western portion of the Maghreb (North Africa).

*Titus Livius
known as Livy*

The Eastern Mediterranean was controlled by Greek Hellenistic kingdoms that were legacies of Alexander the Great's empire. Upon Alexander's death in Mesopotamia, a century earlier in 323 BC, his generals carved his kingdom into three pieces: Egypt was ruled by the Ptolemaic Dynasty; Syria and regions east,

---

1   Ernle Bradford, *Hannibal*, (London: Macmillan London Limited, 1981), XV.

stretching to the Hindu Kush, by the Selucids; and the Macedonian homeland, including mainland Greece, by the Antigonids. Each were now dynasties ruled by the heirs of Alexander's generals who had survived him.

While the Carthaginians fought intermittent wars with some of the Greek city-states for control of Sicily, there was a truce with the Sicilian Greeks and their Hellenist overlords on the eve of the war with Rome. Carthage had control of the western part of the island and the indigenous Greeks controlled the remaining portion. At this time, Carthage preferred to avoid war because it was costly. It ran its empire of the Western Mediterranean, Sardinia, Corsica, Spain, and Western North Africa as if it were a business enterprise.

By the eve of the first Punic War in 246 BC, the Romans consolidated their hold on the entire Italian peninsula. Their southernmost garrisons could quite literally look across the very narrow strait of Messina and see the rich Island of Sicily. Nevertheless, the Carthaginians, with their enormous resources, were confident that their empire was secure. Unfortunately for them, they were wrong.

The First Punic War (264 - 241 BC)

The war lasted twenty-three years, four years less than the Greeks' Peloponnesian War. Yet Livy records that the first Punic War was the longest in history. It was fought

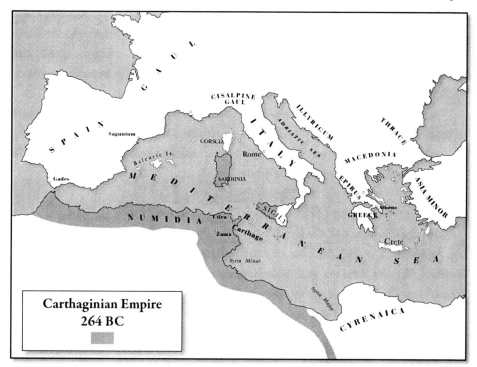

Carthaginian Empire
264 BC

between Rome and Carthage for control of Sicily. Ultimately Rome won and imposed a huge and humiliating indemnity upon Carthage. And, although the Romans left the city of Carthage still standing and able to fight another day, in their prosecution of the first Punic War, they demonstrated and refined many of the attributes that would propel the Roman civilization from a single city-state to the master of the known world.

The spark that set the Punic War ablaze was generated by a group of mercenary thugs, the Mamertines. They were Italians from the area of Campania who traveled to Syracuse and were employed as a sort of professional police force. When their Syracusan sponsor died, they found themselves out of work and began marching up the Eastern Coast of Sicily toward Italy. When they reached the Greek city of Messana, they asked for quarters and the local potentates took them into their homes and treated them as honored guests. Shortly thereafter, in the middle of the night the Mamertines slit the throats of their hosts, took their possessions, and captured their women. When word reached them that the Sicilian Greeks were preparing to make war upon them for their crimes, the Mamertines appealed for aid to the Romans, who were their Italian countrymen garrisoned at Rhegium, just a few miles away on the mainland. So began the Punic Wars that started as a Roman police action aimed at protecting a group of thugs, then escalated into a 120-year life-and-death struggle between Carthage and Rome for the mastery of the Western Mediterranean.

As soon as the Romans landed troops on the island, former enemies, Carthage and the Sicilian Greeks, formed a military alliance to oppose them. When war broke out in 264 BC, the cause of the Mamertines was quickly forgotten. As is often the case in war, the objective escalated and became a struggle to control the major population centers of Sicily, particularly the very wealthy Greek city-state of Syracuse.

The first relatively small skirmish occurred outside the city of Messana where a contingent of legionnaires caused the Carthaginians to withdraw. When the Carthaginian general responsible for the retreat returned home, he was punished in the usual Carthaginian fashion—he was crucified.

Phase One—The Land War in Sicily (264 - 260 BC)

The decisive battle of the first phase of the Punic War was the successful siege of the Agrigentum in 262 BC. The city perched upon a small mountain was massively fortified. Yet the Romans were somehow able to take the formidable fortress in a frontal assault. And in so doing, they sent shock and awe through the ranks of the Carthaginians and their Greek allies, so much so that they never again, in the first Punic War, chose to face the Romans in a conventional land battle. Instead, the allies chose to contest the Romans' presence on Sicily by harrying, ambushing, and retreating, and did so effectively because they controlled the sea and could be resupplied. However, the Carthaginian maritime advantage was about to vanish.

Phase Two—History's First Marines are Born (260 - 255 BC)

According to Polybius, in 260 BC, the Romans were becoming increasingly frustrated by the naval superiority of Carthage until they discovered a stranded Carthaginian quinquereme.[2] With the help of some Greek architects, the Romans made one-hundred copies in sixty days. While the rapidity of their feat of industry may be somewhat exaggerated, the fact that they produced the ships is not in dispute. Moreover, the Romans designed their very first war ships with a new and yet unseen refinement. As we saw at the battle of Salamis, two hundred years earlier, ancient naval warfare was composed of ships whose sole object was to ram the enemy vessel and sink it. The new Roman vessels added a new ingenious technology named the corvus (raven) which was a bridge with a swivel on one end and a massive spike on the other. This allowed the new Roman vessels to draw up alongside an enemy ship and drop the bridge onto it, impaling the spike onto the enemy deck, and allowing the Romans to storm the vessel. The corvus gave the Romans the ability to transfer their superior infantry skills to naval warfare, thus the birth of the world's first marines—men who fought on land and sea.

In virtually their first naval engagement that same year, the new Roman nation defeated the Carthaginians at the battle of Mylae. Flushed with their victory, in 256 BC, the Roman Senate authorized an invasion of North Africa, hoping to pressure the Carthaginians to surrender. The invasion force was ambushed and completely annihilated. Not one man returned. Also in that same year, due to their inexperience in naval warfare, their fleet was moored in an exposed place on Western Sicily where a three-day storm destroyed 75 percent of their ships.[3] Undaunted, Polybius records that in the space of three months the Romans rebuilt their fleet to its original size.

Phase Three—The Romans Defeat Carthage (255 - 241 BC)

In this phase, while the Romans continued to improve their war-making powers, Carthage gradually grew weary of the war because it was expensive. The Carthaginians, whose central organizing principle was wealth creation, during this long fourteen-year phase of the war gradually decommissioned many of their ships and released many of their mercenary sailors from employ. Essentially, they hoped that the war would exhaust

2. Whereas the Persian and Athenian boats that fought at Salamis were triremes, composed of three tiers of rowers, the third-century Hellenistic warship contained four parallel levels of rowers.

3. To put this loss in perspective, in 1940, in the attack of Pearl Harbor, the US lost 26% of its war fleet.

itself. But the Romans, whose central organizing principle was territorial expansion, continued to build their military strength. During the initial years of this phase of the war, from 255-250 BC, the Romans built 200 new ships.

By the time the Carthaginians realized they had squandered their naval superiority, it was too late. In 241 BC, along with some new arriving ships and crews from their allies, they dispatched what was left of their fleet to meet the Roman armada. And in that year, off the western coast of Sicily near the Aegates Islands, their navy was completely destroyed and Carthage was forced to surrender.

The Aftermath of the First Punic War

The indemnity levied against Carthage by the Romans was 3,200 talents of silver.[4] It was also forced to cede all its territory on Sicily to Rome, making these lands Rome's first overseas province. The Syracusans who had gone over to the side of the Romans toward the end of the conflict were allowed to coexist outside the empire as an ally.

But for Carthage things continued to go from bad to worse. Much of their army and navy were mercenaries from surrounding realms, not citizens. Because of the huge indemnity it was forced to pay to Rome, Carthage was unable to pay its mercenaries. Therefore, they converged outside the city, ready for battle, and began preparations to storm the city.

While Carthage commenced the humiliating task of fighting its own mercenary army, the Romans took full advantage of their distraction. In 238 BC the Romans seized Corsica and Sardinia, two major islands off their west coast that were Carthaginian possessions, and thus dramatically extended their new off-shore empire.

The Ramifications of the First Punic War

Carthage lost most of its possessions and was made poorer while Rome gained its first overseas territories and its treasury was engorged. While Carthage saw its navy destroyed, Rome found itself in command of the largest navy in the Mediterranean. More importantly, for the first time, the Romans demonstrated that they could command their navy decisively, a remarkable feat given how new they were to naval warfare. The Romans developed their genius for assimilation. They proved how complete their consolidation of the Italian peninsula was and how their new subjects could be counted on for loyalty, for manpower, and funding. The Romans demonstrated their brilliance at diplomacy by bringing the Syracusans to their side in the closing phase of the war. And most importantly, they displayed a martial ethos that,

---

4.   One talent of silver would have made a man living in the 240s BC a millionaire.

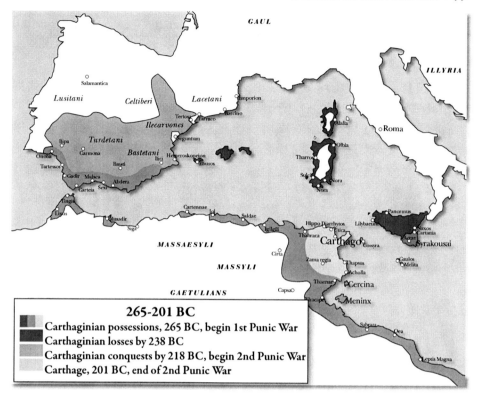

for the next five hundred years, would be characterized by an unflinching commitment to defeat the enemy—no matter how long the war, no matter the cost.

The Second Punic War—Phase 1, Hannibal's Invasion of Italy
(218 - 210 BC)

With their humiliating defeat, made more painful by the annexation of Sardinia and Corsica, the Carthaginians bitterly saw Rome as their mortal enemy. Hamilcar Barca, the commander of the Carthaginian forces and scion of one of the city's most wealthy and powerful families, blamed the weak-willed ruling class for their failure to properly support the war effort. He would have his revenge because he raised a son who would kill nearly 100,000 Romans.

In the years that followed the Great War, Carthage focused its attention west to Spain where there was a mixture of Gauls and Iberians, who were disunified and a good deal more primitive, therefore easily subdued. Additionally, the subjugation of the region was seen by Carthaginians as a means to partially recoup their losses, given that it was rich in silver and timber. As Hamilcar prepared to lead an expedition to Spain, his nine-year-old son, Hannibal, begged to accompany him. According to Livy,

Hamilcar took his son to the temple dedicated to Baal, the Carthaginians' ancestral god, a place where they hurled their infant children into a perpetual fire as sacrifice to their pitiless deity.[5] There he told the boy that if he wished to come with him to Spain and learn to be a soldier, he would have to swear before their ancestral gods that he would never be a friend to the Romans.

Shortly they left for Spain, and by the late 220s, Hamilcar was killed in battle and Hannibal assumed command of Carthaginian forces that gained control of southern and eastern Spain. Hannibal would not see his homeland until he was in advanced middle age. Livy's description of Hannibal gives us an exquisite portrait of this quintessential ancient warrior/commander.

> *He could endure heat and cold alike, and his consumption of food and drink was determined by natural want and not by pleasure. His times of sleeping and waking were not determined by night or day. Many often saw him lying on the ground wrapped only in a military coat amid sentries and outposts of his soldiers. . . . In his dress he was in no way superior to his equals, but he was conspicuous in his arms and his horse. He was always by the far the first in the ranks, foremost to enter the battle . . . last to leave the battle once it had begun.*

During this time the Romans were also on the move. They waged war on the other side of the Alps and were successfully subduing the Gauls, who occupied the southern Mediterranean coast (what is now the French Riviera). As they moved west, Roman expeditionary forces came face-to-face with Carthaginians encamped in Spain. Polybius records that the two empires entered into a treaty. The Romans agreed to not advance south of the River Ebro, acknowledging those lands as the Carthaginian sphere of influence. But in 219 BC, when Hannibal attacked the Spanish port city of Saguntum and the inhabitants appealed to Rome for protection, the second Punic War commenced.[6]

With their navy in virtual control of the western Mediterranean, the Romans were confident that they could easily defeat Carthage this time and commenced planning an invasion of North Africa. But what they could not know was that they were about to face one of history's greatest military minds, and that he would bring the young

---

5.   Tunisia recently lobbied the Western travel media attempting to disprove the facts related to the infanticide practiced by their ancient forbearers. But the archeological record is clear. There are sites near ancient Carthage with hundreds of infant skeletal remains.

6.   Some historians refer to this Second Punic War as the Hannibalic War.

Roman empire to the very brink of destruction. In the spring of 218 BC, Rome's invasion plans were cancelled when Hannibal reached Italy. At the beginning of the march, his forces of 59,000 men were composed of various barbarous mercenaries, the world's finest Numidian cavalrymen, and thirty-seven war elephants.

On the march, his troops suffered losses from bands of warlike Gauls, and crossing the Alps in winter, a nearly impossible logistical feat, proved more costly. According to Polybius, our most trustworthy source, when Hannibal appeared on the Italian side of the Alps, his army numbered only 26,000 starving men. He had lost *33,000 men* yet miraculously every emaciated elephant survived.[7]

Quintus Fabius Pictor, one of our earliest Latin historians, fought Carthage in Italy during the Second Punic War, as a legionnaire. He estimated that in 218 BC, Rome and its allies could muster as many as 750,000 men. Yet, Hannibal believed that if he could defeat Rome's Italian allies in a series of land battles, they would revolt and come over to his side. And when he conquered Rome, he planned to kill all the men, sell all the women and children into slavery, and burn the city to the ground; such was his hatred for Rome. The Romans knew this.

Prior to his first battle, Hannibal gathered to his standard many Gauls who lived in the foothills of the Alps and who considered themselves captive peoples, enemies of Rome. Unlike their Roman adversaries, who were mostly small farmers, the Gauls lived by hunting and plundering. They were equally as comfortable fighting one another as they were fighting an outside foe and were difficult to train and command during the heat of battle.

The Roman cavalry, commanded by Consul Publius Cornelius Scipio, was drawn into an accidental engagement with a contingent of Hannibal's Numidian calvary. The Romans were soundly defeated and Scipio was severely wounded. His son charged into the melee that surrounded his father and rescued him from the field. Young Scipio's rescue would ultimately prove ominous for Carthage.

This first engagement caused many of the Gauls in Scipio's forces to defect to the Carthaginians' side. But before both armies would meet enmass, the elder Scipio's forces were reinforced by those of his fellow consul, Sempronius. A testimony to Roman endurance and discipline, Sempronius had been in the heel of Italy preparing for the invasion of Carthage and marched to northern Italy in forty days.

The two opposing armies were now encamped on opposite sides of the River Trebia. The Romans and allies numbered 40,000, Carthage and allies 30,000. The

---

7. Other Roman historians inflate the size of Hannibal's forces to exaggerate the exploits of the forebears who fought in the Punic wars.

difference was Hannibal. Polybius, who clearly understood the strategy and tactics of ancient warfare, writes:

> *"Any watercourse with a slight bank and reeds . . . can be made to conceal not only infantry but even dismounted horsemen, if a little care is taken to lay shields, with conspicuous devices inside, uppermost of the ground and hide helmets inside them."*

The night before the battle, Hannibal looked down from his camp at the River Trebia and saw across it. Off in the distance, plumes of smoke rose from the Roman camp. He studied an area in front of him on his side of the river, next to the bank, that was populated by tall reeds and rushes, and his plan unfolded.

The following morning, at dawn's first light, Hannibal's light-armed elite Numidian cavalry thundered across the river and began attacking the Roman camp, hurling darts and javelins into the tents of the sleeping legionnaires. When the Romans awoke and began to counter attack, according to plan the African horsemen made an orderly retreat back across the river. Hannibal's aim was to lure the Roman cavalry and the entire expedition across the river where his troops were ready for battle on the overlooking ridges.

With Scipio the Elder wounded and incapacitated, Sempronius was eager to be awarded the credit for crushing the African invasion, and took the bait. He first sent two legions of infantry into the river, then began moving the whole army toward the Carthaginian side. As Livy writes, it was ". . . a day of terrible weather . . . it was snowing . . . and the proximity to the marshes intensified the bitter cold." Despite being groggy from waking just moments earlier and not having eaten breakfast, the Romans showed good discipline. In formation they began wading into the icy swollen river. With sixty pounds of armor and weapons and water rising up to their necks, the crossing was difficult. As they staggered onto dry land and attempted to find their units and reassemble their formations, they were easy targets. The 8,000 Carthaginian javelin throwers and pike men skewered many of them. Still Hannibal, the brilliant strategist, kept the bulk of his forces back. And while they waited for all the Romans to get across, each unit was readied with last-minute instructions from their commanders.

Hannibal placed two wings of elephants in front of the far sides of the long line of heavily-armed infantry composed of Gauls, North Africans, and Spaniards. Next Livy tells us that "Under ominous cold and heavy overcast skies of winter, Sempronius advanced on the enemy in imposing style in order, at slow step." The light infantry on both sides began the battle in heated hand-to-hand combat with the Romans pushing forward at the center. Quickly the Roman flanks on both sides were confronted with elephants and horses. They began to yield and fall back.

Then Hannibal's trap was sprung. Out of the reeds and tall brush on the river bank, where they had hidden since before dawn, Hannibal's most elite special forces rushed toward the back of the Romans' center line that was advancing forward. This stalled the Roman surge. Despite the collapse of their right and left wings and the attack from their rear that rendered appalling loss of life, the Roman center held together and began to retreat toward the river in an orderly formation. On the river bank more Romans were hacked down before they could begin to cross. Only a small portion of the combined Roman armies made the crossing and survived the march down river to the small garrison town of Placentia.

For Hannibal, it was a triumph of his tactics. His starving army had defeated the larger, better-equipped Roman force. Most of his losses were suffered by his newly enlisted Gauls who were poorly trained and had little armor. From the Roman dead and captured, he armed his unruly new enlistments. More important, the path south to the rich Italian farm land, its livestock, grain, gold, women, and slaves were open to his voracious minions. For the first time, he could now see a way to reward his army with their well-deserved plunder.

The news from Trebia incited a near panic among the Roman citizenry. The senate elected two new consuls, Gaius Flaminius and Gnaeus Servilius, and charged them with the muster of new armies to confront the African invaders. Meanwhile, Hannibal marched south hoping to acquire new allies, hoping that city-states controlled by the Romans would defect and join him. His plan was to shatter the Roman confederation that produced its military manpower.

The Africans' elation over their victory at Trebia was dampened when bad news from Spain reached Hannibal. By 216 BC, the Romans gained control of both sides of the Pyrenees, most of Northern Spain, and most of the Mediterranean coast of Gaul. This meant that his expectations of being reinforced by land were now gone. Furthermore, the Romans continued to build upon their dominance of the sea. They intercepted and defeated a Carthaginian naval expedition that attempted to land reinforcements at Pisa. Their dominance of the sea cut off Hannibal's resupply and greatly reduced his ability to communicate with his homeland.

Polybius records that, as he marched south, Hannibal entered Etruria on the western flank of the Apennine Mountains, in a dense marshy area of the Arno River. Many of their pack animals died, bogged down in the mud. Only one elephant survived the battle of Trebia, which Hannibal eventually chose to ride as a sort of mobile lookout post. Of the commander, Livy writes:

> *"Lack of sleep, damp nights, and the air of the marshes affected his head, and since he had neither place nor time for employing remedies, he lost sight of one eye."*

Hannibal's army, isolated and cut off in a hostile land, was constantly presented mortal threats and was totally dependent on the military genius of one man for its survival.

By spring 217, Rome fielded two new consular armies that were nominally ready for battle. Servilius patrolled the Adriatic side of the peninsula, while Flaminius was encamped at Arretium to block the roads leading to Rome. Hannibal's forces avoided both and emerged onto the plane of Tuscany where they began engorging themselves on the rich plunder served up by the undefended rich agrarian cities.

When word reached Flaminius of his Tuscan allies suffering, he broke camp and set off in pursuit of Hannibal. As they reached Lake Trasimene, the Carthaginians learned that Flaminius was just a one-day march behind them. Hannibal halted and ordered his army to hide in the foothills overlooking the lake. The following morning, while a dense mist miraculously enshrouded the Romans marching beside the lake, the Africans swept down upon them in a perfectly executed ambush. The Numidian horses sealed off the rear while the lake blocked any Roman retreat. So sudden was the attack that Livy tells us the Romans were unable to form up in their units and fight with any coordination or cohesion, "... each was dependent on his own valor."

As the heat of the afternoon cleared away the mist, 15,000 Romans, including Consul Flaminius, lay dead or twitching and dying on the flats beside the lake. An equal number of Romans were taken prisoner. Amazingly, Hannibal lost only about 1,500 men. With his second victory, he would certainly have been justified in believing that many of the Italian city-states would be soon coming to his cause. Yet, it was not to be.

Less than one year later, summer 216 BC, Hannibal's motley army met a whole new Roman consular army on a field outside Cannae, a small hamlet in southeastern Italy. The entire Roman 70,000-man army, commanded by new consuls, Amilius Paulus and Tarentus Varro, composed of thousands of new teenage recruits as well as forty- and fifty-year-old senators, was annihilated by Hannibal's force that was less than half its size. Still today, Cannae stands as the largest single-day loss of life in European wartime history.

Again the novice Roman commanders were outmaneuvered by Hannibal. Just as Themistocles used the Persian navy's much larger numbers to their disadvantage, causing them to collide with one another like fish in a bucket, Hannibal trapped the Romans inside an ever-tightening ring of his highly mobile, hardened veterans. His tactics employed that day are still studied by present-day military planners. Again he placed his cavalry on both sides of his line. And with his center line he created an arc which bowed outward and toward the Romans.

Polybius records that the Romans arrived with eight legions of 5,000 men each. And, with the addition of allies from some Greek city-states, the total was between 70,000 and 80,000 men. No Roman had ever commanded such an enormous army in battle. The historian surmises that this may have contributed to the confusion and lack of discipline that resulted in the catastrophe at Cannae. As the two armies stood in formation, poised for the battle, Plutarch records this nervous exchange between Hannibal and Gisco, one of his generals.

"It is astonishing to see so great a number of men."

Hannibal sensed his anxiety and decided to turn it in his own way. "Yes, Gisco, you are right, but there is one thing you have not noticed."

"What is that, sir?" asked the puzzled officer.

"In all that great number of men opposite us, there is not a single one named Gisco!"

The group of generals broke out in laughter, and as Plutarch tells it, this was heard by troops, and with the tension broken, confidence spread throughout the African ranks.

Hannibal ordered his cavalry of Numidians, the finest horsemen of the ancient world, to begin the attack. The Romans were there to meet them with their cavalry on the flanks. But the Romans, relatively unskilled in the art of cavalry warfare, were no match for the Numidians. Romans who were not quickly pulled from their horses and butchered, began to flee, including the Consul Varro.

Nevertheless, as the battle was fully joined, the heavily-armed Roman infantry prevailed and pushed their Carthaginian counterparts backward, collapsing what had been an arc into a u-shaped formation. Into this void poured tens of thousands of Romans. Ominously on each side of this void, stood lines of hardened veteran African infantrymen who waited for their command. By the time the bulk of the Roman infantry had pushed its way into the void, Hannibal dismounted and stood with his retreating infantrymen, disregarding his own safety, and rallied them to cease falling back and to hold their positions. The Numidian horsemen, who drove the Roman cavalry from the field, returned and were sealing off the rear. With this, the African infantry men were given the command to move forward pressing in at the sides, collapsing the area where the Romans were fighting. The Romans found themselves standing inside a vice, pressing against one another in their heavy armor; they soon were unable to even swing their swords.

By the end of the day, there were 60,000 – 80,000 dead or dying Romans on the field of Cannae, including Consul Paulus, Consuls Servilius and Fabius from previous years, and 80 senators (wealthy middle-aged men). Livy records that the Carthaginians lost 4,000 Gauls, 1,500 Spaniards and Africans, and 200 cavalry. He adds that no other nation could have suffered such a tremendous disaster without being destroyed. The great modern historian, Victor Davis Hanson, writes,

> *"What is remarkable about Cannae is not that thousands of Romans were so easily massacred in battle, but that they were massacred to such little strategic effect. Within a year after the battle they could field legions nearly as good as those who fell in August. . ."*[8]

From our sources, we learn that a blood-spattered Hannibal, watching his army strip jewelry, armor, and military hardware from the field of Roman dead, was approached by his Numidian Cavalry general. Maharbal, a black man from the steppes of Africa, said to him, "General, let me have enough troops and we will march on Rome tonight. Who will be left to defend their walls?"

Hannibal decided not to march on Rome. His motivation is not known. No Carthaginian records of his campaign survive. Perhaps, because he had been at war with Rome for so many years, he desired to end it with a negotiated peace, one where Carthage would be compensated by the restoration of its lost possessions. It may simply be that he understood that he had no other option once he saw that Rome's neighboring cities of Campania and Latium would not open their gates to him. Because Rome controlled the seas, he could not be supplied with siege equipment. His army was not large enough to invest a city the size of Rome. Hannibal was forced to keep moving in search of plunder where he could feed his army, such as Roman supply depots. During the entire nineteen years he campaigned in Italy, only one important city, Capua, opened its gates to him. And it paid the ultimate price for its treason when Rome retook the city.

Tarentus Varro, the Roman cavalry commander and consul, found his way back to Rome along with a few surviving cavalrymen from Cannae. Despite their poor performance, they were given a hero's welcome for "not having despaired of the Republic." As Bradford puts it, "It was this flexibility—*the sheer strength and vitality of Rome's political institutions* that was in the end to defeat Hannibal. In Carthage the fate

---

8.   Victor Davis Hanson, *Carnage and Culture: Landmark Battles in the Rise to Western Power* (New York: First Anchor Books, 2001), 111.

of an unsuccessful and cowardly general was well known—he was crucified." 9 In the aftermath of Cannae, the Romans displayed an invincible warrior ethos. They refused to ransom prisoners with the Carthaginians. The Senate outlawed public mourning and generally enforced the Roman code—die rather than yield.

Hannibal conducted the greatest overland invasion in the history of the ancient world, in some aspects, surpassing the feats of Alexander. Smaller inland cities, Casilinum and Nuceria, did fall to him. Yet, he was unable to capture key citadel cities because he could not be reinforced or reprovisioned, and most of the major cities would not defect and join him. Among the major, well-walled, well-defended Greek city-states that remained loyal to Rome were the strategic ports of Neapolis (today's Naples) and Rhegium. These citadels provided much of the Roman navy: men, ships, and great sums of gold and silver.

Hannibal

It seems unlikely that Hannibal ever envisioned a moment in time where, after totally vanquishing his enemy on the field of battle, he was nevertheless unable to dictate the terms of peace. By 210 BC he learned that without the mastery of the sea, his expeditionary force was doomed to unending war. He could not force the Romans and their allies to surrender, such was their martial spirit.

The Second Punic War: Phase 2, The Making of Scipio Africanus
(210 - 202 BC)

By 211 BC, Rome's armies were again numerous enough to starve Capua into submission while, at the same time, station several legions to oppose Hannibal. He was occupied in the south attempting to secure a port for his desperately needed reinforcements and could not come to the aid of Capua, his lone Italian ally. Hannibal established an alliance with Phillip V of Macedon, convincing him to join the Carthaginians' cause lest he be next on Rome's target list. But the Macedonian entry into the war never came. Unable to prevent Capua's fall, Hannibal faced the fact that his diplomacy had failed and his dream of forging an Italian federation capable of isolating and investing Rome, and ultimately conquering her with little effort, was shattered.

---

9.   Ernle Bradford, *Hannibal* (London: The Folio Society, 1998), 120.

The only good news that reached Hannibal that year was that his brother, the Carthaginian general, Hasdrubal Gisco, destroyed two Roman armies in Spain. One was commanded by Scipio the Elder (the general who had been wounded at Trebia) and the other commanded by Scipio's brother. Both Scipios were killed in Rome's attempt to strip Carthage of Spain, its most wealthy province. With his father and uncle's death, came the rise of one of history's greatest generals, Scipio the Younger.[10]

As Bradford points out, ". . . their family tomb reveals that the Scipios had been men of the greatest distinction in Roman history . . . consuls following consuls in a long line of merit on the field of war and in civil affairs." The Scipios were like Hannibal's Barca family, very wealthy and influential. Scipio the Younger was much like Hannibal, born to power, a dauntless commander, and extremely intelligent. As one of the few survivors of Cannae, the power of Hannibal's tactical surprise and maneuver was indelibly imprinted on Scipio's mind.

Ancient Catapults

In typical Roman fashion, the Senate mustered a new army in preparation for a second expedition to Spain. Despite being only twenty-two years old, the Senate promoted young Scipio to General and commander of the expedition. In the spring of 209 BC, Scipio crossed the River Ebro with 30,000 men and invaded Carthaginian Spain. In that same year twelve of the thirty Roman colonies on the Italian peninsula declared their inability to supply any more troops or the money to pay for them, so exhausted were they by Hannibal's invasion. And in that same fateful year, Scipio captured Cartagena (new Carthage), the capital of Spain. His victory proved to be an extraordinary accomplishment for a couple of reasons: it turned the tide of the war, and it demonstrated Scipio's uncanny war making and tactical skills.

Cartagena, like Constantinople centuries later, was built on a neck of land that stuck out into the ocean and was massively fortified on its inland side. But at its rear, on the portion of the citadel that protruded out into the Mediterranean, its walls were much lower and not defended.

Before his first battle in Spain, Scipio demonstrated a genius for diplomacy

10. After commanding the Battle of Zama and defeating Hannibal, he was named Scipio Africanus.

that became one of the hallmarks of Rome's unprecedented rise to hegemony over the ancient Western world. During his march into Spain, he gave audiences to the ambassadors of local Iberian tribesman and learned that many tribes were eager to see Carthaginian rule removed. Scipio instinctively knew how to gain the confidence of foreign populations while assuring them that Roman rule would bestow a strong measure of regional sovereignty. And in so doing, he gained invaluable intelligence.

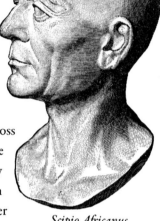

From the local Iberians, he learned that the shallow lagoon bordering the rear of the city could be forded by men in armor when a north wind blew across the surface, lowering its depth. So Scipio blockaded the city with his navy and waited. When the northwesterly winds came, he kept the Carthaginians involved with a partial attack at the inland wall while he sent another intrepid force of commandos to wade across the lagoon to

Scipio Africanus

storm the mostly undefended walls. These precursors to our Special Forces scaled the low walls, burst into the city, and opened the front gates to the main body of Scipio's troops. The Carthaginian commander withdrew to the tower but, with his situation hopeless, he surrendered.

The capture of Cartagena was an extraordinary accomplishment given that, beyond the plunder distributed among his soldiers, it netted huge sums of gold and silver desperately needed by the Roman treasury, vast sums of wheat, barley, and bronze. It also netted items Hannibal had desperately needed to fully subdue Italy— over one hundred of the largest catapults, many rock and spear-hurling machines, tools and equipment for fleet maintenance, and eighteen warships. Moreover, the western sea lanes of the Mediterranean were now firmly back in the hands of Rome.

In victory, the twenty-four-year-old Scipio established a diplomatic template for Roman *statesmanship* so critical to its success in the consolidation of its empire. Instinctively understanding how his victory could become a mechanism for building loyalty to Rome, Scipio made scrupulous lists of his new Spanish prisoners, former hostages of the Carthaginians, and took special care to ceremoniously return them to the emissaries of the tribes from which they hailed. Livy records a number of incidents that have an almost Shakespearean quality. He tells of a sister-in-law of Indibilis, the prince of the important tribe, Ilergetes, who, when she gained an audience with Scipio, fell weeping at his feet, begging for the return of her beautiful young daughters. Scipio complied and sent one of his most trusted aids to accompany them back to their homeland. Livy describes another extremely beautiful maiden ". . . of such beauty that wherever she went, she drew the eyes of everyone . . ." Scipio's fellow officers brought her to him as a gift. When he learned that she was betrothed to a young Celtiberian of noble birth, Scipio summoned the young man, entrusted the girl to him, and said that he wanted no thanks but his pledge to be a "friend of the Roman people."

As Bradford puts it, "Scipio, like all great commanders, took a far-sighted view of the aims and objects of war. The capture of Cartagena was not just a victory to be acclaimed in Rome when the spoils and tribute arrived: it was the beginning of the end (for Carthage)." [11]

Italy Lost (203 BC)

Hannibal's brother, Hasdrubal Barca, was a Carthaginian commander who commanded a Spanish-based largely mercenary army of 30,000 poorly trained Gauls and Iberians. It's not known precisely where Hasdrubal was when Cartagena fell. We simply know that in 207 BC he abandoned Spain and set out for Italy where he marched his troops across Gaul and over the Alps and attempted to join up with Hannibal's forces. His hope was that together he and his brother could inflict a blow even greater than Cannae and smash the Roman alliance once and for all.

With Hasdrubal on his march toward Italy, Scipio was able to defeat what remained of organized resistance in western Spain, bringing the peninsula's vast silver and gold mines under Roman control. And while Rome braced for the second Carthaginian invasion from the north, more ominous news arrived. Phillip V of Macedon was preparing to send an invasion force to aid Hannibal in the south. For the beleaguered Romans and their Italian allies, in 207 BC, their emotions were undoubtedly similar to those of the Londoners during the German blitz—close to mental breakdown. Nevertheless, the Senate authorized a small secret expedition to northern Greece where a group of Roman provocateurs successfully started violent insurrections among a number of the subject peoples of the Balkans who were disaffected with Macedonian rule. The operation was successful. The Macedonians never sailed. Generations later, Romans would look back at this year with inspiration for it being a high-water mark for Roman stoicism.

Due to the horrific losses at Cannae, it was difficult for Rome to find and elect new consuls to carry on the war. After much debate, by June 207 BC, the Senate elected Claudius Nero and Marcus Livius to command two armies—Nero to contain

11. Ibid, 175.

Hannibal in the south, and Livius to meet Hasdrubal in the north. Again, the Romans outnumbered the invaders, plus, they had the advantage of good supply lines, whereas the invaders were dependent on plunder.

When Hasdrubal exited the Alps on the Italian side and began his march south, plundering the countryside, he sent a group of messengers ahead to inform his brother where they should meet and merge their armies. The communiqué was intercepted by Nero who instinctively knew that he must act decisively to cut off Hasdrubal before he could link up with his brother. Nero marched 6,000 of his most elite army north to aid Livius, traveling forty miles a day.

Riders traveling ahead of Nero's force extolled the farming populace of the countryside to give food and water to Nero's men as they marched day and night to join up with Livius. And the Romans obliged, pouring out of their homes, emotionally handing the soldiers bread and water as they trudged north, knowing that their common fate hung in the balance.

The battle of Metaurus took place at night as the Carthaginians attempted to retreat. Hasdrubal learned that both consuls were present, and he feared he was vastly outnumbered, and, moreover, that his brother may have been killed. He hoped to find a better vantage point to determine, if, in fact, he faced both armies. In the confusion of a night battle, his inexperienced force was wiped out next to the Metaurus River. When Hasdrubal saw all was lost, he charged his horse into a vast throng of soldiers and was killed.

Nero proved to be a brilliant commander as well as fearless and decisive. He quickly headed south to resume command of his army that confronted Hannibal at his Bruttian highland redoubt, on the toe of Italy. The night Nero returned to take control of the southern command, a Roman cavalryman was dispatched to the edge of the Carthaginian stockade and threw an object over the walls to the sentries. It was the head of Hasdrubal. When it was brought to Hannibal, he said, "I see there the fate of Carthage."

Hannibal lost nearly all hope of conquering Rome on its home soil. He still retained two vital seaports, Croton and Locri, on the very southern toe of Italy and the support of the primitive local Bruttians who continued to volunteer to serve in his army. For another four years he remained there bottled up by well-trained, well-equipped Roman legions, unable to mount a single campaign.

In 206 BC no major battles were fought in Italy. Scipio continued to consolidate Roman hold over Spain and, by the end of the year, even the ancient Punic trading center Gades (today's Cadiz) on the Atlantic coast, opened its gates to Roman rule.

Scipio set the stage for Rome's great expansion, and he knew it. Before he returned to Rome, he sailed to Numidia[12] and concluded a treaty and an alliance for Rome with the king, Syphax. In so doing, the young general displayed his great statesmanship and his keen strategic thinking. Before he arrived home, he was already planning the conquest of North Africa.

In 205 BC, Scipio returned to Rome triumphant. The city poured out its gratitude and affection for him having endured enormous loss of life and crushing taxation during the thirteen years of war. Scipio was elected consul.

That year eighty Carthaginian ships were captured off Sardinia, reaffirming Rome's ever-growing naval strength. The very rich island of Sicily was finally consolidated under Roman rule. Also that year, Scipio conducted a successful amphibious assault on the port of Locri, stripping it from Hannibal and leaving him just one Italian citadel as his base. After the devastation it suffered over the previous thirteen years, Roman wealth was multiplying rapidly. Despite opposition mounted from many of his political enemies who feared his growing authority, in that momentous year, Scipio convinced the Senate and Assembly to give him the command of an African invasion force.

Carthage Defeated (202 BC)

For Scipio, his plan to invade the Carthaginian homeland was, itself, a military tactic. With Hannibal in Italy, there was always the danger that he would muster new armies from defecting Roman allies and/or gain them from alliances abroad. With his exceptional powers of oratory and his victories in Spain, Scipio implored the Senate to consider he be given an invasion force to mount an attack on their homeland. Carthage would eventually recall the great commander, making the Roman confederation far more secure. And regardless of whether or not Scipio's invasion proved victorious, permanently removing Hannibal from Italy, after 14 years of war, was a long-sought outcome cherished by virtually every Roman. Scipio won his case.

As a testament to the ascending Roman organization, ingenuity, and industry, Scipio, proconsul of Sicily, departed from the port of Lilybaem on the far western shore in spring 204 BC with 30,000 fully-equipped soldiers. They set sail in 400 transports escorted by 40 warships, a massive armada by ancient standards. It was a short voyage to the African shore where they began the task of unleashing vengeance on their arch enemy.

---

12. Numidia occupied the area of today's Algeria and was at this time composed of many rival warring factions, ruled by local warlords, all known for their great skills at cavalry warfare. During the second Punic War, some of the Numidian chieftains allied with Rome, others Carthage. Before the climactic Battle at Zama, Syphax, despite his treaty with Rome, was lured to the Carthaginian side because he had gained the hand of the beautiful, Sophonisba, also of the Barca family.

The arrival of the Romans caused great panic among the Carthaginians inside the city. They had a very small standing army which remained inside to act as its defenders. As always, they were dependent on mercenaries to fill their ranks. When Scipio walked onto the African shore, although Carthage was visible in the distance, no army was there to oppose him.

Upon inspecting the city's enormously tall walls and formidable fortifications, Scipio decided not to besiege it. Instead he plundered the countryside and lay siege to a smaller city, and close ally, Utica. But Scipio was unable to breach Utica's walls. After forty days of siege, a Carthaginian force of freshly recruited mercenaries headed by Hasdrubal Gisco, yet another scion of the Barca family, and his Numidian brother-in-law, Syphax, were reportedly approaching to challenge Scipio. He withdrew to a defensible position on a nearby coastal headland and remained there for a year, resupplied by Rome, from the sea. Like Hannibal in Italy, he was bottled up by local armies who had the advantage of being able to count on local provisional support.

While he forwarded Carthaginian peace proposals to Rome, Scipio continued to work on his strategy and never lost focus on his ultimate goal—the complete annexation by Rome of all Carthaginian lands.[13] He sent envoys to the enemy camps accompanied by senior centurions disguised as low-level adjutants. They reported to Scipio that the enemy ranks displayed low moral and lax discipline.

By Spring 203 BC, he was ready to seize the initiative. In a ruse, he sent a message to the Carthaginian camp indicating that, although his superiors in Rome instructed him to break off negotiations, he was confident he could eventually resume peace negotiations. Hasdrubal sent back a reply that he would be willing to agree to the terms previously discussed. This told Scipio that indeed his enemies' confidence was flagging. He responded by resuming the blockade of Utica. This too was a ruse that masked his true intentions.

On one of the following nights, under the cover of dark, Scipio led his army toward the Carthaginian camp seven miles away. When the Romans arrived around midnight, they had no trouble surprising the sleeping Carthaginians. Soon the camp of reed huts was totally ablaze. As the Carthaginian soldiers emerged unarmed from their shelters, they thought the fire was an accident and were cut down in vast numbers. Hasdrubal and Syphax escaped with only a few thousand survivors. Scipio pursued them and, at the Bagradas, the young Roman general wiped out the remnants of the only army that stood between him and the city of Carthage.

---

13. The English Historian, B.H. Liddell Hart, observed that no man can claim more credit for nurturing the Roman Empire.

In the summer of 203 BC, the Carthaginians sent envoys to Rome with new peace proposals. And despite Roman naval hegemony, they were also able to land a fleet at Croton undetected and evacuate Hannibal and his army from Italy. The great general departed Italy with less than 20,000 men. Of those who made the short voyage, very few had crossed the Alps with him sixteen years earlier. He was now in command of an army of poorly trained Brutians, Gauls, and Roman deserters. The number of ships available for the evacuation was undoubtedly limited. Hannibal had to kill all his horses that had proved so vital to him in his previous victories, lest they fall into the hands of the Romans. As he watched the Italian mainland fall away over the horizon, he must have realized that he knew Italy like few Italians would ever know it. He had fought his way through the entire expanse of the Peninsula, from the Po Valley to the mountains of Bruttia in the far south. He knew Italy intimately, yet he was returning to a homeland he had suffered greatly for and—he could barley remember.

His army landed without incident at Leptis and, while he took up quarters at the fortified city of Hadrumetum, he quickly began recruiting men into his army. Knowing full well how pivotal the Numidian cavalry had been in Italy, Hannibal was distraught by his inability to acquire as many Numidian horsemen from his brother-in-law, Syphax, as he felt he needed for the final battle with Scipio's Romans. He was able to acquire eighty elephants, albeit young untrained animals. And with this, he developed a battle plan where he would place the elephants out in front of his infantry and charge them into the Roman ranks, hoping to sow terror, confusion, and the breakdown of discipline and cohesion.

As the battle day drew closer, Masinissa, Scipio's Numidian ally and rival to the throne, was away from the Roman camp gathering recruits in his rebel homeland.[14] Hannibal's spies reported to him that there appeared to be no cavalry among the Romans. While Scipio patiently waited for Masinissa's reinforcements to arrive, he successfully drew Hannibal out of his quarters by waging a merciless campaign of plunder upon the Carthaginian countryside, the agrarian lands that the new army and the inhabitants of the city relied on for food. In so doing, Scipio brought Hannibal to the battlefield of his choosing, to a wide open field near the town of Zama.

According to both Polybius and Livy, on the night before the battle, two of history's greatest generals met. Both men were multi-lingual and could have spoken with each other in either Latin or Greek. But as modern leaders do to this day, they chose to speak through interpreters, thereby giving each extra time to craft a measured

---

14. Bradford points out a little known fact, that martial prowess of the long extinct Numidians played such an important role in the outcome of the war and therefore upon the direction of Western Civilization.

response. Hannibal opened by offering peace. He offered Rome all disputed lands—Spain, Sicily, Sardinia, Malta—and the guarantee to never make war upon Rome again.

Upon hearing this, Scipio was emboldened. The very fact that Hannibal offered peace told Scipio that his opponent saw his country's position as hopeless. He replied, "If before the Romans crossed to Africa, you had retired from Italy, there would be some hope for your propositions. . . . But the situation is manifestly changed. . . . We are here." [15] Carthage had refused too many Roman offers of peace and abrogated too many truces, which resulted in too many Romans lost. There was nothing more to be said.

Based on their meeting, Scipio knew that he had gained the psychological advantage. Secondly, he learned a great deal from the brilliant tactics employed by Hannibal from the vantage point of the battlefield, from the vantage of a young centurion who had barely survived them. Conversely, Hannibal had no knowledge of how Scipio would conduct himself in battle.

As testament to Scipio's command of events, his meeting with Hannibal postponed the battle by one day, the time necessary for Masinissa to arrive with 4,000 Numidian horsemen and 6,000 infantrymen. It was a hot autumn morning on the African plain as the two armies formed up and faced each other, poised for battle. Although the Roman force was somewhat smaller, its advantage was that it was better trained and disciplined than Hannibal's hastily mustered troops. Moreover, Scipio, having intelligence that Hannibal would try to use his elephants as his force multiplier, made numerous adjustments to prevent them from disrupting his carefully ordered battle plan. Scipio arrayed his cavalry on the outer flanks. Instead of placing his infantry in the usual checkerboard formation, maniples of 120 men, he arrayed them with lanes of lightly-armed men between each maniple who would escape into the safety of the heavily-armed infantry and open gaps for the elephants to run through without any soldiers being trampled.

Hannibal began the battle by ordering his elephant drivers to lead the charge toward the center of the Roman infantry's line. As the entire Carthaginian army charged, each of the 25,000 Romans stood their ground and shouted at the top of their lungs, accompanied by dozens of war trumpeters. This huge sound panicked the young elephants; some collided with one another while others careened off their course and crashed into the Numidian cavalry on Hannibal's advancing left wing. Livy records:

---

15. Ernle Bradford, *Hannibal* (London: The Folio Society, 1998), 222.

"A few of the beasts, however being fearlessly driven into the enemy, caused great losses among the ranks of the light armed, though suffering many wounds themselves. For springing back into the maniples, the light-armed made way for the elephants, to avoid being trampled down, and then would hurl their lances from both sides against the beasts which were now doubly exposed to missiles."

Fortunately for the Romans, the elephants that reached the Roman line were driven toward the left side and into the path of Hannibal's advancing cavalry, sowing chaos there. Masinissa and Gaius Laelius, who commanded the Numidian and Roman cavalry respectively, saw their opportunity and charged into the Carthaginian horses, driving them away from the field. Hannibal's plan to disrupt the Roman disciplined ranks had horribly backfired. Almost as soon as the battle began, he was deprived of his most mobile and decisive forces. The Roman infantry moved forward against the front line of Carthaginians that was composed of Hannibal's least reliable troops, the Gauls and assorted mercenaries. They too began to fall back rapidly and many fled. Behind them, Hannibal had placed his best veteran infantry. Still fresh, they moved up and engaged the Romans in the most elemental brutal hand-to-hand combat. And for a while, the Africans prevailed, pushing the Romans back.

Scipio then sounded the recall trumpets, and as further testament to Scipio's great generalship and Roman discipline, his infantry withdrew and regrouped into their maniples and sub-units and waited for the command to re-engage. While the Carthaginian elite infantry was also regrouping, Scipio sounded the trumpet call to charge. As the two armies resumed their bludgeon work, the outcome remained in doubt until the Numidian and Roman cavalries under Masinissa and Laelius appeared and charged down onto the flanks and rear of the beleaguered Africans. As Bradford describes it, "The horsemen of Numidia, who had served Hannibal so well in the early years in Italy, had finally contrived his ruin. The remnants of the old Guard broke and fled. The battle was over. The Romans had won the war."[16]

The Aftermath of the Second Punic War

Hannibal left the battlefield at Zama with a small escort and repaired to Hadrumetum. He made his way to Carthage to inform his leadership that there was no hope of victory and that holding out would ultimately end in complete defeat. For their part, the Carthaginians still believed their city to be the richest of the Mediterranean

---

16.   Ibid, 226.

The elephant charge in the opening moments of the battle at Zama.

world because, despite the years of war, their commercial trade continued to build and enrich the city's inhabitants. Nevertheless, Carthage acceded to their war hero, Hannibal, and sent envoys to Rome with orders to agree to Roman terms of surrender, whatever they might be.

The terms were shocking, far more onerous than those Carthage agreed to after the First Punic War. The city was forced to pay Rome the enormous sum of 10,000 talents, three times their previous indemnity. All deserters, prisoners, and slaves were to be handed over, and all Carthaginian warships except ten. Masinissa, Rome's ally, was given total rule over Numidia. And Carthage was to never make war upon any other state without Roman authorization.[17] Finally, Rome demanded one hundred hostages be delivered as collateral in the event Carthage abrogated any terms of the treaty.

Although Hannibal was not demanded in the terms of the surrender, he became enemy number one for many in the Roman Senate. Scipio convinced the Senate and Assembly that a good manager was needed in Carthage to ensure that Rome received its full indemnity. Hannibal was elected Chief Magistrate of the city and proved to be as able and incorruptible a statesman as he was a general.

Upon Scipio's return, he was provided a gilded chariot for his triumphant parade

17. This proviso set up the city's final destruction because it meant that Numidia could in affect make war upon Carthage, expand its borders at its expense, while Carthage was powerless to defend itself. It was a proviso that was meant to be broken.

through the streets of Rome. With his successive victories in Spain and in Africa, Scipio embodied some firsts in Roman history. He solidified Roman diplomacy canons that encompassed a robust body of laws that governed its unique system of patronage. He proscribed that conquering generals treat a defeated enemy with compassion and insurrectionists with extreme brutality. He was the first to be given a surname, Africanus, for the lands he conquered, and the first general to enjoy such a long and close relationship with his own army. Previously, men were elevated to the rank of commanding general upon their election to consul. This tradition meant that their commands ended after their one-year consularships expired. Rome had nearly been destroyed by great generalship. Scipio embodied a sea change in Roman attitudes toward military operations.

In stone, Hannibal's sculptor capture's the great general's gaze into eternity

He proved that a great field commander required skill, knowledge, and experience. From this time onward, generals stayed in place until they were recalled.[18]

Scipio's most lasting impact upon Rome was that he led Rome from near catastrophe to a rocklike resolution that enabled the city to conquer the whole Mediterranean basin.

Ironically, Hannibal's greatness, the enormity of his accomplishments during his eighteen-year invasion of their heartland, forged within the Roman people a determination and confidence that, in one generation, propelled them to rule all the lands that touched the Mediterranean. The Romans came to refer to it as Mare Nostrum (Latin for Our Sea).

Carthage, The City That Waited to Die (220 - 146 BC)

Due in part to Scipio's unprecedented stature in public, he attracted a host of political enemies. They coveted his power, detested his magnanimity toward Hannibal and Carthage, and believed that the peace treaty should be rejected and Carthage must be dealt with once and for all. Cato the Elder invariably brought a fresh fig to the

---

18. This change proved effective in the development of Roman military superiority but it also created a danger that would ultimately lead to the career of Julius Caesar and the overthrow of the Republic.

Senate as a prop to illustrate the fact it could have easily arrived via a short voyage from Carthage, Rome's mortal enemy. He would end each address in the Senate with "Carthago delenda est" (Carthage must be destroyed).

Hannibal went about the task of City Magistrate, diligently and skillfully attending to rebuilding his City's commercial accounts. He, too, became increasingly aware that he had amassed many enemies among the Carthaginian wealthy. They blamed him for the war and the terrible cost it had inflicted upon them. Ominously, in 195 BC, Rome sent a delegation to Carthage to charge Hannibal for plotting against Rome with Antiochus, the King of Syria. The king was a descendant of Salukis and one of the generals who carved out a vast portion of Alexander's empire. The Seleucid realm extended from the Near East to the Hindu Kush. Antiochus was ambitiously attempting to reconstitute all of Alexander's holdings under his rule.

Hannibal had no illusions. He knew that his enemies at home would conspire to turn him over to the Romans. So as he had done often on the battlefield, he escaped. On the day the Roman delegation arrived, Carthaginians saw that Hannibal was going about his business as usual. That evening he slipped out of the city to an awaiting ship, crewed by loyalists and with his private fortune on board. Two weeks later, he arrived at Tyre, the ancient home of the Phoenicians and the birthplace of Dido, mother of the city of Carthage. Hannibal spent the remaining twenty years of his life moving from one eastern court to another, even spending time on lawless Crete, then a bastion of pirates.

Now that Rome had consolidated its hold on the western Mediterranean, they were drawn into wars in the East. Powers there feared that Rome would only grow stronger and more of a threat to them. The Eastern Mediterranean was ruled by three dynasties that resulted when Alexander's top three generals carved out pieces of Alexander's empire upon his death.

Phillip V ruled Macedon and Greece. Rome was highly suspicious of him because, after the battle of Cannae, he entered into the alliance with Carthage, hoping to share in the dismemberment of Rome. The Romans brilliantly prevented Phillip V from landing Macedonian armies in Italy at a time when Rome's chances for survival were most in doubt. They did so by fomenting rebellion among subject Greek city-states.

Embassies from Rhodes and Pergamum, small states that suffered from Macedonian aggression, appealed to Rome to make war upon Macedon because Phillip V and Antiochus III, the king of Syria, had entered into a secret non-aggression pact. It had only been two years since the Romans had concluded the long war. But the Senate and Assembly reluctantly sent a force into Macedon. And in 197 BC, a

Roman army defeated a Macedonian phalanx three times its size on Macedonian soil at Cynoscephalae (Dog's Head). In this battle, Roman tactics, specifically the ability to quickly and decisively move small units called maniples, with the authority to act given to their small unit commanders, further established Roman military superiority. Rome could now field a "thinking man's army," able to defeat even well-trained and disciplined armies of much greater size.

The peace treaty imposed by Rome and agreed to by Phillip V stripped him of his holdings and dominion over Greece. While Rome declared the Greeks free, they saw Greece as a protectorate and most definitely part of its sphere of influence, a client state with Rome its patron. Yet the Greeks were soon disillusioned with Roman rule, realizing that they were no freer than was Carthage. They were able to govern themselves locally but disallowed from conducting their own foreign policy. In 193 BC, inhabitants of central Greece, who had conspired with the Romans to foment rebellion against Macedon during the Second Punic war, asked Phillip's rival, the Seleucid King Antiochus of Syria, to aid them in their revolt against their new Roman overlords.

Meanwhile the anti-Carthaginian war hawks in the Roman Senate were advocating for war with the Seleucid Kingdom because word had reached them that Hannibal was being harbored in its court in Antioch. War was declared in 192 BC when Antiochus landed troops in central Greece. In the same year a Roman expeditionary force defeated the Syrian phalanx and drove the Seleucid dynasty from Europe forever. Many in the Roman intelligencia possessed a great reverence for Greek culture and understood that Roman institutions, arts, and architecture were built upon the Greek models that preceded them. Therefore, the Greeks of the Aetolian League in central Greece were subjected to a lesser punishment, rather than one that would have included many executions. Instead, the Romans elected to subdue the population by taking several thousand hostages from among the leading families of the region. Among them was historian Polybius, perhaps our most reliable source for this era of Roman history. Because he was such a highly educated Greek, he found himself adopted by the Scipio family upon his arrival in Rome. He began as a children's tutor but soon became a close confidant of the Scipio men who were members of the most powerful family of the new Empire.

Three years later in 189 BC, the Romans mounted a massive amphibious invasion of Syria and, at the battle of Magnesia, defeated a much larger Syrian force. Roman military superiority was approaching invincibility, or so it seemed to the Romans and their foes alike. Syria, the most populous and richest kingdom ever, was forced by Rome to pay a massive indemnity of 7,000 talents. Additionally, it was banned from all its port cities of the Levant, all its cities and their surrounding lands that touched the Mediterranean.

With Syria's defeat, Hannibal instinctively knew that one of the provisions of the treaty would stipulate that he be handed over to the Romans. As usual, he escaped with most of his fortune and a retinue of loyalists. With the Romans in complete command of the sea, Hannibal knew that his days of eluding capture were coming to an end. After a brief stay on Crete, and with the Romans in constant pursuit, he made his way to the tiny remote Kingdom of Bithynia. Soon, an entire Roman legion surrounded its capital and demanded that its monarch turn over Hannibal. Once again, in his usual fashion, he narrowly escaped (182 BC). This time he drank hemlock and ended his life to prevent his mortal enemy the sublime satisfaction of showcasing him in chains before a victory parade in Rome. So ended one of the most adventurous and heroic careers in all history and mythology.

Roman Justice (146 BC)

In the years between Syria's defeat at Magnesium and the final destruction of Carthage, Rome continued to consolidate its hold on the Mediterranean basin through treaties and mop-up military operations. For the balance of his reign, Phillip V of Macedon obeyed the terms of the Roman treaty. But when he died in 179 BC, his son Persias violated those terms and triggered what is now called the Third Macedonian War (172 - 168 BC).

During this conflict, the Roman general, Lucias Amelias Paulus, defeated the Macedonian phalanx once again at Pidna, the ancestral home of the Greek gods in the shadow of Mount Olympus. According to Polybius, the Macedonians were defeated massively with 20,000 killed as opposed to only 100 Romans. With this victory, Rome broke Macedon into four Roman-ruled provinces. This ended all self-rule by the Macedonians, who, under Alexander, had conquered so much of the known world. Twenty years later, when Rome was forced to put down yet another rebellion, it annexed the territory and made it the Roman province of Macedonia. Macedonian culture was forever extinguished. During this period, the Romans forged an alliance with Ptolemaic Egypt thus subduing through treaty the last major threat to their now awesome military power and wealth.

During the fifty-five years subsequent to the Second Punic War, while Rome expanded its Empire in the east, Carthage made a substantial economic recovery, despite the fact that it was barred from conducting its own foreign policy. But its nemesis continued to be Masinissa, the ruthless and ambitious ruler of neighboring Numidia. He had been placed on the throne by the Romans for his important assistance at the Battle of Zama. He continuously mounted raids upon their lands until the Carthaginians felt compelled to take up arms against him. Making war against Numidia, a Roman client state, was all that was needed by the anti-Carthaginian factions in Rome, men such as Cato the Elder, to convince the Senate that the Carthaginians were in breach of their treaty and that a third and final Punic war should commence.

War was declared and, in 149 BC, a second and much better equipped Roman expeditionary force landed in North Africa. This time its general was Scipio Aemilianus, the grandson of Scipio Africanus who conquered Hannibal. Accompanying him as his personal chronicler was Polybius. At the outset, the Carthaginians sued for peace. But the price Rome demanded—total destruction of their city and the relocation of its citizens ten miles inland—was simply too high. So reluctantly, they elected to resist. Without a large standing army capable of a counter offensive, they were forced to endure a three-year siege, remarkable for the heroic tenacity of Carthaginians. Yet the outcome was never in doubt. In 146 BC the walls were breached and Romans stormed the city to find nearly all the military-age men had been killed. They executed the surviving soldiers and shipped the women and children off to the slave markets. As they had done with Macedonia and later Greece, they decided against creating a client state. Instead Rome annexed both Numidia and the Carthaginian lands, roughly the area occupied by Tunisia today. The lands became yet another Roman province, one so agriculturally rich that it surpassed Sicily as the Empire's granary. In so doing, Rome obliterated both the Numidian and Carthaginian cultures forever.

The irony of Hannibal's great successes on the battlefield was that they brought about the destruction of both Carthage and its neighboring Numidian horsemen.[19] So traumatic was his effect upon the Roman psyche that for one hundred years after his death, Italian women admonished their children by saying, "Hannibal will get you!" Due to Hannibal's brilliant achievements in battle, many Romans who escaped the fields of the dead at Trebia, Trasimene, and Cannae subsequently rose to positions of power and never rested until Carthage was destroyed.

IMMUTABLE #1
*No nation has ever survived once its citizenry
ceased to believe its culture worth saving.
(Hanson's Law)*

---

19. The Numidian horsemen were influential in both Hannibal's victories in Italy and his defeat at the Battle of Zama. In the latter case, Scipio's victory over Hannibal in North Africa was greatly aided by bringing a rebellious portion of the Numidian kingdom to the Roman cause. Few students of history credit this obscure people for having so pivotal a role in the outcome of Western Civilization.

I have demonstrated here that the fall of Carthage was due to its ill-fated decision to make war upon the Romans. In so doing, Carthage was lost, in part, due to the *converse* of the Immutable #1 referenced above. Arguably, no nation has ever held a more firm belief in itself and in its culture than the Romans of the early Republic.

Polybius was a Greek hostage, historian, and confidant of the Scipios, the leading family of the expanding third-century empire. He informs his reader that he was compelled to write his history of the rise of Rome to address the all-important question of how the Romans were able to conquer what was, in his estimation, the entirety of the civilized world. His history begins:

> *"There can surely be nobody so petty or apathetic in his outlook that he has no desire to discover by what means and under what system of government, in less than 53 years, the Romans managed to bring under their rule almost the whole of the inhabited world, an achievement which is without parallel in human history."*

During his own lifetime, Polybius witnessed Rome's rise to Mediterranean hegemony, and was present at the destruction of Carthage. He came to the conclusion that the Romans' secret to their enormous imperialist success was that they possessed a balanced constitution that blended elements of Greek-inspired democracy, as well as ancient elements of aristocracy and monarchy. While its system of balanced, participatory government was a factor, one that we certainly will not discount, the Romans certainly owe the success of their empire to several other factors.

© Jozef Sedmak / Dreamstime.com
Polybius, the Greek Historian

The Brilliance of the Roman Patronage System

By the time Scipio defeated the Carthaginians in Spain, he was able to implement what became a highly evolved form of diplomacy that historians now refer to as patronage.[20] Classics professor Kenneth Harl, of Tulane University, maintains that Rome's patron/client system was the glue that tied the Italian and subsequently all

---

20. We inherit the word from the Romans, even though their system bears virtually no resemblance to today's patronage in America, where the Left rewards union street walkers who "get out the vote."

its conquered peoples together. It was a peculiar, yet brilliant, system for assimilating new subjects very rapidly and eliciting from them almost instant loyalty. Harl believes that the system grew out of the Romans' keen interest in understanding the people they had come to rule. The system does not appear to be codified. Rather, like much of Roman culture, it was the product of an amalgam of precedents that became traditional policies. The importance of the system defies exaggeration when we stop to consider that minus the strength of Rome's Italian confederation, Hannibal would have surely destroyed Rome.

The system worked as follows—once a people was conquered, the commanding Roman general became their patron, their advocate upon his return to Rome. Immediately upon their surrender, warrior elites of the newly conquered were made to understand that the very same general who had defeated them would become their patron and benefactor. Their patron would use his power to advocate for them and ensure that they would get equal protection under Roman law, no matter which magistrate was ultimately assigned to be their provincial ruler.

As *provincials*, opportunities to share in the burgeoning wealth of the empire and ultimately, full citizenship was afforded to them. It was a demanding system that necessitated sending embassies to Rome to maintain or renew contact should the patron die and jurisdiction pass to a son. A patron, out of honor and tradition, would advocate for his provincials' public works projects such as the construction of roads, new ports facilities, military fortifications, and aqueducts. These projects produced wealth in the client provincials, lots of well-paying jobs, and a new phenomenon—a rapidly-expanding middle class.

By the birth of Jesus of Nazareth, the average first-century Roman citizen had obtained a level of affluence well above the peasant tribal warrior. Roman patronage became the engine that produced a level of middle-class affluence throughout the Mediterranean basin that was not eclipsed in the West until the middle of the twentieth century, two millenniums later. And it was this system that enabled a single city-state to command the allegiance of the vast realm.

The Romans of the Republic clearly understood the principle:

IMMUTABLE #6
To hold territory, a state must be populated by those loyal to the central authority. When immigration overwhelms assimilation, the fall is predicted.

The Roman Warrior Ethos

Romans were an enormously disciplined people, adept at the art of war, eager to co-opt new weaponry and methods, a people inured to leaving their farms and going on campaign virtually every spring. They were farmer/warriors who purchased their own armor as a matter of honor, trained themselves and their sons in the art of hand-to-hand combat, and willingly obeyed their generals' command "Conquer or die."

And as Livy observed, there had never been a people who could survive a defeat such as Cannae and continue to prosecute a war. As the result of Hannibal's enormous carnage, the Romans of the early Republic obtained a sort of hyper-warrior ethos, like the British during German blitz of 1942 who emerged with an indomitable ability to settle the score.

Ironically, the rise of Rome can be seen as a direct result of Hannibal's depredations. Despite his devastating victories, he could not break the will of the Romans or the loyalty of their allies, and instead hardened their desire to destroy Carthage. It is not the case that Carthaginians lost their desire to preserve their culture. They lost their civilization because they made the mistake of going to war against a people who had an unprecedented belief in their culture. They lost

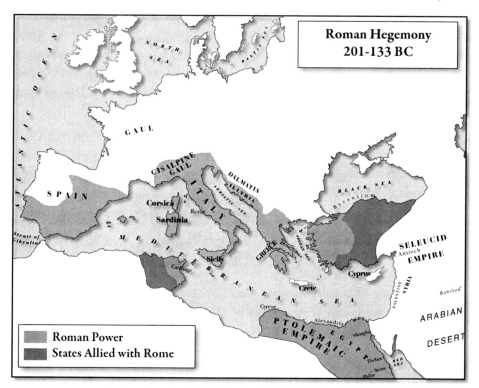

because they could not have foreseen the unprecedented ascendancy of Rome and unwittingly violated this immutable.

IMMUTABLE #10
*Declining civilizations will always face
superior firepower from ascending civilizations
because sovereignty is only temporarily uncontested.*

MODERN COROLLARIES

The Cancellation of the F-22 Fighter Jet

As we saw in the First Punic War, during the late 240s BC, the Carthaginians grew weary of the long war with Rome and made the decision to decommission much of their fleet and release from their employ many of their mercenary sailors. This proved to be an extraordinarily ill-fated decision. They voluntarily ceded naval superiority and *mastery of the seas* to Rome, their mortal enemy. And although it would be another one hundred years before the fall of Carthage, Rome continued to consolidate its naval superiority and mastery of the Western Mediterranean. This decision prevented Hannibal from being reprovisioned and resupplied with new weaponry, especially siege equipment. Essentially, the Carthaginians' decision to cede military control of the seas made them, as a naval trading power, vulnerable to Rome as a naval trading power. That fatefully bad decision set in motion events that led to a huge military advantage for Rome and to the ultimate destruction of Carthage.

By 2008, the year of Barack Obama's election, America had enjoyed air superiority since World War II. And it had been sixty years since a single American soldier had lost his life on the ground due to an attack from the air. Incomprehensibly in 2009, President Obama cancelled the F-22 Raptor jet fighter, which threatens to relinquish American air superiority. As the eminent military historian, Mark Helprin, apocalyptically put it, "Canceling the F-22, the most capable fighter plane ever produced, is yet another act in the tragedy of a nation that, bankrupting itself, is losing its will to prevail." [21]

The mission of the F-22 fifth-generation fighter, in a conflict, is to clear the skies of enemy aircraft. Although each plane costs $142 million, with its stealth, speed, and ultra advanced censors, it is recognized by allies and potential adversaries alike, as the most capable in the world. In 2007 exercises against American fourth-generation

---

21.   Mark Helprin, *Why the Air Force Needs the F-22* (*The Wall Street Journal*, February 22, 2010), A19.

F-22 Raptor, America's lord of the skies,
a weapon system cancelled by President Obama

aircraft, it scored 241 kills to 2. In combat simulations and exercises, our military planners know the F-22 is capable of exploding an enemy plane before it even knows the F-22 is in the area.

So why cancel it, dismantle the production lines, and send all the highly-skilled design engineers and production personnel looking for work? The rational offered by Secretary of Defense Gates, was that the F-35, America's newest plane, can handle two missions—ground attack and sky-clearing. But the F-35 lacks speed and agility and will never clear the sky as well as the F-22. It simply is a lesser plane.

By the middle of this decade, China and Russia are scheduled to have their fifth-generation fighters. When that happens, American military planners cannot be assured that we can prevail in the air. The importance of this cannot be over stated because for a nation to win a war it must dominate the skies. The skies are to the twenty-first century what the seas were to the second century BC Mediterranean.

Also given our experience in World War II, the US knows that it must be prepared to prevail in two separate conflicts simultaneously. The second problem America faces in controlling the skies is the country has too few aircraft. Writing for the Heritage Foundation, Mackenzie Eaglen says "... many of the US Air Force's young pilots fly the same planes their fathers and grandfathers flew in Vietnam. They were once cutting edge but now are old, worn out, and technologically dated." [22]

Eaglen goes on to describe a "Fighter Gap" that is the deficit between the Air

---

22. Mackenzie Eaglen, "Oldest Air Force in History Asked to Do More than Ever Before," The Foundry (blog), February 5, 2010, http://blog.heritage.org/2010/02/01/oldest-air-force-in-history-asked-to-do-more-than-ever-before/.

Force's inventories of air craft and its requirements based on emerging threats. By 2025 the projected deficit will be 540 planes. Air superiority since the latter half of the twentieth century had been to military preparedness what naval superiority had been for two millenniums, stretching back to the Punic Wars. Losing a war, even if limited to just one theater, would be a complete financial catastrophe. And the US has already done the hard part—successfully developed the plane, so why not invest the necessary monies and maintain air superiority? The answer is the same for all modern socialist economies that are in decline; discretionary military spending always suffers to pay for the inevitably-expanding, *contractual* transfers of wealth.

Ambivalent Missile Defense Under the Obama Administration

Since the mid-80s, when Ronald Reagan announced the creation of the Strategic Defense Initiative (SDI), much of the prominent Democrat governing class squandered a good deal of its political capital in an attempt to thwart its development. Their behavior has been an object lesson in a pathology that infects progressives who have, as the expression goes, "evolved beyond their ability to retain their basic instinct for survival." The late Edward Kennedy derided SDI by referring to it as "Star Wars" a delusional costly right-wing program that had no chance of success.

Ironically, his brother, President Kennedy, twenty-five years earlier took the lead in informing the country that it would be "America's destiny to send a man to the moon and bring him home safely." Bundled within Edward Kennedy's dismissal of SDI was a feature of Progressive dogma that rejects American exceptionalism and proudly proclaims that America could one day produce a missile shield capable of defeating a catastrophic nuclear missile attack. The Progressive belief system holds that America should have *no right* to such an unfair military advantage over our adversaries.

To Bill Clinton's credit, he was half-hearted in his attempts to kill SDI. Thanks to diligent Republican efforts in Congress, he was not successful in canceling the program handed to him from President Bush (the Elder). During the Clinton years, however, the SDI program was simply an unheralded line item in the Defense Department budget. When President Bush (the Younger) took office in 2001, he inherited a $4.8 billion a year program. The following year he increased the funding by 60 percent. When he left office, the program had grown to $10.9 billion, and the system, in tests over the Pacific, had shown that it was capable of completing its mission. In so doing, America once again proved to all doubters and nay sayers inside and outside our borders that they were wrong.

On President George W. Bush's watch, the country proved that it could build a system capable of mind-boggling technological precision, "hitting a speeding bullet with a bullet." Although the system still needed to be built out to protect the entire US mainland, Hawaii, Alaska, our allies, and our troops in deployed theaters, all three elements of the system were tested and demonstrated to work, elements that could shoot down a missile—in the launch phase, in outer space, and in the reentry phase. If legitimate history continues to be written in the future, the successful development of SDI will stand as equally historic as America's moon mission for its effects on human evolution.

Enter President Obama.

During his campaign of 2008 he stated numerous times that he "would not weaponize space" and he would not deploy a "costly unproven" missile defense system. In so saying, the new president showed he didn't understand that space had already been weaponized from the first generation of ICBMs developed by the US and the Soviet Union. Secondly, he clearly lacked understanding that SDI could aid him in advancing one of his stated key policy initiatives—his effort to reverse nuclear arms proliferation. Obama vowed to cut $10 billion from the SDI program at a time when its budget was only $9 billion. Moving toward his presumed goal, the unilateral *de*-weaponization of space by the US, he historically authored the first *cut* in missile defense spending. He reduced the program by $1.4 billion to $9.3 billion, and egregiously eliminated key components of the system vital for intercepting ballistic missiles in the boost phase, such as the Kinetic Energy Interceptor (KEI) program.

Next, in a display of abject prostration, in 2009 President Obama cancelled missile defense treaties signed by President George W. Bush with two staunch allies, Poland and Czech Republic. These treaties allowed the US to base long-range interceptors on East European soil, installations designed to protect the Eastern US from attacks from rogue nations such as Iran. During the Bush Administration, the US requested basing rights from the Polish and Czech governments. They agreed, despite the discord they suffered from their own anti-American leftist constituencies.

Obama's cancellation of the treaties, in response to intimidation by Russia's Putin, profoundly embarrassed the Polish and Czech governments. Putin made it clear in his first meeting with Obama that he considered the Soviet Union's former East European satellites to be his sphere of influence. It was whispered, but not corroborated, that Putin threatened America's new president with war in East Europe if the installations went forward. What is known is Obama cancelled the treaty shortly after meeting with Putin. He announced that the US would protect Europe with ship-based interceptors located in the Baltic and Mediterranean seas, systems that are not robust and can only intercept short-range missiles.

Candidate Obama stated over and over during his campaign that he would repair America's reputation damaged by the unilateralist right-wing policies of his predecessor. He intimated, as Jimmy Carter did in the 1970s, that he would succeed in calming world tensions by a kinder, more informed, and more accommodating foreign policy.

The first test of his new foreign policy came with his meeting with Putin who clearly had taken measure of the man and had found him wanting. Obama thought he could charm the former KGB commander, soliciting his aid in containing Iran and in bringing its ruling Mullahs to a position where they would see the futility of their nuclear ambitions. In this high stakes game of poker, the pot was large and Putin took it all. Obama gave up the missile defense of his own homeland, alienated important allies, made himself look weak, and got nothing.

In the aftermath of this debacle, the largely obsequious American press failed to ask the president: Will the US be able to protect itself from long-range nuclear missiles that Iran has proven it possesses? Are you still committed to unilaterally disarming the United States? If so, isn't that an abrogation of your duties as Commander in Chief?

Had it not been for the ambivalent Left and the influence of its political class during the last half century, it seems doubtful that, in 2010, the country would have arrived at both the brink of insolvency and unable to defend itself from a rogue regime's ballistic missile attack.

IMMUTABLE #3
Appeasement of a ruthless outside power always invites aggression.
Treaties made with ruthless despots are always fruitless and dangerous.

America's War Against Its Own Intelligence Community

As we saw in the wake of their horrific defeat at Cannae in 207 BC, the Romans sent a small secret expedition to northern Greece. A group of Roman provocateurs successfully started violent insurrections among a number of the Greek city-states who were subject peoples of the Macedonians. It was this successful clandestine operation that prevented Phillip V of Macedon from reinforcing Hannibal with troops and necessary siege equipment for the capture of the Roman citadel. Rome lost almost all its standing army. It can be argued that the Romans' ability to launch a successful covert operation against Macedon made the difference between their total destruction and their ability to survive and fight another day.

One of the shibboleths of the American Left is that President Kennedy was assassinated in 1962 by sinister forces within the government. Another is the belief that one of those forces was, and continues to be, the CIA. Arthur Herman writes,

"The Left discovered that recounting horror stories about the CIA was a useful way to discredit Richard Nixon. Over time, criticizing the CIA became a fixation all its own." [23] As early as 1964, leftist journalists published books like *The Invisible Government* by David Wise and Tom Ross. Over the next four decades, they and a continuous string of imitators such as Seymour Hearsh of the *New York Times*, obsessively asserted there was a secret cabal headed by the CIA running the country's foreign policy and carrying out the darkest of American aspirations.

During the Carter administration, Congress launched a full-scale investigation of the CIA with the Church Committee hearings and the Rockefeller Commission. In 1976 alone, one-third of the agency resigned. Carter himself made it plain that he was at war with his own intelligence service. He personally issued a twenty-six page directive detailing all the activities forbidden by the agency. Six hundred positions in covert espionage were shut down. In 1978, Congress passed the Foreign Intelligence Surveillance Act (FISA) that required a court order for electronic monitoring of foreign nationals, even those located in the US. These rules remained unamended and played a key role in the CIA's failure to uncover and stop the 9/11 attacks. Moreover, by 9/11, the US did not have a single human asset (native informant) inside the two most dangerous powers in the Middle East, Iraq and Iran.

The remaining seven years of the Bush (GW) presidency, the role and stature of the intelligence services were greatly restored. After 9/11, the President's first meeting *each* day involved his review of a one-page synopsis culled from reports generated by all sixteen intelligence agencies. Despite the depredations suffered by the American intelligence agencies that culminated in 9/11, history will record that the Bush presidency overcame the handicap. He led two successful invasions of hostile Middle Eastern countries, and on his watch, there were no subsequent attacks on American soil.

KSM, Waterboarding, and Gitmo

On March 1, 2003, nineteen months after 9/11, two dozen Pakistani tactical assault forces burst into a safe house and captured the mastermind Khalid Sheikh Mohammed (KSM). There they found a wealth of data on computers, cell phones, and in documents. The terrorist mastermind of 9/11 was not given a lawyer. Instead he was spirited away to an undisclosed third country and to a secret CIA "black site." At first he was defiant, contemptuous of his captors, and refused to talk. He was then waterboarded.

At first his resistance was impressive but eventually the techniques worked. He

---

23. Arthur Herman, *The Thirty-Five Year War on the CIA* (*Commentary Magazine*, December 2009, 12.

told his de-briefers about active al-Qaeda plots and provided information leading to the arrest of those poised to carry them out. He even held classes explaining al-Qaeda's operating structure, financing, communications, and logistics, and he identified safe havens and travel routes. His information yielded 6,000 intelligence reports shared by our allies across the world.

One of the plots KSM revealed, then thwarted by the CIA and FBI, was the plan to fly a plane into Library Tower, the tallest building in Los Angeles. Thousands of people living in LA owe their lives to the interrogators of KSM. The information derived from KSM also led US and British agents to preempt the 2006 attack that would have seen seven jets departing from London explode over US and Canadian cities. Had this plot not been stopped, it may have dwarfed 9/11 in American loss of life. Finally, KSM led US and allied intelligence services to locate and roll up many terrorist cells, both in the West and Middle East. It is not quantifiable the number of lives saved by the success of the KSM interrogations.

Additionally, President George W. Bush authorized Guantanamo Bay (Gitmo), on the western tip of Cuba, to be used as a detention and debriefing center, and the facility where military tribunals for terrorists, most of them captured off the battlefields of Afghanistan and Iraq, be held. It was the perfect facility outside the country so the detainees would not be allowed the benefit the constitutional protections afforded American citizens. Surrounded by water on three sides, it made escape and attack from outside terrorists nearly impossible.

With respect to the detention and interrogation program at Gitmo, the former CIA director who served under both Clinton and Bush, George Tenet, stated, "I know that this program saved lives. I know this program alone is worth more than what the FBI, the Central Intelligence Agency, and the National Security Agency put together have been able to tell us." [24]

Yet, on January 22, 2009, in his first substantive action as the newly inaugurated President of the United States, Barack Obama issued Executive Order 13491, closing the advanced interrogation program, despite urgent requests from the five living former CIA Directors, many top officials from various intelligence agencies, and his own director, Leon Panetta. The new president ordered the release of four Justice Department memos on April 16, 2009, memos that described in detail the techniques used to interrogate KSM and numerous other high-value terrorists imprisoned at Gitmo. As Marc Thiessen characterized it, "With these actions, Barack

24. Josh Gernstein, *Tenet: Aggressive Interrogations Brought US Valuable Information* (*New York Sun*, April 26, 2007).

Obama arguably did more damage to America's national security in his first 100 days of office than any other president in American history." [25] The memos written by CIA staff attorneys directed then President George W. Bush as to what the law allowed the Agency to administer during interrogation. These were guidelines the new Bush administration desperately needed to know in the aftermath of 9/11, fearing another imminent attack. Today many have forgotten that 9/11 was followed by the arrival of anthrax-laced letters delivered to members of Congress and that fear swept the nation's capital during the fall of 2001.

The men who wrote the memos were patriots, dedicated to helping the President defend the country, yet stay within the law. For their service, President Obama's Attorney General appointed a special prosecutor to consider criminal charges. This directive had a devastating effect on intelligence service officers across the world and put the country in great danger. If the West is to survive this war against militant Islam, it will need to rely on skilled intelligence officers far more than in any other previous conflict. Moroever it must resist the violation of:

IMMUTABLE #4
*If a people cannot avoid continuous internal warfare,
it will have a new order imposed from without.*

---

25. Marc A. Thiessen, *Courting Disaster: How the CIA Kept America Safe and How Barack Obama is Inviting the Next Attack* (Regnery Publishing, 2010), 92.

CHAPTER THREE

The Fall of Rome

AD 476

The Roman Empire in the fifth century had disintegrated in the West
because the government could no longer tax the citizens and
because they were no longer willing to support
the administration necessary to defeat the barbarians.
KENNETH HARL

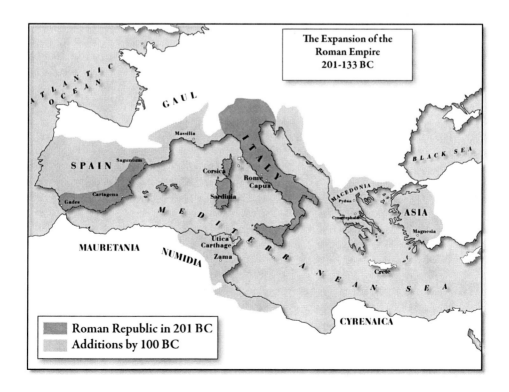

The Romanized Frankish Centurion
(Depicted in Historic Fiction)

On New Year's Eve, AD 406, as the pre-dawn eastern skies showed a hint of light above the black outline of the forest, young Marcus Risconius stood at his post on the ramparts of a wood and earthen Roman fort built on the banks of the Rhine near the ancient city of Treverorum.[1] In the bitter cold, he had remained awake the entire night, knowing full well that the punishment for falling asleep on his watch was to be clubbed to death by the men of his own unit.

As a centurion, he commanded a regiment of fourty men. Over his uniform of helmet, breast plate, grieves, and skirt he wrapped himself in several threadbare blankets. As he stood gazing out at the dozens of fires stoked by the Germans across the river, he wondered if any of them might be a relative, an uncle, a cousin, or a grandmother.

Marcus was eighteen years old. He had taken on a "Latinized" name adapted from his father, Riscobald, a Frankish warrior chieftain and able cavalry commander. Riscobald had secured the settlement of his entire village within the dwindling safety of the Empire.

When Marcus was still an infant, his father negotiated a treaty with the provincial Roman authorities. A bargain much like ones struck over the past fifty years by thousands of tribes of Franks, Sueve, and Alans. The bargain was that a German warlord and all the able-bodied men of his village agreed to serve in the Roman military in exchange for resettlement rights for his village. Marcus's father had been killed one year earlier while conducting reconnaissance inside

Germania, somewhere out in the still unmapped territory across the river.

Marcus was more fortunate than all the other German-born boys who grew up in his small newly constituted Roman village because his father trained him in the military arts, and provided him with tutoring conveyed

When Rome was gaining its empire

---

1.   Today's city of Trier.

lovingly by Sextus Illyrius, a Christian monk who had once been a soldier in the army of the Emperor Valens. Sextus had lived through the battle of Adrianople.

By the time Marcus was twelve years old, he had learned to speak Latin, thanks to his tutor. He had read Cicero, the histories of Livy, and the "Meditations" of Marcus Aurelius, the man he believed was the greatest of all Roman Emperors and whose name he chose as his own. As a boy, he came to understand the enormity of the Empire and its mythical accomplishments, and thrilled to the idea of one day going on campaign and marching in a victory procession in Rome. He dreamed of commanding an entire legion, becoming an equestrian, becoming a provincial governor, marrying into a Senatorial family, and raising a son who would one day become Emperor.

Despite the fact that he was born a "barbarian," he understood that, as a Roman citizen, he was an inheritor of twelve centuries of a civilization that produced unprecedented levels of—agriculture, architecture, horticulture, cuisine, arts, literature, law, political structure, martial superiority, and wealth. He believed that the world might never know anything that would exceed the Pax Romana (Latin for Roman peace) and the brilliant predictability of the Roman world, a world he feared was becoming only a memory.

He joined the army at age sixteen, the year he accepted the toga of manhood. He was a member of the limitanei, the frontier guards whose units were stationed in forts along the banks from the upper Rhine to the lower Danube. These two great rivers formed the northeastern border of the Empire and ran a thousand miles from the North Sea to the Black Sea. In just two years, his bravery in fighting the constant invasions of his own countrymen earned him the rank of centurion. Each day, as he inspected his men, he would mentally contrast them to the boorish brutes across the river. As their commander, he made sure that he held to the Roman ideal—clean shaven, resolute, with the hard physique of Greek statuary.

Yet for Marcus, into his ideal world of Roman perfection, intruded a realization that the present Empire was clearly breaking with its past. Throughout northern Gaul, Roman currency was practically nonexistent. Too often, when the soldiers stationed at his fort were not occupied with repelling German invaders, they were ordered to set upon their own countrymen *inside* the empire and confiscate their food, livestock, and whatever stores were available. It had been just a few months since his mother and sister, who lived on a small farm a few miles from the fort, had been forced to turn over to the legionnaires almost all their pigs and only cow, leaving them destitute.

As was his habit to pass the long hours while on watch, he recited whole passages he memorized from the copied manuscripts his teacher, Sextus, loaned him, particularly the military accounts of Tacitus, Polybius, and Livy. This morning, as he wrapped his arms tightly around his torso to keep from shivering, he recited lines from Livy. In his *Histories*, Livy quotes another centurion addressing the Roman Senate 600 years earlier:

"I am Spurius Ligustinus of the tribe Crustumina, and come from Sabine stock.[2] My father left me half an acre of land and a little hut in which I was born and bred and I am still living there. As soon as I came of age, my father gave me his brother's daughter to wife who brought nothing save her free birth and chastity together with her fertility which would be enough for any wealthy home. We have six sons and two daughters, both already married.

I joined the army in the consulship of Publius Sulpicius and Gaius Aurelius.[3] I served two years in the ranks of the army which was taken across Macedonia in a campaign against King Philip.[4] In the third year, Flaminius promoted me for bravery to centurion of the tenth maniple of hastate.

After the defeat of King Philip and the Macedonians when we had been brought back to Italy and demobilized, I immediately left for Spain as volunteer with the consul Marcus Pocius." [5]

"I enlisted a third time, again as a volunteer in the army set against the Aetolians and King Antiochus.[6] And when Antiochus had been driven out and the Aetolians had been crushed, we were brought back to Italy. Thereafter, I saw two campaigns . . ."

"Four times in the course of a few years I held the rank of Chief Centurion. Thirty-four times I was awarded the honor of bravery by generals. I have been given six civic crowns.[7] But even if I had not

---

2. People who lived in central Italy and absorbed by Rome two centuries earlier.

3. In the Roman Republic, during this period, the Senate elected two consuls each year to be its most senior elected officials. Because they were elected for only one year and shared the position shows how important it was to the men of the Republic that they avoid being ruled by a tyrant.

4. This was the campaign in the Balkans of 199 -198 BC.

5. Kenneth Harl of Tulane University says he is a brave guy. In this period of Spain, large armies starved due to limited plunder on the edge of the Empire and tough barbarians wiped out small armies.

6. Still another conquest eastward, this time Greece.

7. This is an award for saving the life of a fellow legionnaire on the battlefield.

*completed my service.[8] and if my age did not give me an exemption.
I would never claim an exemption.[9] I shall make it my business to see
that no one in the army outdoes me in bravery which is always what I
have done, as my commanders as well as my fellow campaigners can
testify." [10]*

Next, as he often did, Marcus reviewed and relived great Roman battles.
On this morning it was the Battle of Adrianople, the catastrophic defeat where
his elderly tutor, one of the few Roman survivors, had fought. Marcus, on
many occasions, asked his teacher to repeat and expand upon every detail of
the battle. He conducted a sort of "thought experiment" while on watches or
prolonged marches; he would put himself in the place of the Emperor Valens,
the general who commanded the Romans and was killed. And with this exercise,
Marcus would build a new strategy, change the battle plan, and lead his legions
to victory.

Thirty Years Earlier—The Eve of the Disaster at Adrianople

During the decade of the AD 370s, along the frontier of the Western Roman
Empire on the eastern side of the Rhine and Danube Rivers, lived an array of Germanic
peoples. The shadowy origins of the tribes of Franks, Alemans, Sueves, and Goths
remain obscure given their universal inability to write their own language. They were
uniformly warlike people who augmented their farming and hunting with raids upon
each other, as well as periodic raids into Roman territory across river.

During the middle decades of the fourth century, many of the tribes periodically
forgot what is was like to be defeated by Roman legions. They entered imperial lands,
attacked farms, and carried off livestock, booty, and anyone they could capture for
slaves. This necessitated a response from the Emperor, albeit usually a slow one, due
to the long distances messages had to travel to and from Rome. Rome generally
responded with punitive raids, its legions would burn the guilty villages and massacre
men, women, and children until the tribal chieftains came begging for mercy. This
scenario greatly benefited the provincial estate owners and merchants of the violated
region. The price the Roman provincial authorities exacted for peace always involved
cheap access to captured slaves and compulsory tribute, usually in the form of livestock.

---

8. He served 20 years.
9. With four sons he could legally receive an exemption from military service by sending his sons to the conscription.
10. Livy.

Additionally, the Roman legionnaires were ordered to scour the encampments of the defeated tribe, capturing the most robust boys to be carried off to military training facilities and converted into Roman soldiers. The great proto-feudal estate owners of the period, who had tenant farmers working for them, were glad to pay a tax rather than send any of their employees off to the army. They were happy to do so as long as they could see that the Empire was doing its recruiting on the other side of the river. For much of the fourth century, as Alessandro Barbero writes, "The war against the barbarians was a business, like any other; all it required was proper management." [11]

The Goths, who defeated Valens, were a semi-nomadic Indo-European people originally from Scandinavia. A much taller people than the average swarthy Roman, they were fair skinned and blond haired. They had learned farming techniques mainly from their trade contacts with the Romans, and were generally very good soldiers, although they lacked the technology to conduct siege warfare. They also did not build or dwell in cities.

Sometime around AD 370, while temporarily settled in the Balkans, they came under attack from a new fierce and terrifying enemy from the Asian steppes, the Huns. Ammianus Marcellinus is our best source for this period.[12] He tells us these primitive Hun horsemen were the quintessential warrior nomads, who "nourished themselves with raw meat that they warmed between their thighs and the backs of their horses." He writes, "They are like fugitives, taking along with them the wagons in which they live. In these wagons, their wives weave their horrible garments, lie with their husbands, give birth to their children. . . . If asked, none could say from whence they came. . . . Like beasts without reason, they make no distinction between right and wrong."

In the summer of AD 376, under the command of Fritigern, the entire nation of terrified and hungry Goths appeared on the far bank of the Danube. They were across from Roman guard posts and near Marcianople, the capital of Roman Thrace, that was one of the twelve dioceses into which the Empire was divided. The Roman emissaries sent to their makeshift camps learned that much of the Gothic lands in the Balkans had been ravaged by the Huns, and that the Goths sought safe passage across the Danube and refuge inside the Empire. Their message was sent from the emissaries

---

11. Alessandro Barbero, *The Day of the Barbarians: The Battle that Led to the Fall of the Roman Empire* (New York: Walker & Company, 2005), 14.

12. The surviving books of Ammianus' history, *Res Gestae*, cover the years AD 353 to 378. As an experienced soldier, he is the mostly highly placed and traveled historian of the period. Ammianus entered the army when Constantius II was emperor of the East, and served under Ursicinus, the governor and magister militum of Mesopotamia. Ammianus accompanied Ursicinus to Gaul to put down usurper, Claudius Silvanus, who declared himself Emperor. He also accompanied him on two expeditions to the East.

to the commanders of the guard forts, to the military governor, and then to Valens, the Emperor of the Eastern Empire, who was in Antioch campaigning against the Persians.[13] The message in essence read—what do we do with these people?

Although Ammianus was not present at the meetings held in Antioch with Valens and his circle of advisors, his reconstruction of the Emperor's decision to grant the Goths their request provides us a wide window into the society of the Western Empire of the late fourth century. Ammianus tells us that everywhere in the West manpower was in short supply and entire provinces were depopulated because *crushing taxation had made the land not worth cultivating.* Large areas of the empire had become state-owned but lacked inhabitants to work the land. The admission of the Goths onto these state lands would allow the Empire to rebuild a portion of its tax base in the region.

Secondly, Valens reasoned that some of the Goths could be settled on large estates to become tenant farmers. During this period Roman law had elaborated the status of the serf who was technically a free man, but barely, given that he was obligated to remain on the land owned by his lord.[14] Thirdly, the Emperor needed conscripts for his armies. The Goths offered him a huge pool of recruits, young men inured to the hardship of battle and campaigns, and their officers. And fourth, he thought that their desperate situation worked to his advantage. As refugees who were dying of hunger, they were in no position to negotiate terms they were given. Valens mistakenly believed that their desperation rendered them passive and a non-threat.

We don't know exactly how long it took for the Goths' request to reach Valens in Antioch and for his acceptance to arrive back in Marcianople on the desk of Lupicinus. Because of the large distance and the primitive communications of antiquity, we can assume that it was many weeks, if not several months. By the time the Romans had been commanded to admit the Goths, built the necessary ferry systems, and had begun to ferry them across the river, the refugees were uncontrollable due to desperate hunger.

Another historian of the period, Eunapius, a Greek, records the chaos that ensued. He tells us that the Roman plan conveyed by Valens was to disarm all the men and segregate the crossings, first the adolescent males, next adult males, then adult women and children. Food was to be immediately supplied the Goths on both sides of the river while the disposition of the population was administered. Instead the corrupt soldiers

---

13. As Goldsworthy, author of *How Rome Fell*, points out, the Empire was actually ruled by three Emperors. The West was ruled by Gratian, the oldest son of Valentinian I who had died a year earlier, and his four-year-old brother Valentinian II who was proclaimed Augustus, the title of Emperor, by the armies of the Danube. So chaotic was the West that the group of senior bureaucrats in charge were content to run the government with an infant and an adolescent Emperor as nominally in charge.

14. Ammianus clearly demonstrates that the feudal system of the nobleman and his indentured serfs stretched farther back into European history than the medieval age as commonly thought.

and bureaucrats took advantage of the remoteness of their outpost and decided upon theft and extortion. For those Goths who had a little money, they were able to pay bribes to their corrupt Roman handlers so their entire family could cross together. Those who paid bribes were fed and allowed to keep their weapons. But for most, they tragically traded their children for food and passage. Some wretched families were forced to forfeit a child in exchange for dog meat. As Eunapius puts it, "They (corrupt Romans of Thrace) had all decided to fill their houses with domestics and their lands with shepherds and to exploit the situation to satisfy their every desire."

Soon, the immense size of the desperate population of refugees began to alarm the Romans. Massed on the west bank of the Danube was the largest reception of immigrants ever admitted into the Empire. While their orders were to disperse the Goths to various areas throughout the interior, this would clearly take time. Food supplies and sanitary conditions were practically nonexistent. The population of ten thousand people dying of hunger could not be contained by a small garrison of soldiers on the outskirts of the Empire.

The Goths Revolt

One evening, while their countrymen were dying of hunger and they awaited orders, Fritigern, the Gothic prince, and retinue were invited to dine with the Thracian Governor, Lupicinus, at his residence in the walled capital, Marcianople. During the banquet, a large crowd of Goths amassed outside the city gates, desperate to enter the city and barter for food. When Roman centurions appeared and attempted to disburse them, the throng descended and killed the Romans, stripping the bodies of armaments and valuables. Ammianus tells us that when a messenger came into the dining hall to inform the Governor of the situation, although he was "heavy with wine and sleep," Lupicinus surreptitiously gave the order to have all the Gothic leaders' guards waiting outside in the hall, killed.

When the crowd sensed that its leaders were not coming out of the city and fearing the worst, the Goths began to besiege the walls, attempting to storm the city. Fritigern and company, realizing what was happening and that their lives hung in the balance, dissembled their concern and implored their Roman hosts to send them out to calm their people. Their subterfuge worked. They were released. As soon as the Gothic princes were outside the city walls, they leapt on their horses amid the roar of the countrymen and shouted, "The Romans have broken their agreement!" It was a very black day in the increasingly sordid history of late Roman antiquity.

For the next several months, the starving Goths ravaged the Thracian countryside, killing famers and carrying off their livestock, food stores, and possessions.

Lupicinus, who may have planned to kill all the Gothic leaders the night of the banquet, incorrectly thought that a leaderless throng of Goths could be easily dispersed, compounded his treacherous mistakes. Rather than request reinforcements, Lupicinus decided that sending a report to Valens informing the Emperor that he had crushed the rebellion, was a far better career move.

He gathered what troops he could, roughly 10,000 from the region, and headed out into countryside. He believed that Roman military superiority would overwhelm the barbarian rabble. What he did not realize was that the tide was turning against Rome. Inside the Empire, there were men of Gothic descent and others, who were swarming to the rebel Gothic banner. They sensed that Rome was losing control of the region. They hated the government and were eager to participate in, and profit from, its liquidation. As the Italian historian, Alessandro Barbero points out,

> *"Thrace was filled with Goths. Some of those who lived there were prisoners of war, compelled to work as tenant farmers on the imperial estates; some, naturally, were slaves, the same Gothic slaves who had flooded the markets for many years; and some were whom their parents had bartered just a few weeks earlier in exchange for something to eat. All of them deserted or fled at the first opportunity and joined their people serving as guides for the warriors, leading them to the richest villages where reserve supplies were stored. . . . There were also many inhabitants of Thrace who no longer felt loyalty to an empire that crushed them with taxes and yet was unable to defend them in a time of danger. People arrived at the Goths' encampments daily."*[15]

While we don't have a good detailed description of this first battle with Gothic rebels, we know that the Lupicinus forces were routed totally and the dead Romans provided the Goths with a great deal of armor for their future campaigns. It was recorded that the commander, Lupicinus, seeing his legions being overrun by the far more determined Goths, was one of the first to ride away from the field of battle. No longer could it be said that the Roman generals led from the front.

Flushed with their victory over the world's greatest military, Fritigern led his army to a nearby lesser city, Adrianople.[16] He knew that it held large stores of food and gold, his forces had no siege equipment and could not breach it walls. Failing the siege, his

15. Alessandro Barbero, *The Day of the Barbarians: The Battle That Led to the Fall of the Roman Empire* (New York: Walker & Company, 2007), 57.

16. Today's city of Edirne near the border of European Turkey and Bulgaria.

army took up quarters nearby in the western quarter of Thrace. His rebels pillaged small farms and undefended hamlets to obtain food. This gave him time to wait and see what the Romans' next move would be.

For the next year, the Thracian countryside continued to be ravaged by the Goths. All across the province, terrified rural Romans were forced to flee their lands and take up residence as refugees inside the walls of garrisoned Thracian cities. Meanwhile the adolescent Emperor of the West, Gratian, was consumed with a campaign in northern Germany against a confederation of Aleman tribes. By spring AD 378, Valens, Emperor of the East, was forced to end his campaign against the Persians and return to his palace in Constantinople, the capital of the Eastern Empire.

There he found that his unpopularity with his subjects was manifest. He attended a chariot race and was jeered by the crowd. He saw very plainly that he needed a victory over the Goths whose raids of the surrounding Thracian lands had reached all the way to the perimeter of the great city's walls. Moreover, he knew that if he did not defeat the Goths, he would surely meet the fate of so many Roman emperors of the previous two centuries—murdered by his own soldiers and replaced by their current favored general.

Valens left the capital and marched his army west toward the Balkans. On the night of their arrival at Adrianople, Valens held a war council with his generals. He wanted to confirm that they should attack the Goths on the following day. Several of his generals told him to wait. Valens had received word that Gratian's victorious army was only a few days away, after its great victory in Germany against the Aleman tribes. The Goths were camped on the bank of what the Bulgarians today refer to as the Tundzha River, at the base of Rhodope Mountains where today, on the border with Bulgaria, there is the Turkish village, Muratcali.

This was not what Valens wanted to hear. Gratian was Valens' nephew and still a boy. As a matter of personal survival, he needed a victory over the Goths and could not afford to share it with an adolescent Emperor of the West.

The Battle of Adrianople (August 9, 378)

The day prior to battle, a Gothic envoy, including a priest, appeared with a message from Fritigern requesting negotiations.[17] After reading the letter, Valens sent the emissaries away without a response. At dawn the following morning, Valens' army began its march toward the Goth's position. The hilly terrain lacked roads and, combined with the heat of the day, made the march difficult. When the Goths came into view, what Valens saw was a huge circle of wagons drawn tightly together on the

---

17.   At this time, many of the Goths were Aryan Christians as was Valens.

top of a hill with all the Barbarians, warriors, women, and children hidden inside the barricade. As Barbero writes, "Slowly, methodically, in response to a precise sequence of commands, the Roman infantry began to deploy in order of battle within sight of the wagon ring, while the cavalry spread out on the flanks and pushed forward, as if to feel and perhaps encircle the enemy."[18]

The Goths flooded out from behind their protective ring of wagons and, as they formed into their ranks, they shouted insults and taunts at the Romans who responded with a deep lowing of the "barritus" (a derisive battle cry aimed at belittling the barbarian). This combined with ten thousand Romans' banging their spears and swords against their shields, raised an ominous din that reverberated up the gently sloping battlefield. The Roman cavalry, on both the right and left flanks, failed to hold their horses at bay and edged closer and closer to the Gothic warriors who stood bristling for battle. The Roman archers, who had moved into range, let their first volley of arrows fly into the enemy position. Still neither commander gave the order to attack.

Once again, the Goths sent an envoy out from behind their lines that the Romans allowed to gain access to Valens. Ammianus was not present at the battle but fervently concludes that Fritigern used this stratagem as a delay tactic because he was waiting for his cavalry to return. He had sent them out

Roman Helmets

to forage several days earlier. Valens received the diplomatic envoy and left his army standing in battle-ready formation, in the heat of the day, while he treated with the enemy.

We can assume that the Roman legionnaires were losing their resolve, as they stood in their ranks, and became increasingly hot, thirsty, and fatigued. Surely, Valens saw the Gothic offer of peace too attractive to reject out of hand. He was well aware that the empire, particularly in the western provinces, was in desperate need of manpower to work the state-owned fields and to man the forts along the frontiers. Therefore, it certainly must have occurred to him that slaughtering thousands of these able-bodied men would be a horrible waste.

As the shadows lengthened across the battlefield and his men remained standing in battle-ready formation, Valens sent a message back to Fritigern that he wanted to

---

18. Barbero, p.101.

negotiate with him face-to-face. Suddenly, the Gothic cavalry, composed of hardened Hun, Alan, and Gothic riders, appeared.

Earlier that day, from higher ground in the foothills, the Gothic horsemen had seen the dust cloud of the approaching Roman army. They had ridden back to their Gothic camp through the bed of the Tundzha River that was only a few inches deep during this time of year. By doing so, they generated no dust and stealthily arrived on the battlefield without the Romans even knowing that they existed.

Seeing the Romans massed in front of their camp, the Gothic horsemen seized the advantage and charged the Roman cavalry arrayed on Valens' left flank. Suddenly, a huge din and an enormous cloud of dust enveloped that side of the battlefield. What soon became apparent was that the surprised Roman cavalry had collapsed backward on top of its own infantry.

Although the left flank of his army was in disarray, the bulk of Valens' infantry held its position, then began fighting its way forward against the Goths, killing many. They pushed up the hill toward the wagon encirclement while Goth archers and slingers fired rounds into them at near point-blank range. Had Valens made adequate decisions during the confusion of a battle that began almost by accident, the Romans probably could have broken through the wagon encirclement and routed the Goths inside their encampment. But to the horror of the forward infantrymen, they turned and saw that none of their compatriots on horse or foot had followed them up the hill. No one had their back. While the balance of the Romans engaged in individual hand-to-hand duels, the more numerous Gothic cavalry began to envelop Valens' most experienced foot soldiers in a vast net. Soon the bulk of Valens' elite infantry found itself in the same situation that their ancestors faced at Cannae a half millennium earlier. "The foot soldiers," Ammianus writes, "stood in the open, their companies so crowded together that hardly one of them could pull his sword or draw back his arm. The clouds of rising dust blotted out the sky which resounded with ghastly cries." [19]

The Gothic and Hun cavalry charged into the Romans over and over. Despite the fighting spirit of the Roman infantry elite, they could not hold out indefinitely. Weary, tormented by thirst, tripping over their wounded and dead, with spears broken and shields riddled with arrows, their ability to hold off wave after wave of cavalry charges fell apart. As dusk descended into night, the Roman infantry was running away while the Gothic cavalry rode them down, slaughtering all that they could catch.

Before he could escape into the darkness, Valens found that he was practically

19. Ammianus Marcellinus: *Roman History, Volume I, Books 14-19* (Loeb Classical Library No. 300) (English and Latin Edition) by Ammianus Marcellinus and J. C. Rolfe (Hardcover, Jan 1, 1950), 29.

alone with his generals. Seeing that the battle was lost, they took refuge among the last remaining infantry regiments and attempted to retreat in good order. Soon the generals around him were fleeing the scene as well. Only the late hour that the battle commenced allowed some of the Romans to escape in the cover of dark.

Valens' body was never found. The loss to the Empire was staggering. A huge cadre of veteran soldiers from the East lay dead on the Thracian countryside. Numerous distinguished generals and members of the Emperor's cabinet were lost as well.

Marcus and the Frozen Rhine —(Depicted in Historic Fiction)

Twenty-eight years after the disaster of Adrianople, Marcus was lost in his thoughts, reliving the battle that had been described by Sextus so many times. He envisioned the odyssey of his teacher when, as a young soldier, he was wounded at Adrianople, escaped at nightfall, and made his way through the Thracian countryside. He gained his admittance to Gratian's army and an audience with the Emperor, learned to live with strange recruits from German tribes he had never encountered, traveled with them north to defend Illyricum, and eventually settled in northern Gaul.

The frigid night was dissolving into a grey dawn. The young centurion's fort stood a few yards back from the beginning of a tall sandy bank that sloped down to the water's edge and looked across the half-mile wide Rhine River. From his rampart, in the dim light, on the far side of the river, just beyond the bank, Marcus could make out figures huddled around a fire. They were draped in crudely-fashioned animal skins. The men's hair was braided and dressed in grease. They were dirty; they stank and bellowed at each other incoherently. An elderly troll-like woman, wrapped in filthy hides, stirred a cauldron, slicing rancid meat and bits of roots into the concoction. The Germans gathered around the fire were decoys; left to distract the Romans billeted in Marcus's fort from what was happening that morning.

Marcus craned his neck forward. In shock he saw that the river was not flowing; it was standing still—frozen! He looked downstream and saw, off in the distance, vast numbers of dark forms running across the solid surface of the river. He swung his head to his right, and upstream, there too he could see even more figures moving across the ice.

The young centurion bolted from his post and sprinted down the wooden steps to the fort's dirt floor. As he raced across the dark courtyard toward the entrance to his commander's quarters, he blew into his battle whistle, issuing a series of three short bursts. This signaled to his regiment that an attack was imminent and that all men were to report to their battle stations immediately. In moments, the men of Marcus' regiment were at their posts in full armor. To his dismay, the commander of Marcus' fort, along with a second regiment billeted there, had not returned from their expedition across the river.

All that day, as the most senior officer on duty, Marcus assumed command and walked the ramparts of his fort, making sure that each soldier knew that he was expected to fight as if he were two men. Yet he knew that with such a small number of defenders, even a small band of determined archers armed with "fired" arrows could easily burn the fort down. He did not have enough men to rush outside the compound and repulse such an attack. But the attack never came.

Under overcast skies, the ice held and the invasion continued throughout the day until it became clear to the young centurion that the barbarians were bypassing his fort and heading inland for soft targets and easy plunder. Each time Marcus walked the western ramparts of the fort, he paused to survey the rising plumes of smoke coming from the direction of the inland villages.

The following day, a bloodied survivor from Treverorum was admitted to the fort. In his audience with Marcus, he gave Marcus the worst news of the centurion's life. The entire village had been raised, all the buildings burnt to the ground, and all the inhabitants, with their possessions and livestock, taken with the barbarians into the interior. As he struggled to hold back the tears in front of his men, the young centurion's thoughts turned back to the last words he had spoken to his sister and mother, knowing that he would never see them nor his teacher again.

The Aftermath of Adrianople, The West Begins Its Decline

Financing the administration of its empire was not a problem when Rome was expanding. Each newly conquered realm had their gold and silver reserves transferred to the Roman treasury. Its lands and other assets could be parceled out to regional commanders and the rank and file soldiers as a form of payment. Once Rome ceased conquering new realms in favor of consolidating its hold upon its vast lands, financing the administration of its empire became problematic.

During the late second century and early third centuries AD several Roman Emperors attempted to inflate the Empire's wealth. They recalled some of the outstanding gold coinage, secretly melted it down, and reissued it with leaden cores. In each case, this tactic was nearly catastrophic. The secret became instantly common knowledge among the Roman citizenry who reacted by refusing to accept the Empire's coinage in exchange for his goods and services. This in turn meant that the Emperor could not pay or provision his own armies. Each time the Roman debasement was attempted, all bogus coinage was again recalled and reissued with the lead removed.

IMMUTABLE #8
Debasing the currency always destabilizes the governing authority.

While the empire avoided the pitfalls associated with currency debasement, after its loss at Adrianople, the Western Empire began its disastrous decline toward destruction.

As soon as Gratian, the young emperor of the West, learned of the defeat and the death of his uncle, he collected the survivors he encountered from Valens' army. He immediately reversed direction and traveled north into Illyricum (the northern Balkans of today's Croatia and Bosnia). With the death of his uncle, Valens, he was resolved to defend the West and hoped he could prevent the spread of the Gothic menace to his half of the Empire.[20]

The very next day following the battle, Fritigern marched to Adrianople where Roman deserters told him that Valens deposited a large cache of gold necessary for the provisioning of his army. Ammianus tells us that Valens left a regiment of 300 soldiers behind to help secure Adrianople. But the municipal government was too afraid to allow the regiment to enter the city. By 10:00 a.m., when the Goths appeared outside Adrianople, the 300 legionnaires were entrenched outside the city's walls. Upon seeing the approaching army, the Romans deserted their position enmass and tried to join their ranks. The Goths, perhaps still crazed by battle, admitted them and instantly killed them all.

Ammianus spends a good deal of his last book describing the plunging morale of the Roman armies in both the East and West. He enumerates the various regiments and even select groups of officers who deserted to the Goths and other barbarian tribes. He writes of another group of deserters fighting for the Goths. From a select group of officers, the candidati, made up an elite contingent of the Emperor's personal body guards. During the Goth's unsuccessful siege of Adrianople, a group of these men went to the city during the night. They announced they were Roman, prisoners of the Goths, and had escaped and wished to join forces with the defenders there. Their actual plan was to gain the trust of the Romans defending Adrianople and, at

---

20. During the second half of the fourth century, Roman soldiers would nominate a new emperor. He would rule semi-legitimately a portion of the Empire, usually but not always the Eastern or Western half. For all their brilliance, the Romans never developed a smooth bloodless system for succession.

their first opportunity, set fires so the Goths could successfully storm the fort. When questioned, their stories were contradictory, so they were tortured, confessed their plot, and promptly beheaded.

For the next few days, Fritigern's besiegers were met with hails of arrows and large boulders propelled by war machines, and they concluded that they could not capture a walled city without siege equipment. For Rome it was all a profoundly dismal event.

Ammianus closes his work with an account of the battle because, as Barbero puts it, "The symbolic value of Adrianople seemed conclusive to him; as for what would follow, he said, let some other, younger writer record it if he choose . . . (for the historian) the history of the Empire finished there, as if it had come to a full stop."[21] The battle technically occurred in Thrace, on the soil of what was the Eastern Empire, and resulted in the death of an Eastern Emperor. And with the benefit of hindsight, we can see that the Romans' defeat at Adrianople set in motion a chain of events that led to the fall of the Roman Empire in the West. To use a phrase Winston Churchill was fond of, "The beginning of the end."

When hoards of barbarians stormed into the Western Empire on New Year's Eve AD 406, it had been fully twenty-eight years since Adrianople. But the defeat had proved seminal, an event that had caused profound trauma. Romans were not shocked by the news from Adrianople because an Emperor had been killed. For two hundred years many emperors, challengers and usurpers had been killed in palace coups and in civil wars. What was shocking for Romans all across the Mediterranean was that it called into question the Empire's manifest destiny. To be a Roman was to believe that the Empire's military would ultimately always defeat its barbarian enemies. Now that assumption was utterly called into question.

Gratian—The Last Effective Emperor of the West

In AD 375, Gratian had been elevated to emperor at the death of his father, Emperor Valentinian I.[22] During his father's eleven-year reign over the Western provinces, he proved a tireless and able administrator. As commander-in-chief he successfully maintained the integrity of the massive Western frontier that was increasingly under siege. Valentinian I selflessly appointed his brother, Valens, as co-emperor of the East to better manage the vast Empire. Valentinian I was known for meeting out severe and cruel punishments for those he deemed guilty of malfeasance and for his uncontrollable rages. While on campaign in Valeria, in a fit of apoplexy,

21. Barbero, 118.
22. The title used by Romans was Augustus. To conform with modern usage, this book uses Emperor.

Valentinian I died. On his deathbed he convinced his senior officers and key bureaucrats to elevate his son, Gratian, age 7, and his stepson, Valentinian II, age 4, as co-Emperors of the West. An inheritor of his father's leadership skills, by age 17, Gratian led armies on successful campaigns against enemy tribes inside *Germania*.[23] Had the insipid and craven Valens simply waited for Gratian's army to arrive before attacking the Goths, the downward trajectory of Roman/European history might very well have been avoided or at least postponed.

Roman Coinage

While encamped in Illyricum, it fell to Gratian and his advisors to choose a new emperor of the Eastern Empire. In AD 379, they appointed Gratian's top general Theodosius, his *magister militum*, master of the soldiers and named him Co-Augustus of the Eastern Empire. He was a Spaniard from a very illustrious line of Roman military men. His first order of business was to rebuild the army and restore order in Thrace. He moved into temporary headquarters in Thessalonica. Over the next two years he forged a peace with the Goths at an enormous cost to the long-term security of the Empire.

He recruited vast numbers of Goths into his new legions. He allowed them to form all-Gothic regiments, reporting to their own commanders. He domiciled them in completely autonomous regions of Thrace, in new Gothic homelands that were also completely tax exempt. Additionally, he paid the Gothic soldiers in these new regiments an exceptionally high rate of military pay. These initiatives placed a higher financial burden on citizens of the region who were not tax exempt. Thus Theodosius made the rebellious Goths a separate, favored group of people living among the heavily-taxed citizens upon whom they had visited atrocities and mayhem only a few years earlier. Soon a deep resentment against the barbarians became evident among the Roman citizenry of Thrace and around the Empire. But for Theodosius, it seemed a small price to pay if it meant that he could retain his control over the East.

In AD 381, with the Empire nominally at peace, Theodosius moved into the palace in Constantinople, a city that was far richer than Rome, for that matter, richer than any other in capital in the West. He and his court lived lavishly on a grand scale. The balance of power had permanently shifted to the much wealthier East. By AD 383, he and Gratian developed a good working relationship as equal co-Emperors and, in that year, concluded a formal peace treaty with the Goths. What they could not

23.   The previous year he defeated the barbarian tribe Lentienses at Argentaria.

see was that the more vulnerable Roman West was moving closer to its fall because the Empire showed the Barbarian world that rebellion would be rewarded—for the Goths, extortion paid off.

That same year, Gratian lost his life. His tutor, Ausonius, described him at twenty-four as possessing a "mens aurea," a golden mind. He was extremely well-read, a superb athlete, a master horseman, and, according, to his tutor a "supernatural hunter" who could kill a lion with a single arrow. In AD 383, Roman general, Clemens Maximus, serving in Britain, was proclaimed Augustus by his troops. Learning that Gratian and his army were in Paris, Maximus landed in Gaul and rushed to face the young Emperor in an effort to usurp the throne. On a field outside the city the two armies met. Both forces contained regiments of cavalry and infantry. Unexpectedly, Gratian's largely Moorish cavalry defected at the last moment to Maximus. The young emperor's army was routed. He escaped but was captured in Lyon. On August 25, under the promise of safe conduct, Gratian was murdered at a banquet. Incessant, never ending civil war had liquidated the West's last effective Emperor.

Theodosius—The Last Emperor to Rule a United Empire

Theodosius received the news of Gratian's death with profound shock and sadness. He naturally felt a deep devotion to the young charismatic man who elevated him to be Co-Emperor of the East. Due to pressures on his Eastern frontier from Ardashir II, the Persian King, and from the Huns to his north, he could not embark immediately on a campaign against Maximus and reluctantly acknowledged him. Privately, to his close advisors, he vowed to destroy him when the first opportunity presented itself.

The West was dysfunctionally ruled by a usurper in Gaul and boy emperor, Valentinian II, in Italy. In AD 388, the boy Emperor and his mother, Justina, spent a winter in Thessalonica with Theodosius. The "Empress behind the throne" brokered the marriage of her daughter, Galla, to the recently widowed Theodosius.[24] With that marriage, Justina and Theodosius fused both families and united the empire for the last time. That same year, Theodosius led an army north into Illyricum, into what is today Bosnia, where Maximus was headquartered on the Sisak river. Despite his army's long march, his troops swam the river in full armor and stormed up onto the far bank and defeated the usurper's irregulars from Gaul.

Four years later, AD 392, Arbogast, a Frankish master of the soldiers, made arrangements to murder the boy Emperor, Valentinian II. He used his position to

---

24. A chronicler of the period, Zosimus, in his *Historia*, writes that Theodosius was at first reluctant to make war on the usurper, Maximus, but Justina convinced the widower by offering him his very attractive daughter who pled with him to do so.

elevate a Roman puppet of supposed noble birth, Eugenius, to Emperor. In response, during the summer AD 394, with an army of 20,000 Gothic mercenaries, Theodosius located the usurper's troops at the River Frigidus near Trieste. He defeated them in a bloody two-day battle and beheaded Eugenius, who had murdered his nephew.

The battle contained an almost supernatural vindication for Theodosius. Several years earlier he issued an unprecedented decree, making Catholicism the official religion of the realm and outlawing all Christian variants such as Aryanism and pagan cults. On the second day of fighting, a gale force wind came up out of the East, at the backs of Theodosius's troops, and straight into the faces of the enemy. Its force was so great that Eugenius' army was blinded by flying debris and unable to throw spears or loose their arrows. The largely pagan troops became so dispirited that many simply surrendered to what they saw was their enemy's more powerful god.

On the eve of Theodosius' departure for the campaign, his young second wife, Galla, died, probably in child birth. At the conclusion of the battle, he traveled to Milan, which had replaced Rome as the city most often occupied by the Emperor, and issued another fateful decree. Because Valentinian II was killed before he had married and produced any heir, the obvious course was to formally divide the Empire among his two sons, giving the elder, Arcadius, the East and Honorius, the West. The enormous demands of his office had taken their toll. Shortly thereafter, in his fiftieth year, Theodosius died.

Honorius was ten years old when he ascended to the Western throne and exhibited none of his father's managerial skills as he aged. With the division of the two empires, the West was cut off from any financial aid it might otherwise have received from the wealthier East. In AD 395, Rome and Constantinople became forever separate capitals with their separate courts, armies, senatorial elites, and treasuries—two separate states with often competing interests. During his sixteen-year reign, Honorius worked tirelessly and effectively to unite the Empire that was constantly at war with invaders and itself. Yet in officially dividing the Empire and awarding the co-emperorships to his weak and ineffectual sons, Theodosius further set in motion the events that would doom the West.

Additionally, within the army that Theodosius had assembled and led to victory at the Frigidus River, were two actors who played leading roles in the fall of the West. The first was Stilicho, the Emperor's master of the soldiers and second in command. He was the son of a Vandal warlord and married to Theodosius' niece, Serena. He became the first in a line of German commanders-in-chief, *magisters militum*, who, during the next seventy-five years, took control of a collapsing Western Empire while a succession of boy puppet emperors succeeded to the throne. The second actor was

Alaric, a brilliant young Gothic general, who led a small nation of his countrymen into Italy and sacked Rome.

Since Adrianople, the old system of recruitment and conscription had ceased to function. Fewer Romans were willing to become lower-paid soldiers, serving in an army with higher-paid foreign mercenaries. Saint Jerome denounced the emperors who relied on barbarian soldiers as running an empire with feet of clay. "Just as in the past, there was indeed nothing stronger and more solid than the Roman Empire, so now, at the end of time, there is nothing weaker; for whether we fight civil wars or foreign wars, we need the help of barbarian peoples." [25]

The West would soon descend into chaos.

Alaric Destroys Rome's Sovereignty over the West

In AD 395, with the vacuum created by the Emperor's death, ominous events occurred in rapid succession. First, Honorius was only ten years old so Stilicho was in complete control of the levers of power in the West. He plotted his next moves, if he was not crowned supreme Emperor over the whole of the East, in a quest to seize a portion of the Eastern Territory from Constantinople. Second, the very dim-witted eighteen-year-old Arcadius, once introduced to the startlingly beautiful Frankish girl, Eudoxia, instantly asked for her hand. She accepted and began a long line of Byzantine Empresses who were known to be beautiful, worldly, and ambitious. Eudoxia was also rumored to entertain whole strings of lovers.

On the day of the great wedding, April 27, 395, twenty-five year old General Alaric, the commander of all the Gothic troops domiciled in Thrace, took the opportunity to go into revolt. He learned that virtually all the regular Roman army units of the East that Theodosius had led on the campaign against Eugenius were still in Milan. This left the entire area of the Eastern Empire, west of the Bosphorus, virtually defenseless. It was too great an opportunity to pass up.

Alaric began pillaging the countryside under the pretext that it was he, not Stilicho, who should have been promoted to *magister militum*. When his Gothic marauders reached the gates of Constantinople, Arcadius' senior advisor, Rufinus, secretly met with Alaric and paid him off with a large sum of gold. [26] The Goths turned south, passed through the historic defile of Thermopylae, pillaging Greek cities in Boeotia and Attica. Few towns escaped their wrath. Even the ancient Greek port, Piraeus, was destroyed.

---

25. Saint Jerome was an enormously influential Illyrian priest who first translated the Bible into Latin.
26. Essentially, Alaric was not acting as both commander and king of the western Goths. He knew that if he could secure a formal command in the Roman army, he could provide food and provisions for his nomadic people.

The chronicler, Zosimus, records that when the Goths reached Athens, Alaric's courage faltered due to a vision where Athena and Achilles appeared fully dressed in their battle armor and scowled down at him as they patrolled the ramparts of the mythical ancient city. Bypassing Athens, he went south across the Isthmus of Corinth into the Peloponnese, systematically sacking Sparta and the other rich cities of the central plain. When they turned north, near Olympia, Stilicho had a large enough army to surround the Goths. Yet for some reason, perhaps because he thought that he could one day use the Goths for his own ends, Stilicho allowed them to escape rather than annihilate them when he had the chance. Despite the devastation the Goths had visited upon Thrace, Macedonia, and Greece, Stilicho's attitude was that those losses were not his worry. They were provinces of the Eastern Empire and, thus, Arcadius' problem.

Every year thereafter, Alaric's Goths went on a rampage and demanded that Constantinople pay him off. He knew that he could not conquer Constantinople, the most heavily fortified city in the Western world. He extorted large sums of money from Theodosius' other worthless son, Arcadius. Ultimately, in AD 401, Alaric chose to go north and invade Italy. Traveling slowly with their families and all their worldly belongings, the invading Goths were an entire nation on the move, headed toward Milan, the provisional capital of the West.

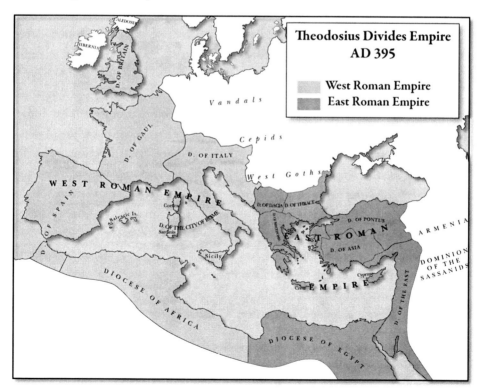

When he received word of the Goths' imminent arrival, Honorius fled the city to a hideout in Piedmont. On Easter Sunday AD 402, outside the city of Pollentia, today's village of Pollenza, Stilicho again met Alaric in battle. The battle lasted an entire day, ending indecisively. Claudian maintains that Stilicho pursued the Goths and defeated them near Verona.[27] Yet once again, he allowed Alaric and a portion of his army to escape back into the confines of the East.

Like the Taliban of today, hiding out in Waziristan, Alaric remained in southern Illyricum on the frontier between the East and West for the next three years, plundering for supplies as he needed them. In AD 405, Claudius Claudianus tells us that Stilicho granted Alaric the title he sought, Master of the Soldiers, and commander of the Eastern armies. But the court in Constantinople refused to honor this promotion because it implied that Stilicho had authority over the East.

Secondly, that same year, a new nation of Goths under King Radagaisus launched a deep raid into Northern Italy. These Goths spoke the same language as Alaric but had no other connection to him. They came to be called the Ostrogoths (Eastern Goths). Zosimus tells us that their troops numbered 400,000. This, like many reports of troop strengths during late antiquity, was a massively inflated figure. But whatever the size of the invading force, Zosimus also tells us that the great general, Stilicho, summoned and assembled regiments from Gaul and Italy, and utterly destroyed the invaders.

At this point it is necessary to analyze the relative strength of the Roman Army during the first decade of the fifth century.

Notitia Dignitatum, The Roman Army on Paper (AD 405)

A copy of this remarkable document from the late fourth century survives today. First produced in AD 395, at the time the Empire was being divided upon Theodosius's death, it is an accounting of both the civil and military Roman bureaucracies. Its formal title, *Notitia Dignitatum omnium, tam civilum quam militarium,* "The list of all offices, both civil and military," provides a detailed look at the size and scope of both the government and the military of the late Empire. Yet, with respect to the military, it may also be a huge deception.

In Goldsworthy's *How Rome Fell,* he includes a chart, The Command Structure of the Roman Army in the Notitia Dignitatum.[28] It shows that, according to the Romans' own internal records, in AD 395, the year that the Empire was officially divided, the West maintained 19 cavalry, 83 infantry regiments, and 18 *limitanei*

---

27. Claudius Claudianus, a Roman chronicle who worked for Emperor Stilicho.

28. Adrian Goldsworthy, *How Rome Fell: Death of a Superpower* (New Haven: Yale University Press, 2009), 287.

(frontier guards).[29] And the chart shows that there were 43 cavalry, 114 infantry, and 15 limitanei in the East.[30] Although the regiments of late antiquity became much smaller than its predecessor, the legion, the above numbers nevertheless indicate a very large number of men in arms, perhaps as many as 600,000, an army twice the size as was available to earlier emperors such as Marcus Aurelius.

Goldsworthy observes that the existence of this massive army is hard to reconcile given the course of events in the fifth century. As the disastrous century wore on, the Roman army seems to be invisible and whole regions of the West are undefended and overrun. He postulates that many of these regiments, or large portions of them, may have existed only on paper and remained in existence so that a few generals and their staffs, who supposedly commanded them, could continue to reap the commensurate privileges and salaries. Or perhaps the regiments were composed of men trained and able and were waiting for sufficient funds to call them up from leave, funds that too often were in short supply. Thirty years earlier, Ammianus laments the many desertions of the Romans serving under Valens, and the Moroccan cavalry defected to Maximus (the British userper), caused the defeat and death of Gratian. With the collapse of the West about to unfold, we can't help but conjure the image of Adolf Hitler in his bunker, planning his great counter offensives with divisions that ceased to exist.

The Invasion of Gaul and the Execution of Stilicho

A later edition of the *Notitia Dignitatum,* published in AD 405, records that Stilicho had 181 regiments under his command in the West, with 48 stationed in Gaul. Ironically, that year a new British challenger, Constantine, was in the region. His troops proclaimed him Emperor of Britain and, like Maximus two decades earlier, took his army into Gaul and seizied territory. The few regiments in Gaul, that remained loyal to Rome, were occupied with limiting the damage caused by Constantine's presence. The balance of the regiments, formerly stationed in Gaul, were in Italy in the aftermath of the Gothic invasion. The entire province was relatively defenseless.[31]

When the Rhine River froze on New Year's Eve, 406 AD, a "who's who" of Germanic barbarian tribes, Alans, Burgundians, Vandals, Franks, and Sueves stormed across the ice. Practically unopposed, they first overran and plundered communities near the Rhine then pushed into the interior with their newly acquired booty and

---

29. The limitanei, frontier guards, were regiments assigned to forts along the Rhine and Danube.
30. The length of the Danube defended by the East was shorter than the Rhine and required fewer forts.
31. The soldiers of the limitanei were lesser soldiers, trained to defend forts that were important because they were used as food and equipment depots and where gold currency was stored.
    But they were not capable of mobilized open field battle.

Roman slaves. The invasion was so massive and successful that by spring AD 407, nine months after the great crossing, the Vandals moved all the way across the Pyrenees and conquered Roman Spain. In little over a year, except for a few highly-fortified cities in Gaul and the provinces of the Italian peninsula, all formerly tax-paying communities of the Western Empire were under the control of new masters, the Barbarians.

In AD 407, Alaric took advantage of the situation and led his army north into Italy. He sent emissaries to Stilicho demanding 4,000 pounds of gold, lest he ravage the towns and countryside of northern Italy. Stilicho messaged back that he would pay the sum, as he still held onto the belief that Alaric and his army could somehow become allies of the West and a bulwark against the East.[32] When he informed the Senate of his need for such a large sum of money, one senator was quoted as saying, "This is not a treaty; it's a pact of slavery."

Previously, despite being half-Barbarian, Stilicho was seen as a great general and a hero of the Empire. Now he was blamed for the loss of the Western provinces, Gaul and Spain, as well as the man who now wanted to empty the treasury to pay a bribe. He became very unpopular, especially among the powerful elite who orbited the Emperor, Honorius. In AD 408, while Stilicho was in Ticinum putting down a rebellion of army officers who refused to be deployed to Gaul, he was ordered to Ravenna where Honorius had recently installed his court. When Silicho arrived, he was arrested. He refused to fight, although his loyal entourage wished to do so. He briefly escaped and received sanctuary in a church. He was lured out with the promise that his life would be spared. Honorius promptly had him executed. Stilicho had the opportunity, like so many generals before him, to launch a civil war in an effort to save himself, but he appears to have rejected the idea in favor of putting the good of the Empire above his own life.

Upon Stilicho's death, a bloody purge followed; men, wives, and whole families of Stilicho's inner circle were killed. Even his son was hunted down and killed. Those officers loyal to Stilicho who escaped, promptly deserted to Alaric. Olympius, who replaced Stilicho, presumably had a hand in convincing Honorius to execute him. He also convinced the twenty-one-year-old Emperor to renege on the payment to Alaric.

Ominously, two other events took place in AD 408. A new army of Goths headed by Alaric's brother-in-law, Athaulf, invaded the Empire and arrived in the Balkans, greatly expanding the Gothic forces bristling for war. Meanwhile, Honorius and Olympius failed to make war preparations to meet the building Gothic threat.

---

32. The Romans term for these Barbarian commands was federates, *federati*. They were incorporated as autonomous entities serving under their own commanders.

The Sack of Rome (AD 410)

During the winter of AD 408-409, Alaric's newly expanded army once again moved north into the Italian peninsula. The army swarmed and pillaged its way south until it arrived at the gates of the West Coast city of Portus, the harbor city that supplied Rome with food and goods from its overseas trading partners. Encountering little resistance, the Goths captured the city and cut off all food shipments to Rome. Over the next eighteen months, Alaric's army mounted three sieges of Rome, each ending in a stalemate. Honorius, cowered in Ravenna, whose defenses amounted to disease-ridden swamps and marshes that surrounded the city. There he was able to make only the feeble gesture of sending a small contingent, some 4,000 troops, to aid in manning Rome's walls. Some sources tell us these troops were ambushed and massacred on their way. But it may very well be that they deserted. No one knows. What is clear is they didn't show up.

Our sources are frustratingly imprecise in what happened in the spring AD 410. What is known is that Roman army regiments located in Italy, many of which were all-Barbarian units loyal to Stilicho, simply disappeared. Certainly some defected to Alaric while other non-Barbarian regiments presumably went home. Meanwhile the Gothic hoards under Alaric continued to grow in size, taking on defectors, runaway slaves, and the displaced farmers and craftsmen unable to earn a living in the collapsing economy. Alaric's most pressing problem was finding the means to feed his massive flock. At this very late date, he still hoped to gain a contract and a command from the Roman government so that he could induct his men into the army and reward them with land and money. He still believed in the greatness of the Empire.

When news arrived that the city of Rome had been sacked for the first time in 800 years, the civilized world was shocked.

Unlike his loyal barbarian general Stilicho, Honorius had neither the ability nor the military assets to lead an attack on the invaders, nor would he deal with Alaric. The hapless emperor's envoys were said to have blustered they had innumerable warriors ready to attack him.

To which Alaric remarked wryly, "The thicker the grass, the more easily scythed."

Realizing that he could not be duped, the emissaries asked him what his price was for departure. Alaric told them that his men would sweep through the city, taking all gold, all silver, everything of value that could be moved, and all barbarian slaves.

"But what would that leave us with?" they asked hysterically.

Alaric paused, "Your lives."

The citizens inside Rome were left in a very untenable position because the city was out of food and had no professional garrison to defend its vast walls. It appears that the city's elders made the decision to surrender. On the night of August 23, 410, the Gothic army entered through the Salarian Gate and, for the succeeding three days, sacked Rome for the first time in 800 years. When news of the sack reached the capitals around the Mediterranean, the civilized world was profoundly shocked.

Alaric, who was an Aryan Christian and a Roman citizen, ordered a somewhat respectful sack where churches were not to be burned and the usual wholesale slaughter of military-age men and the rape of their women were forbidden. However, given that some of his soldiers were men whose families had been purged in the wake of Stilicho's execution, his orders were not uniformly followed. Of the sack, Gibbon writes:

> "*The brutal soldiers satisfied their sensual appetites without consulting either the inclination or the duties of their female captives . . . it is not easy to compute the multitudes who, from honorable station and prosperous fortune, were suddenly reduced to the miserable condition of captives and exiles.*" [33]

Gibbon goes on to describe the methods that the Goths used to strip the populace of its wealth. All over the city, people were pulled from their homes and summarily put up on auction blocks. Family members were forced to bid for the release of their father or mother, lest they be hauled away, never to be seen again. This proved an effective method to milk the treasure from the citizens, who no doubt were doing their best to hide what they could, jewels, money, etc. The Goths were able to collect an enormous amount of booty before they headed south, further plundering their way across the Italian countryside.

---

33. Edward Gibbon, *The Decline and Fall of the Roman Empire*, Book One, Chapter 31, Abridgement by D.M. Low, (New York: Harcourt Brace and Company,1960), 455.

Alaric died later that same year, unsuccessful in his quest to create for his army and his people full Roman citizenship. His life was that of a hero from a Greek tragedy. He killed what was most dear to him, the concept of Rome.

The West Descends From Chaos to Dissolution

Most historians consider AD 476 the date when the Roman Empire in the West officially ceased to exist. That year, after a series of puppet boy emperors ascended to the throne, a child with the ironic name, Romulus Augustulus, was deposed by the German warlord, Odoacer.[34] But this was only a symbolic act. For the sixty-seven years that intervened from the sack of Rome to the removal of "Little Augustus," Roman authority over the Western provinces, and even Italy itself, was mostly fiction.

Upon Alaric's death in AD 410, his brother-in-law, Athaulf, became king of the Goths. In AD 411 he negotiated a settlement with the quisling Honorius that gave his people (and the army who had sacked Rome only one year earlier) a treaty, called a foedus. It made the Visigoths (Western Goths) federati, and with this came a settlement in southern Gaul, north of Marseilles. Rome again rewarded rebellion and settled a hostile, unassimilated people inside its borders.

Meanwhile, the Vandals and Sueves plundered their way across Gaul, crossed the Pyrenees, and moved swiftly into all the quarters of the Iberian Peninsula, efficiently dividing up the plunder and extortion. The Notitia Dignitatum lists sixteen Roman field regiments in Spain which, if they actually existed that year, apparently did nothing to even slow the invaders down. The horrific level of chaos experienced by the inhabitants of Western Europe during the intervening years between the sack of Rome in AD 410 and the deposition of Augustulus in AD 476, can be broadly demonstrated by the careers of three men: Aetius; Gaiseric, King of the Vandals; and Attila the Hun.

With respect to the Huns, the Romans had little or no knowledge of these nomadic horsemen of the Russian steppes until the Goths began massing on the banks of the Danube during the middle AD 370s, begging for sanctuary inside the empire. Toward the end of Ammianus' chronicles, we get a description that reeks of Roman superiority, but is nevertheless compelling reading.

> *"They (the Huns) have squat bodies, strong limbs, and thick necks, are*
> *prodigiously ugly and bent that they might be two-legged animals. . . .*
> *Still their shape is human but their way of life is so rough that they have*

---

34. Romulus was the mythic founder of Rome. Augustus was the man who constituted the Empire after the fall of the Roman Republic. Augustulus means little Augustus.

no use for fires or seasoned food, but live on roots of wild plants, half-raw flesh of any sort of animal, which they warm by placing it between the thighs and backs of their horses. . . . They have no buildings to shelter them, not so much as a hut thatched with reeds . . . like unreasoning beasts, they are entirely at the mercy of their maddest impulses. They are totally ignorant of distinctions of right and wrong . . . they are under no restraint from religion or superstition." [35]

The average Hun was also an incredible athlete. Without the benefit of stirrups, he was able to ride his pony at full speed into a melee of armed foot soldiers, steering his animal with his legs while firing arrows from his bow with deadly accuracy at armor piercing velocity.

By AD 440, Attila and his brother, Bleda, assumed command of the Hunnish hoard that had driven out or conquered all the Germanic speaking people within a large swath of land in and around the great Hungarian plains.[36] Attila had this portion of Europe well in hand by AD 441, which he ruled from his redoubt in Aquincum (modern day Budapest). From there he commanded devastating raids into the poor beleaguered Balkans and Thrace, the same god-forsaken region that suffered so much at the hands of the Goths forty years earlier. When the Huns stormed into a lightly defended village or captured a relatively well-defended city, it was said that there was not left one stone piled atop another. It was leveled, all the populace who resisted killed, the rest taken into slavery, and every item of value, down to the smallest knickknack, taken. The Huns perfected the act of *total* plunder. So horrific were they that Attila earned the moniker, *Scourge of God*, that he wore with pride. Some chroniclers wrote that they questioned the validity of Christianity if their god would abandon them so totally to such hoards.

In addition to the total plunder of Greece and the Balkans, Attila was able to extort huge sums of gold from the Eastern Emperor, Theodosius II.[37] Meanwhile he also hired his warriors out to the Western Empire that needed extra troops to fight campaigns against the German invaders. The alliance between the Eastern and Roman Empires was totally broken.

Aetius was born into a military family from the Balkans, an area that produced

---

35. Ammianus Marcellinus, *Histories, Book XVII*, 20

36. The country of Hungary is named for these invaders.

37. By AD 450 the fortifications around Constantinople were the most formidable of any city from ancient times to modern times. The Huns had siege equipment that their captive European population had constructed for them. But the walls of Constantinople were simply too massive for them to breech.

many emperors of late antiquity. He rose to Master of the Soldiers in AD 435. While he never tried to elevate himself to emperor, he was the most powerful man in the West for thirty years. His entire adult life was engulfed by never-ending war, crisis, and chaos. He served under an impotent emperor, Valentinian III, and fought with the Huns and against the Huns. He fought against the Franks, Alamanni, Burgundians, Roman challengers, and an army of Bagaudae, the Roman homeless revolutionaries.

But Aetius will be most remembered as the last Roman General to win a battle on European soil. In AD 451, at the battle of Chalons in northern Gaul, he led his motley assembly of barbarian armies—contingents of Franks, Burgundians, and Visigoths to a bloody stalemate with the Huns. But Aetius was not able to pursue the Huns because Gothic King Theoderic was killed in the battle, and his army wanted to return to their permanent homeland in the Aquitaine where they could determine who would be successor to the throne. With limited resources and little time to prepare, Aetius succeeded in preventing much of Gaul from utter destruction.

Attila withdrew, repairing to his capital in Budapest, and immediately made plans to invade Italy the following year. While Aetius proved himself a fine general, the battle demonstrated that Europe was no longer Roman. His army was composed of nearly all German troops, speaking their native tongues, and reporting to their own regiment warlords or royalty. By the middle of the fifth century, Roman units played an ever smaller role in the defense of the Empire. It was no longer fashionable among the Roman elite to serve in the military, and most avoided it.

The following year, spring AD 452, Attila's hoards moved west from the Hungarian plains, then south, invading Italy. Like biblical locusts, they crossed the Julian Alps as they did a decade earlier in the Balkans. They descended upon the ancient capital of Aquilea which, despite its formidable walls, fell to Huns' siege machinery. Next they devoured the largely undefended cities of Padua, Mantua, Vincentia, Verona, Brescia, and Bergamo, and arrived at the gates of Milan, a long-time, wealthy imperial capital.

After a long siege, it too fell. Again the Roman armies of the West were not in Northern Italy to rescue the besieged cities. Aetius was still in Gaul, desperately trying to raise armies. He was unable to come to the rescue of Northern Italy largely because the Germans would defend their new homelands in Gaul, but were not willing to defend Italy. Roman power continued to evaporate.

As the Huns moved south from Milan and into the Italian heartland, one of history's most remembered meetings occurred. At the Po River, Pope Leo I and two aged Senators met the small, impish warlord, Attila, and convinced him to leave. As Aetius and his German allies saved Gaul one year earlier, the rest of Italy was saved from destruction. It is not known what Leo said, but Attila's decision to return to Hungary probably had more to do with his instinct for survival than the Pope's impassioned eloquence. Chronicler, Hydatius, tells us: "The Huns who had been plundering Italy, were victims of divine punishment, being visited with heaven sent disasters, famine and some kind of disease."

The Huns never developed sophisticated logistics and supply lines. So despite their ability to capture cities and plunder them, they still had difficulty feeding their huge army. With continued close quarters associated with long campaigns, fatigue and disease were a constant. Attila's army probably suffered dysentery and food shortages. Given that Valentinian III was, at the time, cowering in Ravenna behind its marshes and unable to do anything, Leo's mission bolstered the authority of the papacy immeasurably, literally for centuries to come.

Immediately upon his return to Budapest, Attila married yet another woman, a daughter of a German chieftain. He married often as a means to form alliances. The night of his wedding, he uncharacteristically drank to excess and the "Scourge of God" went off to meet his "boss." With his death, his many sons fought among themselves and his empire collapsed very quickly. Two years later, in AD 454, just as Stilicho had been executed by Honorius, Aetius was summoned to Ravenna and murdered by Valentinian III. The very next year, Valentinian III was murdered in a plot that ended all pretensions of a legitimate royal succession to the throne. With Aetius dead, there was no legitimate imperial army anywhere in the West.

During the 430s AD, the Vandals were led by Gaiseric, a very able general and king. He gained control of a fleet of ships in southern Iberia and landed his army in North Africa. He first captured Mauritania and Numidia (today's Morocco and Algeria). But in AD 439, he captured Carthage (in today's Tunisia) that had become the second largest city in the West.[38] The Vandals became the only invading German nation to become a naval power. They conquered much of the land in western North Africa; Gaiseric's Vandals stripped away the West's primary food source and its largest surviving tax base. Also they officially ended Rome's naval dominance of the Western Mediterranean that lasted six hundred years and proved so vital to the Empire's great expansion during the second century BC. Not satisfied, in AD 455, one year after Aetius' execution, Gaiseric took advantage of his new found maritime hegemony. He landed an expeditionary force near Ostia and sacked the city of Rome for a second time. This was not a respectful sack as Alaric's was. It reportedly lasted fourteen days and was thoroughly pitiless and brutal. Before his departure, he

---

38. The original city was razed in 146 BC, six hundred years earlier. The citizens who occupied the (New) Carthage were largely Romans or Romanized citizens who bore no relation to the original Phoenician settlers who founded the city around 800 BC.

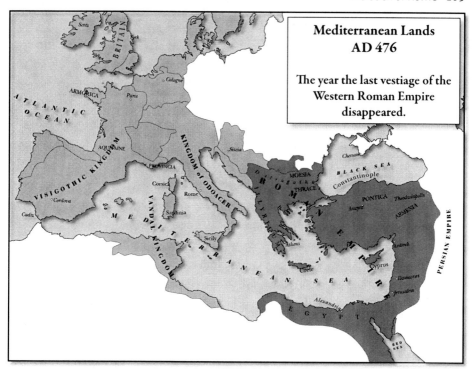

Mediterranean Lands
AD 476

The year the last vestiage of the
Western Roman Empire
disappeared.

removed thousands of captives including the Emperor Valentinian III's widow and two daughters.

The fictional empire persisted for another twenty-one years. During that time eight new emperors appear in the record. Like Stilicho, a German named Ricimer, became commander of the soldiers. He was the real power (what little there was) behind the throne and continually made and unmade emperors. He even executed Emperor Majorian (AD 457-461), for failing to win a sea battle against Gaiseric.

In AD 476, a Danubian chieftain, Odoacer, arrived outside Ravenna and sent a message to the boy Emperor, Romulus Augustulus. He requested a federate status and land for the settlement of his soldiers and families. Before the boy Emperor could give a response, Odoacer's Danubian army seized the final Roman capital and dismissed the boy to his retirement. Then Odoacer sent the Emperor's imperial insignia to Zeno, the Eastern Emperor in Constantinople as a signal that the Danubians would submit to the power of the East. Due to Zeno's problems with insurrectionists in the East, he never marched against Odoacer nor acknowledged him. Nevertheless, Odoacer took up residence in the palace in Ravenna and began to rule Italy as its monarch. The last vestige of Roman authority over Western Europe was gone.

The Message and the Aftermath

The brutal message of the first sack of Rome in AD 410 was that imperial government in the West was incapable of preventing it. For the next seventy years leading up to Rome's final dissolution, there continued to be incessant challengers to the throne, generals proclaimed Emperor by their troops and who started new civil wars. There continued to be royal family inheritors (usually children or pitifully inept court dandies) installed on the throne. These were ruling in Ravenna over a powerless court, senate, and a myriad of useless officials. After 410, the Empire could not maintain security or even collect taxes except in pockets of territory in and around some fortified cities. As a city official and private citizen living in Gaul, Spain, and even Italy, you were on your own. You made what deal you could with the Roman or German warlord who seemed to be in control of your immediate surroundings and prayed that he could keep the next wave of plunderers at bay.

Cities which had been the backbone of the empire continued to shrink in size. Rome, at its zenith, had eleven aqueducts bringing water to the city from sixty miles away on arches, some one-hundred feet tall. What astounds us even more than grandeur of Rome was the Empire's cities with paved streets, public baths, and stadiums for sporting events. There was every manner of diversion from regularly spaced fountains, to drinking establishments, bath houses, gambling parlors, and brothels. The city of Pompeii had fourteen dry cleaners. The level of affluence an average Roman citizen enjoyed in a first-century Roman city—disposable income, free time, and associated amenities—would not be eclipsed in the West until the middle of the twentieth century. Yet the archeological record shows that cities in the Western Empire had been shrinking for much of the fourth century (but not in the East). With the collapse of Roman authority, at the beginning of the fifth century, city populations plummeted. The great public edifices in the West were turned into quarries as wealthy Romans walled off their country estates and recruited their private militias and indentured serfs.

There is a school of modern revisionist historians who maintain that the fall of Rome was not really a fall but a *transformation*, that the German invaders represented a largely peaceful transition to a new civilization. They hold this view because they are invested in a leftist devotion to pacifism. And they are dead wrong. In the aftermath of the sack of Rome in AD 410, life in western Europe was a wretched daily battle to survive for the middle class Roman merchant and poor farmer.

The expertly engineered Roman roads that linked southern Scotland to Persia, once safely traveled due the power of the Empire, were the scenes of personal tragedy for many. Lurking along the Empire's vast network of highways were myriad bands of highway robbers, increasingly composed of the ruined and dispossessed, who formed proto-Mafiosi brotherhoods, combined with the Emperor's highway police who also extorted bribes from travelers desperate to find places of greater safety. It was customary for Romans to entrust their children to shepherds, traditionally kindly older men who watched over their flock while babysitting the young playing in the countryside outside the cities. Now in desperation, many once trustworthy shepherds succumbed to snatching children and raising them as slaves until they could be sold to German slavers.

As barbarian attacks became commonplace, the West imperial government went into the business of confiscating farms and land. After a farmer's records would be lost in a raid, the Emperor's enforcers, the *discussores*, descended on the ravaged, disoriented farmer, demanding he show proof of ownership. These confrontations generally ended in imprisonment or execution, all in the name of stealing property from its own beleaguered citizens.

In the AD 440s, Salvian, a priest living near Marseille, gives us an "on-the-ground" haunting report of the suffering experienced by the average Roman citizen at the hands of both the invading Barbarians and the complicit rump imperial government in Ravenna. He writes:

> *"Where now is the ancient wealth and dignity of the Romans? The Romans of old were powerful: now we are without strength. They were feared: now it is we who are fearful. . . . Our enemies make us pay for the very light of day, and our right to life has to be bought. Oh what miseries are ours! To what a state we have descended. We even have to thank the barbarians for the right to buy ourselves from them. What could be more humiliating and miserable?"*

In Summary

Someone has likened the study of history to peering through a keyhole in a locked door leading into the Palace of Versailles. Given that limited view, some objects are seen very clearly, others are completely obscured so we can only guess as to their existence. In this regard, there are some things that we know very definitely about the fall of the Western Empire.

Just four years after the great barbarian crossing of the frozen Rhine and after two years of brutal war and plunder that ravaged the god-forsaken Iberian Peninsula, Hydatius recorded in AD 411 the terms by which Spain was divided up among the Vandals, the Sueves, and Alans.

> *"After the provinces of Spain had been devastated by the blows I have described, through the mercy of God the barbarians turned to the making of peace, and divided the provinces for settlement amongst themselves. . . . Those Spaniards who had survived the disasters, subjected themselves to slavery under the barbarians who ruled the various provinces."* [39]

From our fifth-century source, Hydatius, we observe several truths about the fall of the West. He tells us that much of the Roman Europe was consolidated under barbarian rule long before the rump government in Ravenna was dispatched and the boy emperor, Romulus, removed in AD 476. Secondly, we understand that Hydatius was exaggerating when he referred to the Spaniards who "subjected themselves to slavery," because earlier in the passage, he told us that the cessation of warfare was the result of "the mercy of God." From this we can deduce that the barbarian invasion was horrific, no doubt a hellish period of looting and butchery. Moreover, we know that under the new German masters, taxes continued to be levied upon the Latin-speaking gentry. Once the new overlords found that most of the citizenry could not pay any tax, their land was confiscated and distributed to the men of the victorious armies. With German rule, came peace, albeit at a very steep price.

Why Did Rome Fall? Gibbon and The Short Answer

So *why* did Rome fall?

The question has been hotly debated by each successive generation of Western historians since Edward Gibbon published his first volume of *The Decline and Fall of the Roman Empire* in 1776, the fateful year for the British Empire. Oddly, in that year, his book created a greater stir among the British imperialist subjects in England than did the news emanating from the restive American colonies. The average Englishman of his day drank deeply of the Roman experience depicted by Gibbon because he understood that Britain had supplanted Rome as the largest empire ever amassed by a single people. With his magisterial epitaph, Gibbon earned his place among the greatest historians of all time. He assembled the ancient texts and was able to read and translate them from the ancient Greek and Latin. No English language history was more comprehensive. His eighteenth-century prose was so magnificent that, one hundred years later, a young Winston Churchill memorized long passages from *The Decline,* as a method to elevate his own oratory. Gibbon writes:

---

39. Hydatius, *Chronicle,* entry 41.

"The Italians, who had long since renounced the exercise of arms.[40]*Majorian (the Western Roman Emperor from 450-461) like the weakest of his predecessors, was reduced to the disgraceful expedient of substituting barbarian auxiliaries in the place of his unwarlike subjects."*[41]

And in these passages, Gibbon observes that toward the end of their Empire, even in Italy, the Romans were no longer warriors and were no longer willing to fight and protect their homeland. In Gibbon's conclusion as to *why* they lost their martial spirit, he succumbed to his own prejudices. He was correct in observing that by the dawn of the fifth century, the average Roman in the West, and especially the hierarchy, had lost their "*civic virtue.*" By this he meant they had lost their martial spirit and even their willingness to contribute to the defense of the Empire. Our sources from the period make this observation clear.

Gibbon writes, "*The decline of Rome was the natural and inevitable effect of immoderate greatness. Prosperity ripened the principle of decay.*" In this construct, he concludes that Roman wealth softened the empire's inhabitants and made them incapable of the rigors of war. In the second portion of his construct, he allowed his animus toward the Catholic Church to cloud his judgment. He writes, "*The clergy successfully preached the doctrines of patience and pusillanimity; the active virtues of society were discouraged; and the last remains of military spirit were buried in the cloister.*"[42] He concludes that it was the effect of Christianity that preached passivity and focused the individual on life in the hereafter that was paramount in eroding the Romans' will to resist the barbarian invasions.

Why was Gibbon wrong about the cause of the Romans' loss of martial spirit and consequently their empire? The answer lies in the fact that the Roman Empire of the East—the empire we now refer to as the Byzantine Empire—was far wealthier and more Christian than the West, yet it survived for nearly another millennium.[43] Therefore, the proper question to ask is—Why did the Western Roman Empire in Europe collapse while the East survived for another thousand years?

My short conclusion—The Romans of the West did not lose their martial spirit,

---

40. Edward Gibbon, *Decline and Fall of the Roman Empire*, Chapter 35, 490.
41. Ibid, Chapter 36, 502.
42. Ibid, General Observations.
43. The last vestige of the Roman Empire disappeared May 29, 1453, when Turkish armies breached the walls of Constantinople, murdering most of the remaining inhabitants and enslaving the survivors. No Roman was spared.

and consequently their empire, due to the wealth of its ruling class or the adoption of Christianity. They lost their empire due to their adoption of:

- A fifth-century multiculturalism that admitted vast numbers of non-Latin speaking peoples that opposed assimiliation.
- Oppressive taxation that severely undermined patriotism and the desire to serve.

My in-depth conclusion will be described when we look at the Immutable Laws the Romans of the West violated on their road to extinction.

IMMUTABLE #6
To hold territory, a state must be populated by those loyal to the central authority. When immigration overwhelms assimilation, the fall is predicted.

In allowing a large tribe of Goths to settle in Thrace, the Emperor Valens set in motion events that led to the Empire's total defeat at Adrianople and ultimately the sack of Rome. Remember, it was in Thrace, an Eastern province, where the Goths first settled. After they migrated into Italy and sacked Rome, it was the *West* that granted this same band of brigands a homeland in southern Gaul. This proved to the barbarian world that *rebellion would be rewarded*.

In the East, the disastrous policy of settling whole tribes inside imperial borders was abandoned. Moreover, the East never lost its devotion to the realm. The citizens of Constantinople proudly proclaimed themselves *Romans* until the last day of their empire in AD 1453. During the second, third, and fourth decades of the fifth century, the policy of the West was to admit vast numbers of Germans into the Western Empire. Under the terms of formal treaties, they allowed Roman localities to be plundered and ultimately enslaved by these new arrivals. Consequently, in large swaths of the West, Romanization and a commensurate loyalty to the central government disintegrated. The result was that often whole Western regiments failed to report for battle while others defected to the German side.

IMMUTABLE #4
If a people cannot avoid continuous internal warfare, it will have a new order imposed from without.

Going all the way back to the time of Julius Caesar, Augustus, and Constantine I (the Great), civil war was a constant feature of the Roman Empire, especially in the West. Yet, somehow the average Roman, if he were not conscripted or wounded in the fighting, simply shrugged and went about his business. But by the beginning of the fifth century, constant civil war was clearly taking its toll. Ammianus put it succinctly, "What fury of foreign peoples, what barbarian cruelty, can be compared to the harm done by civil wars?"

Despite the brilliance of Roman civilization and all its political savvy, it never created a method of peaceful transition from one ruling family to the next. The immense power of the throne was tempting. Too many generals proclaimed themselves Emperor, even when the Empire was under siege. And, for whatever reason, the West produced more usurpers than did the East. From AD 395 to 476 the East was ruled by four Emperors. Theodosius II ruled for forty-two years. During that same period, the West was ruled by eleven Emperors.

Stock footage by [snem] / Pond5.com
Caesar Augustus
The Great Boy Emperor

Due to constant civil wars, Western armies of the late fourth century were increasingly absent, unwilling to face barbarians with less equipped, smaller armies. Civil war drained manpower and fed the spirit of failure. As we saw during the first decade of the fifth century, when Alaric's Goths marched toward Italy and the hoards of Germans crossed the frozen Rhine, a rebellious Roman army in Britain proclaimed Constantine (the challenger, and not so great) Emperor. In AD 405, the British pretender crossed the English Channel and plundered Roman hamlets and took territory in Gaul. Had Stilicho been able to count on Constantine and his British legions to aid in the defense of Rome, perhaps Alaric could have been defeated before he entered Italy, the sack of the city prevented, and the Western Empire preserved. History is, of course, filled with "what ifs."

IMMUTABLE #5
When a free people, through taxation, is deprived of
its ability to acquire wealth and property, collapse is presaged.

During the fourth century, in the years leading up to the debacle of Adrianople, the Western Roman hierarchy was hard at work financially destroying both its poor farmers and its middle class. From the writings of a very wealthy land owner and poet, Ausonius, we gain an understanding of how this occurred. Born about AD 310, he grew up on and ultimately inherited two exquisite country estates in Bordeaux and Aquitaine, located in southern Gaul.[44] Historians of the period contend that much of his work was plagiarized from Cicero and some of it bawdy in extreme. The volume of his poetry and chronicles gives us a rather robust picture of what life was like in the fourth-century declining Empire of the West.

Apparently his family's estates were profitable enough to operate without him. He began his career as a gramaticus, a professor of Latin in Bordeaux, one of the Empire's great universities. The American historian, Thomas Cahill, writes that when Ausonius' fame as a brilliant teacher reached Valentinian, he was summoned to Milan and became tutor for the Emperor's son, Gratian. He also accompanied the Emperor on a campaign in Gaul against the invading Germans. As the official chronicler of the expedition, he wrote a poem about his own participation in the spoils of war—the sexual services of, Bissula, a German slave girl.

Upon Valentinian's death, Gratian assumed the throne (one of three claimants at the time) and Ausonius was elevated to Quaestor sacri palatii, the emperor's chief of staff. By some calculations, Ausonius lived to be ninety. Yet almost never, in all his voluminous descriptions of fourth-century Roman life, did he mention a commoner by name other than the slave girl. He seemed detached from the plight of those beneath his station.

From Ausonius we learn how the Western Empire drained its financial life blood. It created a middle-class designation of bureaucrat, the curialis, that was tasked with tax collection. The great landowning families and powerful bureaucrats were usually members of the senatorial class. They were exempt from paying taxes and from soiling their hands with tax collection. This task fell upon curialis, typically small landowners or middle-class merchants, a class of people whose station passed from the father to his eldest son, a station one was born into and could not escape. It was a cruel trap because each man was assigned a quota to collect from the inhabitants of his immediate vicinity. Originally they formed the nucleus of the middle class, members of city councils (curiae), and were respected benefactors of their townships. Those days disappeared. They became imperial agents of oppression. Their duties earned them the unremitting hatred of their peers. Further, any shortfall in their assigned collections, they personally had to make up.

---

44. The latter region today, the Dordogne, is still dotted with magnificent castles (chateaux) now owned by the state and operated as museums, reminders of a wealthier time long gone.

By the middle of the fourth century, the curialis, originally formed from a prominent segment of the Roman middle class, were disappearing. Some were able to bribe their way out of their curial rank, gaining positions in the army, the bureaucracy, granary managers, or aqueduct repairmen. But most, driven to desperation, were forced to borrow funds from the only source available, the local lord. The landowner was happy to make the loan given that his new debtor was supposedly his tax assessor and collector. Now that the poor curialis owed his local landlord money, he forfeited what little authority he had to collect tax from his creditor. And of course, when inevitably the curialis defaulted, his small farm or business would be added to the lord's network of estates, while the man's poor family became indentured serfs.

As the West created more barbarian fiefdoms, many of the fugitive curialis found refuge among the subjects of German warlords on whose estates Roman sovereignty no longer pertained. Without the curialis, the Western Empire was forced to use its own army to gather what taxes it could from its beleaguered poor and withering middle class. Consequently, this arrangement made middle and lower class Romans hate the regime and refuse conscription into the army. The landed estates evolved into independent colonies with lord, army, artisans, and serfs, untouchable by the supposed sovereigns running the Western Empire.

IMMUTABLE #7
With the loss of fiscal solvency comes a loss of sovereignty.

From Salvian, in the fifth century, we hear of an uprising of the Bagaudae in Spain and in Western Gaul. This large band of roving landless desperados were driven to banditry and rebellion by the excessive levels of taxation and the empire's inability to protect them. They were former Roman farmers and small merchants, men who comprised the body and martial spirit of the armies that held out against Hannibal, defeated Carthage, and conquered lands from Scotland to the Euphrates River. They were Roman citizens who rebelled against the suicidal empire then were destroyed by a German-born commander and his army of German conscripts.

The officials of the Western Imperial Government were utterly corrupt. They exempted themselves and their families from taxation and military service, and they forced the lower classes into the military and wantonly confiscated their property. As the fifth century wore on, there simply was not enough money to pay the military. The middle class had largely disappeared. The remaining poor landowners were unwilling to serve in the army and had no money to pay in.

MODERN COROLLARIES

The UN

At his death, the Emperor Theodosius elected to divide his empire between his two sons. This divided the authority over the treasury and the military among two states. Today America is dangerously relinquishing its sovereignty to the massively corrupt international body, the United Nations. At great cost in lost lives and treasure, we are expected to protect the free world and liberate a portion of the enslaved world every time it causes chaos to erupt. The world community, via the UN, constantly chips away at our authority to defend our vital interests, and we continue to submit.

The US has not yet allowed the Southwest to be repatriated to Mexico, or to form a breakaway Spanish-speaking rump state, Hispoamerica. Yet with each successive administration, the US freely cedes more and more control over its own military to the UN. In a world where Iran, the leading sponsor of Islamic terrorism, is about to become a producer of nuclear weapons, this is suicidal and must be reversed.

The US would become more beholden to the UN during the balance of President Obama's term. He made it abundantly clear in his campaign that, in contrast to his predecessor, he will be more compliant to world opinion.[45] While it is true that both Bush presidents went to the UN and lobbied the Security Council for the authority to make war on Iraq, it should be remembered that Bush the Younger took the country to war without UN authorization.[46] This, among other things, earned him five years of unremitting harsh criticism from both the American Left and the membership at the United Nations. While Obama and the American Left attacked Bush for what was arguably treasonous political advantage, they were also fellow travelers with the United Nations that attacked an American president because he violated international law.

During the Iraq War, stories surfaced in the European press that a UN sister organization, the World Court, considered issuing Dick Cheney and Donald Rumsfeld indictments for war crimes. Similarly, it should be remembered that George W. Bush pushed back against world opinion and nominated John Bolton to be our UN ambassador. Like Jeanne Kirkpatrick, appointed by Reagan, Bolton exhibited a healthy contempt for the anti-Semitic, anti-American representatives of the UN.

Obama wasted the first eighteen months of his presidency in a humiliating attempt to convince Iran to give up its decades-long nuclear weapons program. He was further humiliated in July 2010 by the very weak set of sanctions imposed on Iran by

---

45. Foreign policy is the area where our executive branch has the greatest unilateral authority.

46. Bush the Elder received authorization from the UN to remove Saddam Hussein from Kuwait. The authorization was only for his removal, not his overthrow. The Bush-led coalition complied.

the UN. This resulted directly from the fact that Russia and China, members of the all-powerful Security Council, were both business partners with Iran. Russia even sold Iran state-of-the-art air defense systems designed to knock down Israeli aircraft should a strike on Iranian nuclear sites occur.

Shortly after the tepid sanctions were imposed, Leon Panetta, Director of the CIA, was summoned to Congress to report on the efficacy of our Iran policy. When asked if he thought the UN sanctions would be successful in dissuading Iran from producing nuclear weapons, he dourly replied, "Probably not." Despite the constant threats by the Iranian theocracy to destroy the US, we have allowed ourselves to be rendered impotent by the UN. This must change as America's survival is at stake.

The Environmental Movement

We have surrendered much of our sovereignty to the international climate change advocates, many who are US citizens, including their grand poobah, Al Gore. The core of this movement is the old guard, anti-capitalist, Marxist crowd posing as environmentalists. To conclude that the movement is driven by small "c" communists, realize that with the fall of the Soviet Union, they needed to disguise themselves as members of another cause. Secondly, understand that the global warming (or is it the "climate change") movement is both a thinly-veiled redistribution movement and perhaps the largest con ever. Consider that its proscription is exactly that of Marx, Vladimir Lenin, Stalin, Fidel Castro, and Saul Alinsky—through legislation, indoctrination, new versions of the Kyoto treaty, or a Cap and Trade bill—it aims to confiscate wealth from the producers and those who have assets, and transfer it to their collectivist allies on a massive world-wide scale. In the process, the movement hopes to grab the levers of power and take control of the bureaucracies that conduct the transfer of wealth across the whole of the developed world. While the movement proclaims its deep concern for "working families" (workers of the world unite!) it will further impoverish the small farmer, the independent trucker, and the elderly living on a modest fixed income by driving up the cost of fuel and electricity. While environmentalists claim to be able to turn down the temperature of the planet, like the fifth-century Roman ruling class, through a myriad of other new taxes they will drive the poor and the middle class toward modern serfdom.

As the new ruling class of left-wing internationalists, environmentalists, and crony capitalists is at work running America, we can see that, in amassing their power, they are gradually stripping away the country's military strength. Over the past three decades, since the fall of the Soviet Union, a larger and larger portion of the electorate has been convinced to vote for politicians who have thrown in the power grabbers. In so doing, these politicians, allied with the environmentalists, have put the country at great risk.

Due to scare tactics based on politicized science, we have dangerously reduced our own domestic energy production, energy necessary to power our economy and fuel our worldwide military readiness. We do not have enough resources, oil, coal, or electricity to stage a blockade of Iran. Like Western Rome of the fifth century, on paper we have the military might to take down the Iranian regime. We just lack the fuel.

It could be that President Obama feared that if he had ordered a blockade (like the one ordered by President Kennedy during the Cuban Missile Crisis) it would have drastically reduced oil deliveries from the Persian Gulf to the US, and to our key allies. His left wing environmental polices had produced such a fragile and dependent economy that he felt powerless to confront Iran.

China

During President Obama's first trip to China in November 2009, our American sycophantic press had difficulty suppressing the fact that the meetings with President Hu Chintao and China's key ministers did not go well. With extreme irony, communist China, who owns approximately a trillion dollars of our debt, gave our young president a stern dressing down.

Chinese officials made it clear that they saw the Obama Administration's huge deficits and massive new spending programs as threats to the value of their investment. It does not require an advanced degree in economics to know that we are on a course to inflate our way out of our commitments to our creditors, thereby reneging on our side of the bargain and turning our lenders' returns into losses.

The Chinese let Obama know that they were not happy about his whole approach to governance. In fact, it was rumored that they told him there was not enough liquidity in the world to finance the sort of spending he was advocating. Moreover, to his devaluation of their dollar denominated investments, they informed him that wars have been fought over less. No wonder he looked thoughtfully glum when photographed walking the Great Wall by himself. So much for Obama's banal promise to make the post-Bush world love us.

As Brent Baier, a journalist who made the trip to China put it, "The difference between John Boehner [then House Minority Leader] and the Chinese is that they have real power over us." Today investors must worry about the possibility of what some obliquely call the "debt event." What if the Chinese suddenly led a stampede of investors out of US treasuries, what would that mean to our national security?

Multiculturalism Overwhelms Assimilation

In the summer of 2010, the politicized Attorney General's Office filed a law suit against the State of Arizona. The crime—passing a law that authorized Arizona state and local law enforcement personnel to enforce national immigration law. This was unprecedented in our nation's history.

Both parties and both Bush presidents contributed to a gradual diminution of American sovereignty by the decades-long open borders policy and the subsidization of illegal immigration.

Approximately twenty percent of failing Mexico, 10 million of its citizens, are already in the United States, either full- or part-time. This massive influx has produced a new hybrid culture in huge enclaves of the Southwest—not Mexican nor American. In Los Angeles County a child can be born, grow up, die, and never learn to speak English. As we saw in AD 376 Thrace, disaster ensued when the Romans began their policy to admit enmass foreign nationals without a program to assimilate them.

The vast unchecked illegal migration across our southern border is driving down wages in numerous industries, creating massive unemployment in various business sectors, and is providing a conduit for potential Islamic terrorists to import components for WMD devices. It puts low-skilled Americans out of work, bankrupts school systems, hospitals, and even municipalities. Ultimately it may well threaten American sovereignty over portions of the Southwest that a majority of Mexicans claim as their country, a northern region of Mexico they call Azatlan.

IMMUTABLE #6
To hold territory, a state must be populated by those loyal to the central authority. When immigration overwhelms assimilation, the fall is predicted.

The American Left Commits Acts of War Against America

While they did not lead armies against their own countrymen as did Constantine, the fifth-century Roman usurper from Britain, leading congressional Democrats such as Kerry, Kennedy, Chris Dodd, John Edwards, and Nelson Rockefeller spent half a decade publicly accusing the US Commander-in-Chief of taking the country to war on the basis of falsified intelligence. During the 2004 Presidential election, candidate John Kerry heightened his rhetoric accusing President George W. Bush of "lying us into war." Did he and other Democrat Bush accusers not know that their many inflammatory statements were immediately translated into Arabic and posted to radical Islamic recruiting websites? Their statements vilifying their own country were a great aid in rallying young Muslims from all over the Middle East who traveled to Iraq and joined the fight against the invading infidel armies. Their exhortations led to a greater American death toll.[47]

It did not seem to concern them that:

- Saddam Hussein was the only living head of state to use chemical weapons (WMDs) twice: once against another Islamic country, Iran; and a second time, against his own people.
- After the fall of Baghdad in 2003, top US weapons inspector, David Kay, reported that his team found more than a dozen facilities capable of producing chemical weapons.
- It was an established fact that Saddam Hussein attempted to assassinate President Bush (the Elder).
- All our allied intelligence agencies warned us that Iraq was at work producing weapons of mass destruction.
- This is the most serious accusation that can be leveled against a sitting President, charging that he sent men and women to their deaths, based on a lie and for ulterior motives. The charge, if substantiated, would be tantamount to accusing a sitting President of high crimes or treason.

Conversely, it did not seem to concern them that the charge, if made falsely by an elected official of the US government, would itself be an act of treason, especially if made during war time. Such accusations are tantamount to aiding and abetting the enemy. Future historians will no doubt grapple with the question—did Congressional Democrat leaders commit treason during the Iraq War years?

Oliver North wrote his book, *American Heroes in the Fight Against Radical Islam (War Stories),* based on his experience as an "imbed" in the Iraq war. He writes that two weeks after the fall of Baghdad, in the town of Baji, the 66th Armored Regiment came upon one of Saddam Hussein's enormous ammo dumps. Quickly, the regiment's commander realized that the insurgents were coming to steal the ammo. He ordered his troops to set up ambush points along the roads leading into the massive complex. Pitched gun battles erupted nightly. Recapping one night's fighting, North writes:

"When we arrived, the platoon commander who triggered the ambush is

---

47. This is not the first time John Kerry found himself drawn into arguably treasonous activity as a means to elevate his stature with the Democrat party.

*reviewing with his soldiers what happened. The bodies of 14 men, nearly
all dressed in black, are lying on or near a rutted dirt road that enters
the ammo dump from the East. . . . According to identity documents,
only two are Iraqis. Of the remaining 12, four are Jordanian, three are
Syrian, two are Egyptian, one is Saudi, and two are Lebanese."* [48]

During his campaign, in 2007 and 2008, Barack Obama incessantly pronounced
that the centerpiece of his "change" agenda would be the repair of our international
reputation that was so badly
damaged by President George
W. Bush's illegal and misguided
war in Iraq. This assertion,
uttered for the consumption
of his far-left contributors and
a compliant media, clearly
illustrated his belief that a lie
told often enough becomes a
fact. North's American Heroes
shows Obama's mantra was a
disservice to those who fought
that war—Americans, Iraqis,

US Army Photo by Spc. Daniel Herrera

*US soldiers became both conquerors and
goodwill ambassadors during the Iraq War.*

Afghanis, and allied soldiers. A huge lie—it was defamation of those who gave their lives.

North's account, just one of many, showed conclusively that American troops in
the Iraq invasion were fighting a force of Islamists from all over the Muslim Middle
East—disparate Sunni jihadists of the Muslim Brotherhood and al-Qaeda, Wahhabi-
subsidized Mujahideen, disenfranchised Baath party members, and Shiite militias
aligned with Iran. While they obviously didn't all report to bin Laden and al-Zawahiri
or operate through a centralized command-and-control structure, they all had one
thing in common; they were terrorists willing to kill Americans, terrorists who relished
the torture and murder of fellow Muslim men, women, and children. North makes
it clear that George W. Bush, like the Roman general Scipio who defeated Hannibal
in Africa, moved the war against the planet's most vicious terrorists from New York
City to the Middle East, a battleground of his choosing. He also made clear that the
American Democrat leadership shamelessly contributed to an Islamic call to arms.

---

48. Oliver North, *American Heroes: In the Fight Against Radical Islam (War Stories)*
     (Nashville: B&H Publishing Group) 2008, 124.

Past presidents who knew war, such as Washington and Lincoln, would certainly see Congressional officials who actively work to aid and abet an enemy during wartime— guilty of treason, having committed an act of war against their own country. It was a violation of:

IMMUTABLE #4
If a people cannot avoid continuous internal warfare,
it will have a new order imposed from without.

Destruction of the Middle Class and Economic Chaos

In AD 161, during the reign of Emperor Marcus Aurelius, there were about 3,000 officials and bureaucrats in the Roman imperial government. By the abdication of Emperor Diocletian in AD 305, there were 35,000. In the same intervening years, taxes rose from what the small farmer could produce in two days a month to half his monthly output. By mid-fourth century, the empire exacted such an onerous level of taxation that many of its citizens defected, abandoned their lands, and joined the Barbarian invaders. Rome was in violation of:

IMMUTABLE #5
When a free people, through taxation, is deprived of
its ability to acquire wealth and property, collapse is presaged.

In the essay *America's Ruling Class: And the Perils of Revolution*, Angelo M. Codevilla, Professor Emeritus, Boston University writes,

> *"As over-leveraged investment houses began to fail in September 2008, the leaders of the Republican and Democratic parties, of major corporations, and opinion leaders stretching from the National Review magazine on the right to the Nation magazine on the left, agreed that spending some $700 billion to buy the investors' "toxic assets" was the only alternative to the US economy's "systemic collapse." In this, President George W. Bush and his would-be Republican successor John McCain agreed with the Democratic candidate, Barack Obama. Many, if not most, people around them also agreed upon the eventual commitment of some 10 trillion nonexistent dollars in ways unprecedented in America. .*

. . The public objected immediately, by margins of three or four to one." [49]

For Professor Codevilla, America is in the grip of a new "ruling class" where the "differences between the Bushes, Clintons, and Obamas are of degree, not kind." [50]

While much of his construct has merit, a single benchmark must be kept in mind—the average **annual** budget deficit during the eight years of the George W. Bush presidency became the bi-**monthly** deficit under Obama. The members of the ruling class who have always unabashedly sought unlimited power through the expansion of government spending and taxation, by 2010, were explicitly Democrats.

Secondly, it should be remembered that Obama proclaimed in his inaugural address that he would "fundamentally transform" America. Perhaps he meant that he intended to crash the American capitalist, free-market economy and replace it with a Marxist command and control system. No one in our media bothered to ask our new president what he meant by his proclamation that he would transform the country— from *what to what*?

The private-sector economy continued to contract during the first two years of the Obama presidency and millions of private sector jobs were lost. The administration recklessly spent a trillion dollars in Keynesian "stimulus bills" and approved new spending programs that dramatically increased the Democrat-voting public workforce and ominously set in motion annual trillion dollar deficits indefinitely into the future—debts the next generation will not be able to pay.

By Obama's inauguration in January 2009, the federal workforce reached 17 million employees. This did not include the vast number of state, county, and municipal employees whose salaries, pensions, and benefits are paid by the private sector. For every employee at the EPA, Energy Department, or the Des Moines Public Works Department, there is a second employee, retired from that position, collecting a sumptuous pension and benefits—all subsidized by the taxpayers. Like the Roman Senatorial class of the fifth century that sucked the life blood out of their middle and lower classes through confiscatory taxation, America's ruling class of Democrat politicians merged with the public sector workforce, and the American Senatorial class rewarded them handsomely. According to the US Office of Personal Management, the average federal worker earned 77 percent more than the private sector worker *whose wages were confiscated to pay government employees' salary.*

In 2010, Obama set in motion government spending programs that, by the

---

49.   Angelo Codevilla, *America's Ruling Class: And the Perils of Revolution* (*American Spectator Magazine*, online edition, July-August 2010).

50.   Ibid.

end of the decade, would exceed all the deficits amassed from George Washington's first budget through the last budget of George W. Bush. But that would only be the monetized deficit that in 2010 passed $14 trillion. When all the unfunded liabilities associated with Medicare, Medicaid, Social Security, federal, state and local pension funds were added in, the real American indebtedness was over $100 trillion, *twice the total private net worth of the United States*, or roughly **$350,000 per American**. This was the debt burden before adding the cost of Obamacare (his healthcare takeover) and the new President's other massive spending agenda.

The American middle and lower classes pay a lower percentage of income taxes than do those at a higher income. This arrangement is a ruse. Just as in fifth-century Rome, the American rich are not the ones bearing the real burden of repaying the staggering new debt obligations, because they can purchase exemption. They will force the lower and middle classes to pay for their own subjugation through higher payroll, Medicare, Social Security, gasoline, and utility taxes, and the new Obamacare taxes, mandatory insurance policies, and the dreaded VAT (value added taxes).

As to why Rome fell, Gibbon references chronicler Zosimus, who recorded that "Popular monasteries spread over the adjacent country . . . and for the benefit for the poor, the Christian monks had reduced a great part of humanity to a state of beggary."[51] From the passage we deduce that infant Catholicism provided a blessed refuge for the dispossessed, destitute Romans who could not find shelter inside the walls of the local warlord or could not morally support the life of banditry. Similarly, thanks to the assistance of our ruling class, the American dependent class continues to rise alarmingly. In a study commissioned by the Heritage Foundation, and conducted by William Beach, the number of Americans dependent on government for their basics of survival, food, housing, and medical care rose 12-fold since 1962.[52] Beach reached two chilling conclusions if the trend continues—The country will lose its competitiveness economically and militarily, and it will pass the tipping point when it will be politically impossible to restore our competitiveness.

Our economic system that is dependent on foreign creditors, such as China, may break down. Like the middle and lower class fifth-century Romans, those expected to pay the tab in the form of new fees and a myriad of taxes, hidden and unhidden, will renounce their fealty to the American enterprise because they will simply run out of money.

51. Edward Gibbon, *The Decline and Fall of the Roman Empire*, 514.
52. William Beach, *Relying On Government Coming to Tipping Point,* http://www.heritage.org/Research/Commentary/2010/03/Relying-On-Government-Coming-to-Tipping-Point/.

IMMUTABLE #1
*No nation has ever survived once its citizenry
ceased to believe its culture worth saving.
(Hanson's Law)*

Arnold Toynbee wrote that all great civilizations rise and fall and that an autopsy of history would show that all great nations commit suicide. I don't agree. Not all civilizations commit suicide. The Romans of the West did not willfully destroy themselves. Rather, as Gibbon puts it, they simply lost their civic virtue and with it, their martial spirit. Other fallen civilizations simply made a fatal mistake. In the case of Carthage, their fatal mistake was their decision to make war upon a far more ascendant people, the Romans, not willful suicide.

Yet, in 2008, slightly over half of all Americans who voted in the Presidential election seem invested in the Democrats' suicide pact. Virtually all the immutable laws violated by the European Romans of the fourth and fifth century, with minor semantic modifications, can be construed as agenda items embraced by today's American Left. How did the Left come to hold its many suicidal pathologies?

How the Professional Left Lost Its Civic Virtue

At the height of the Cold War, on a bitterly cold day in January 1961, John F. Kennedy proclaimed to the world in his inaugural address,

> *"Let every nation know whether it wishes us well or ill, that we shall pay any price, bear any burden, meet any hardship, support any friend, and oppose any foe to assure the survival and success of liberty."*

Kennedy was the last American president to draw strong support from both parties, the Left and the Right. The country was united in a singularity of purpose.

November 22, 1963, two and a half years later, President Kennedy was assassinated by an American defector to the Soviet Union, Lee Harvey Oswald. On that horrible day, from Dallas to Washington DC aboard *Air Force One*, Lady Bird Johnson, the Vice President's wife, urged Jacqueline Kennedy to change out of her blood-spattered clothes. "No," Jacqueline replied more than once, "I want them to see what they have done."

Her response begs the questions—exactly who were "they?" And what did "they" do?[53]

---

53.   James Pierson, *Camelot and the Cultural Revolution: How the Assassination of John F. Kennedy*

James Piereson, in *Camelot and the Cultural Revolution*, persuasively makes the case that President Kennedy's assassination was the exact moment when liberalism began to lose its complete and total dominance over American political orthodoxy. More importantly, it began to lose its grip on reality and its adherents were unable to distinguish truth from their own mythology.

Piereson points out that Liberalism grew out of and supplanted the earlier, pre World War I political ideology, Progressivism. It was a moralist movement comprised of independent workers, farmers, and small businessmen who were dominated by big corrupt urban political machines, labor unions, large companies, and robber barons. Woodrow Wilson was an outspoken Progressive who took the country to World War I for the moralistic reason that we should "make the world safe for democracy." It was not that we needed to protect any national interest.

Later, the great depression generated an enormous distrust of big business, swept away the old political paradigms, and gave birth to a new philosophy of governance, liberalism. Unlike progressivism that was embraced by various members of both parties, liberalism attached itself solely to the Democrat party and eventually became its official credo. Its first manifestation was FDR's New Deal.

By the end of World War II, it was the fastest growing political philosophy in the country. It advocated that government should not break up large commercial industrial enterprises to promote the interests of the small farmer and small businessman. Instead, liberalism accepted the reality of big business, and responded by building even bigger government bureaucracies to regulate and control it.

The most prominent champions were FDR and Harry Truman. Progressives became the leaders of the FDR and Truman administrations and the preeminent American post-war historians and intellectuals. The most influential liberal historian was Arthur Schlesinger Jr. who wrote liberalism's credo, *The Vital Center*. He later became a cabinet member in the Kennedy administration and part of the young President's inner circle.

By 1950, liberalism's core tenant was that government, the public sector, could and should regulate every aspect of the private sector—the economy, small business, big business, morality, race relations, and even personal economic outcomes. It maintained that it is the government's responsibility to manage income disparities among individuals to ensure that the "gap between rich and poor" did not grow too large.

While it did not use overt Marxist phraseology, *for each according to his need, from each*

Shattered American Liberalism (New York: Encounter Books, 2007), 89.

John and Jacqueline Kennedy, November 22, 1963, moments before
the two bullets fired by Lee Harvey Oswald struck the President

according to his means, this was a central pillar of liberalism. It proudly advocated the
redistribution of wealth, while ambivalent about how the US should use its power to
halt Communist expansion. While liberalism proclaimed itself to be anti-communist,
it rejected nationalism and, by 1955, it was internationalist and accommodationist to
Soviet expansion.

Liberalism, according to its most authoritative proponents, held that those who
did not subscribe to its tenants were *conspiratorial, bigoted, and delusional.* Moreover,
as Schlesinger proclaimed in his book, *The Vital Center*, liberalism was no longer a
belief that resided on the political spectrum to the left of anything. Despite the fact
that the country elected aging war hero Dwight Eisenhower, a Republican, to two
terms as president, by the close of the decade, polling data confirmed that liberalism
had became the central organizing American political philosophy.

In 1951, the alternative to liberalism, modern conservatism, was born with the
graduation of an audacious student from Yale, William F. Buckley. His book, *God and
Man at Yale*, grew out of an alumni day address that he was poised to deliver but was
prohibited from doing so. The essence of Buckley's thesis was that the liberalism that
dominated the Yale faculty was overwhelmingly hostile to Judeo-Christendom and
capitalism and something should be done about it. The book drew a storm of angry

negative reviews from prominent literary and academic figures such as McGeorge Bundy. It made Buckley, at age 26, a national figure and the preeminent spokesman for a new, albeit fledgling, philosophical and political movement—conservatism.

By 1954, the nation's capital was in an uproar over the hearings conducted by the House Committee for Un-American Activities. It's chairman, Joe McCarthy, contended that the government was not doing enough to stop penetration by a hostile Soviet Union and that something should also be done about it. Buckley picked the unfolding drama to publish his second book, *McCarthy and His Enemies*, co-written with his brother-in-law, Brent Bozell. The book's careful examination of numerous cases pursued by McCarthy, enraged the Liberal establishment even more than had his first book. As Elliot Abrams wrote recently, "It was in the McCarthy era that the iron triangle of liberal bureaucrats, a liberal press, and liberal Democrats in Congress was first evident." [54] While the iron triangle destroyed McCarthy, Buckley gained greater notoriety and more converts to the conservative cause throughout heartland America, where most were unabashedly anti-communist.

One year later, in 1955, Buckley founded his magazine, *National Review*, and hired Whittaker Chambers, the celebrated Communist defector whose testimony corroborated much of McCarthy's accusations. In his excellent requiem to Buckley, John O'Sullivan wrote that "Bill's philippics against the "new Republicanism" of Eisenhower and Richard Nixon . . . set a high standard for invective." [55]

Buckley wrote, "The Eisenhower approach was designed not to solve problems, but to refuse, essentially, to recognize that problems exist, and so, to ignore them." [56]

By inauguration day, January 1961, with the new President as their representative, liberals could credibly proclaim that theirs was the central and *dominant* political philosophy in the country. As Piereson puts it, "Liberalism was without doubt the single most creative force in American politics . . . (it) owned the future." [57]

Yet, oddly enough, Kennedy was not a liberal. He championed civil rights, a liberal cause, like his father. Yet he was much more a conservative. He was a staunch anti-communist and authorized several assassination plots aimed at Fidel Castro, and an invasion of the island of Cuba. He even brought the country to the brink of nuclear war with the Soviet Union. In the modern, post World War II era, he stands alone in his adulation by both American Right and Left. In the year of his death, he was making preparations to establish a beachhead in Vietnam to confront communist

54. John O'Sullivan, *Man of Thought, Man of Action* (*National Review*, March 24, 2008), 20.
55. Ibid.
56. Ibid.
57. Ibid, 1.

expansion in Southeast Asia. As the words from his first inaugural speech convey, he was a nationalist who believed that America's manifest destiny was to spread freedom and to stand with anti-communist freedom fighters everywhere.

He was not an accomodationist nor a redistributionist. Instead he initiated a massive tax cut that did not pass in Congress until a few months after his death. It brought the top tax rate of 91 percent down to 65 percent. It was the largest tax cut by any nation, ever. And it produced extremely favorable results by expanding the US economy and in turn, created greater military power. In short, it was Kennedy's twin initiatives—non-appeasement foreign policy and lower taxes—that formed the two most important pillars of conservative orthodoxy, initiatives that Ronald Reagan incorporated into his platform. He defeated an incumbent liberal president, toppled the Soviet Union, and touched off an expansion of the US economy that ultimately reached 25 percent of the **world** GDP.

Pierseon notes that by the late 50s, the vast majority of historians, political science professors, and intellectuals were liberals. They portrayed the right as irresponsible "conspiracy nuts" and reactionaries because they mistakenly believed that the United States was infiltrated and threatened by Communists. So powerful and dominant was the influence of liberal intelligencia and its coalition of bureaucrats and politicians that the word McCarthyism became a noun in the American lexicon meaning: *unfairness in investigative technique.* They saw the American Right as being irrational and dangerous in its avid opposition to Communism. Moreover, they held themselves and their movement as more rational, given their "well-informed" rejection of the right wing's obsessive notion that there was a domestic threat posed by Communism.

When their leader, JFK, was killed by a committed Communist, it posed a crisis for liberals, from which Piereson contends (and I agree), they have not recovered. It threatened to falsify their world view. Jacqueline Kennedy's pronouncement that she would wear her blood spattered dress for the DC press, so America would see what "they" had done, became the formula for how the liberal establishment responded to the assassination. In thousands of op-ed's, speeches, and treatises across the country, the massive liberal establishment proclaimed that JFK was a *martyr*, killed by a "climate of hate," and was "a victim of bigotry." Within a week of the president's death, the former First Lady invited Theodore White of *Life Magazine* to come to the Kennedy compound in Hyannis. She pressed the compliant journalist assigned to memorialize the Kennedy presidency to emphasize the Camelot motif, and memorialize her husband as an American Arthur, the man who died both on behalf of and at the hands of his own people. For Jackie and the Left, he was not a victim of communist infiltration. There was no place in their new mythology for Lee Harvey Oswald.

His identity and act of assassination were not possible, by definition in the liberal world view. Ironically, although it was they who claimed the mantle of superior rationality and accused the Right of conspiratorial hatred, nearly every liberal leader, including Schlesinger himself, proclaimed that Kennedy was really a victim of a *climate of hate*, spawned by a nebulous force. If pressed for the true villain, they would say that Kennedy was a *victim of the radical Right*. The American Left became so pathologic that they continue to see their political enemies as a greater threat than external enemies—Soviets who targeted our cities with thousands of nuclear weaponized missiles or militant Islam seeking to detonate smuggled nuclear weapons inside our cities.

Additionally, in the years following Kennedy's death, liberalism made the leap from irrationality to its ultimate weakness—loss of civic virtue. Prominent liberal authors and pundits suggested that Oswald was not really a committed Communist, but a contract assassin hired by an agency of the *American* government. This would not be the last time that prominent liberals in leadership roles would accuse the country of egregious crimes. It would be just the beginning.

John Kerry and Our Loss of Martial Spirit

In the 2004 presidential election, Kerry was defeated in the "swing" state of Ohio by fewer than 60,000 votes. It was the votes of these few Ohioans in a US population of nearly 300 million that prevented John Kerry from ascending to the presidency in 2005. Almost half the country voted for arguably the most anti-military presidential candidate ever nominated by a major American political party, this during wartime and only three years after 9/11. For nearly four decades, John Kerry has been one of the most influential figures in shaping the evolution of the American Left's anti-martial nature. No other individual played a more decisive and continuous role in the anti-military movement mounted by the Left, since it rejected the martial ethos of FDR, Harry Truman, and Kennedy.

On April 12, 1971, Kerry began his ascent within the ranks of the ruling class with his testimony before the Senate Fulbright Committee. Under oath, he stated that American soldiers had "raped, cut off ears, cut off heads, taped wires from portable telephones to human genitals and turned on the power, cut off limbs, blew up bodies, randomly shot at civilians, razed villages in a fashion reminiscent of Genghis Khan." Moreover, he asserted that these men who told him that they had done these things could not be charged with war crimes, because it was the *unwritten policy of the military and the US government* to coerce them to commit atrocities in Vietnam on a massive scale.

While Kerry was lying to Congress, Ion Mihai Pacepa was overseeing the Soviet's misinformation campaign aimed at bringing down the West and reporting to Yuri Andropov, the head of the Soviet KGB. Pacepa was still the highest-ranking intelligence officer to ever defect from the former Soviet bloc. In 2004, he wrote a pre-election article for *National Review* and asserted that Kerry's testimony before the Fulbright committee was clearly plagiarized—an obvious word-for-word parsing of the KGB's most common sloganeering, accusations, and phraseology. The former KGB General should know. He ran the Soviets' main propaganda shop in Bucharest where he and his agents produced and disseminated thousands of anti-US, anti-war news releases that were gobbled up by the leftist European media outlets. For Pacepa, Kerry's phraseology was not just a coincidence; his "razed villages reminiscent of Ghengis Khan" stands out as a signature example.

General Pacepa, once a master propagandist and now an American citizen, wrote that the Soviet disinformation campaign was enormously successful. It unmistakably inspired Kerry's senate testimony, was parroted by a gullible US media, and created a lasting effect for leftist intellectuals and politicians in America. As Pacepa put it, so effective was the operation, the American mainstream press still depends upon Europe for guidance, such things as "sane and frank" criticism of the Bush (GW) administration's war policy. As proof of its lasting success, he writes, "Anti-Americanism in Europe today is almost as ferocious as it was during Vietnam." France and Germany insist we torture the al-Qaeda prisoners held at Guantanamo Bay. *The Mirror*, a British newspaper, confidently reported that President George W. Bush and Prime Minister Tony Blair "killed innocents in Afghanistan." The Paris daily *Le Monde* put Jean Baudrillard on its front page asserting that "the Judeo-Christian West, led by America, not only provoked the [September 11] terrorist attacks, it actually *desired* them." [58]

In 1971, none of the senators on the Fulbright committee thought to ask Kerry if he committed an atrocity, or witnessed any, while he was in Vietnam. Thirty-two years later he debated John O'Niel, the swift boat veteran and co-author of *Unfit For Command*. Kerry was forced to admit that, for the duration of his short tour, he had not witnessed *any* US service men committing war crimes.

In his testimony before Congress, Kerry said that the entire foundation for his charges was derived from a meeting held in Detroit that was called the "Winter Soldier Investigation." He attended and listened to one *supposed* veteran after another recount their war crimes, each one more horrific than the next. However, investigative journalists have since proved that many of the supposed vets who testified at the event in 1971 were frauds. Either they had never even been to Vietnam or were falsely using names of veterans who had. Many were just operatives, and the important question is—operatives from where or from what?

---

58. Ion Mihai Pacepa, *Kerry's Soviet Rhetoric* (*National Review Online*, February 26, 2004).

Part of the answer can be derived from the true identity of Kerry's then close associate, Al Hubbard, head of VVAW. He claimed to be a decorated Air Force captain wounded in Vietnam. Actually he was a staff sergeant who *never* served in Vietnam. Hubbard, an African-American, also professed strong ties to the Black Panthers. What was less known was his membership in the People's Coalition for Peace and Justice (PCPJ), a branch of the Soviet financed, Stalinist Socialist Workers Party whose entire charter was the "national mobilization to end the war in Vietnam."

The American radical Left/anti-war movement born in the late sixties was the offspring of the American Communist party. Leading radicals of the period, like Kerry, were naturally sympathetic to regimes such as North Vietnam, Cuba, and the Sandanista-run Nicaragua. Many of the intellectuals in their midst, such as Ronald Radosh and David Horowitz, were in fact sons and daughters of committed communists.

John Kerry cannot escape his association with committed communists. He wears the label of unrepentant sympathizer and has always been a powerful advocate, others would say—asset—of communist causes and regimes. As the national spokesman for the VVAW, he became the most influential champion of anti-American, Soviet produced disinformation that was instrumental in turning the American public against the Vietnam War. He with Al Hubbard, a known communist operative, and the VVAW membership influenced American foreign policy favorable to the goals of communist powers, are the avowed enemies of the US.

As a senator from 1984 to the present, Kerry voted against most the country's new and vital weapons systems including: the B-1 and B-2/Stealth bombers, the Apache helicopter, the patriot missile, and the F-14 and F-15 jets. He cast over fifty votes against missile defense, appropriations which were instrumental in allowing the US to bankrupt the Soviet Union. In short, he proved to be a very effective asset. Bui Tin headed the delegation of army officers who formally accepted the surrender of South Vietnam in 1975. He later defected to the West and has publicly stated that the anti-war movement headed by Kerry and Jane Fonda "was essential to our strategy."

More important, in 1970, Kerry met with the North Vietnamese delegation headed by the mercurial Madame Binh and Lo Duc Tho, two of the founders of Indochinese communism. This violated the US Constitution, Article 18, section 953, that prohibits negotiating with foreign powers. When confronted with FBI documents obtained by the Freedom of Information act, the Kerry presidential campaign admitted what he had done in Paris. At the precise moment Henry Kissinger and US negotiators were securing a cessation of hostilities, Kerry convinced the North to fight on instead of accepting a North/South divide. A treaty would have kept our South Vietnamese allies from being ravaged by the North. After the Kerry meeting, the North Vietnamese position hardened. The war dragged on—thousands of Vietnamese and Americans lost their lives.

A year after Kerry's meeting with the North Vietnamese in Paris, July 1, 1971, they offered a seven-point plan that would free our POW's if the US agreed to surrender and leave. Twenty-one days later, Kerry called a press conference on behalf of the VVAW and urged President Richard Nixon to accept the plan.

So important was Kerry to their cause, when Communist Vietnam opened its "War Crimes Museum," in 1984, the government placed a photo of Kerry with a plaque that described his "heroic contributions." Kerry's ongoing anti-American activities that were pivotal in the the North Vietnamese securing America's defeat, are of inestimable importance now. In a question and answer exchange at the end of the Fulbright hearings, Kerry was asked what he thought would happen in South Vietnam if America surrendered. He replied, "Having done what we have to that country, we have an obligation to offer sanctuary to 2,000 to 3,000 people."

While campaigning for president in 2004, Kerry advocated for America to capitulate again—this time abandoning the government and freeing people of Iraq, leaving them and their country's oil revenues to the tender mercies of al-Qaeda, Iran, and assorted jihadists. As recently as July 2007, in a banal display of self denial, Kerry said, "We heard that argument over and over again about the bloodbath that would engulf the entire Southeast Asia and it didn't happen." The fact is, when the Democrat controlled Congress cut off all funding to South Vietnam in 1974, a holocaust befell the region and approximately two million Cambodians, Laotians, and Vietnamese lost their lives.

Had George W. Bush committed a slip of the tongue or a minor gaffe like his father did in a debate with Bill Clinton when he was seen glancing at his watch, it's quite possible that John Kerry would have been our 44th president.

To say that he exhibits and mirrors a constituency that, like the Romans of the fifth century, lacks martial spirit would be a colossal understatement. We can imagine that if legitimate history is still being written a century from now, Kerry will likely be as important a figure as is Benedict Arnold. In 2111, junior high school textbooks will mention Kerry as a man who committed treason during the Vietnam War and nearly became president during the Iraq War.[59]

To appreciate the depth of its commitment to unilateral disarmament and dismembering of the American military ethos by the American Left, consider that John Kerry launched his political career in a 1971 testimony before the Senate. There he accused the entire military operation in Vietnam—from the commanders

---

59. My intention is to display a picture of both Benedict Arnold and John Kerry side by side.

to foot soldiers—of being guilty of war crimes. Thirty-three years later, while Kerry was its nominee for President, at the premier of Michael Moore's Fahrenheit 9/11 in Washington DC on June 23, 2004, nearly all the Congressional Democrat leadership turned out for the black-tie event. Reporter Byron York covered the premier. He asked Terry McAuliffe, Chairman of the Democratic National Committee, if he believed as the movie alleged, that President George W. Bush went to war in Afghanistan not to overthrow the Taliban and rout al-Qaeda but to benefit his business cronies who wanted to build a natural gas pipeline there.

McAuliffe said, "Yes, I believe that after seeing the film." [60]

In September 2007, the commanding general, David Petraeus, in a congressional hearing, informed the world that the US was making real progress in Iraq. David Gelernter who observed the hearing, recorded that the Democrat congressional leadership made it clear, for the entire world to see, including the jihadists plotting our destruction, that the leaders of the American Left are pacifistic globalists, and certainly not nationalists. They accused a four-star general, who daily risks his life in an active theater of war, of being a tool and a liar. In so doing, they echoed a sentiment that Democrat leaders have betrayed for over four decades. As Gelernter puts it:

> *"The Democrats are not unpatriotic, but their patriotism is directed at a large abstract entity called The International Community or even (aping Bronze Age paganism) the Earth, not America . . . Liberals are loyal to philosophical abstractions—and seek harmony with the French and Germans. Conservatives are loyal to their own nation, and seek harmony with their Founders and heroes and guiding principles."* [61]

Robert Kaplan who spent a great deal of time in the Iraq War, puts an even finer point on the distinction between the Right and the modern Left as manifested by their attitudes toward the current war in the Middle East and nationalism:

> *"That international society has ideas to defend—ideas of universal justice—but little actual ground. And without ground to defend, it has little need of heroes."* [62]

---

60. Jay Nordlinger, *Podhoretz at War*, A Review of the Norman Podhoretz's book, *World War IV*, (*National Review*, September 24, 2007), 55.

61. David Gelernter, *Defeat At Any Price* (*The Weekly Standard*, Sept. 24, 2007), 24.

62. Robert Kaplan, *Modern Heroes* (*Wall Street Journal*, Opinion, October 4, 2007), A19.

PART TWO

The Rise of Islam

Immutable Laws
Governing the Fall of Civilizations

1   No nation has ever survived once its citizenry ceased to believe its culture worth saving. (Hanson's Law)

2   In battle, free men will almost always defeat slaves. (Herodotus' Law)

3   Appeasement of a ruthless outside power always invites its aggression. Treaties made with ruthless despots are always fruitless and dangerous.

4   If a people cannot avoid continuous internal warfare, it will have a new order imposed from without.

5   When a free people, through taxation, is deprived of its ability to acquire wealth and property, collapse is presaged.

6   To hold territory, a state must be populated by those loyal to the central authority. When immigration overwhelms assimilation, the fall is predicted.

7   With the loss of fiscal solvency comes a loss of sovereignty.

8   Debasing the currency always destabilizes the governing authority.

9   When a civilization accepts the propaganda of its enemy as truth, it has reached the far side of appeasement and capitulation is nigh.

10 Declining civilizations will always face superior firepower from ascending civilizations because sovereignty is only temporarily uncontested.

CHAPTER FOUR
The Fall of the Christian Middle East
AD 632-732[1]

> When you meet the unbelievers on the battlefield,
> strike off their heads and,
> when you have laid them low, bind your captives firmly.
> THE KORAN—SURAH 47: VERSE 4

In his praise of the book, *The Decline of Eastern Christianity under Islam* by Bat Ye'or, a Coptic Christian from Egypt, Father Richard Neuhaus wrote that Muhammad is the only founder of a major modern religion whose life falls with an era of pedigreed historical inquiry. Islam's spectacular spread was brought about by brutal military conquest, rapine, spoliation, and slavery. Its culture was derived from the vanquished.

In 2011, nearly a decade after 9/11, insurrections broke out all across the Muslim Middle East. For some in the West, this seemed to buoy hope that the threat posed by resurgent militant Islam was dissipating. It is not.

On March 7, 2011, Representative Peter King of New York began a hearing on the threat of indigenous terrorism. He said that Attorney General Eric Holder had shared that he authorized undercover agents to enter American mosques. The FBI and law enforcement agencies were, at an increasing frequency, uncovering plots by radicalized American Muslims to attack targets inside the US.

Globally, since 9/11, there have been over 10,000 terrorist attacks perpetrated by Muslims upon non-Muslim populations. What if only one percent of the world's 1.3 billion Muslims are active jihadists? This would mean that thirteen million souls

---

1. The fall of the Christian Middle East commenced with the death of Muhammad in AD 632 and included the conquest of the Levant, large portions of today's Turkey, Persia, all of North Africa and Spain, and was only turned back at the battle of Poitiers in AD 732.

awake each morning and plot the destruction of the West—an army larger than the combined World War II Axis powers of Germany, Italy, and Japan.

For anyone who cannot believe there are such a vast number of Muslims plotting to attack the West, consider Abdel Baset al-Megrahi, the "Lockerbie Bomber" who killed 220 innocent non-Muslims over Scotland. When he was repatriated to Libya in 2010, he was met by crowds at the airport and given a hero's welcome. Ponder the fact that when the images of Americans leaping to their deaths from the burning Trade Center Towers were transmitted to Islamic enclaves from Damascus to Falls Church, Virginia, the Muslims celebrated.

The question is *why*? What commands a Muslim to take up arms against the West generally, and America specifically?

The answer is that he is driven by four powerful motivations:

First—the Koran and other religious texts command that he militarily defend his culture from what he can clearly see as corruption heaped upon Islam by an ubiquitous Western press, internet, commerce, and pop culture.

Second—history. He longs for Islam's past greatness which Islam absorbed from those it conquered. The Bedouin invaders produced practically no scholars or inventors of their own.

Third—the example of the Prophet who was a ruthless warlord and whose life cannot be judged. Muhammad's life is the standard by which all others are judged. Islam teaches the Muslim from childhood that the ruthless conquest of the unbeliever (infidel) is blessed and that those who resist are evil.

And finally—Islam attacks the West because, for most of its fourteen centuries, it always has.

The Historical Prophet

I am indebted to Robert Spencer who explains in his book, *The Truth About Muhammad*, how it is that there is no "comparable religious figure's life and times so well recorded as Muhammad's." [2] Modern historians can paint a fairly accurate portrait of him due to the events recorded in three large bodies of records. They are the *Qur'an*, the *Hadiths*, and the *Sira*.

The Qur'an

Virtually all Muslim chroniclers of the period believed that the Qur'an was

---

2. Robert Spencer, *The Truth About Muhammad: Founder of the World's Most Intolerant Religion*, (Washington DC: Regnery Publishing, 2006), 20.

revealed to Muhammad over the twenty-three years of his prophethood, that it was delivered to him in separate visitations by the Angel Gabriel, and that the verses are literally the word of God. His followers, who grew to tens of thousands of warriors—the Sahabas—memorized the verses and recited them to each other and to the Prophet. Upon Muhammad's death in AD 632, the first Caliph, Abu Bakr, commanded that the verses be compiled in book form.

The Qur'an

Spencer makes the fascinating observation that "reading the Qur'an is like walking in on a conversation between two people with whom one is only slightly acquainted." [3]

The Hadiths

Due to the fact that the Qur'an is disjointed and often obtuse, early Muslim writers wrote elaborations which gave context to the verses of the Qur'an. These are the hadiths.

Muhammad Ibn Ismail al-Bukhari (AD 810-870) travelled the Middle East and collected 300,000 of them. Upon close examination he published about 2,000 which he determined were reliably written by a person close to Muhammad. The Arabic word for reliable is *sahih*. Bukhari's collection is *Sahih al-Bukhari* and is a major source about Muhammad's life.

Sahih Muslim was collected by Muslim Ibn al-Hajjaj-Qushayri (821-875). He is considered by Islamic scholars to be the definitive authority on the life of Muhammad.

The Sira

The *Sira* is the biography of Muhammad. The Prophet's earliest biographer, Muhammad ibn Ishaq ibn Yasar (often called Ishaq), appears to have written a very careful and comprehensive work.

Some events in Muhammad's life, although they may appear in all three texts, may be somewhat fictionalized. To what extent is not known given the fourteen centuries that have elapsed. But as Spencer so aptly points out, despite the fact that it may not be completely possible to separate fact from fiction, the important thing for us to understand is that a composite "portrait of Muhammad has over the centuries passed

---

3.   Ibid, 21.

into the general consciousness of Muslims." [4] His is the life of the perfect man, the life by which all others are judged.

The Life of the Prophet

The Prophet was born in Mecca in AD 570 and, due to the Hobbesian world of sixth-century Arabia, he was quickly orphaned. His grandfather arranged for him to find work in the merchant-run camel caravans of his tribe. At the age of twenty-five, he married a somewhat wealthy widow fifteen years his senior and worked for her as her chief camel driver before rising to the post of full partner.

The Bedouins, (Muhammad's first converts) from whose culture Islam was derived, made most of their money from the raid of caravans and camps. His first successful raid was against a trade caravan headed to Mecca.

During this period, his early biographers record that he met Jewish merchants and Christian monks where he was introduced to anthropomorphic monotheism. Then in AD 610, at age forty and while in a meditative trance, Muslims believe the Angel Gabriel appeared to him proclaiming that he was the "Messenger of God." [5] At first he was reluctant to act upon the vision, fearing that he was possessed by demons. His wife, Khadija, convinced him of the truthfulness of the revelation and in so doing became Islam's first convert. As Serge Trifkovic writes in *The Sword of the Prophet*:

> *"From that time on, at increasingly frequent intervals, Muhammad received 'revelations' such as hearing of sounds, perspiring on a cold day and losing consciousness, . . . these later gave rise to the suggestion that he was an epileptic. . . . Sometimes the texts of the revelations were written down and others he carried in his heart, that is, in his conscious mind and were recorded later."* [6]

At this time, the Quraysh tribe controlled Mecca and was very prosperous. They derived hefty profits by their stewardship of the temple of Kaaba where a stone (perhaps a meteorite) was, and still is, worshiped. Positioned on the crossroads between two empires to the north, Byzantium and Persia, and citadels to the south in Yemen and Ethiopia, they were the custodians and tax collectors of a large commercial center. As

---

4.   Ibid, 28.

5.   Ibn Ishaq, *The Life of Muhammad*, trans. A. Guillaume, (New York: OUP, 1980), 155.
     Ishaq is considered the earliest biographer of Muhammad.

6.   Serge Trifkovic, *The Sword of the Prophet: Islam; History, Theology, Impact on the World*
     (Regina Orthodox Press), 14.

Muhammad became known and preached to a small group of his Meccan followers, the Quraysh city elders began to see him as a seditious threat to the profits they earned from the pilgrimages made to their city's temple. He slowly became a despised and unwanted outcast.

To add to his troubles, in AD 619, his wife and his protective uncle died. Fearing for his safety and that of his followers, he sought refuge in Medina, where his fortunes changed. As a fiery orator and an outsider, he was able to arbitrate a truce between three warring factions, the indigenous Arabs, the recent immigrant Arabs, and the Jewish settlers who had prospered there from trade and agriculture. A constitution of Medina was drawn up that regulated relations among the factions, including Muhammad's small following. It stated that disputes would be arbitrated by the "Prophet." The little house that was eventually built for him become a place where his small and growing flock could come and pray.

Most of his original cadre of followers were not interested in finding employment in Medina. They wanted revenge upon the rich Meccans who had dishonored them. Moreover, this dishonor was only a pretext for Muhammad's nomadic Bedouin followers whose livelihood was largely derived from their raiding camps and caravans. Unlike some of the Arabs of antiquity who learned to make a living as farmers or merchants, the mark of manhood for the Arab nomads who followed Muhammad was the possession of arms, obsession with honor, and claim to pastures, camels, and women. Robbery and murder outside the protective confines of one's clan were simply the means to an end." [7]

It was upon the ethos of the ruthless raid that Muhammad founded Islam.

As time passed, Muhammad's combined position of authority and prophetic oratory made him the de facto ruler of Medina. After three years in his adoptive city, he was ready to make war against his home city and his own clan.

In 623, with an eerie, apocalyptic symmetry, he led his young religion's first three terrorist attacks against Meccan caravans which were traveling past Medina on their way to Syria. (The symmetry stems from the fact that fourteen of the nineteen hijackers gained entry into the US via Meccan travel agencies located very near where these seventh-century terror attacks took place.) These initial raids were so unsuccessful that they were not even able to steal a camel.

Then early AD 624, Muhammad led a raid on a caravan from Yemen: killed one man, took away a lot of booty, and captured two prisoners—one who was ransomed for eighty pieces of silver. The success of this raid was largely due to surprise, given

7. Ibid, 17.

that it took place during the holy month of Ramadan, a period that was ". . . a time of truce generally respected even by the most pugnacious of brigands. . . (But) this did not present a problem for Muhammad, however, who had just received a revelation allowing warfare even during Ramadan." [8]

When he returned to Medina after his victory, he set in motion the phenomenon we see today in most Islamic countries—the complete blending of mosque and state.

Because of the strength of his army and their ability to effectively carry out raids, and because of his harsh treatment of the losers, a state of fear descended over the city. Informants attempting to curry favor brought Muhammad word of inhabitants who did not support Islam. Many murderous reprisals were carried out. For the Medinans, their choice would be the same as for all the peoples ultimately conquered by Islam, conversion, servility (quiet submission), or death.

From this point (AD 625) forward in Muhammad's life, Jews became the target for extermination. Originally, when he was preaching peacefully in Mecca, Muhammad thought that the Jews could be converted. He was wrong. Many of the Jewish merchants he encountered were learned, very religious, and viewed the teachings of this uneducated camel driver with contempt. This slight hardened into a fierce vengeance and hatred which gave rise to the numerous virulently Jew-hating revelations and passages in the Koran:

> And among the Jews too are those who would listen fondly to any lie...
> These are they whose hearts Allah has not been pleased to purify; they
> shall have disgrace in this world, and in the Hereafter they shall have
> severe punishment. [9]

On March 15, 624, Muhammad lead a raid comprised of three hundred men against a Meccan caravan returning from Syria. Near the town of Badr, forty Meccans were killed and sixty taken prisoner. It was the Prophet's first major victory over his *own* kinsman. [10] After their victory Muhammad's poorly trained herdsman had several engagements with Meccan soldiers and suffered sound defeats before retreating to Medina. So the Prophet, in need of another victory, turned to softer targets—Jewish settlements outside Mecca, some within his Medina redoubt.

---

8. Ibid, 35.
9. The *Koran*, Surah 5, verse 42.
    Additionally the holy Qur'an contains no less than three passages, 2:63-66, 5:59-60, 7:166,
    that refer to disobedient Jews as the descendants of "apes and pigs."
10. *Sahih Al-Bukhari*, Volume 4, Book 52.

He laid siege on the Banu Nadir tribe, a Jewish settlement in Medina, and eventually drove them from their homes and farms, all of which was confiscated by the Muslims. (Two years later, he attacked the Banu Nadir in their new settlement and made them Islam's first indentured people.) Muhammad, based on God's revelations to him, developed a policy where he took one-fifth of all the spoils, which made him a wealthy man. The Jewish plunder distributed to his followers convinced most of those in Medina who had not yet converted to Islam to join. Now Muhammad was wealthy with a consolidated position, and he had a good number of fighters eager for rape and plunder under his command.

In early 627, the Meccans and Quraysh elders realized that Muhammad was a force that had to be eliminated. They amassed a huge army, by Arabian standards, of over 10,000 men and began to ride toward Medina. Muhammad's earliest biographer, Ibn Ishaq, records that some of the Jews who were expelled from Medina and others from settlements around Arabia joined the Meccan army. This adds another reason why Jews are held in contempt by Muslims today.

Muhammad received word of the impending attack, ordered trenches dug around the city, and withstood a twenty-five day siege. As soon as the Meccans withdrew, he attacked the last Jewish tribe allied with the city of Medina, the Banu Qurayza.

It is recorded in the *Koran* that Allah sent a new revelation to the Prophet that instructed him to kill the Jews because they had broken their promise to not aid the armies from Mecca. Muhammad addressed them in terms that have become familiar usage for Muslim radicals speaking of Jews today—language that also made its way into the *Koran*, "You brothers of monkeys, has God disgraced you and brought His vengeance upon you." [11]

While the prophet was overseeing the decapitations, "He caught a glimpse of Rihana, a beautiful Jewish woman, whose husband and father were massacred before her eyes just hours earlier. Muhammad asked her to become his wife. She refused. So he took her as his unwilling slave and concubine." [12]

Other sources record that, on that day, many unspeakable tortures preceded the executions of the men. Because the event is so well-documented in the Koran, as Robert Spencer observes, ". . . it established a precedent that was enshrined in Islamic law, *Sharia*, which gives Muslim captors the right to kill or enslave their non-Muslim prisoners (with the full blessing of God) as they deem expedient." [13]

---

11. The *Koran*, 5:59.
12. Ishaq, *The Life of Muhammad*, 464. Muhammad's earliest biographer writes, "Then he sent for them and struck off their heads in those trenches as they were brought out to him in batches."
13. Robert Spencer, *Onward Muslim Soldiers* (Washington DC: Regnery Publishing, 2003), 160.

"By the summer of 627," Trifkovic records, "Muhammad's prestige and authority were truly unassailable. He had transformed himself into an absolute ruler." Sources tell us that he had a passion for women, and he had at least fifteen wives, the youngest, (we even know her name) Aisha, was seven years old and still played with dolls when he first took her for his wife. Due to the prophet's example, polygamy and the forced marriage of female adolescents are widely accepted practices throughout the Muslim world even today.[14]

By the winter of AD 628, the prophet's armies were attacking and pillaging smaller Jewish and pagan settlements around Arabia with varied success. And Muhammad was eyeing his most coveted prize—the conquest of Mecca, his home town—and the submission by the ruling Quraysh tribe to his will. This would be a sublime vindication and ecstatic payback for the former camel driver. While his emissaries negotiated with Mecca and he contemplated its sack, he negotiated a ten-year truce. In this agreement the Meccans agreed to relinquish all protection agreements and alliances they had with surrounding Jewish and pagan settlements. This, in effect, bought ten years worth of security while throwing their former allies to the dogs.

One year after signing the ten-year truce with Mecca, the Prophet had conquered enough of Mecca's former allies, a goodly number of whom he converted and who had joined his army. He knew that he had the strength to besiege and conquer Mecca. So he broke the treaty on the pretext that Mecca had attacked one of his allied cities. As Muhammad amassed his army of ten-thousand men outside its walls, the Meccans knew that they had no chance to withstand an extended siege and that they had been had. They sent an emissary, known to every faithful Muslim today, Abu Sufyan, to meet with the Prophet and to agree to terms. There would be no war, only capitulation.[15]

On January 12, 630, the victorious band of bandits and brigands (the first Muslims) rode into Mecca and proclaimed all of Arabia to be Muslim. The Arabs of Mecca who embraced the prophet were given honorable positions in the army and government. The Jews of Mecca and throughout the Arabian Peninsula were enslaved or murdered.[16]

Muhammad died at age sixty-three, two years after the fall of Mecca. Besides the chronicles of his life, conquests, and revelations enshrined in the *Koran* and hadiths, one of his most lasting legacies is his concept of *jihad*, the word used so often by Osama bin Laden's followers and imitators post 9/11.

---

14. Trifkovic, 40-43.

15. Ibn Hisham, *Biography of the Prophet*, Part Four, 289.

16. Ibn Warraq, *The Quest for the Historical Muhammad*, (New York: Prometheus Books, 2000), 197.

The Sword of Islam

Soon after the Prophet was dead, Muslim armies stormed out of the Arabian Desert and conquered Syria, Egypt, and Persia. Damascus fell in 635, substantial portions of today's Iraq and Jerusalem in 638, Caesarea (today's Israel) in 641, and Armenia in 643. The conquest of Egypt took place during the same period. The Muslims won decisive victories in the Maghreb (North Africa) over the Byzantines at Sufetala in Tunisia in 647. By 709, they had complete control of all the African coastline touching the Mediterranean. By 711, they had subdued Spain and were moving into France.

Muslim marauders rode into a vacuum left by the Persian and Byzantine empires which were exhausted from having fought one another for twenty-six years (602-628). As Roger Crowley writes in *1453*:

> *"Motivated by the word of God and disciplined by communal prayer, bands of nomadic raiders were transformed into an organized fighting force, whose hunger was now projected outward beyond the deserts's rim into a world sharply divided by faith. . . . By the 630s Muslim armies started to appear on the margins of the Byzantine frontier, like ghosts out of a sandstorm. They traversed the harsh empty quarters, killing their camels as they went and drinking the water from their stomachs— to emerge again unexpectedly behind their enemy. They attacked, then retreated into the desert, lured their opponents out of their strongholds into the barren wilderness, surrounded and massacred them."* [17]

The Roman Empire of the East (termed Byzantium today), headquartered in Constantinople, was simply unable to exercise any real authority outside Western Turkey, Greece, and the Balkans. The Arabs conquered the relatively defenseless Christian Middle East and Africa simply because they could and because it paid well. They were compensated as Muhammad had proscribed; every man was allowed to retain the plunder of those whom he had slain with his own hand, including women and children, with the rest thrown into a stock. They were further motivated by a religious zeal—their plunder and conquest was blessed by Allah.

Slaughters occurred in most of the initial waves of conquest. During the Muslim invasion of Syria in 634, thousands of Christians were massacred. In Mesopotamia, between 635 and 642, monasteries were ransacked and monks and villagers slain. In

---

17. Roger Crowley, *1453: The Holy War for Constantinople and the Clash of Islam and the West*, (New York: Hyperion, 2005), 10-11.

Egypt the Coptic Christian towns of Behnesa, Fayum, Nikiu, and Aboit were put to the sword, the men were killed, and the women and children sold into slavery as a means to pay a tax imposed upon the dhimmi (the non-Muslims living in conquered lands). Other cities in North Africa, such as the once Christian city of Tripoli, were pillaged in AD 643, where Jews and Christians alike were forced to hand over their women and children to the Arab army. They were told that they could deduct the value of their enslaved family from the poll-tax, the *jizya*.[18]

Sophronius, the Bishop of Jerusalem, in his sermon on the Day of Epiphany 636, writes for posterity of the ravages wrought by the Arabs. He tells that thousands perished in AD 639, victims of the famine and plague that resulted from the pointless destruction of the Christian and Jewish farm lands.[19]

Before his death, Muhammad spoke often to his followers about his fervent dream of conquering the great Christian citadel which he referred to as "Ceasar's City." During the four decades after the death of Muhammad (AD 630s-670s), many of the Christian lands of the Greek-speaking Middle East were stripped away from the Roman Empire, what we today refer to as Byzantium. The mostly Roman Catholic provinces of Syria, Phoenicia, Palestine, and Egypt had fallen to Islam. By 674, with a captured fleet of ships and mostly captive crews, the Muslims began a four-year siege of Constantinople, the capital of Christendom.

Despite their fleet being greatly outnumbered, the Romans held out. The five miles of massive walls around Constantinople, completed almost three hundred years earlier by the Roman Emperor, Theodosius, in 390, still rendered the city the most impregnable fortress in the known world. Therefore, it was necessary for the attacking Muslims to defeat the Roman navy to starve the city into submission.

In response, the Romans produced a secret weapon called "Greek fire." It appears to have been a petroleum-based product that could be sprayed on the surface of the water and ignited. Chroniclers tell us that the Romans burned up three separate Muslim armadas this way. When a fourth Muslim fleet deserted, the siege finally ended. This proved to be a decisive event in the history of Muslim aggression against the West because it was Islam's first major defeat. (The next was fifty years later at Poitiers.)

The great Roman citadel would fight Islam continuously for another 775 years.

---

18. Ibn Khaldun, *The Muqaddimah: An introduction to History*, trans. Franz Rosenthal (Princeton University Press, 1986), 20-330.

19. Bat Ye'or, *The Decline of Eastern Christianity under Islam* (Fairleigh Dickinson University Press, 1996), 44. Ms. Ye'or, a non-Muslim, was born in Egypt and is the world's authority on the history of Islamic dhimmitude (the treatment of non-Muslims in Islamic lands).

The Battle to Save Christendom

In AD 732, exactly one hundred years after Muhammad's death, Charlemagne's grandfather, the Frankish warlord Charles Martel, stopped the northwestern advance of Islam in the French countryside at a battle fought near the small city of Poitiers. In so doing, historians believe that he saved Western Christendom.

The Battle of Poitiers (AD 732) —(Depicted in Historic Fiction)

The valley, surrounded by the stately green and brown hills of the Frankish countryside, might have given an imperceptive observer an utterly false sense of serenity that morning. As the dawn was beginning to pierce the darkness, Charles noted a familiar eerie quiet hanging over the valley, owing to the fact that the birds in the area were silent, frightened by his army that was amassing on the Roman road to Tours and by the Saracens who were preparing for battle just over the horizon on the ridge above.

This must surely be the day that Rahman (Abd al Rahman al Ghafiqi, Emir of Spain) will attack me, Charles thought. For six days, Charles sent his scouts up to an adjacent bluff to watch Rahman's men while the mounted Saracen warriors had been watching his army from the edge of their camp. Unless a large body of Arab reinforcements had come in under the cover of darkness the night before, he judged the two armies to be roughly the same size, between twenty- to thirty-thousand men each.

So that he personally would not be an easy target for the Saracen archers, Charles dismounted and, in the still dim light, sent his horse off the battlefield with his squire. He walked between two rows of men near the front of the formation and took up his position inside the first phalanx positioned nearest the enemy ridge.

His battle dress was very similar to the Greek hoplite soldiers who fought at Marathon. His Germanic battle costume had changed little since the days when they were the Rhineland tribes of Batavians, Chattans, Riparians, and Alamans, peoples now fading into the shadowy past, that confederation of tribes the Romans called the Franks. He was a proud Germanic warrior who came from the eastern side of the Rhine, from a people never subjugated by the Roman Empire. He led an army of heavy infantry of hardened Teutonic tribal warriors.

Charles was clad in simple armor so as to be indistinguishable from the rank and file of his army. He wore a conical helmet, out of which poured two long braids of red-brown hair that reached nearly to his waist, and a coat of mail that hung to his knees. A vest of animal skins covered his upper body.

His leather shoes were secured by long leather straps which crossed each other around his shins and above his knees. In one hand he carried a round shield with its boss drawn out to a point and in the other, he carried a fifteen-foot pike with a sharp iron tip. On his belt, there was a Frankish battle ax, a dagger, and a double-edged sword, all sheathed in leather.

His face had a reddish flush with piercing pale blue eyes and a mustache that hung three inches below his cheek bones that contained some conspicuous long grey members. His face was weathered but contained no battle scars. Although his adult life had been one consumed by near constant war, Charles had never been wounded and had never been in a losing battle. He was powerfully built and, like the majority of his tribesmen assembling on the green meadow, he stood over six-feet tall and would tower over the mostly five-foot tall Bedouin scouts who were beginning to be arrayed on the overlooking bluffs, mounted and ready for battle. Charles was thirty-two.

He was more troubled than he had ever been in the moments before a battle. As was his habit, he prayed, or at least he tried. The relationship Charles had with his God had been a practical one. Charles spoke a "barbarized" Germanic Latin. He could neither read nor even write his name. His confessor and tutor, an Anglo Saxon monk, Benedictus, taught him to say his prayers in the pure Latin of Virgil. On the evenings of this campaign to the Aquitaine, he also read to Charles from the Roman historians, Polibius, Livy, and Tacitus.

Charles could not comprehend the omniscience of his God. He believed that his prayers and those of his soldiers and subjects needed to be delivered in the classic Latin of the Pope in Rome for the Lord to heed them. And for God to hear his entreaties, Charles believed that his

Ann Ronan Picture Library / Heritage Images

Charles Martel

prayers needed to be spoken in the same language that Virgil and the Pope in Rome spoke. Benedictus, who had been commissioned by the Pope to convert the pagans of Gaul, had accompanied Charles on two previous campaigns in central Francia, the new name being used for the region of independent duchies and counties that made up the area north of the Alps and west of the Rhine.

Now, on the cusp of battle, Charles was too nervous to pray or even remember the prayers that Benedictus had taught him. If there is only one true God, he thought, certainly He favors the enemy. Why else had so many Christian lands, Syria, Palestine, Egypt, Spain, and Septimania (the Pyrenees Kingdom) fallen to the sword of Islam?

If there is one true God, Charles thought, He must favor them. "How can I possibly win today?" the great warrior asked himself. Then mused, "If He does favor them, I will certainly die today." At that thought, remorse began to weigh upon his spirit. All his adult life, Charles had fought and killed men, pagans and Christians alike, some of whom had even grown up in neighboring villages of Austrasia, even men from his own clan. Was his quest to bring order and a common rule to these lands of Francia worth their lives? He dreaded the answer.

When he awoke earlier that morning, Charles prayed that God would forgive him and somehow give him a sign that He favored his cause, a sign that He was a Christian God and not the Saracens' god. "God, give me a sign that I am worthy," he tried to pray under his breath. As he did so, he noticed his mouth was very dry, so much so that his tongue was swollen and he a felt an overwhelming nausea that he hoped the warriors around him could not see.

On a road the Romans had built between Poitiers and Tours, Charles' army was arrayed in five phalanxes, two on one side of the road and three on the other. His army, like a single organism, sensed that this would be the day the battle would start. Some of Charles' newest soldiers were more eager than their brothers-in-arms for the fighting to begin. These were the men of Poitiers who had joined Charles' army after their village fell to the Saracens two weeks earlier, before the Austrasians arrived. These new soldiers were those who had escaped the village. Many had lost loved ones and neighbors, either killed or captured, at the hands of the Arab horsemen who had stormed the unfortified village and looted the church and monastery.

Many of the men of Poitiers stood and prayed as well; they prayed that they would kill the captors and be reunited with a wife, son, or daughter, who were held captive there behind the ridge in the Saracen camp. Nearly all the men of Poitiers begged Charles to be placed on the front-line of the phalanx and be given their own iron-tipped pikes so that they could be the first to face the Arab cavalry charges. In the gathering light, Charles held back his tears as he thought of these men of Poitiers who were so desperate in their grief, fearing that too many would not survive the day to free their families.

Adb al Rahman, Emir of Andalusia (Islamic Spain) awoke around the same time Charles found himself unable to pray. He stood for several minutes, contemplating the dark sleeping form of his Jewish slave girl, Ximena. Outside he could hear his army stirring, stoking their morning fires, and muttering about the battle to come. He turned and walked outside his tent and brought back inside a burning branch which gave off just enough light so that he could see Ximena's face in the darkness. Between blankets of luxuriant bear fur, she lay naked on a Persian rug. She was restrained at her ankles and wrists by leather straps which led to stakes driven into the earth off the edge of the rug. She awakened when he entered the tent and shined the light in her eyes.

A year earlier, in an early morning raid, her father and two brothers were captured and beheaded. She and her mother were taken as slaves and were entrained to be sent across North Africa and back to Syria. Word reached Rahman of the recently captured beautiful Jewess. Upon seeing her, he decided to keep her as his concubine while he was in the north leading raids into Francia. Ximena was seventeen.

She possessed eyes the likes of which he had never seen. Rahman had more than a dozen concubines in his harem in Cordoba, the Islamic capital of Spain, and had been offered and refused hundreds of other slave girls, products of the Islamic conquests of northern Iberia, the Pyrenees, and the Mediterranean Coast of Aquitaine. He had never beheld a woman whose eyes could hold him in its grip. Each iris was a luminous emerald green with a band of darker green around its outer rim. What held him transfixed was not simply their utter jewel-like beauty but the staggering emotion they conveyed: rage, hatred, and horror. Her gaze penetrated his warrior soul and had the odd effect of enslaving him to her. Knowing that the Prophet had captured a Jewish wife, Aisha, it was his dream that she would become his willing princess and that he would take her to Damascus to meet the Caliph. He dreamed that they would travel there by the northern route across conquered Islamic Europe.

Charles' Austrasian warriors were the Teutonic recipients of an ancient oral tradition. For centuries they recounted, over their campfires, legends of their ancestors who they believed were the descendants of Troy, descendants from the men and women who found their way to Germania after the Greeks had conquered the city. In the early morning before the battle, they must have watched as the gathering light revealed more and more Bedouin horsemen forming up in their ranks on the ridge.

Presently, they witnessed what no one born in Northern Gaul or Germania had ever seen—a massive Saracen cavalry charge. Ten thousand horsemen began galloping down from the ridge, shrieking at the top of their lungs, some brandishing swords, others riding with bows. Charles had given the order to stand firm and to remain in tight formation so that his soldiers' shields would touch one another and would provide a solid wall against the volleys of arrows. The front row of men crouched behind their shields while the men in the inner rows held their shields over their heads, creating a protective roof.

As Rahman's arrows began to fly into Charles' phalanx, most were deflected by the bronze shields. Few men fell. As the Islamic riders reached to within fifty paces, the men of his front rows hurled their pikes at the oncoming unarmored horses, mortally wounding many and causing several hundred of the others to stumble or fall. Horrific braying erupted. At the same time, hundreds of Saracens were thrown forward, over the heads of their falling mounts onto the ground, only to shriek more loudly as they were trampled by the wave of riders behind them.

Next, the Austrasians in the second and third rows of Charles' phalanx quickly moved up and replaced the front row and aimed their pikes outward toward the onrushing horsemen. A wave of several hundred riders crashed into Charles' front line creating a near deafening explosion while horses and riders were impaled. In this first charge, the Saracens failed to create an opening in his phalanx where Charles stood commanding the battle.

In the space of a few moments, Charles was able to judge that his front line had held firm with minimal losses inflicted by the enemy's arrow men. As he looked to his right, he could see the phalanx commanded by his cousin, Dragobert, had also withstood the charge on it at its front flank, inflicting large losses on the Saracen horses and riders, and he could see that they were moving forward approaching the slope which led up to the Saracen encampment. He could also see that they managed to stay in formation while passing over the quivering mass of wounded men and thrashing horses which issued huge braying noises.

As the day wore on, Charles' five phalanxes sustained frontal and lateral attacks by the mounted Saracens. Their charges were aimed at panicking the Teutonic ranks, with the aim of causing their lines to break into disorganized leaderless pockets, so that they could be struck down from sword blows and shot in the back by arrow men. Charles' phalanxes held and their formations were not breaking down, so determined were the Franks to kill the Saracen invaders.

What Charles could not see was that the discipline among Rahman's troops was breaking down. This was the result of a panic that was infecting the Arabs and North Africans as they began to see that it was possible they might lose this battle. And in so doing, might also lose the vast stores of plunder and slaves that they had amassed over the previous eighteen months of campaigning in Southern France. The panic spreading among Rahman's warriors stemmed from the desire of each man to get back to camp, gather his plunder and head back to the safety of the lands on the other side of the Pyrenees. Temporal greed was overtaking their lust for infidel blood.

Rahman rode along the crest of the ridge at the head of about two-hundred mounted elite riders who were his bodyguards. As he was about to issue the command to charge, he glanced off to his right and could see hundreds of his Saracen riders retreating back up the hill while one of Charles' phalanxes was pushing them slowly up the hill. With that he shouted to his men to charge that forward column of Franks. Two hundred elite riders began to gallop down the ridge toward Dragobert's advancing soldiers. Leading the charge, Rahman had closed to about fifty feet from the Franks when an airborne pike struck him just above his groin on his right hip, penetrating through him, his saddle blankets, and into his horse. This caused his horse to stop suddenly, throwing him to the ground. In the fall, the pike tore itself out of his flesh, leaving a gaping hole in his right hip which gushed blood. One of

The fanciful painting of the Battle of Poitiers by Charles Steuben (1788-1856). Note the depiction of Charles Martel in the Conical helmet and a Semitic looking woman evocative of the author's heroine, Ximena.

his bodyguards saw that he had been wounded and thrown, rode up and hoisted him on his mount. Rahman knew that he was mortally wounded and ordered his adjutant to take him to his tent. He had an overwhelming desire to be with his personal belongings, including his beloved slave, Ximena, before he died.

As Rahman and his bodyguard mounted the ridge and approached his tent, thousands of Saracens were swirling around them, screaming at one another, while desperately trying to gather their belongings and captives, and make their escape before the Franks could converge on the camp.

When Rahman entered his tent, he was unable to stand and ordered his bodyguard to carry him to the rug next to where Ximena lay under her animal skins. Knowing that the Arab commander was near death, the bodyguard quickly left the tent without a salute or even a farewell. He had his belongings to collect.

Ximena had been a captive for nearly a year and was from a small coastal village near the major port city of Narbonne, which had fallen several years earlier. The Koran forbade the killing of the infidels if they surrendered to the warriors of Allah. But the citizens of Narbonne had chosen to fight the Arabs because word had reached them that other villages in the Pyrenees had surrendered only to learn that they would have to sell their children into slavery in order to pay the gizya, the Arabs' tax levied on the infidels.

After its fall, all the surviving men of Narbonne were killed. All the women and children were taken as slaves. The residents of Ximena's village were bypassed when Narbonne fell. But two years later, in a surprise raid, the luckless souls of Ximena's village were not given the option of surrender. Rahman needed to provide his army with plunder and, especially, slaves as a means of payment for their service. Slaves were more easily acquired than minted gold pieces.

With the gaping wound on his side bathing his lower body in blood, some of which was already turning brown, Rahman rolled his head toward his beautiful slave and looked at her with a longing, helpless gaze, a look which asked for tenderness and forgiveness.

During the day, Ximena had been able to work herself free of the leather straps that bound her. Free to move around his tent while he was away at the battle, she found his dagger that she knew he kept in a satchel next to his bed. She had now hidden it under her rug. If the Saracens had won the day and defeated the Franks, her plan was to wait until Rahman returned to his tent. After he had raped her and gone to bed, she would kill him with his own knife and make her escape into the forest. Now, listening to the chaos going on outside the tent, she knew that the Saracens had lost the day, that they were in full retreat, and that Rahman was dying right before her eyes. With all the crescendo of confusion, she concluded that, with the impending invasion of their camp, the Saracens would overlook collecting the commander's concubine.

Seeing his utter helplessness, she sat up, exposing her naked breasts, and, brandishing Rahman's own dagger, she spoke to him for the very first time in perfect Arabic, "My father and brothers whom you killed await you! They are the saints who will throw your filthy soul into hell!" With that, she slammed his dagger into the center of his chest and his ghost made an audible sound as it left his lifeless body.

Charles looked up to see one of his warriors, Theabald, whose father had been a boyhood friend, approaching him though the shambles of the Saracen camp. Theabald held a rope led to Ximena's bound wrists. As he pulled her behind his horse towards Charles, she struggled to straighten the Arab commander's tunic she had taken from Rahman's tent. She had no sandals for her feet. She had been rehearsing, for the entire year of her capture, the speech which she was about to deliver. Charles spoke a Latinized Germanic tongue. Ximena had a great gift for languages, a gift that her father recognized would have made her a much better manager of his import business than even he. She had the ability to rapidly master many of the tongues of the Mediterranean and commanded a powerful aura with her speech, especially in the company of men.

Theabald called out to him. "Sire, the prisoner is a Jewish slave girl who wishes to speak to thee."

When she reached him, Ximena looked up at Charles and waited for both horses to come to a complete stop. Peering deeply into Charles' eyes, she said slowly and loudly in Gallo Roman, "Sire, I have spent an eternity as Rahman's slave. I know the Saracens' plans. I beseech you, keep me so that I can tell you what they will do next. I know what the Arabs think. Please Sire, if you keep me I will help thee to capture all these lands and make Francia yours alone. I will be your concubine if that is what you wish. You need me."

When she said, "You need me," the sound of Ximena's voice and gaze produced an overpowering sensation that time was standing still. It also had the effect of muting the sounds of his army's mopping-up operations—the sounds of summary executions necessitated by the fact that Charles forbade the taking of slaves and by the fact that food provisions were extremely limited. Her presence was for him a profound religious experience. He surmised that the Lord had spoken to him through the vessel of this strange and beautiful slave woman.

While he looked into her eyes and into eternity, Theabald broke into his reverie, "Sire, what shall I do with this prisoner?"

"Order a rider to take her to the abbey in Tours. Tell the Abbotess that I asked that the slave girl be given residence there, and I will visit in a few days."

"Yes, Sire."

Before the soldier could lead her away, Ximena said, "Will I see you there my Lord?"

"Yes," he said as he watched her being led away, escorted to where she could be outfitted with a horse for the one-day ride to Tours.

The battle that day had raged for over twelve hours, and in that time Charles had been delivered from his purgatory of doubt, a doubt in his Christian God. Now he saw himself as the commander of men who had beaten the anti-Christ, and at the same time, saw that he had been visited by the spirit of the Lord. In a mystical fashion, the vision of this beautiful Jewish slave girl caused him to comprehend the indomitable, yet compassionate, nature of his God. He saw that the God he worshiped was the same deity worshiped by Christians and Jews, and the same God who favored his cause.

From that day forward, the Carolingian dynasty of Germanic warrior kings Charles, Pippen (his son), and Charlemagne (his grandson) consolidated a vast new Holy Roman Empire that stretched east of Pyrenees and north of the Italian Alps to the Baltic and the North Sea. It would provide a permanent bulwark against further Islamic conquest emanating from Europe's southwestern flank. Edward Gibbon wrote in *The Decline and Fall of the Roman Empire, Volume 7*, that had Charles lost at Poitiers, the boys of Oxford, in his day, would have been learning their lessons in Arabic. The nineteenth century British military historian, Edward Creasy, wrote that Poitiers was the "salvation of Europe" and that "The progress of civilization and the development of nationalities and governments of modern Europe from that time forth went forward in a not uninterrupted, but ultimately certain career." [20]

Unrelenting Islamic Jihad

As Robert Spencer points out in *Onward Muslim Soldiers,* "Jihad is the central duty of every Muslim. Modern Muslim theologians have spoken of many things as jihad: defending the faith from critics, supporting its growth and defense financially,

---

20. Sir Edward Shepherd Creasy, *The Fifteen Decisive Battles of the World: From Marathon to Waterloo,* first published in 1852, (Dover Books on History, Political and Social Science, 2008) 167.

even migrating to non-Muslim lands for the purpose of spreading Islam. But in Islamic history the doctrine of violent jihad is clear and is founded on numerous verses of the Qur'an." [21]

In the *Qur'an* (Sura 9, verse 5) the Angel Gabriel speaks these words, transmitted to the Prophet from God, "Then when the sacred months have passed, slay the idolaters wherever ye find them, and take them captive, and besiege them, and prepare for them each ambush."

By the middle of the ninth century, a consolidated Francia had blocked the Islamic armies from any further push into northern Europe. However, in the Mediterranean basin, they continued to take vast territory. By 840, the armies had conquered and plundered Sicily and the lower half of the Italian peninsula, reaching all the way to the Tiber River. The defenders of Rome prevented the Muslims from breaching the city's walls and destroying the city; however, the Arabs sacked and desecrated the graves of the early popes in the original basilica of St. Peter that was outside the city walls at that time.

Muslim armies continued to slowly and relentlessly push eastward, and by 1200 they had conquered huge portions of the Hindu world—the Punjab, Sindh, Delhi, and Doab.

Byzantium Postponed the Islamic Conquest of Europe

Justinian, who many historians regard as the last great Roman Emperor, came to the throne in Constantinople in 527 BC and ruled the Eastern Empire for thirty-eight years. (Modern historians have adopted the convention of referring to the Roman Empire of the East as Byzantium. The name is derived from the Greek fishing village, where in 330 the Emperor Constantine I had chosen to found the capital of the Roman East.) A half century after the fall of the Roman West in 476 BC, Justinian, in concert with two of history's most resourceful generals, Belisarius and Narses, conquered numerous Barbarian kingdoms. This returned to the Empire some of the lost western provinces in North Africa, Spain, and Ostrogothic Italy. It had required a twenty-year-long effort that cost the Empire dearly. Citizens of the Eastern Empire were subjected to crushing taxation to finance Justinian's wars. Many were driven to destitution.

In Justinian's defense, he assumed that his reconquest of the European provinces of the West would be a quick and profitable venture. He planned to take over their tax bases and reconstitute the former wealth of the once great Empire. But two things, which he could not have predicted, destroyed his grand plan.

---

21. Robert Spencer, *Onward Muslim Soldiers* (Washington DC: Regnery Publishing, 2003), 5.

First was the fact that the former Western Empire had morphed into a vast collection of proto-feudal estates which retained their own standing armies and which could not be easily and profitably forced to pay taxes even if their king had signed a treaty with the Romans. In fact, the lords in command of these newly reacquired barbarian baronies exacted bribes from Constantinople as payment for their supposed loyalty. Feudalism would become a permanent feature of medieval Europe precisely because it proved so successful in resisting imperialism. The reconquest of the West was very much a pyrrhic victory for Justinian, effectively impoverishing his formerly wealthy Eastern citizenry and weakening the Empire's authority over its realm.

Secondly, in 541, a horrific plague struck the Middle East and Europe. The disease approximated the black death of the Middle Ages. By 545, as many as two-thirds of the inhabitants of Constantinople had died. The plague caused a demographic collapse, drastically eroding the empire's tax base.

At the death of Justinian in AD 565, Eastern Rome's control over its reacquired African and European provinces was fiction. Outside the Balkans and Anatolia (Turkey), the nominally reacquired provinces were essentially independent and on their own. Moreover, between the years 602 and 628, the Romans and Persians exhausted themselves in near constant war. By the 630s, a decade after the Prophet's death, when the Arab armies stormed into the Christian Middle East, what they found was a vacuum of central authority. So rapid was their conquest that, by 635, the Roman Emperor, Heraclius, abandoned all of Syria. The great Christian citadels of Damascus, Antioch, and Aleppo would forever become Islamic. Over the next two decades, Jerusalem, Armenia, Egypt, and Persia also fell.

In 669, forty years after Muhammad's death, the Caliph Mu'awiyah dispatched a large army and a captured fleet of 400 ships to Dardanelles. With orders to lay siege to Constantinople and to stay for as long as it would take to bring *Rum* (Arabic for Rome) out of the *Dar al-Harb* (House of war) and into the *Dar al-Islam* (House of Islam).

Despite a five-year siege, the Byzantines won because the Romans defeated their Islamic attackers for two important reasons. First, they possessed enormous fortifications constructed by Theodosius during 378-390 BC. Second, they deployed a secret weapon—Greek fire, a petroleum-based product that was projected through high-powered siphons from the prow of their ships. Once ignited, Greek fire had adhesive properties and would even burn on water. An anonymous chronicler wrote that this extraordinary inferno, ". . . burned the ships of the Arabs and the crews alive." While the fleet was being immolated at sea, the Byzantines surprised the Arab army stationed ashore and destroyed them. Very few men who set out on the campaign returned to announce the glorious deeds of Allah's warriors.

A subsequent attack mounted against Constantinople in 717 with over four times the number of ships (1,800) and 80,000 men, had an even more disastrous outcome for the Arabs. The Muslim's failure to take the city was the first major setback for the apostles of Islam. Combined with their loss at the Battle of Poitiers fifteen years later, the three defeats represented an initial high-water mark for the Muslim conquest of Western Christendom. For the West, it was a theological victory. The age of the first great jihad was over. No Muslim armies would amass outside the walls of Constantinople for another 650 years.

Yet, had any of these three battles been won by the Muslims, the forward march of Western Civilization may well have ceased. For the next several centuries, Islam would consolidate its imperia over its vast conquests: the Middle East, North Africa, Spain, and Persia. With the certain knowledge that Muhammad's prophecy would be fulfilled—victorious Muslim armies would one day venture north to conquer Christianity, making the infidel submit to Islam.

The Rise of the Turkic Horse Archer

It was the emergence of the Turks that reawakened the spirit of jihad, oddly enough, amongst the Muslim populations that they raided in Iran and Iraq. Toward the end of the ninth century, the Turks poured out of the Steppes, the vast grasslands east of the Black Sea, which stretched to China. They were nomadic warriors and, like their Arabian forbearers, they lived by herding flocks and by raiding their neighbors. Booty was their business—cities their enemy. Their use of the bow and the mobile tactics of horse warfare gave them superiority over the settled peoples of the Muslim Empire.[22]

The Arab historian, Ibn Khaldun, romanticized the initial wave of Turkic invaders who were of the Seljuk Tribe, dubbing them the new Bedouins, much like the men of Muhammad's inner circle:

> *They always have weapons. They watch carefully all sides of the road. They take hurried naps only . . . when they are in the saddle. They pay attention to every barking and noise. Fortitude has become a quality of theirs, and courage their nature.*[23]

Around the beginning of the tenth century, the Caliph in Baghdad, seeing that the

22. Roger Crowley *1453: The Holy War for Constantinople and the Clash of Islam and the West* (New York: Hyperion, 2005), 23.

23. Ibn Khaldun, *The Muqaddimah: An Introduction to History, Volume 1*, trans. Franz Rosenthal.

Turkic invaders could become an asset, captured and enslaved large numbers of them for use in his army. While the Seljuks maintained much of their tribal identity and love of nomadic warfare, they quickly embraced the militant Islamic faith which suited their warrior ethos and sanctified plunder. Their military prowess eventually allowed them to dominate their Arab overlords in Persia. By the middle of the eleventh century, men of Seljuk-Turkic ancestry ascended to the throne in Baghdad and established a ruling dynasty over what is now the Muslim Middle East and Persia.

By the 1060s, new waves of Turkic invaders from the Steppes were traveling north of the Islamic/Seljuk Middle East and began raiding softer targets in Byzantine cities and villages throughout Anatolia (Turkey). In March 1071, the Byzantine Emperor, Romanus Diogenes, personally led an army into Anatolia in an attempt to crush the invading terrorists. However, at Manzikert, the far eastern edge of Anatolia, he encountered the excellent Seljuk army commander, Sultan Alp Arslan. The Sultan did not wish to do battle as he was on a campaign to destroy the detestable Fatimid Caliph, a Shiite dynasty ruling Egypt. Arslan offered a truce which Romanus refused. The Romans were badly defeated in the ensuing battle, due in large part to the skill and mobility of the Turkic horse archers. Romanus survived to be ransomed, deposed, blinded, and sent off to a monastery.

For the Byzantines, the Battle of Manzikert was a defeat of epic proportions, placing their empire into a near permanent decline. New Turkic invaders poured out of the Steppe, and, unopposed, ravaged farms, hamlets, and cities across Byzantine Anatolia until they reached the Mediterranean Sea. In the space of a decade, various Turkic warlords were ruling the entire peninsula. Western chroniclers of the period even began referring to the region as *Turchia*.

At its zenith, Byzantium had controlled the whole of the Eastern Roman Empire. Now it had been reduced to a few municipalities across the strait in Northern Anotolia, the City of Constantinople, Greece, and a portion of the Balkans. To make matters more desperate, some Turkish generals served on the side of some Byzantine factions involved in civil wars, which further weakened the withering empire.

The Crusades Effectively Postponed the Advance of Islam

With the Byzantine's defeat at Manzikert, the wholesale loss of Anatolia, and the loss of the Holy Land and Christianity's holiest sites in Bethlehem and Jerusalem, for the first time, the Emperor in Constantinople wrote letters and sent envoys to the Pope in Rome pleading for military assistance. In 1095, Pope Urban II preached to a crowd of knights and assorted mercenaries, adventurers, and opportunists at the city of Clermont, exhorting them to begin a reconquest of the Holy Land. With this act, the Crusades began a two hundred year counter offensive against Islam. The official objective was to recapture the holy relics and sanctuaries from the barbarian Muhammadans. Additionally, the Crusaders' mission was to capture and hold fortified cities. Jerusalem, where the Church of the Holy Sepulcher was located, was the primary target. These citadels would be taken as a means to house and protect the Christian populations which were stranded inside the now Islamic Levant and subject to the whims of their new Islamic overlords. The final objective, which proved pivotal to the salvation of the West, was to mount an effective counter offensive. From a military point of view, the crusades were successful in halting almost four hundred years of Islamic aggression against the West.

The Crusader armies, despite the long distances traveled and the difficult logistics involved in provisioning their armies, were initially successful in recapturing the once-Christian citadels of the Levant: from Edessa in the north to Antioch, Tyre, Acre, Haifa, Caesarea, and Jerusalem south to Gaza. By 1150, new Crusader monarchies and baronies were divided among four states adjacent to the eastern shore of the Mediterranean: Kingdom of Jerusalem, County of Tripoli, Principality of Antioch, and County of Edessa.

Each of these new largely autonomous kingdoms were now comprised of Christian baronies which took on the aspect of ancient Greek city-states. Together these fortress Crusader kingdoms halted Islam's advance upon Europe. For the 200 years marked by the beginning of the first Crusade until the fall of Tyre in May 1291, the last of the Crusader kingdoms, Islam did not conquer a single square mile of new lands inside Christian Europe. Additionally, while the Crusades went forward, Islam was also losing lands to Christian armies that they had controlled for centuries in Spain, Southern Italy, and Sicily.

Despite the fact that the Crusades were both effective and a perfectly justified counter measure to four hundred years of Islamic aggression, the Christian West committed sins in their own conduct. On July 15, 1099, Crusader armies breached the walls of Jerusalem and killed all its inhabitants, indifferent to age or gender.

In the most egregious act of self-flagellation in the history of Medieval Christendom, a Genoese armada headed for a crusade in Egypt detoured into the Sea of Marmara, ostensibly to be reprovisioned by their ally Constantinople. In April 1203, the Genoese armada, under Enrico Dandolo, attacked and nearly destroyed the unsuspecting city of Constantinople. For a period of nearly sixty years, the Byzantine Empire lay dismembered with various factions forming colonies in Greece and in Anatolia. It was not until 1261 that Byzantine forces recaptured the city from the Genoese and found the infrastructure in shambles.

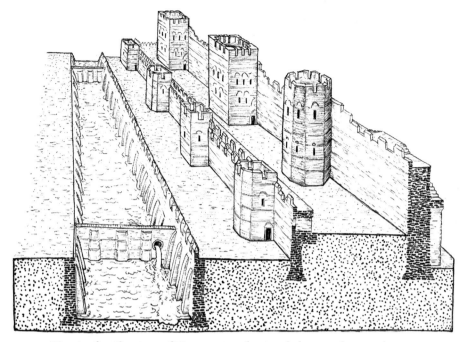

*The city fortifications of Constantinople exceeded any in human history
and protected the city for over a millennium*

To his credit the Roman Catholic Pope Benedict wrote a letter in 2010, addressed
to all members of the modern Greek Orthodox faith, and offered his sincere sorrow
for such a sinful act committed by men of his faith eight hundred years earlier.

Genghis Khan Saved Byzantium to Fight Another Day

Crowley writes, "Two years after the sack of Constantinople (by the Genoese
crusaders), a tribal leader called Temuchin succeeded in uniting the feuding nomads
of inner Mongolia into an organized war band and received the title of Genghis Khan
meaning *Universal Ruler.*" [24]

Shortly after, the Mongol hoards assumed the mantle of the most ferocious and
ruthless barbarians. They swiftly plunged a large swath of the civilized world into chaos—
ravaging Persia, parts of Syria, and Armenia on their way to Eastern Europe. As a result,
a new wave of displaced peoples flooded into Anatolia, this time fleeing the Mongol
invasion and making it a "wild west" of lawless raiders and plunderers. Some tribes were
able to capture small fleets and raided Byzantine coastal cities across the Dardanelles on
the European side. But most fought among themselves and raided one another.

---

24. *1453*, 29.

Out of this toxic soup of warring nomadic horsemen emerged the Turkic tribe warlord, Osman, who gave his name to the Ottoman Empire. During the late 1280s, Osman's tribe (nameless to history) occupied the last few remaining Byzantine cities in the far northwest corner of the Anatolian peninsula. When his tribesmen looked across the tiny Bosphorus (Istanbul Strait) that separated Asia from Europe, they saw Constantinople, the citadel of a superior culture. Its towering walls rose out of the sea, with colorful banners on top fluttering in the breeze. Huge armadas of ships were again entering and exiting the safeguarded port. The golden dome of St. Sophia, the world's largest church, shimmered in the sunlight. It was the glimmering symbol of what Islam would be when the warriors of Allah one day would make it submit to their will. According to a Turkic warlord, Osman, had a dream where he saw his ancestors would one day rule from the great citadel and it would be the capital of the world. The *hadiths* contained many allusions to its conquest, "You will certainly conquer Constantinople." ". . . excellent will be the emir and the army who will take possession of it."

Ominously, during the 1280s, in the midst of Byzantine civil wars and an ever declining tax base, the Emperor Andronikos made the suicidal decision to disband the imperial navy. This insane directive sent his unemployed sailors and ship builders to seek work with the surging Ottomans. It proved to be a catastrophic act of governmental malfeasance.

In 1302, Osman won his first battle against Byzantine forces. This brought him prestige and new recruits to his cause. With greater numbers of men, the Ottomans surrounded the city of Bursa (on the Anatolian side of the Bosphorus). Lacking siege equipment, they were able to starve out the inhabitants with a seven-year blockade, but not before Osman died.

His son, Orhan, captured the city in 1326, making it the first Ottoman capital. In 1329, Orhan defeated the hapless emperor, Andronikos III, at the city of Pelekanos, which ended Byzantine support for its last Anatolian cities. They fell in quick succession—Nicaea in 1331, Nicomedia in 1337, and Scutari the following year. Except for small isolated Christian and Jewish enclaves, Christian rule had now been expunged from both Asia and the Maghreb.

As Crowley writes, the speed with which the Ottomans gained control over the Turkic tribes of Anatolia and Syria during the 1340s seemed to the Muslim faithful as providential as the conquests by the Arabs seven centuries earlier. It seemed that this was the new era, the *Gazi*. The fabled Turkic horse archer from the Steppes, inspired by the word of Allah, would fulfill the prophesies of Muhammad. All who resisted God's chosen warriors would be conquered or destroyed. A Muslim chronicler of the period,

Ahmeti, perhaps put it best, "The Gazi is the sword of God, he is the protector and refuge of the believers. If he becomes a martyr in the ways of God, do not believe he has died—he lives in beatitude with Allah, he has eternal life."

The Fall of Constantinople

On May 29, 1453, Constantinople, the last great city of the Roman Empire, fell under the leadership of the Ottoman Sultan, Mehmet II "The Conqueror." A description from inside the city's walls that day survives—a diary of a Venetian ship's doctor, Nicolo Barbaro. He describes the last moments of Byzantine Emperor, Constantine XI, who fought beside his Greek-speaking Roman soldiers on the city's walls and was cut down in the breach. The account includes the butchery that followed. "The Turks put the city to the sword as they came, and everyone they found in their way they slashed with their scimitars, women and men, old and young, of every condition, and this slaughter continued from dawn until midday. . . . They sought out convents and all the nuns were taken to the ships and abused . . . some of them preferred to throw themselves into wells and drown." [25]

With the fall of the Roman Empire of the East in 1453, Muhammad's command to conquer Rum was heeded, his prophecy fulfilled. Islam had eliminated the Christian civilization of Byzantium. Istanbul, situated on European soil, would become the new capital of Sunni Muslims. The soft underbelly of Central Europe was now exposed, and Islam would begin its next great push to subjugate all of Europe and expunge Judeo-Christianity from existence.

Yet Western Christendom must remember that most of its

Fatih the Conqueror, with warriors of Islam. Dead Christians lie strewn in the foreground.

25. Nicolo Barbaro, *Giornale dell'Assedio di Costantinopoli 1453* (Vienna, 1856). trans. J.R. Melville Jones *Diary of the Siege of Constantinople 1453*, (New York, 1969), 320.

early saints were from the Middle East. Its greatest theologian, St. Augustine, was an Egyptian from Alexandria. St Paul was a Roman citizen born in southern Anatolia (on the today's southern Turkish coast). The West must remember the citizens of Constantinople whose government was Roman, whose faith was Orthodox Christian, and whose culture was Hellenic. They succeeded in halting the Islamic advance for seven hundred and fifty years, an accomplishment to which we owe our current way of life and our exalted standard of living. For seven, often brutal, centuries, the citizens of the Roman East guarded Europe's southeastern flank, protecting Christendom from conquest by the ruthless armies of the Islamic Middle East.

MODERN COROLLARIES

Islamic War Against the Infidel and the Ruse

On August 31, 1993, immediately after Yasser Arafat signed the Oslo Accords with Bill Clinton, a treaty that granted Israel the right to exist, Arafat flew to South Africa and addressed Muslim congregants at a Johannesburg Mosque. Speaking in Arabic, he comforted his audience, letting them know that they need not despair, that he was only implementing the "Quraysh Model." And in so doing, he was referring to what all Muslim children know from their studies of the Qur'an, the *hadiths* and the *Sira*, all of which record the Prophet's most glorious of deeds—the conquest of Mecca.

What Arafat meant by citing the "Quraysh Model" is what Muhammad's biographer, Ishaq, refers to as the Prophet's *hudna* (Arabic for truce). Hudna is, for all Muslims and for Arafat's audience, a word pregnant with meaning. It has nothing whatever to do with peace. Rather, it signifies a truce that the Muslim warrior knows his enemy will not be able to keep. Therefore a hudna (Arafat's "Quraysh Model") for Muslims is merely a ruse to make infidels believe they are safe until the warriors of Allah gather enough strength to conquer them.

Based on the example of the Prophet and the exhortations to violence in their sacred texts, in the mind of the Muslim, there is no peace with the infidel—only a temporary cessation of hostilities. Any peace treaty that the Muslims may make with the infidel is merely a truce and a ruse, which should be made with cleaver trip wires, designed to be broken when the time to strike is nigh.

Soon after his speech in Johannesburg, Arafat returned to the West Bank and launched a vicious several-year intifada where thousands of innocent Jewish civilians were killed on buses, in cafes, and in community centers. In his speech at the Johannesburg Mosque, Arafat was simply pointing out that, for modern Muslims, modeling the Prophet and his behavior was a praiseworthy trait in their ongoing war to destroy Israel. Arafat was proud of the fact that he had deceived President Clinton, the Israelis, and the Western press and couldn't resist boasting about it to his Muslim audience.

In Arabic, the word which signifies the righteousness of Muslim duplicity is *taqqiya*. Established again by the deeds of Muhammad and his followers, it refers to the Islamic precept which holds that it is not wrong to deceive or lie to the infidel. In fact, if it is necessary to lie to gain advantage over the sinful, it is mandatory. Even today's politically correct Wikipedia records that the practice of dissembling the truth before the infidel is central to the advancement of the Muslim faith:

> *"One of the few books devoted to the subject, At-Taqiyya fi'l-Islam (Dissimulation in Islam) makes it clear that taqiyya is not limited to Shi'a dissimulating in fear of persecution. Written by Sami Mukaram, a former Islamic studies professor at the American University of Beirut and author of some twenty-five books on Islam, the book clearly demonstrates the ubiquity and broad applicability of Taqiyya:*
> *'Taqiyya is of fundamental importance in Islam. Practically every Islamic sect agrees to it and practices it. . . . We can go so far as to say that the practice of Taqiyya is mainstream in Islam, and that those few sects not practicing it diverge from the mainstream. . . . Taqiyya is very prevalent in Islamic politics, especially in the modern era."*

Based on the example of the prophet's glorious deception and ultimate conquest of Mecca, Allah commands the modern Muslim to negotiate a peace with the infidel until he is strong enough to conquer him. As Robert Spencer points out, Islam is the only major religion with a developed doctrine of deception. In the Koran, Allah commands, *Take not the unbelievers for friends of helpers the unbelievers. . . . If any do that, in nothing will there be help from Allah.* (The Qur'an, surah 3, verse 28)

Al-Bukhari recorded, in his collection of *hadiths,* two statements which expand upon this commandment made by close associates of the Prophet, Abu Ad-Darda: "We smile in the face of some people although our hearts curse them." And Al-Hasan, "The Tuqyah (*taqiyyah*) is allowed until the day of Resurrection." (Sahih al-Bukhari, vol. 8)

Arguably the penultimate modern example of the Taqiyya-based ruse was Ayatollah Khomeini's seizure of Iran in 1979. His deception has enormous implications for what will befall the world if it becomes the model for the new government that will replace

Hosni Mubarak's Egypt. While Khomeini plotted an Islamist totalitarian takeover of Iran after the fall of the Shah, he reassured an easily duped the Western press. Just months before his triumphant return to Iran, he told the British Guardian, "I don't want to have the power of government in my hand."

Soon after Khomeini assumed power, vast numbers of the secularists active in the Iranian revolution were murdered or disappeared. Today, the Iranian regime is the leading sponsor of world-wide terrorism. It is developing a nuclear weapons program and an electromagnetic pulse weapon, either of which could destroy America. For the devout Muslim, the use of taqiyyah is a key tactic in his religious quest to conquer the infidel.

The Ruthlessness of Jihad

Alvin Schmidt states that today *Reliance of the Traveller: The Classic Manual of Islamic Sacred Law Umdat Al-Salik* is the primary manual for the body Islamic jurisprudence called Sharia law. It is a book which virtually all modern Sunni scholars agree is the definitive source for legal Islamic rulings. It states: "*Jihad* means to wage war against non-Muslims, and is etymologically derived from the word *mutahada*, signifying war to establish the religion." [26]

> *There are numerous references in Reliance that cite verses from the Koran which command of the devout Muslim that he wage warlike jihad against the infidel: Fighting is prescribed for you (surah 2: verse 216); Slay them wherever you find them (surah 4:verse 89); Fight the idolaters utterly (surah 9:36).*

In essence, Muslims are urged to undertake jihad against enemies, dividing the spoils of the battle among the combatants. Under its "Rules of Warfare," Islam commands that, "It is not permissible to kill woman or children unless they are fighting." But there is no prohibition against capturing, raping, or enslaving women and children which, of course, were major features of its previous conquests. [27]

One of Muhammad's most lasting legacies is his concept of *jihad*. And the essence of jihad is ruthlessness. How else can we explain Palestinian parents allowing their own children to be employed as suicide bombers? The American philosopher, Lee Harris, writes that the Islamic attack on 9/11 was an age-old attack of the ruthless.

---

26. Alvin Schmidt, *The Great Divide*: *Failure of Islam and Triumph of the West* (Boston: Regina Orthodox Press, 2004), 220.

27. Ibid, 221.

Lee observes that, "It is endemic of civilizations that they forget what it was that made them successful. Civilizations rise and fall and, in each case, the fall was not inevitable but due to decisions—or lack of decision—of the human beings whose ancestors had created the civilization for them but who had forgotten the secret of how to preserve it for their children." [28]

The Ottoman horse archers were "Restless, mobile, and tribal, and lived by herding flocks and raiding their neighbors." [29] Harris concludes that civilizations have a way of turning men into peaceful cosmopolians—the large-scale version of the peaceful community which leaves its proverbial doors unlocked and finds it hard to imagine that there still exist those ruthless enough to threaten that tranquility. And as Tony Blankley points out, "Stability is an illusion. Change is all."[30] It is civilizational forgetfulness that heightens the probability of attack, moreover *invites* it. As long as there have been peaceful civilizations to plunder, there have existed the ruthless. And only in a Hobbesian world of complete savagery are there no ruthless.

For Harris, what is the essential nature of the ruthless man? He is the one who says to his enemies of the civilized world, "I will not only risk the prospect of having to take your life in order to take from you what I want, but I will also risk the prospect of losing mine." The ruthless cannot be appealed to with reason or with the offer of mutually beneficial treaties. He only wants your submission and your assets and cannot be appeased.

After the horrors of World War I, the Second World War saw the loss of sixty million lives. Thirty years later, the Soviet Union raised the stakes of ruthlessness even higher with its Brezhnev Doctrine which maintained that the Soviets would defend any possession, no matter how small or insignificant, with the full weight of their nuclear arsenal.

Although the modern jihadists employ ruthlessness as their primary tactic, it is much older than Islam. It emanates from the darkest aspects of human nature and man's loyalty to the small band of warriors, a massively powerful urge transmitted by DNA from tribal millennia, an urge which fuels human martial spirit, good or perverse. Very small bands of ruthless thugs have always been able to take over very large submissive peaceful civilizations. In the twentieth century alone, small bands of Brown Shirts captured Germany and a small, yet committed, cell of Bolsheviks,

28. Lee Harris, *Civilization and Its Enemies: The Next Stage of History*, (New York: Free Press, 2004), XVIII

29. *1453*, 24.

30. Tony Blankley, *The West's Last Chance: Will We Win the Clash of Civilizations?* (Washington DC: Regnery Publishing, 2005), 22.

Russia. Harris writes, "We may blame ruthlessness on someone's upbringing or culture or economic status. We never dream of identifying it for what it is—a strategy that works." [31]

When Muhammad was ostracized from his home city of Mecca and sought refuge in Medina, he had only seventy adherents. Ten years later, he ruled the entire Arabian subcontinent. He was the utterly ruthless warlord who successfully took over the rule of a largely submissive population precisely because he could not be appeased.

As Robert Spencer puts it, "The Qur'an and its prophet are guides for Muslims and valid for all time. To admit any shame at the exploits of Muhammad would be to judge Muhammad." [32] In our attempts to understand the nature and gravity of the threat we face, we need to confront the reality of Muhammad's life together with Islam's central creed which, based on his example, canonizes *ruthlessness* in the spread of Islam.

In the late 1930s, Neville Chamberlain embarked on a policy of appeasement of Adolf Hitler, desperately hoping that his diplomacy would dissuade the Fuehrer from his dream of conquering Europe. His policy of appeasement invited Hitler's invasion precisely because Chamberlain violated the following immutable law:

IMMUTABLE #3
Appeasement of a ruthless outside power always invites aggression.
Treaties made with ruthless despots are always fruitless and dangerous.

Over the last several decades, too many American leaders have demonstrated a spectacular blindness to history's warnings. They seemed unaware that, during the seventh and eighth centuries, nearly the whole Christian Middle East was expunged by a ruthless wave of pitiless Islamic armies. And they clearly didn't understand that ruthlessness cannot be appeased. Consider the Oslo Accords which President Clinton negotiated with Yasser Arafat, the father of modern Islamic terrorism. The entire process gave Islamic terrorists everywhere legitimacy and was an abject act of appeasement.

During the final eighteen months of Bill Clinton's beleaguered presidency, Arafat met with the President of the United States more often than all other heads of state *combined*, so desperate was Clinton to leave office with the legacy of having brokered a Middle East peace. In the final hours of Clinton's presidency, Arafat telephoned Clinton to tell him he was a "great man." Clinton recounts in his own memoirs that he

---

31. Harris, *Civilization's Enemies*, 66.
32. Robert Spencer, *Islam Unveiled* (Encounter Books, 2002), 56.

responded vehemently saying, "I am not a great man, I am a failure, and you have made me one." [33]

As President of the United States and leader of the free world, Clinton should have known that, in the person of Arafat, he had been duped into endless and utterly fruitless negotiations by an implacable, ruthless Islamic enemy. He did not understand until it was too late to save his place in history.

Similarly, shortly after his inauguration, President Obama sent what he hoped would be a private letter of appeasement to the Iranian government. As Dore Gold, former Israeli ambassador to the United Nations, stated in a 2009 interview he gave with a San Francisco radio station, the letter was exposed when Iranian President Mahmoud Ahmadinejad publicly wrote back, "We say to you that you are in a position of weakness. Your hands are empty. You can no longer promote your interests from a position of strength." As Gold explained, "What the administration saw as a magnanimous gesture was seen as total weakness by the regime in Tehran."

Well before the city-states of Greece fell to the Macedonians in 343 BC, the attempt at appeasement had been an attending factor in the fall of many civilizations. The fall of the Christian Middle East came about because it was attacked by a ruthless outside aggressor *which could not be appeased.*

The House of Permanent Internal War

On June 17, 656, just twenty-four years after the death of Muhammad, Ali ibn Abi Talib, Muhammad's cousin and the husband of his daughter Fatima, and a group of rebel soldiers from Medina, murdered the *Khalifa* (successor in Arabic) Uthman while he sat reading the Qur'an. Ali, who had been waiting impatiently in the wings to become Muhammad's successor, proclaimed himself Caliph. In May 660, Mu'awiyah, a governor of Syria, declared Ali unfit to rule and declared himself ruler of all Islamic lands which included the Levant, Arabia, and Egypt. That year Ali was stabbed to death in the mosque in Kufa. This consolidated Mu'awiyah's power and made him the first of the Umayyad caliphs and the first caliph to send an army to attack Constantinople. The murder of Ali and the resulting schism between the Islamic Shiites and Sunnis proved to be of incalculable importance as it pertains to the survival of the West, even to this day.

In 660, most Muslims swore their allegiance to Mu'awiyah. They followed the sunna, the way of the Prophet, and became Sunni. Those who followed Ali came to be called *Shi at Ali* (the party of Ali) or Shiites. As we will see in *The Fall of the Ottomans*,

---

33. John F. Harris, *Ties that Bind* (*The Smithsonian*, September, 2005), 22.

the never ending war between the two houses of Islam would serve to prevent the Ottoman Empire from conquering the Hapsburg Empire in 1683 and quite possibly the whole of Europe. Had the armies assembled outside the walls of Vienna been composed of *both* Ottomans and Persians, the saga of Western Civilization may have ended there.

In 2010, while Iran feverishly continued its nuclear weapons development, copies of high-level cables stolen by an American low-level military operative were distributed to the world-wide media by an Australian website, WikiLeaks.org. Among the thousands of pirated communiqués were those sent from Arab diplomats to the American government requesting American military action against Iran. These demonstrated that the Sunni monarchs and dictators in Egypt, Jordan, and Saudi Arabia feared Iran far more than they feared or hated Israel.

To survive the threat of a resurgent militant Islam, the West must strive to keep Islam at war with itself. It must encourage, give aid and sanctuary to those forces inside Islam who will stand up and fight those among them who long for the seventh century. The West must take advantage of Islam's penchant for internal war and actively support reformers who will fight those who believe in the Islamic conquest and domination of the infidel. Given the enormous population of Muslims worldwide, Islamic ruthlessness must be destroyed from within. We in the West must seek to destabilize those factions in the Islamic world that seek to destabilize and destroy us.

Immutable #4
*If a people cannot avoid continuous internal warfare,
it will have a new order imposed from without.*

CHAPTER FIVE

The Fall of the Ottoman Empire

1918

The salvation of the West may again
rely on Islam's penchant for overreaching.
BERNARD LEWIS

On September 12, 1683, for the first time in over two hundred years, the Ottoman Empire suffered a crushing defeat by European armies while attempting to conquer even more lands for Allah. With their defeat at the battle of Vienna, the Ottoman empire inexorably began to contract, culminating with its dismemberment at the end of World War I.

Bin Laden did not pick a random date for his attacks on the World Trade Center, the Pentagon, and the US capital. As a pious Muslim, he knew the Islamists' version of history. September 11 was, and is, a very important anniversary for the new *mujahedin*.[1]

On September 11, 1683, Islam reached an important high-water mark. It was the actual *day* when the Ottoman Caliphate ruled the largest portion of the European continent, and the largest number of European infidels were subject to its administration. The king of Poland, Jan Sobieski, in command of European allied armies, defeated a vastly larger Muslim invading army at Vienna and began the nearly uninterrupted decline of the Ottoman Empire.

Bin Laden's selection of that specific day was his signal to Muslims worldwide, who also knew the significance of the anniversary, that Islam would resume its holy conquest of the infidel and reassert its rightful rule over the West. The attacks would right the wrong committed 318 years earlier.

---

1.   Muslim fighters, from the same Arabic root as *jihad* meaning to struggle.

There are a number of hadiths which quote Muhammad as issuing prophesies that Islam would one day conquer Constantinople, "Excellent will be the emir and the army who will take possession of it." [2] There are others who refer to the fact, according the words of Allah, Islam would conquer all of *Rum* (Arabic for Rome and meaning all of the West). For the illiterate, semi-barbarous Bedouins who followed Muhammad, the City of Constantinople had a profound gravitational pull.

For these men of the Middle Kingdom of the seventh century, Constantinople was a dazzling symbol of a great civilization, possessed of wealth, refinement and prestige, whose domains stretched far beyond their comprehension. The conquest of *Rum* was more a concept for the Bedouins than a single military target. Their goal of conquering the lands of *Rum* has essentially remained unchanged.

To this day, Muslims wish to conquer the West because they know their culture is inferior. They fervently want to fullfil the prophesies of Muhammad and the commands of their sacred texts. Their desire to conquer the infidel is a means to achieve a practical objective. This primal urge can be summed up by the fact their culture could not even produce the cell phones on which they plot to kill us.

The Makings of Modern Islamic Rage

Despite the commands of the Qur'an to conquer the unbeliever, from the late seventeenth century battle of Vienna to the present, the Islamic world has lost its empire and has fallen further and further behind the West in terms of wealth and technological advancement. In 1560, the ambassador, Ogier de Busbecq, wrote to his boss, the Holy Roman Emperor, "When the Turks are finished with Persia, they will fly at our throats, supported by the might of the whole East."[3] The ambassador also noted, that while the Ottomans had begun to copy Western weapon designs, *they printed no books* including their own Qur'an. In fact, they didn't employ clocks, watches, or standard weights and measures. Strangely, the ambassador noted, the Ottomans seemed to have made a conscious decision not to educate their own populace.

This prescription for self-imposed illiteracy still commands wide acceptance by the Islamic world today. It is creating a collective rage among Muslims, who witness, via an ubiquitous Western media, a vast technological/prosperity gap between the West and those who follow the path of Islam.[4]

---

2.   Muhammad al-Bukhari, *Sahih al-Bukhari* (from his collection of hadiths, collected and originally published around 860).

3.   *The Turkish Letters of Ogier de Busbecq, Imperial Ambassador at Constantinople,* trans. Edward Seymour Foster (Oxford, 1927), 112.

4.   A gap that President Obama apologizes for and seems determined to close.

In an extremely uncharacteristic act of self-examination, a consortium of researchers commissioned by the twenty-two member Arab League in 2002, produced the report *Arab Human Development*. The report found that in 1999, all twenty-two Arab countries translated *only* 330 books, one-fifth the number of Greece. Consequently, the report noted, non-petroleum-based exports from all twenty-two Arab nations were below that of tiny Finland. Therefore it's easy to imagine that when the Western world inevitably converts from a combustion-engine/petroleum-based economy to one based on a new energy paradigm, the Arab world will devolve back to something approximating the seventh century, to that medieval time that the militant Islamists tell us they so long for.

Princeton University's Professor Bernard Lewis, described as "the doyen of Middle Eastern studies," provides a very pointed answer to why most of the Muslim world elected not to participate in the Enlightenment and the resulting industrial and technological revolutions.[5] He writes for the Muslim:

> *"All problems are ultimately religious and all final answers therefore religious. The final answers (to problems) given by traditional writers were always to go back to our roots, to the good old ways, to the true faith, to the word of God... (but) compared to Christendom, the world of Islam had become poor, weak, and ignorant. And the primacy and therefore the dominance of the West was clear for all to see, invading the Muslim in every aspect of his public and—more painfully—even his private life."[6]*

Due to the worldwide reach of Western media and the internet, well before 9/11 and long before the Middle East erupted in revolution, the superiority of the West could no longer be hidden by Muslim monarchs and dictators. It was obvious for even the lowliest of their subjects to see. The centuries-old prescriptions "go back to the old ways" and "trust in the word of God" had clearly failed. The Muslim world was destitute and weak. So for Lewis, and other Middle Eastern observers, it is this sense of failure and loss of empire, combined with supremacist religious texts, that causes the Muslim to experience a cognitive dissonance resulting in collective rage. This rage has caused many to burn down embassies, riot over the publication of cartoons, and attack Western institutions.

---

5. Bernard Lewis, FBA, is a British-American historian, scholar in Oriental studies, and political commentator. He is the Cleveland E. Dodge Professor Emeritus of Near Eastern Studies at Princeton University. He specializes in the history of Islam and the interaction between Islam and the West. He is especially famous in academic circles for his works on the history of the Ottoman Empire.

6. Bernard Lewis, *What Went Wrong* (Oxford University Press, 2002), 43, 151.

Assigning Blame to Keep Control over Muslim Populations

Professor Lewis writes that it has long been a feature of Islamic thought to assign blame to external forces to explain its reverses in fortune both past and present. Beginning in the 17th century, as their empire ceased expanding and their territories began to be stripped away, the favorite scapegoats were the Mongols. The 13th century invasions were seen by Islamic chroniclers as the underlying cause for a coarsening of their once superior civilization. This belief, however, fell prey to common sense.

Later Islamic texts show a rise in nationalism that was imported from Europe. In this construct, Arab chroniclers blamed the decline of the Islamic world on the profligate rule of their overlords, the Turks. The Turkish commentators blamed the loss of their ancient glories on the "dead weight of Arab past." After the fall of Vienna and the resulting military losses that proceeded throughout the 18th and 19th centuries, Ottoman commentators and historians assigned blame to various indigenous ethnic groups.

With the British and French conquests and the colonization of much of the Middle East during the 19th and 20th centuries, Muslim chroniclers, and later newspapers, came up with a new and more plausible scapegoat to assuage Muslim pain—Western Imperialism. This contains enough irony to be laughable. Clearly it had not occurred to past or present mainstream Muslims that their conquests of Western Christendom, Turkey, Syria, Palestine, Egypt, North Africa, Spain, southern Italy, and central Europe were anything but positive? Given the warlike example of the Prophet, and the violent commands of the Qur'an, how could their conquest be anything other than a beneficent method of showing the infidel the true way?[7]

The domination of the Middle East by the British and the French was brief—less than fifty years in the late 19th and early 20th century. During their period of subjugation, living standards for most Muslims remained squalid. Their overall subservience to the West has, until very recently, remained a constant, even after the European rulers departed. Ironically, while hatred for the West continues to be encouraged by state-owned Muslim media, Muslim states have been uniformly happy to accept our assistance in developing their oil fields and to receive our foreign aid.

For a period after World War II, Middle Eastern rage against imperialism was transferred from its former Anglo-French rulers to the hegemonic influence of the US. With the collapse of the Ottoman Empire at the close of the First World War, the Islamic world suffered further humiliation due to its universal support for both the Axis Powers in World War II and the Soviets during the Cold War.[8]

---

7. See aggressive warlike verses of the Qur'an cited in chapter *The Fall of the Christian Middle East.*
8. Wikipedia.

For the most part throughout the Middle East, the real "demonic" source for Islam's appalling state of decline, according to Muslim journalists and intellectuals, is the same force that is behind the economic and military power of the hegemonic United States—the Jews. This mainstream thought is preached to children in the madrassas, taught to students at leading Middle Eastern universities, and espoused by state-run Islamic news organizations. The prevalence of an abject, murderous anti-Semitism was made clear for all to see when Iranian head of state, Ahmadinejad, continuously threatened to "wipe Israel off the map." Yet not one Muslim leader nor Islamic ambassador to the UN ever issued a single condemnation of him for his repeated threats of genocide. Tragically, it became clear. Too many in the Muslim world agree with Ahmadinejad when he refers to Israel as the "little Satan" and the US as the "Great Satan."

The Ottomans' Continued Rise After the Conquest of Constantinople

For over a millennium, since the time when Muhammad's seventh-century successors first rode out of the Arabian Peninsula, Islam has waged constant war against the unbelievers and taken lands for Allah. By 1500, the Sunni branch of Islam, administered by the Ottomans, ruled lands from Syria and Iraq, across the Magreb to the Atlantic. And on the European mainland, it ruled all of Greece and the Balkans. By 1529, the Ottomans began their first siege of the imperial Christian capital of Vienna and were not successful in taking the city. They lost that battle because the Sultan, Selim "the Grim," was temporarily distracted from his conquest of Europe, feeling obliged to wage wars against his Islamic rivals both in Egypt and in Persia.

Selim's armies fought Persia to a stalemate. They were victorious against the Mamluks of Egypt, incorporating within the Turkish Ottoman Empire, Egypt, and the holy citadels of Islam, Medina, and Mecca.[9] Most important for the ultimate survival of Europe, *Persia remained an enemy of the Ottomans.*

As Bernard Lewis writes in *What Went Wrong*, [from 1500 onward] "The Ottomans and the Persians continued to fight each other until the 19th century. By that time they no longer constituted a threat to anyone except their own subjects." [10]

Lewis points out that, during those 180 years leading up to the battle of Vienna in 1683, various and successive Persian Shahs and ambassadors made overtures to the monarchs in the West—the Pope, the Dodge of Venice, the Holy Roman Emperor, and the Queen of England—seeking an alliance with them and against the Ottomans,

9.   Phillip K. Hitti, Professor Emeritus, Princeton University, *History of the Arabs, From the Earliest Times to the Present* (London: Macmillan & Co., sixth edition, 1956), 710.

10. Bernard Lewis, *What Went Wrong* (Oxford University Press, 2002), 9.

but to no avail. The Western powers were too busy fighting wars among themselves. Fortunately for us moderns living in the West now, the Sunni Ottomans and the Shiite Persians were also at war with one another and not united in the conquest of Europe.

By 1526, under the Sultan, Suleyman the Magnificent, the Ottomans immobilized the Persians and embarked on the conquest of the West. In that year, at the battle of Mohacs, Islam conquered portions of Hungary. Three years later, in 1529, Suleyman's armies attempted to conquer Vienna in what was then seen as the struggle for the mastery of Europe. Although the Ottomans lost, they were not destroyed and viewed the setback only as a delay, not a defeat.[11]

Later in 1571, the Ottomans suffered an enormous defeat at the maritime battle of Lepanto. The Turkish ruling elite at the court in Constantinople passed it off as only a *naval* battle. As the Muslims saw it, they still ruled the land where taxes could be levied and slaves taken. They underestimated the significance of the Europeans' new war ships which were built on a more massive scale than those of the Islamics'. European shipping was now global. They piloted more technologically sound ships, and, in one battle, nearly destroyed *the entire Ottoman navy*. Yet the Islamic sources of the 1570s record that few in the capitals of Islam were worried because they still controlled the land. As Bernard Lewis puts it, "Turkish pashas were ruling Budapest and Belgrade, and Barbary Corsairs from North Africa were still raiding the coasts of England and Ireland." [12] In the Ottomans' view, the naval battle of Lepanto was merely a setback in Islam's inevitable march to complete domination of the infidel.

Life for Non-Muslims in Islamic Europe

For the next 112 years (1571-1683), the Ottomans ruled a vast and wealthy empire which included millions of ruthlessly subjugated Europeans. Due to the current embrace of multiculturalism by many in the American media and academia, it has been established as conventional wisdom, through a relentless campaign of historical revisionism, that Islamic rule in Europe was tolerant of its non-Muslim minorities. But as John Schindler puts it his book, *Unholy Terror*, ". . . the truth is darker and more complex." [13]

Schindler spent a great deal of time in the Balkans, in the nineties, as an undercover agent for the National Security Agency and knows the Balkans and their history. He points out that the Ottomans strictly observed the aspect of Islam that describes any portion of the world outside Muslim rule as the *dar al-harb* which translates—land

---

11. Ibid, 11.

12. Ibid, 11.

13. John Schindler, *Unholy Terror: Bosnia, Al-Qaida and the Rise of Global Jihad* (Zenith Press, 2007), 21.

of war. European Muslims today still refer to non-Muslims as *harbi*, by definition, the enemy. Christian subjects living inside Muslim Europe were also dhimmi, which Schindler defines as "the unbeliever who submits to Islam, accepts Muslim protection, and pays the poll tax to the Muslim state."[14] The poll tax, called the *jizya*, was oppressive and was imposed even on widows and orphans. Moreover, dhimmis were required to wear a parchment on their clothing that proved they had paid the latest tax, a demeaning practice later adopted by Nazi Germany.

The dhimmi natives living in the Balkans or elsewhere in the Ottoman Empire were not second-class citizens as we modern Westerners understand the term because they had *no rights.* According to the Muslim legal code, sharia law, dhimmis had no legal standing in courts of law. They could not bear fire arms. They could not testify against Muslims because, by definition, they were deemed untrustworthy. Hence Muslims could commit crimes against dhimmis with impunity. Due to Islam's repressive sexual taboos, a common offense was rape. If a Christian or Jew was accused of blasphemy, a Muslim accusation could not be countered and the penalty was death. Marriage or sex between Muslim women and dhimmi men was punishable by death for both parties. But the converse was not true. Muslims often took dhimmi women, employing coercive tactics, and converted them through forced marriage. As testament to their contempt for their non-Muslim subjects, any Muslim who converted to the faith of the "inferiors" would be killed. Shockingly to most Westerners is the fact that apostasy was and still is a capital crime, punishable by death, in much of the Muslim world, in Saudi Arabia, and even in countries we have liberated, such as Afghanistan.[15]

Schindler found out from his years in the Balkans,

> *"The most hated aspect of Ottoman rule was the one . . . whose memory lingers most sharply, even today, and was the practice of devshirme— the blood tax imposed on Christians. . . . The Ottomans annually levied male children as tribute, every year up to one-fifth of Christian boys in Bosnia—usually aged fourteen to twenty were forcibly taken from their families . . . and shipped to the imperial court in Istanbul to become warrior-slaves in the Janissaries, the sultan's elite guard. . . . The annual*

14. Ibid.

15. The death sentence for apostasy is a universal feature of sharia law which no scholar of Islamic jurisprudence disputes given the numerous references to it in the Qur'an and in the hadiths. The Prophet said, "Whoever changed his Islamic religion, kill him, Sahih Al-Bukhari 84:2:57. Citations from the Sunni version of sharia law make the condemnation of apostasy a cornerstone of Islamic thought, stating that "when a person who has reached puberty and is sane voluntarily apostates from Islam, he derves to be killed. *Reliance of the Traveller, 081.1, 08.4.*

*levy became a focus of horror among Bosnian Christians. At a fixed
date, every father had to gather his sons in the main square of the local
village and allow the authorities to select the best to be sent away . . .
resistance brought instant death . . . some fathers disfigured their sons to
prevent their enslavement."* [16]

Muslim rule of Europe, for its European subjects, was brutal. In other parts of
non-Islamic Europe during the Ottomans' zenith, whole fishing villages on both the
Mediterranean and Atlantic coasts would disappear, captured by landing parties of
Islamic pirate slave traders whose harvests of men women and children would arrive in
the bustling slave markets of Tripoli, Cairo, or Constantinople.

The Struggle for the Mastery of Europe

By 1676, the Ottoman Sultan Mohammad IV (aka Mehmed IV) had appointed
his son-in-law, Mustafa Pasha, to be Grand Vizier. This position in the Ottoman
capital of Istanbul embodied the equivalent of a supreme commander of the armies,
a secretary of state, and chief of staff. Mustafa earned the endearing moniker of Kara
(Dark) Mustafa for his cruelties. In the early spring of 1683, Mohammad IV the Sultan,
mustered an army of 270,000 combatants and, with a huge entourage of attendants
and camp followers, he personally led a march of a half million men from the city
of Adrianople north to Belgrade. There, in the Serbian/Islamic capital of Belgrade,
Mustafa the Dark took full command of the enormous throng with orders to march
north through Hungary and not to return until Vienna had fallen and the head of the
Hapsburg Holy Roman Emperor, Leopold, was severed and delivered to the Sultan.

On his way north through the Hungarian countryside, Mustafa met little
resistance while his army laid waste to the villages, plundering them and taking large
numbers of slaves, particularly women. Meanwhile the Hapsburg Emperor, Leopold,
sent urgent messages to the King of Poland, Jan III Sobieski, pleading with him for
help. [17]

It had been one hundred and fifty years since the Ottomans had besieged the

---

16. Ibid, 23.

17. Fifteen years earlier, in 1673, General Jan Sobieski defeated the Ottomans in their bid to conquer his
homeland in the battle of Chocim. While the joyous news of that battle spread across their country,
Poles learned that their beloved king, Michal Korybut Wiśniowiecki, had died one day before the
battle. This made Sobieski the most popular person in the state. The following year, on May 19, he
was elected the new monarch of the Polish Commonwealth. Jan Sobieski was crowned Jan III,
King of Poland, February 2, 1676. On the eve of the battle for Vienna, he was still capable of leading
his people in battle at fifty.

city. Mustafa was now in command of a far larger and better equipped army in this, the second attempt at taking Vienna. It would again be left to the Hapsburgs of the Austrian Holy Roman Empire and whatever allies they could muster to prevent the rest of Europe from coming under Islamic rule. The European Christians were outnumbered. The Ottomans controlled a population (and tax base) of fourteen million while Spain contained five million and England only two and a half million subjects. With the fall of the Hapsburgs and Vienna, the vast heartland of Europe would be vulnerable to conquest.

By the time the armies of the Grand Vizier Mustafa reached the Austrian flatlands beneath the walls of Vienna in the summer of 1683, Muslim and European chroniclers recorded that the defeat of Europe by the Ottomans seemed inevitable. This would be the Western infidels' last stand. We know from Turkic records that the Ottoman Sultan, Mohammad IV, believed that one more victory over the infidel could mean the death of Christendom. This final conquest and destruction of Christendom, which seemed so close at hand in 1683, represented for him a divinely inspired work still unfinished for the followers of the Prophet.

Just days before Mustafa's army arrived at the walls of Vienna, the Austrian Emperor Leopold and his following of sixty thousand Austrian nobility fled, leaving only a garrison of eleven thousand men under its governor, Stahremberg. and Polish general, Lubomirski, to defend the city. On the day the huge Turkish army arrived, it surrounded the walled city, and began to construct its siege operations. Three horsemen rode out onto the flat plain in front of the city's main gate, set up a small catapult, and began firing messages attached to rocks into the city. Each read "Surrender now and you will be saved. Open your gates and turn your churches over to us. If you resist the will of Allah, your leaders will be killed and your women and children sold into slavery. Fight and you die! Surrender and you live!"

The bombardment of Vienna began June 1683. A great many of the defenders were killed over the long and horrible summer of that year.

The Battle for Vienna (Depicted in Historic Fiction)

In mid-August, Sobieski received, at the palace in Warsaw, an emissary, the papal legate, Cardinal Pentucci. His message sent from the Pope in Rome was dire—the survival of Christianity was dependent upon what Poland would do now. In expanding upon the contents of the Pontiff's letter, the Cardinal was forceful and blunt.

"Jan, child of 'God, if you do not help us, the church will suffer and perhaps even vanish. I must also remind you that Poland will vanish, and most cruelly. If you think Turkish occupation of Hungary is brutal, think of what it will be like if Turkey takes Poland. They will remember the humiliating defeats you visited upon them at Podhajce and Chocim. The Sultan remembers and will avenge them in strange and terrible ways. You who aroused Turkey are not free to stop the battle now. If Vienna falls, Krakow and Warsaw will be next and we shall never see Poland again."[18]

Understanding that Vienna could soon fall, Sobieski hurriedly mustered an army of fifty-eight thousand of his countrymen and began the march south to meet Moustapha. In route, he was joined by dukes of Lorraine and independent German duchies whose musters swelled the ranks of the allies to one hundred and nine thousand. Still, the Christians would be outnumbered by the Muslims roughly three to one, not counting those destitute defenders still alive inside Vienna. By the time Sobieski began his march, some of the defenders on the broken walls of Vienna were women and children.

While the Polish king and his allies marched toward Vienna, Moustapha did not realize that he was losing control of his army. With many breaches in the walls of the city, his generals, as well as his rank and file Islamic warriors, knew that, if all their army was commanded to attack, it could easily overwhelm the city. Yet Moustapha refused them the opportunity of an all-out assault. He kept a large portion of his army, including the entire Tartar cavalry, away from the siege, bombardment, and undermining operations. He did this out of personal monumental greed. His harem consisted of fifteen hundred concubines, attended by twice as many servants. His household was guarded by seven hundred black eunuchs. His servants, horses, and cattle numbered in the thousands. Due to this payroll, he needed a way to personally extract huge sums of wealth from Ottoman conquests. Therefore, he did not want his army to storm Vienna because he wanted the city to capitulate. This way he alone, not the army, would control the treasure and the captives inside the city walls. If the city fell to two hundred and seventy thousand Islamic fighters, its treasure and slaves would fall into their hands. He needed a way for it to fall into his hands alone. In short, it was due to this one man's epic greed that the fall of all Islam began.

Late in the afternoon of September 11, 1683, Jan Sobieski, King of Poland, reached an opening near the summit of Mount Kahlemberg with a retinue of his mounted generals and their elite bodyguards. This allowed them to look

18. James A. Michener, *Poland* (New York: Random House, 1983), 141. For the battle of Vienna sequence, the author is greatly in debt to this brilliant and very important historical research.

down upon the fortress of Vienna, see the enormous Turkish encampment with its several thousand brightly colored tents, the majestic Danube meandering off over the horizon, and the city's vast surrounding farmlands.

Mounted beside him in ceremonial battle armor reminiscent of Roman mounted generals were: Charles the Duke of Lorraine with 28,000 Austrians; Prince Waldeck with 23,000 Bavarians, Thuringians, and Saxons from surrounding German states; Count Alecksander Olesko from Sobieski's home town in the Ukraine, and Krystoff Jonare from Lithuania. Each man commanded an army mustered from his respective homeland. With Poland, the Ukraine and Lithuania a single commonwealth, Sobieski and his allied generals represented an imposingly large portion of Central Europe.

What Sobieski could not tell his allies was that Poland was nearly bankrupt. After fifty years of constant warfare with the invading Muslims and their Tartar allies, the Polish treasury was nearly depleted, so much so that the young king feared he might not be able to continue provisioning and paying his army. But Jan Sobieski was an incredibly resourceful general.

And for a few moments, as he studied the Turks' encampment and siege operations below, the highlights of his life, leading to this moment, flowed across his consciousness. After graduating from Nowodworski College in Krakow in 1646, he and his brother, Marek, spent two years traveling in Western Europe where he learned French, German, and Italian in addition to his Latin. His language skills would later prove vital to his military career. In 1648 war broke out with invading Turks and Tartars, when he was only nineteen. He

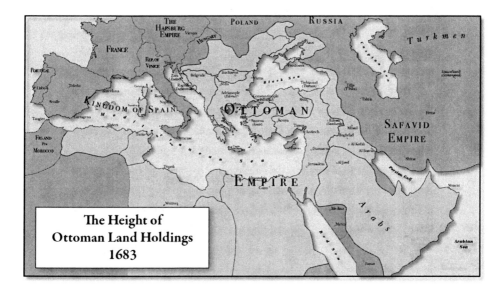

The Height of Ottoman Land Holdings 1683

and his brother were recalled by the Polish King John II Casimir and given small commands. They fought battles at Chmielnicki and Zborow and recaptured the fortress cities for Poland. Jan distinguished himself, and sadly his beloved brother was captured and died in Turkish captivity. After commanding a larger regiment at the Battle of Beresteczko, King John sent him to Constantinople as an envoy, part of a Polish delegation which negotiated a treaty with the Ottomans that was nothing more than a cease-fire. There the young emerging military prodigy spent his time intensely studying the Turkish language, war methods, and tactics.

In the 1650s, during a lull in the fighting along the Polish/Turkish fronts, Sobieski rose to the highest ranking field commander in Poland. In 1666, war was renewed as the Turks once again resumed their relentless attempt to conquer Poland, a conquest which the Muslims saw as their right and duty. This time Sobieski led the entire Polish army to a victory at Podhajce in 1667. And it was with this victory that he became recognized as the first and only European commander who could be relied upon to consistently defeat Turkish invaders in land battles. Since Islam had begun its conquest of Western Christendom in the seventh century, eight hundred years earlier, Sobieski's continued and sustained military success against the Muslims was unprecedented.

About this time, Islamic chroniclers were beginning to refer to Sobieski as the Lion of Lehistan (their term for Poland). Five years later, in 1673, as commander-in-chief under the Polish King Michael, he defeated the Turks, yet again, at the battle of Chocim, recapturing the ancient fortress for Poland. On the very day of the battle, the King died. When news of Sobieski's victory spread throughout the country, he was universally seen by the Poles as their nation's savior. Six months later, he was elected king by the Polish diet (term for congress/assembly). He was forty-seven.

Over the next seven years, Sobieski's reign saw constant warfare with the Turks along Poland's southern border. During this time, he was able to hold most of the fortress cities. More important, he spent the time completely reforming the Polish military, replacing the infantryman's pike with battle axes, creating two classes of cavalry—the dragoons and hussars, and creating greater firepower from his artillery. He sensed that a massive invasion by the Ottomans of Poland was inevitable. As he looked down upon the Ottoman encampment, he knew that God had guided him and directed him to this moment.

As the sun was beginning to set, bathing the panorama below in an increasingly soft yellow light, he sat motionless on his horse, peering through his hand-held telescope at the Tartar operations and camp below. At length, his observations caused him to feel an immeasurable elation. He estimated that the Ottomans' vast sprawling camp contained over a half million souls. Yet incredibly, there were no defenses built and no breastworks. Even bridges across the Danube were still standing and leading into the camp while everything seemed in confusion. What he could not see was that there were also three thousand Tartar cavalrymen encamped behind a dense stand of trees two miles south of the Turkish camp. Finally, after a very long silence, he said to his generals, whose horses were now arrayed behind his, "This commander knows nothing of war; we shall certainly defeat him." [19]

"My king, we are outnumbered three to one, are we not?" asked Krystoff, the Lithuanian general.

"Over half that camp are eunuchs, cooks, slaves, and harem girls. And they will create chaos when we breach Turks' defenses," Sobieski said as he pointed one hand toward the valley below. He glanced back toward the Turkish encampment for a few moments, and turned to his generals, "Do the Turks know that we are here?"

"They do," said Alecksander as the other generals nodded in agreement. And while darkness began to gather around them, Sobieski began querying his generals regarding their armies' readiness to carry out his battle plan. Then a mounted adjutant appeared, carrying a note for the commander. As the boy and his horse breathed hard from their long ride up the trail, he handed the note to the powerfully-built, fifty-five year old King of Poland.

The note was from the Polish General Lubomirski who commanded the defenders inside Vienna. It said, "We are so heartened to learn that you, the Christian allies, have arrived. I have sent one of my most trusted aids out a secret subterranean exit with the hope that he could slip through the Turkish lines to deliver this urgent message. Yesterday, as I stood in front a small home at 22 Anna Gasse Strasse, I was shocked to hear the distinct sounds of engineers (sappers) chipping away underground, several hundred yards inside the city's walls. There must be a honeycomb of tunnels under the city by now. We cannot know how long before they install the gunpowder charges and the city begins to explode."

Sobieski read the note and spent a few moments digesting its meaning, and

---

19. Alexander Hidden, *The Ottoman Dynasty* (Nicholas H. Hidden, 1912), 221.

said to his generals, "The Muslims' undermining operations are nearly complete.[20] The city might soon fall. We cannot afford to wait. We attack tomorrow."

That evening, Moustapha also called a war council of his generals to issue his battle plan. Inside his sumptuous tent, complete with separate apartments to house his multiple bedrooms and a large harem, Khan Murad, the commander of the Tartars, was among those summoned by Moustapha to receive their orders for the coming battle. The Grand Vizier told his generals that the battle was to commence in the morning and that it was sure to be the greatest Islamic victory since the Prophet conquered Mecca. He informed his generals that the sappers had been ordered to bring the charges into the tunnels, to detonate them, and to collapse the walls in the morning. As soon as the walls fell, the Janissaries would then take the city. The Turkish army and Tartar cavalry would repel and defeat the Poles and Germans. "Tomorrow is the day, you, the armies of Allah, will conquer two infidel kingdoms! The Austrians and Poles will be our subjects, their women and children, your slaves!" Moustapha exhorted them.

Among the generals listening to Moustapha's battle plan was the Tartar commander, Khan Murad. He was a descendant of the elite mounted warriors from the Russian steppes, a nomadic tribe that two hundred and fifty years earlier was united by Genghis Khan, founder of the Mongol invasions. Suddenly and without warning, they swept into central Europe, bypassed the walled cities and castles, and pillaged the undefended villages. In the intervening two and a half centuries, most of the Tartars did not intermarry with the native populations. They remained nomadic, had not become European or Ottoman and instead retained their martial equestrian ethos. The Khan was a short, lean, and finely muscled cavalry officer. His skin was dark brown, as were his Asian eyes. He wore a linen shirt, felted trousers, an animal skin caftan, and a conical fur cap. While he stood at the rear of the assembled commanders, he looked at the lavish furnishings of the Grand Vizier's tent and listened to his words with mounting contempt.

Earlier in the day, when reports reached Moustapha that the fighting over female slaves had again resulted in several Turkish soldiers' deaths, he ordered all of the several thousand Christian female captives to be put to death. Those unfortunate souls had been taken from the Austrian villages on the army's route north from Budapest and had been savaged for months,

---

20. On the scene Polish chroniclers recorded that Sobieski planned to give his armies a day to rest and attack Mustafa on the 13th. He changed his mind when he received intelligence that indicated the Tartars had nearly completed their tunneling operations in preparation to set and detonate charges. If that were to happen before Sobieski could attack, the city would be lost.

This wanton cruelty was even more than the Khan could abide. Furthermore, the Grand Vizier's bejeweled tent and feminine taste in silken clothes caused his blood to boil. As he looked at Moustapha's emerald studded dagger and sheath, he guessed that this ornament was worth enough to feed his army of three thousand horsemen for a year. Moustapha's order that the Tartar warriors be located outside the main Turkish encampment was the most unforgivable of the many insults the Tartar chieftain had suffered at the hands of the Ottoman Empire.

When all the other generals had departed the tent, Khan Murad remained and stood in front of the entrance, glaring at the Grand Vizier with a look of seething hatred. Moustapha walked slowly up to the Tartar, fingering his long black beard, while he attempted to wear a look of sublime confidence. Avoiding any deferential courtesies, the Khan shouted, "You have placed me and my people in danger by keeping us away from the Poles. While they were pulling their canons through the forest, my riders could have destroyed them!"

"You will destroy them tomorrow," Moustapha said slowly and calmly.

"You should not have brought us here to Vienna. Because of you, the Austrians, the Germans, and the Poles are united against us. And now we face the Polish King, Sobieski, who is the best infidel general in all of Europe!" Khan shouted, pointing at the slender Grand Vizier who towered over him, "You seem determined to lose this war!"

Moustapha was unable to speak. His face contorted in rage as he focused on his overwhelming desire to behead this little impudent Tartan mongrel.

Khan shouted, "Don't think that you will have the pleasure of killing me because you will not be able to find me." Before the Grand Vizier could speak, the Tartan turned and disappeared into the darkness.

Khan Murad rode like the wind out of the Ottoman camp, through the forest to the clearing where his army was encamped. He shouted to his generals, seated by their fire, "Tonight we ride!" And with that order began a whirlwind migration of the Tartars from Europe. He led his nation out of Austria, across Hungary, through the forests of the Ukraine, across Russia to the endless expanse of the Central Asian Steppes, their ancestral homeland. Never again would European armies face in battle the enormously effective Tartan horsemen, the once elite warriors of the Mongol invasion.

That night, September 11, 1683, what Moustapha also did not know was that his engineers (then called "sappers") were also disserting the Ottoman cause. Perhaps because the Prophet did not need gunpowder to subdue the Arabian

Mounted Polish Hussars

peninsula, the craft of undermining and collapsing a besieged city was not one that the Ottoman armies had mastered or even bothered to understand. Therefore, all of the Ottomans' engineers were Europeans, specialists hired from Italy, Holland, and France. Athough they had been ordered to detonate their charges the following day, demolishing the southern-facing walls and much of the city, they uniformly decided to defect when word reached them that the Christian armies had arrived and that the great Polish general, Sobieski, was their commander. The sappers were mercenaries who had formed no allegiance to the Ottoman Empire. Moreover, they knew they would be singled out for very harsh forms of execution reserved for traitors, should the Ottomans be defeated.

So, the gunpowder charges were not brought up to the tunnels which led to the chambers under Vienna's walls, and the Christian engineers were deserting and making their way, under the cover of darkness, to the German and Austrian encampments.

On September 12, 1683, several hours before dawn, Sobieski awoke, prayed, and placed around his neck the portrait of the Virgin of Czestochowa. Next, by candlelight, he wrote last minute notes to his key commanders, and summoned his adjutant who, in turn, sent the notes by riders to Prince Waldeck and Charles of Lorraine. Sobieski's Polish troops were now in place and would form the right wing, while the Austrians commanded by Charles would attack from the left wing, and Waldeck's Germans would advance from the center, facing the most seasoned Turkish regulars whose line was the deepest. As dawn's early light began to illuminate the massive Turkish camp, Sobieski stood behind the new hastily-constructed ramparts and surveyed its fifteen thousand brightly-colored tents. He studied the twenty thousand Janissaries dressed in armor, poised beneath the city walls. And he heard the sounds of sixty thousand horses who fidgeted nervously sensing the ensuing conflagration. Then, with a wave of his hand, his heralds signaled the attack.

As the three Christian infantries marched toward the enemy, twenty-five thousand Turkish regulars poured out of their center position to engage

Waldeck's Germans. They ran to take up positions behind small stone walls that laced back and forth among the vineyards, walls that made advancing in formation difficult. Next, Sobieski's regular Polish ground troops were met by the on-rushing Turkish left flank. This initial collision produced an enormous explosion that was a blend of cannonade, swords, and battle axes crashing against bronze shields, and thousands of mens' cries and shouts. The loud sounds enveloped Sobieski's senses, and caused the movement of humanity to proceed, over the next few minutes, in a kind of hypnotic slow motion.

For two hours both armies were bogged down in fierce hand-to-hand fighting with neither side achieving an advantage. Then Sobieski's army, which had fewer obstacles and flatter ground than their allies, began to move the Turks slowly back. With this, the Austrians on the far opposite flank, who faced thinner lines of resistance, also began to slowly move the Turks backward toward their camp. This gave Waldeck's Germans encouragement to push forward, despite the difficulty of their situation. They did this by employing their troops and canons in spectacular synchronization. As the Germans approached each wall defended by masses of Turks, the infantry stood their ground; bombadiers fired their small cannons which blasted the wall to rubble, allowing brave men to charge through the breaches. Conversely, Sobieski saw that all three of his armies were suffering no incoming cannon fire. Mustapha had reserved all his available cannons for that day's bombardment of the city. He fully expected to be storming the city by early in the day. He calculated that the explosion of Vienna would rupture the Christians' battle plans and make them vulnerable. The explosion never came.

By noon all three allied armies were moving forward inexorably and performing similar feats of synchronized bombardment and heroic infantry charges. Their progress was good enough to allow Sobieski the chance to send a rider with notes to his commanders, Charles and Waldeck, congratulating them on their progress with encouragement to keep moving. Charles messaged back to him, "When do you send the Hussars forward?" The Hussars were the finest cavalrymen in all of Europe, an elite force that made up a new Greek phalanx of lightening speed, men who rode armored stallions and carried long pikes, men who could ride with amazing precision. Charles messaged back that he could not send them in because the terrain was too rough.

The Christian armies' advance slowed to a crawl as the afternoon wore on and the ground in front of them became more difficult with small barns, abandoned cottages, and rock walls forming defensible positions for Turks. In studying the battlefield from Mount Kahlemberg the previous afternoon, the allied generals could clearly see that if they were successful in pushing the Turks back through the area of vineyards and abandoned buildings, there would be roughly a thousand yards of flat open ground leading directly to the Turkish camp. Sobieski hoped to reach the flat ground by the end of the first day of battle, make camp just off its edge, and resume his attack on the second day. His plan was to save his Hussars for the second day of the battle.

By late afternoon, the three allied Christian armies began again to push through the obstacle-ridden terrain, with the Poles moving the fastest. Suddenly amidst the smoke and confusion, Sobieski realized that his forward line had reached the level ground. He could see that his forward troops were standing no more than a thousand yards from the Turkish camp! Meanwhile, Moustapha galloped back and forth just behind his front lines and shouted orders for men to move to shore up his left flank which was succumbing to the Polish advance. This in turn, thinned the line in front of Waldeck's Germans who continued to decimate the Turkish regulars with high-precision canon fire.

With only two hours left of daylight, the Germans also reached the flat open plain. Additionally, they were breaking holes in the center of the Turkish line, allowing portions of Waldeck's infantry to emerge on its other side, without any combatants in front of them. A mounted adjutant then came galloping up to Sobieski, shouting at the top of his lungs over the enormous din, "The Germans have broken free!"

Sobieski threw his spyglass up to his face to see if he could corroborate the report. He saw two hundred yards away, through the cloud of dust, the melee and abject confusion being wrought against the center of the Turkish line. Some of the Turks were being assaulted from the front and back, while others were running toward their encampment. With that, Sobieski screamed to his adjutant, "Hussars to the front!" Next, he rode back and forth along the rear of his lines, shouting to every cavalry officer to prepare for a charge.

On his command, three thousand Hussars spurred their horses to galloping speed, headed toward the center of the Turkish line. They maintained an extremely tight formation, each holding a gleaming fifteen-foot pike as they charged. They were followed by five thousand superior cavalry and thirteen thousand horsemen composed of petty noblemen and farmers who were good riders and well-trained military men. It was largest single cavalry charge in the history of European warfare and was a demonstration of Sobieski's military genius.

The charge impaled and instantly killed several thousand Turks and conscripts, and ruptured a massive hole in their defenses. And with that nearly every Turkish fighter, except the five thousand Janissaries who held their positions at the base of the city's walls, began a full-scale retreat toward their camp. As they ran with their backs to their mounted pursuers, many more Turks were hacked down. Moustapha galloped ahead of his retreating hordes and attempted to rally them to take up positions at the edge of the camp. Some regrouped and took up defensive positions. Many Turkish regulars and conscripts did not heed the general's command and instead began looting the nearest tents or running for their mounts.

Soon, the Germans and the Polish infantrymen began a hurried march in formation toward the Ottomans' camp with some of the disengaged cavalry on the outside flanks. As they approached with pikes and battle axes at the ready and with darkness gathering, full-scale panic and looting enveloped the Turkish army. Moustapha looked to his left and saw a Bulgarian hurriedly looting an officer's lavish tent. He shouted at him, "You! Get back to your position!" And when the lowly conscript did not even acknowledge the command, the Grand Vizier knew all was lost. He then shouted to his bodyguard to take what they could. He looked back toward Vienna, wondering how it was that its walls were still standing, and rode away from the battlefield.

As Sobieski's and Waldeck's armies captured the last straggling Turkish looters inside the sprawling camp, Charles' Austrian army was still attacking the Janissaries positioned below the city walls. Surrounded, the Janissaries, in their customary manner, fought to the last man. Most of them had been absconded, as young boys, from villages in Turkish Hungary or the Balkans. They had been trained by their kidnappers to grow up as ruthless Muslim soldiers, the sons of anguished Christian parents they no longer remembered.

Through the gathering darkness, the starving inhabitants inside Vienna could see the Turks retreating. This set off a spontaneous flood of emaciated men and boys who ran out of the city's main gate toward the portion of the abandoned encampment which contained the Turks' buffalo and livestock. So crazed by hunger, they ran directly past their liberators without greeting them, in a near rabid desperation to kill and butcher some of the animals. Sobieski, seeing this, rode promptly toward the vast livestock pen. There he beheld the pitiful sight of a Venetian man who had just run up to a buffalo, slashed its throat, involuntarily fell upon the still dying beast, and was ravenously drinking its warm spurting blood.

As he watched the pitiful scene, Sobieski began to issue an order to his mounted adjutant, "Find Count Lubonski and tell him to bring some men here with sharp swords." Before he could finish his order, a man appeared on foot, and stood beside his horse. In the gathering darkness, he saw a man whom he had not seen since college—General Lubomirski. He had left Poland twenty years earlier to marry a Venetian princess and had commanded the defense of Vienna for this long and brutal summer. He was gaunt and frail—and alive. Sobieski dismounted. They hugged and wept.

By nightfall, the entire Turkish encampment was completely in the hands of the Christians. The size of the spoils was unprecedented in European warfare. There were more than seven hundred cannons, forty thousand horses, twenty thousand mules, two thousand camels, one hundred thousand bags of corn, vast numbers of prisoners, and seventeen million crowns, all left in the camp by the fleeing Turkish invaders.

Sobieski was used to living modestly while on military campaign. When he first entered Mustapha's abandoned headquarters, he was astonished by what he saw: a golden basin for washing his hands, a marble tub for bathing, walls draped with silk, and hundreds of hanging swords and daggers studded with jewels. It was what he would later call a "voluptuous effeminacy." No self-respecting commander would allow himself this kind of debauchery, he thought. When he walked into Moustapha's harem chambers, he found the corpse of a beautiful Circassian slave woman so highly prized by the Ottomans. Undoubtedly to prevent her from falling into the hands of the victors, her head had been severed and it lay in a pool of blood and at a grotesque angle to her body. For the first time, on a day where he had already witnessed so much death, Sobieski rushed outside the tent and vomited.

He spent much of the night overseeing the exhausting task of allocating the Ottoman plunder—some of the spoils went to the allied soldiers, while the largest portion was apportioned fairly to government treasuries. Sobieski elected to break away from the necessary mendacity of the task and rode out of the camp to inspect the burial of the fallen Janissaries.

This drawing of a Janissary frightened the Ottoman Emperor, Mehmet. It mysteriously conveyed a three-dimensional figure in defiance of Islamic law.

When he arrived at their position by the city's southern walls, where they had made their last stand only a few hours earlier, he found a priest whom he recognized as Piotr. The priest was praying over the Janissaries, dead young men who were from Christian families. By the light of the priest's torch mounted on its stanchion, Sobieski could see that many of the fallen were clearly boys as young as fifteen or sixteen. "Greetings, Father. Your entreaties to the Almighty were clearly heard today. The Polish nation is grateful," he said reverently.

"My King," Piotr said, "I have found one soldier alive. It is for you to decide his fate. Please follow me over here."

Sobieski dismounted and followed the priest, who led him down a row of dead, those that Piotr and his fellow priests had placed there in preparation for cremation. "Here he is, my King," he said holding the torch over the boy who lay on the ground still in his armor. Sobieski could see by the torch light that the wounded Janissary was very young. He had only a few whiskers growing from his chin and none emerging from his cheeks. His long dirty-blond hair protruded from his helmet, and the blue of his terrified eyes reminded the general of the Aegean Sea on a cloudless day. "What is your name, my boy?"

"Muhammad!" he shouted with his voice cracking. "Please kill me! I wish to be martyred in the name of Allah!" he sobbed.

"Your name is not Muhammad. Where are you wounded?"

As the boy broke into inconsolable sobs, Piotr said to Sobieski, "He was unconscious when I found him. I suspect that he was knocked down, but that he is in good health, my King."

"Good," Sobieski said to the priest. "Please see that he is fed and made ready for the trip back to Warsaw. I wish to learn a few things from this boy." He walked back to his tethered horse, mounted, and rode into the darkness toward Moutapha's tent. Once inside it, his total exhaustion allowed him to fall into a dreamless sleep.

The Beginning of Islamic Decline (September 12, 1683)

Turkish chronicler Silihadar recorded the Ottoman defeat: *This was a calamitous defeat, so great that there has never been its like since the first appearance of the Ottoman State.*[21]

When Sobieski entered the city of Vienna the morning of September 13, he was greeted by tearful, joyous ovations of the surviving inhabitants. For the Viennese, the Polish liberator was their savior sent by God. For the allied victors, it seemed that the tide of history had turned in their favor and that God had saved them from death or slavery. Two days later, the allies marched out of Vienna and headed east in the attempt

---

21. Silihdar Findikli Mehmed, *Tarih Vol. II,* 87.

to liberate what was left of their Austro-Hungarian prisoners and to catch up with and capture or kill what was left of the invading Ottomans.

When Mustafa halted his retreating army beside the River Raab, near the Hungarian city of Gran, he deepened his debacle when he ordered several of his best generals to be beheaded as punishment for their abysmal performance in the battle for Vienna.

Six weeks later on October 27, 1683, Sobieski's Polish army and their allies from the Duchy of Lorraine, finished the job of annihilating the invading Ottoman army. They killed fifteen thousand Turks, captured thousands of prisoners, and confiscated what remained of the army's stores and war material. With this victory, to the overwhelming joy of its Christian inhabitants, they liberated the city of Gran that had been under Islamic domination for nearly two centuries. Mustafa, along with a tiny vestige of his massive army, escaped the battlefield and made his way to the capital of Islamic Hungary, Buda. There, on the orders of the Sultan, Mustafa was beheaded.

One hundred and fifty-four years earlier in 1529, the Ottomans tried and failed to conquer Hapsburg, Vienna. On that campaign, they were successful in conquering much of Hungary, Serbia, and some of Poland and greatly expanded their domination of Central Europe. Had they conquered all of Poland, Turkish dominion on European soil would have cut a swath from Greece, on the Mediterranean, to the Baltic Sea.

With their loss at the battle for Vienna, the Ottoman Empire, the standard bearer for all of Sunni Islam, began a nearly uninterrupted descent into its own servitude, culminating with its final dismemberment at the end of World War I in 1918.

Western Europe Finally Unites

As soon as the news of Mustafa's defeat and the destruction of his army spread throughout, the capitals of Europe—Austria, Venice, Poland, Tuscany, Malta, and Russia—declared war on the Ottomans. In March 1684, the Pope dubbed the new alliance the Holy League and blessed its mission. Over the next fourteen years, (1684-1698), the Ottomans suffered a series of defeats that resulted in the loss of much of their European holdings outside of Greece and nearly all its lands west of the Dardanelles.

Under the Czar, Peter the Great, the Russians ejected the Ottoman armies from the port city of Azov, the Russians' first holding on the shores of the Black Sea. Their loss of the Christian lands in Europe was accepted with bitterness within the Ottoman court in Constantinople. But those Christian European lands were fairly recent conquests, ruled by Turkish governors and largely inhabited by infidels.

The loss of Azov caused bitterness and alarm because it represented the first time since the Crusades that the infidel ruled in a predominantly Islamic land. The Crusades were a very distant memory. A portion of the Ottoman homeland—which had been Islamic since the eighth century—had been stripped away and worse, the *believers were now ruled by the infidel.* From the Islamic point of view, Allah was simply not supposed to let this happen. Moreover, its conquest made Russia a Black Sea maritime power that posed a further threat to the Turkish homeland, even its capital of Istanbul.

The Beginning of the Ottomans' End

Beyond the Ottomans' propensity to fall prey to a hubristic overreach, there was another lesson bundled within the epoch-making battle for Vienna, which marked the beginning of the end for the Ottomans' empire. And that is the very old lesson taught to us moderns by the Greek historian, Herodotus, considered the father of Western history. He was the first European who sought to find the *causes* for events and who chronicled the Persian wars (popularized by the movie, *300*, portraying the Spartans' stand at Thermopylae). In compiling his *Histories* of the Persian wars, he sought specifically to find out how such a small number of men of Greek descent were able to defeat the vastly larger Persian armies and navies.

His answer is an immutable lesson for the ages.

IMMUTABLE #2
In battle, free men will almost always defeat slaves.
(Herodotus' Law)

The men who filled the Christian ranks at Vienna were not conscripts as most of the Ottoman army. They were volunteers or career military men who fought to save their homes, their families, their way of life, and their *freedom* from Muslim invaders who aimed to enslave them. The Europeans fighting at Vienna were the spiritual descendants of their Greek ancestors who fought at Marathon and Thermopylae, and rowed the ships at Salamis. Like the ancient Greeks who invented democracy, the Poles *elected* their king and commander.

That summer day outside Vienna, the Ottoman soldiers' only motivation was plunder. Moreover, the rank and file Muslim warriors knew that even their plunder was actively being withheld by their unelected and despised general, Mustafa. The Christians won because they fought as free men—not as slaves.

During the eighteenth-century, Russia and the European powers went back to fighting wars among themselves that resulted in the Ottomans holding onto portions of their empire, mainland Greece and the Balkans. And the gap between the Ottomans and the West, in terms of military power, continued to grow. In 1774, the Russians defeated the Ottomans in a series of battles which resulted in their annexation of all the Crimea. Like the port of Azov, this represented a much larger portion of Islamic homeland stripped away with believers being conquered and ruled by the infidel. Bernard Lewis, who studied the original Turkish archives, records that eighteenth-century Islamic chroniclers, in the face of relentless military defeats, were incessantly querying as to what had gone wrong; who had done this to us?

It would certainly be an oversimplification to state that the cause for the fall of the Ottomans was the result of an immensely flawed civilization which ultimately produced immensely flawed commanders-in-chief. After all, the Ottoman Empire was able to dominate much of the Middle East and Southern Europe for five hundred years.

By the eve of the battle for Vienna, the Ottoman Empire was ruled by sultans who were products of succession. The first-born boy of the Sultan would only survive to reign if he murdered *all* his brothers who would otherwise be contenders for the Crown. With the number of slave women in the harem at the Sultan's disposal, this would mean that the new heir's *first acts* as a nascent ruler of the Ottomans was to kill his numerous brothers and half-brothers. The Ottoman succession modality was a hallmark of a cruel, murderous, and dysfunctional empire.

Although the Ottomans conquered a vast portion of Western Christendom, its weaknesses were many and strengths few. Its primary strength lay in its Turkish cavalrymen who descended from nomadic warriors. They were feared far and wide, known as being exceedingly fierce fighters with an ability to endure extremely harsh campaigns. In David Fromkin's masterful work, *A Peace to End All Peace: The Fall of the Ottoman Empire and the Creation of the Modern Middle East*, he explains that the Ottomans never outgrew their origins as marauding warriors. They enriched themselves by capturing wealth and slaves when invading new territories. It was the only way they knew to make money. When the conquests turned into defeats, the essence of Ottoman existence was lost. The Turks had mastered the arts of war but not those of government.

West and Resurgent Islam Approaches a Battle-for-Vienna Moment

Daniel Pipes, Director of the Middle East Forum and one of the West's most eminent commentators on the Islamic threat wrote, in January 2007:

> *"Should Islamists get smart and avoid mass destruction, but instead stick to the lawful, political, non violent route . . . it is difficult to see what will stop them."*

In this statement, Pipes holds out one counterintuitive hope for the West—that the Islamists *will overreach* and attack us with weapons of mass destruction (WMD).

The Final Consignment to the Dust Bin of History

As David Fromkin observed in *A Peace to End All Peace*, on the eve of World War I, the Ottoman Empire was a fiction. For a long time, its Sultans had not even comprised a single ethnic group. While they spoke Turkish, they were half-slaves, the descendants of Christian slave women from the Balkans or central Europe. Among their non-Islamic subjects were Roman Catholic, Greek Orthodox, Armenian Catholic, Armenian Georgian, Jewish, Protestant, Maronite, Samaritan, Nestorian, and Monophysite peoples. Even their Islamic subjects were enormously fractured and antagonistic. They were Arabs, Egyptians, Syrians, and many smaller groups from Mesopotamia whose histories and ethnic backgrounds caused them to chafe under the rule of the Ottomans.

While the Islamic faith was followed by the majority of their subjects and provided somewhat of a unifying effect, the Ottoman Sultans were Sunnis and proclaimed themselves successors to the Prophet Muhammad. At least seventy-one sects of Islam were resident inside the fractious realm, most of whom *did not* believe that the Ottoman Sultan, the son of an infidel slave girl, was the true Caliph and legitimate successor of the Prophet. This was particularly true of the numerous non-Sunni sect of Shiites.

By the dawn of the twentieth century, European travelers came to the Middle East to visit biblical sites, tour excavations, or see nomadic people living in the same manner as did their ancestors who roamed the deserts in the time of Abraham. In essence, they came to witness the past. So too, were the Ottoman ruling elite, in Constantinople, living in the past. Fromkin also points out that "Ottoman officials continued to pretend, for example, that Bulgaria formed part of the empire long after losing control of that territory in 1878, and counted Egyptians as among its subjects even after Britain occupied Egypt in 1882." [22]

The census statistics were totally unreliable. The Ottoman holdings were the lands that today comprise Turkey, Syria, Israel, Lebanon, Jordan, and the Arabian peninsula, a land mass six times the size of Texas with an estimated population of between twenty to twenty-five million. Their ability to provide administrative control over these lands was, to use Fromkin's term—chimerical.

---

22. David Fromkin, *A Peace to End All Peace: The Fall of the Ottoman Empire and the Creation of the Modern Middle East* (Avon Books: New York, 1989), 35.

Although they posted garrisons of infantry around their empire, this was merely a facade. The empire itself was a facade. Centralized authority was a fantasy. Once outside the few cities, Ottoman rule vanished and local sheikhs, nomadic warlords, were in charge. It had reverted to its ancient character, where local tribes, clans, and sects were in a near constant state of war with one another. Many districts were controlled by no authority other than thieves and cut throats. "The rickety Turkish government was even incapable of collecting its own taxes. . . . On the eve of the First World War, only five percent of taxes were collected by the government; the other 95 percent was collected by independent tax farmers." In other words—stolen.

MODERN COROLLARIES

Prior to their first attempt in 1529 to conquer Vienna, the Ottomans had a war with Persia that ended in a stalemate and left both Islamic realms considerably weakened by the conflict. The Shiite Shah Ismail of Persia, who lost many soldiers and great treasure in that war with the Sunni Ottomans, sent a letter to the Hapsburg Emperor, Charles V, asking that he consider forming an alliance with Persia to fight the Ottomans. Although no such alliance was forged, what proved decisive was that Persia and the Ottomans were *not* allied in the last great Islamic conquest of Europe that culminated in the battle of Vienna. Moreover, the Shiite and Sunni houses of Islam have continued to make war with each other to the present day. In so doing, the world of Islam, what they refer to as the *dar al Islam*, has for over two hundred years violated the following immutable law which inexorably contributes to the disintigration of civilizations.

IMMUTABLE #4
*If a people cannot avoid constant internal warfare,
it will have a new order imposed from without.*

What the West should learn from the Ottomans' defeat at Vienna, and ultimate fall, is the understanding that if the co-religionists—the Persian Shiites and Ottoman Sunnis—had joined forces rather than made war upon themselves, Western journalists today might well be writing their commentaries in Turkish or Arabic. Had the Persians and Ottomans united in the war to impose Islam upon the infidel, the combined strength of their land armies would likely have led to Islamic hegemony over Europe and quite possibly the destruction of Western Christendom.

If we conclude that the Muslims' propensity to make war upon themselves saved 17th century Europe from Muslim conquest, might we construe that our ability to foment intenal strife within the current Muslim world is a necessary survival strategy now? The answer is clearly—yes.

We can observe the efficacy of this survival technique in the successful prosecution of World War I by the allies against the German-allied Ottoman empire, as well as in George W. Bush's war against Saddam Hussein's Iraq. In World War I, while the fighting raged in the European trenches, the British Middle East field operation based in Cairo was joined by a brilliant Oxford-educated "Arabist," T.E. Lawrence, whose task it was to train, equip, and most importantly, *inspire* the Arab revolt.

At the outset of the war, he organized and commanded a few thousand primitive Islamic Bedouin horse- and camel-mounted warriors from the Arabian Peninsula, the Islamic heartland, to fight a guerilla war against a vastly larger mechanized army of Islamic Turks. Essentially Lawrence became a field commander in an operation that pitted *Islamic* freedom fighter against *Islamic* Turkish overlord, an operation which finished the work of dispatching to history the militant Islamic Ottoman Empire.

Similarly, the Iraq war employed the exact strategy as that of T.E. Lawrence, it gave Iraqis the option to choose freedom and prosperity over jihadism, which required an alliance with the USA. George W. Bush's war strategy finally proved successful with his "surge" that essentially made use of Islam's natural tendency to make war on itself.

The Iraq war has had the fortunate outcome of splintering many Muslim factions. Sunni Baathists were pitted against the newly liberated Iraqi Shiites. Moderate Shiites fought Iranian fundamentalist Shiites, Kurdish separatists fought Iranian theocrats. By 2011 in Iraq, there were sizeable populations of Kurds, Shiites, and Sunnis who are united and sided with the West. As a result of the allied toppling of the Baathist regime in Iraq, the Islamic imperialists lost an important ally and suffered a staggering propaganda defeat.

While the Western media continued to castigate the Bush (GW) administrations for employing such a strategy, history may well record that it proved as essential as a delaying tactic as were the Ottoman/Persian wars for our European ancestors.

The Ottomans Chose Illiteracy

In *Carnage and Culture*, Victor Davis Hanson chronicles many of the great battles of human history and makes the case for what I have synthesized into one of my immutable laws that govern the collapse of civilizations.

IMMUTABLE #10
Declining civilizations will always face
superior firepower from ascending civilizations
because sovereignty is only temporarily uncontested.

As we contemplate the Ottomans' loss at the battle of Vienna and their subsequent path to extinction, it's important to consider that the Ottomans and the balance of the Islamic world did not experience a Renaissance or Enlightenment, nor did they participate in the educational, philosophical, and industrial revolutions. Throughout the Middle Ages, neither the Ottomans nor other Islamic realms had knowledge of the New World, nor any means to travel there safely, any holdings, or any new world markets.

They began to lose their empire because the Western militaries that they confronted were increasingly superior to theirs due to technology and wealth. European scientific advances created better weaponry and economies that allowed French and British kings to equip their armies with mobile cannons, advanced personal weapons, and armaments.

With the loss of Vienna, the Ottomans could scarcely afford to pay their soldiers from the late 17th century onwards. As a further indicator of their declining civilization (soon to face superior firepower) the Ottomans never evolved a system of meritocracy. Grand Viziers, for example, were always appointed by the Sultan from his own family. They purposefully prevented half their population, Islamic women, from being educated. Moreover, as Bernard Lewis observed, whenever Ottoman fortunes were in decline, the prescription of its elders was always to go back to old ways and to find solutions in Islam's ancient sacred texts. Despite their entireties, Allah failed to defend them from those who wished to be liberated from Islamic aggression and Muslim rule.

The Consequences of Overreach

The Ottomans now found themselves under attack from an ever-growing array of better educated, better armed, and better commanded hostile powers. The Ottoman overreach was characterized by its Grand Vizier, whose monumental greed compelled him to plunder an entire capital city for his private use, this so that he could retain his thousands of slaves, attendants, and concubines. In so doing, he deprived his own army of its share of the spoils. Additionally the Ottomans' overreach was characterized by the hubris of its Sultans and ruling elites who mistakenly believed that Allah would grant them victories endlessly, no matter how many infidel kingdoms they attacked, in rapid succession or simultaneously.

By the late 1690s the Ottomans began to sue for peace and on January 12, 1699, they signed the Treaty of Carlowitz. The Ottomans suffered the ignominy of signing the accord in Voivadina, a land newly recaptured from the Turks, and they agreed to terms dictated to them by the victors. This strange new form of speaking to the infidel called *diplomacy* was utterly foreign to them because no such treaty had ever been negotiated by the Ottomans. For a millennium, through their religious elders, they had been taught to despise the infidel. It was incomprehensible to the average Ottoman that the Christians could command superior war-making powers.

Khalid Sheikh Mohammed (KSM), in March 2007, testified at his military tribunal, that he was the "operations manager" for 9/11. He also confessed to planning and carrying out many other al-Qaeda attacks: the beheading of Daniel Pearl, the first World Trade Center bombings in 1993, the Bali bombings which killed 202 people, and the November 2003 attacks in Istanbul against Jewish and British targets. He confessed to having plans to attack targets in South Korea, Singapore, Thailand, Philippines, Israel, the Philippians, the Panama Canal, Brussels, London, and even the Straits of Hormuz. He confessed to assassination plots aimed at killing former presidents Carter and Clinton, as well as Pope John Paul. And most ominously, he confessed to overseeing a group which was at work on biological weapons and dirty bombs.

While it's generally acknowledged that KSM was the operational planner of 9/11, most Americans take little stock of the testimony of a semiliterate scruffy thug, especially since he was waterboarded prior to his confession. Others see it as further proof that the West is truly in dire straits.

We should be heartened by the KSM confession, even if some of it strains credulity. Much of it has been corroborated over the intervening years by intensive investigation. It is encouraging because it shows that the jihadists are not going to heed Daniel Pipes' admonition, that they are going to overreach and, in fact, are actively attempting to detonate a WMD somewhere in the West.

KSM's list of targets reminds us of the many realms targeted by Ottoman Sultan, Mohammad IV, and Grand Vizier Mustafa, of the 1680s. In their overreach, they managed to lose the battle for Vienna and managed to bring about the alliance of, and declaration of war by, Austria, Venice, Poland, Tuscany, Malta, and Russia. This was a consortium of powers whose existence, or, at least vital interests, had been attacked by the Ottomans. In essence, the Ottomans' overreach extended to their believing that God was on their side, that they were therefore invincible, and that infidels were godless and destined to come under their rule. Secondly, they overreached in creating too many enemies, some of whom were equally as ruthless as they, like the

Russians. After the battle of Vienna, the Ottomans retained their seat of power in Constantinople for another two hundred years, and yet their empire continued to be relentlessly hollowed out. From that battle onward, it was ultimately doomed.

We must hope that Bin Laden, al-Zawahiri, the theocrats running Iran, Hamas, Hezbollah, and Mohammed Badie, the head of the Muslim Brotherhood, are the modern reincarnations of Mustafa the Dark. Like Mustafa, they believe that God will bless their unbridaled jihad against the West, blessing them with unlimited connubial bliss should they be martyred. In bin Laden's 1998 Fatwa he wrote:

> *"We—with God's help—we call on every Muslim who believes in God and wishes to be rewarded to comply with God's order to kill the Americans and plunder their money wherever they find it."*

It was widely reported that bin Laden stated, "It is the duty of the Islamic faithful to acquire and detonate weapons of mass destruction in western lands as a means to conquer the infidels."

What was less widely reported is: that the name Osama had replaced Muhammad as the most popular name for babies in the Middle East, that bin Laden is widely viewed as a mythic hero of the faith, that on 9/11 there was dancing in the streets *throughout* the capitals of the Middle East and in Islamic quarters of Western Europe.

Warren Buffett, a principle in several reinsurance firms, knows as much as anyone about systemic risk. He stated the likelihood that the West will sustain the detonation of a chemical, biological, or nuclear weapon is 100 percent. It's time for the West to finally remove its gloves. We must hope that, like Mustafa and the Ottoman Sultans, resurgent militant Islam will underestimate the West.

While history is not an exact roadmap for the future, it is the only navigation aid we have. Therefore, we must hope that the resurgent Muslims of today are showing the exact same signs of primitive hubris displayed by their coreligionist ancestors. It's impossible to know exactly how their overreach will take place or how many of our beloved we will lose before the West rises up and unites around our common Judeo/Christian heritage and develops a superior strategy for defending our lands and our culture.

If history is our guide, today's Islamic militants betray a strong likeness to Mustafa, commander of the Ottoman army in 1683.

In this, there is hope.

PART THREE
Resurgent Militant Islam

Immutable Laws
Governing the Fall of Civilizations

1 No nation has ever survived once its citizenry ceased to believe its culture worth saving. (Hanson's Law)

2 In battle, free men will almost always defeat slaves. (Herodotus' Law)

3 Appeasement of a ruthless outside power always invites its aggression. Treaties made with ruthless despots are always fruitless and dangerous.

4 If a people cannot avoid continuous internal warfare, it will have a new order imposed from without.

5 When a free people, through taxation, is deprived of its ability to acquire wealth and property, collapse is presaged.

6 To hold territory, a state must be populated by those loyal to the central authority. When immigration overwhelms assimilation, the fall is predicted.

7 With the loss of fiscal solvency comes a loss of sovereignty.

8 Debasing the currency always destabilizes the governing authority.

9 When a civilization accepts the propaganda of its enemy as truth, it has reached the far side of appeasement and capitulation is nigh.

10 Declining civilizations will always face superior firepower from ascending civilizations because sovereignty is only temporarily uncontested.

CHAPTER SIX

The Modern Islamic Threat and Our Forty-Fourth President

"We have a strategy drawn up for the destruction of Anglo-Saxon civilization."
HASSAN ABBASSI, SENIOR ADVISOR
to KHAMENEI, IRANIAN SUPREME LEADER

"Islam isn't in America to be equal to any other faith, but to become dominant.
The Koran should be the highest authority in America,
and Islam the only accepted religion on earth."
OMAR AHMAD, CAIR

In June 2011, ten years after 9/11, Catherine Herridge documented in her book, *The Next Wave: On the Hunt for Al Qaeda's American Recruits,* the existence of a massive new wave of terrorists who were American citizens, radicalized in American mosques, planning spectacular attacks from inside the US. She ends by writing, "A new homegrown plot with links to international terrorism was documented, on average, every two weeks." [1]

In March 2011, Peter King, House Chairman of the Homeland Security Committee, began hearings on the radicalization of the American Muslim. Prior to and during the hearings, Democrat members of the U.S. Congress made half-hearted attempts to discredit the Republican Congressman for "singling out" Muslims. Given the volume and severity of the Muslim attacks carried out or interdicted inside the US since 9/11, the Left and their other allies, the American Muslim groups like CAIR (Council on American-Islamic Relations) made little effect on public opinion. Most

---

1. Herridge, Catherine, *The Next Wave: On the Hunt for Al Qaeda's American Recruits,*
    (New York: Crown Forum, 2011), 223.

Americans understood that it was not Buddhists or Hindus, or Evangelical Christians who attempted to detonate car bombs in Times Square or shoot people inside military installations. They instinctively understood that while our constitution guarantees the freedom to practice one's religion, it does not grant the right to advocate for the violent overthrow of the US government.

What too many Americans failed to comprehend is that Islam, at its core, is an aggressive supremacist faith. So reviled is the Infidel, by the Muslim faithful, that Islamic law forbids him to set foot in the holy cities of Medina or Mecca. Islam's core tenant holds that the Infidel must be conquered by any means possible. Moreover, dying in the attempt to subdue the Infidel is the most blessed of acts. As the country approached the ten-year anniversary of the 9/11 attacks, what most Americans did not fully comprehend was how deeply militant Islam had penetrated and compromised American institutions, our government, and even the White House.

While the Storm Gathered, the West Refused to See it

Ten years earlier, on July 26, 2001, in a backwater US Embassy in Baku Azerbaijan, a high-level Iranian security official, Hamid Reza Zakeri, walked in. He told the receptionist that he wanted to speak to the CIA because he had information related to the security of the United States. He explained to the station chief, "Joan," that in his capacity as a high-level security officer at Iran's Ministry of Information and Security (MOIS) headquarters, he observed "Arabs" training pilots and briefing them on their appointed targets. He even described models that were on the table in the meeting room—the *World Trade Center*, the *White House*, the *Pentagon*, and *Camp David*. He told her that the attack was coming from the air, that Arab pilots had already left for America, and the date for the attack was 9/11/01.

Joan called for backup. Several days later a senior CIA officer, "George," arrived from headquarters to debrief the "Baku walk in." He immediately decided that Zakeri was peddling lies, paid him $200, and told him to get out. The information that could have saved 3,000 lives was never passed up the chain-of-command."[2]

In 2003, Stephen, a British spy and self-styled "Lawrence of Arabia," was on the ground inside Iraq weeks prior to the US-led invasion and saw the evacuation of WMD stockpiles and production equipment. Stephen observed the operation being

---

2 . Ken Timmerman, *Countdown to Crisis: The Coming Nuclear Showdown with Iran* (New York: Crown Forum, division of Random House, 2005). With photos and documents included in the appendix, the author makes a solid case that Zakeri, the "Baku walk in," was a highly credible informant. His information passed to the author was corroborated by other reports given to Timmerman from defectors, sources (spies) still inside Iran and independent intelligence reports.

conducted by non-uniformed Russian Special Forces (Spetsnatz), who loaded drums of poison gas and biotoxins on huge eighteen-wheelers destined for Syria and Lebanon. He sent his reports directly to Deputy Undersecretary of Defense, John Shaw. His network was so good that he tracked the shipments to specific villages in Syria, to hospitals in Beirut, and, in some cases, to the specific doctor who received the drums.

Shaw also received corroborating reports of the Russian evacuation operation directly from the Ukrainian head of intelligence, General Ihor Smeshko. The agency refused to work with the CIA or any conventional US intelligence agency for fear of leaks that would result in great political peril. The reports received from the Ukrainians actually named the former head of the KGB, Yevgeny Primakov, as the man who headed up the WMD evacuation operation. It even revealed the code name, Sarandar (Russian for emergency exit).[3]

Nevertheless, Shaw's reports were spiked as "Israeli disinformation" by anti-Bush saboteurs in high places inside the CIA and the Pentagon, so that the Democrats, Kerry's campaign, media, and international Left could continue its all-out relentless war against George W. Bush for his supposed crime of taking the country to war without proof that Iraq had WMDs.

In 2007, three left-wing saboteurs, National Intelligence Agency executives, Brill, Vann Van Diepen, and Fingar, produced a National Intelligence Report (NIE). It stated that in the fall of 2003, the United States Intelligence agencies had "high confidence Tehran had halted its nuclear weapons programs."[4] This was a humiliating reversal for the Bush (GW) administration that had increasingly issued warnings that Iran was getting dangerously close to producing nuclear weapons. As news of the report circled the globe, the subtext once again was that "Bush the war monger" had it wrong, and he didn't even know what his own intelligence service knew.

The report, from the Left-wing saboteurs' perspective, was a very successful operation. It destroyed any negotiating leverage America had with Iranians. It further damaged the country's credibility with our allied intelligence services. And most important, it took the military option off the table for an already beaten-down Bush (GW) administration. The assessment was written to prevent a Republican president from launching a successful military strike upon a dangerous rogue state, because, if Bush did so, it would have burnished his image, making it more likely that a Republican president would succeed him. Although the NIE report was ultimately discredited by virtually every one of America's allied intelligence agencies, the treasonous objective

3.   Ken Timmerman, *Shadow Warriors, The Untold Story of Traitors, Saboteurs, and the Party of Surrender,* (New York: Crown Forum, 2007), 194.

4 . *National Intelligence Estimate,* United States Office of the Director of National Intelligence, 11/2007.

was met.[5] One could argue that the production of this report was so potentially destructive by rogue members of our government, that it was tantamount to an act of treason.

Resurgent Militant Islam Inside the US Today

Pew Research did the largest study of American Muslims ever conducted in May 2007.[6] The company surveyed 55,000 people, conducting the interviews in English, Arabic, Farsi, and Urdu. While the multiculturalists at Pew tried to put a happy face on their study, giving it a upbeat title, the report revealed horrific warnings for Americans. For example, in its summary they concede that "just 40% of Muslim Americans say groups of Arabs carried out the 9/11 attacks." They reported that 5% were willing to say out loud to a pollster that they had a favorable opinion of al-Qaeda while another 27% refused to answer the question. With two to three million American Muslims in the US at the time of the study, between 500,000 and 750,000 Muslims (roughly one in four) favored the actions of their coreligionists who attacked the U.S. on 9/11 and are actively seeking to detonate WMDs in our cities.

Globally there are 1.2 billion Muslims. Abdel Baset al-Megrahi, better known as the Lockerbie Bomber, killed 270 people by blowing up flight 103. Released by the Scottish government in 2010, he was greeted by adoring crowds and given a hero's welcome in Tripoli. From this and so many similar indicators, we can surmise that there are hundreds of thousands, if not millions, of jihadists who wake up every day plotting to destroy the West, and who are financially supported by a much larger host of fellow Muslims.

As described in the beginning of this book, Muhammad was a ruthless warlord. The founder of Islam massacred his enemies in battle, beheaded his male captives, and took their women as concubines. We know he said, "He who leaves the religion, kill him."[7] Consequently, *Reliance of the Traveler*, the single most authoritative book of Sunni jurisprudence says, "When a person who has reached puberty is sane and voluntarily apostatizes from Islam, he deserves to be killed." [8] Furthermore, over the fourteen centuries since Muhammad's death, Islamic scholars have all agreed that there are no aspects of the Prophet's life that can be questioned. Rather, his life is the standard by which all other lives are to be judged.

We can conclude that there is nothing "radical" about militant Islamists at all—

---

5. *Wall Street Journal*, Review and Outlook, Intelligence Fiasco Footnote (February 18, 2008).

6. Pew Research Center, *Muslim American:Middle Class and Mostly Mainstream*, May 2007.

7. *Sahih al-Bukhari*, Volume 9, bk 87, no. 6878.

8. *Reliance of the Traveler*, 08.1 - 08.4.

they are simply imitating the Prophet. Of course, this is not to say that all Muslims are militant terrorists. As Bernard Lewis points out, "Although not all terrorists are Muslim, nearly all terrorists are Muslim."

At the same time that Islamic warriors were ravaging southern France in AD 732, there were millions of peaceful civilian Muslims of the Caliphate going about their business, living in the newly conquered, formerly Christian, capitals of what are today Syria, Egypt, Lebanon and North Africa. Those peaceful Muslims were (as most are today) unconcerned that their jihadist brethren murdered and pillaged the European infidels in the name of expanding the lands of Islam (dar al Islam). Likewise, the jihadists, pillaging Europe in the beginning of the eighth century, were no doubt secure in their belief that they were merely following the blessed example of the Prophet and those of his followers who had already subjugated two-thirds of Western Christendom.

Unlike Jesus, who commanded his followers to "teach all nations," the prophet prescribed war on the unbelievers. By 2011, numerous covert studies conducted by Arabic and Urdu speaking counterintelligence operatives have determined that the vast majority (3 out of 4) of American Imams preaching in the 2,300 US mosques were inciting insurrection and jihad. This is because the US is the great prize. For militant Islam, America is the only nation standing in the way of their dream of a worldwide jihad to establish the new Caliphate. The fact that the citizens of the United States do not demand that their government shut down those Mosques preaching sedition and insurrection is in itself a violation of:

IMMUTABLE #1
No nation has survived once its citizenry ceased to believe its culture worth saving.
(Hanson's Law)

But there has been a positive development. As the ten year anniversary of the 9/11 attacks arrived, more and more Americans had awakened to the realization that tolerance of those who advocate the eradication of their way of life is the activity of cowardly fools.

The Rise of the Terror Masters In Iran

Since the fall of the Shah in 1979, Tehran, the Shiite capital of Islam, has made it no secret that it is at war with the US and that it intends to kill Americans on a massive scale.

In February 2008, Imad Mugniyah was blown into globs of protoplasm, by a car bomb on a well-to-do Damascus street, in close proximity to the Syrian intelligence offices.[9] His long and storied terrorist career was made possible by the ascendancy of Tehran as the world's headquarters for Muslim terrorism. Although no person or entity took credit for the hit, much was already known about the "high-value target." CIA agent, Robert Baer, during the Clinton years, was one of a very few American intelligence officers able to penetrate the Islamic terror networks. In his landmark book, *See No Evil: The True Story of Ground Soldier in the CIA's War on Terrorism*, he proves that Iran provided training, finances, logistics, and diplomatic cover for militarized Muslims who attacked the United States continuously from 1979 to the present. And even more ominously, the Shiite Iranians have partnered with Sunni state-sponsored terrorist organizations to do so. He proved that the two strains of militant Islam had united in terrorist operations against the West.[10]

With their extensive contacts inside American intelligence services, Baer, Ken Timmerman, Steve Emerson, and Jack Cashill have produced a comprehensive trove of evidence that shows the '83 bombings of our embassy and the Marine barracks in Beirut, the '96 Khobar Towers bombing in Saudi Arabia, the '96 downing of TWA Flight 800 off Long Island, and the *9/11 attacks*—all have very identifiable Iranian fingerprints on them. Mugniyah, a Lebanese Shiite, was the Iranians' point man. For twenty-five years, he was the regime's perennial liaison to the various terrorist teams who carried out the most spectacular attacks against Israel and the US. Mugniyah provided the Iranians with the perfect operative who had both an unquenchable thirst for killing the Infidel and complete plausible deniability.[11]

The CIA, FBI, and two separate European intelligence agencies also confirmed that Zakeri (the "Baku Walk in" described earlier) was employed at Iran's Ministry of Intelligence and Security (MOIS). His job was to coordinate the physical security for the regime's most senior leaders and their important foreign visitors.[12]

During the first half of 2001, Zakeri escorted Ayman al-Zawahiri, al-Qaeda's number two man; Saad, Osama bin Laden's eldest son; and their entourages to several major "planning sessions" in and around Tehran. There al-Qaeda's men met

9. BBC News, *Bomb Kills Top Hezbollah Leader*, February 13, 2008.

10. Robert Baer, *See No Evil, The True Story of A Ground Soldier in the CIA's War on Terrorism* (New York: Three Rivers Press, 2002), 8-257.

11. To understand how Iran has played a central role in terrorism world wide since 1979, as banker and often the central planner, please read: *First Strike: TWA Flight 800 and the Attack on America* by Jack Cashill; *Countdown to Crisis: The Coming Nuclear Showdown with Iran* by Ken Timmerman; and *The War Against The Terror Masters* by Michael Ledeen.

12. Ken Timmerman, *Countdown to Crisis*, 7-16.

with the regime's most senior leaders; the five mullahs of the Leadership Council, the Supreme Leader Khamenei, and Rafsanjani. Zakeri overheard al-Zawahiri say to some Iranian officials that his mission in Iran was to build a movement of Sunni and Shiite cooperation and to prepare for a *major operation* against the United States.[13]

On May 4, 2001, Saad bin Laden attended a meeting where the specifics of the 9/11 attacks were presented, and the Iranian regime decided to provide the operational assistance. Zakeri produced a memo from the Iranian leadership with guidelines for joint operations with al-Qaeda. It stressed that the Iranian regime should limit its relations with al-Qaeda to just two people, al-Zawahiri and Imad Mugniyah.[14]

Even the whitewashed politically correct 9/11 Commission Report made a few faint and timid allusions to the "... 8 to 10 al-Qaeda muscle operatives" flying in and out of Iran in 2000 and 2001, and to a "senior Hezbollah operative" (Mugniyah) accompanying them.[15]

During the 1970s, while the Shah was a close American ally in the cold war, Ayatollah Khomeini operated out of France. He distributed vast numbers of sermons to mosques and receptive congregations in Iran and other Shiite enclaves throughout the Islamic world. As a result, it was common knowledge throughout the Middle East that Khomeini had a five-step plan to conquer the West and destroy the Great Satan (the US). Andrew Young, Carter's ambassador to the UN, called Khomeini a "saint."

When the government of the Shah of Iran fell in February 1979, the Carter administration, in partnership with a pliant and gullible press, was successful in convincing the Western public that the Shah was overthrown by the Iranians due to his *repressive* rule. Yet the new Khomeini regime loudly proclaimed, for anyone who bothered to listen, that Iran had become too modern, too *tolerant*. Shortly after the regime took power, student mobs stormed the US Embassy.

As Americans watched the hostage drama on television night after night, no one could know then that what we were seeing was only a *preview* of what the Iranian mob meant by "Death to America." What we know now is that, true to his plan to destroy Israel, Khomeini quickly partnered with Syria's Hafez Assad, to create Hezbollah, one of the world's most dangerous terrorist organizations. This was a truly ominous

---

13. Ibid.

14. Ibid.

15. 9-11 Commission Report, *Final Report of National Commission on Terrorist Attack Upon the United States*, official Government Edition, 240-241. Composed of representatives from both parties, the report reflected and appalling display of our ruling class "circling the wagons" In order to protect their own. Not one person in any branch of government was found guilty of malfeasance in the wake of the worst attack on the US since Pearl Harbor.

development because the governments of Syria and Iran, one Sunni the other Shiite, became partners—what Michael Ledeen calls the new *Terror Masters*.

After seizing power, Khomeini appointed Sabena Rezai, a hardened young resistance fighter, to form a new intelligence service. It became the Republican Guard or Pasdaran. The Supreme Leader tasked him to create a secret police force that was separate from, and not answerable to, the provisional new government. Their first operation was to find and round up all the remnants of the Shah's government and murder them. Khomeini also immediately instituted the practice of public hanging and stoning.[16] The Islamic world's first terrorist state, like all totalitarian regimes, would first rain terror on those inside its own borders who did not wish to conform. The incarceration, torture, and murder of Iranian prisoners of conscience and non-conformists continues to be massive and widespread today.[17]

At Khomeini's death on June 3, 1989, Ali Khamenei, a minor cleric, was elevated to Supreme Leader. Ali Akbar Rafsanjani, the wealthiest man in Iran, was named president.

Rafsanjani effortlessly played a double game, like all Islamist enemies of the West, due to his prestige as both a cleric and an internationally known businessman. He convinced the easily-duped Western media and craven Western governments that he was a moderate and a reformer. At the same time, he sent teams of hit men out of the country to assassinate Iranian expatriate opposition leaders. One month after he assumed the presidency, he pretended to negotiate a truce with Kurdish leader, Abdolrahman Ghassemlou, in Vienna and his Kurdish Democratic Party of Iran. Then he authorized Abdelrahman's murder. In addition to sponsoring other high value "hits" in Europe, he personally signed off on major attacks on US assets—the Khobar Towers bombing in Saudi Arabia and 9/11.[18] As late as 2011, he was still one of the driving forces behind Iran's mad dash to acquire nuclear weapons.[19]

Al-Qaeda and Iran—Sunnis and Shiites Ominously Unite

By mid-2002, Taliban and al-Qaeda fighters—who were not dead or captured—escaped Afghanistan. They were hiding in either the tribal regions of Western Pakistan or in its province of Baluchistan. In July, President Pervez Musharraf announced that

---

16. Feydoun Hoveyda, *The Second Death of Ayatollah Khomeini*, National Committee on American Foreign Policy.
17. Larry Kelley, *A Message from the Iranian Resistance to President Bush*, October 11, 2006, http://larrykelley.com/2006/10/11/a-message-from-the-iranian-resistance-to-president-bush/.
18. Nineteen American service men were killed in the Khobar Tower attacks of 1996.
19. Ken Timmerman, *Countdown to Crisis*, 15 -185.

he was sending commandos into those regions to capture bin Laden who had a $25 million bounty on his head.

Richard Miniter, author of *Shadow War*, learned, from his intelligence sources on the ground in the Middle East, that bin Laden sent an audio tape to the Iranian Supreme Council pledging to put al-Qaeda under the service of Iran in exchange for safe harbor and funding. After the fall of Tora Bora, satellite images confirmed movements of convoys moving from Southern Pakistan and Afghanistan into Iran. First bin Laden's four wives, then Saad, bin Laden's then heir apparent, then al-Zawahiri, and finally, on July 26, bin Laden himself crossed into Iran at the border crossing near Zabol. For the next seven months Iran denied that there were any al-Qaeda operatives inside the country. Then on February 21, 2003, Foreign Minister Kharrazi stated that the Iranian government had arrested over 400 al-Qaeda members and that Iran was "holding them in jail."[20] While bin Laden would ultimately find permanent residence status in Pakistan, Iran provided safe harbor for significant remnants of al-Qaeda, cadres of hardened terrorists that the regime warehoused for use in future attacks against Israel, the US, and its allies.

By fall 2010, it became abundantly clear that it was dangerously absurd for President Obama to think he could negotiate with the Mullahs running Iran. The radical theocracy had spent decades attacking the US and untold billions of dollars sacrificing economic growth to develop a nuclear weapons program aimed at the destruction of the West. Obama's initial attempt was grossly naïve and a clear violation of:

IMMUTABLE #3
Appeasement of a ruthless outside power always invites aggression. Treaties made with ruthless despots are always fruitless and dangerous.

The Iranian Electromagnetic Pulse Weapon

A seven year study, commissioned by Congress, was delivered in Spring 2008 to the House Armed Services Committee by Chairman Dr. William Graham of the Claremont Institute. The report revealed that a terrorist group could plausibly move a barge near the US and, from the safety of international waters, launch and detonate a nuclear tipped missile into our atmosphere. In the blink of an eye, our electrical grid would be destroyed—crippling "military and civilian communications, power, transportation, water, food," and virtually every other vital infrastructure. The report

20. Richard Miniter, *Shadow War: The Untold Story of How Bush Is Winning the War on Terror*, (Washington DC: Regnery Publishing, 2004), 18-19.

warns that America would be reduced to a "pre-industrial society" where barter would be the only form of commerce and where "Nine out of 10 American would not survive the first year after the attack." [21]

In short, a *single* EMP weapon has the potential to destroy the United States. Iran has repeatedly stated, "It is both desirable and achievable to bring about a world without America," and has been testing EMP delivery systems and missiles from platforms on the Caspian Sea. Iran's development of nuclear and, especially, EMP technology is *the* greatest threat to this country posed by the resurgence of militant Islam.

The Rebirth of Militant Islam and the Muslim Brotherhood [22]

In their 2009 book, *Muslim Mafia*, coauthors David Gaubatz and Paul Sperry exposed the Muslim Brotherhood as the worldwide Islamist hand behind *all* Sunni terrorist groups. As the world's largest and most dangerous Islamist organization with offices in 88 countries, it is largely funded by the Saudi government. Additionally, *Muslim Mafia* exposes the "Brothers'" secret plan for the eventual Islamic domination of the United States.[23]

> *"By 1948, only thirty years had passed since the collapse of the Ottoman Empire. In that year, an influential Egyptian writer, Sayyid Qutb (pronounced Kuh–tub) set sail from Cairo to New York City. His trip was financed by powerful Egyptian friends who were also conspiring against the dissolute monarch, King Farouk, who was a puppet of the occupying British government, and who had put out a warrant for the seditious writer's arrest. Also in that year, five Arab armies were in the final stages of losing the war to prevent the establishment of the Jewish state within Islamic lands, (a defeat that) not only stunned the Arab world but the shame of that experience would shape the Arab intellectual experience more profoundly than any other in modern history."* [24]

Qutb's writing espoused a new Islamic fundamentalist ideology, a movement, and

21. W.R. Graham, Chairman, *Commission to Assess the Threat to the United States from Electromagnetic Pulse (EMP) Attack*, delivered in testimony to the House Armed Services Committee, July 10, 2008.

22. Larry Kelley, *Islamist Infiltration*, excerpt (*Townhall Magazine,* May 2010), 44 -50.

23. David Gaubatz, Paul Sperry, *Muslim Mafia: Inside the Secret Underworld That's Conspiring to Islamize America*, (Los Angeles : WND Books, 2009).

24. Lawrence Wright, *The Looming Tower: Al-Qaeda and the Road to 9/11*, (New York: Alfred A. Knopf, division of Random House, 2006), 201.

an organization—the *Muslim Brotherhood*. Founded by an equally influential Egyptian, Sheikh Hassan al-Banna, the goal of the Brotherhood was to convert Egypt into an Islamic state.[25] Al-Banna was a man of action. In just two decades since its founding, his organization had hundreds of thousands of members across Egypt and throughout the Middle East. He and Qutb saw the movement as a kind of counter society, challenging every norm of Western secular politics and culture. The Brothers built their own schools, hospitals, and factories. Ominously, al-Banna taught that it is the nature of Islam to dominate—not to be dominated—and to impose its law on all nations.[26]

While in the United States, Qutb began writing a book filled with revulsion for what he saw as spiritual wasteland of sexual licentiousness and materialism. He was threatened by promiscuous American women that he encountered, believing that only by resisting their exceptional powers could he find salvation.[27]

In 1949, Qutb was still in the US. His book, *Social Justice in Islam*, was about to be published. He was shocked to learn that al-Banna had been assassinated. The Egyptian government killed al-Banna out of self-defense because the Brothers were embracing violence—blowing up movie theaters in Cairo and murdering British and Egyptian officials.[28]

With al-Banna's death, Qutb became the leading voice of the new Muslim fundamentalism and blamed America and the West for al-Banna's murder. Qutb wrote, "The white man in Europe or America is our number one enemy. . . . We are endowing our children with amazement and respect for the master who tramples our honor and enslaves us. Let us instead plant the seeds of hatred, disgust, and revenge in the souls of these children. Let us teach them that the white man is the enemy of humanity, and that they should destroy him at the first opportunity." [29]

In August 1950, Qutb returned to Egypt, fully radicalized and determined to violently overthrow the regime. By this time, the Muslim Brotherhood had one million members in a country of eighteen million.

January 1952, the Brothers fomented a riot which saw 750 buildings incinerated and thirty killed in the center of Cairo.[30] September 1952, the government was seized in a military junta, led by Gamal Nasser, a young army colonel. For the first time in 2,500 years, Egypt was ruled by Egyptians. The military plotters coordinated the coup

25. Ibid.
26. Ibid.
27. Ibid.
28. Ibid.
29. Ibid. 223.
30. Ibid.

very closely with the Brothers. In fact, one of the officers, Anwar Sadat, who succeeded Nasser, was himself a Brother.

While Nasser invited Qutb to be an advisor to his Revolutionary Command Council, the alliance was short lived. Nasser's dream was to found a pan-Arab modern socialist state with Cairo as its capital. This had nothing to do with a new theocratic Caliphate—the dream of Qutb and the Brothers. Their mutual hostility toward democracy was about all they had in common. In October 1954, while Nasser was speaking to a huge assembly and the country listened on the radio, a number of Brothers opened fire on him. Miraculously, Nasser escaped injury. The regime immediately captured and hung the conspirators, rounded up thousands of Brothers, and placed thousands in concentration camps. Qutb was given a life sentence.

Nasser thought he had destroyed the Brotherhood. Instead, Qutb, who suffered torture in prison, became the hero in a kind of passion play for the new Islamic fundamentalists. Through family and friends, bits and pieces of Qutb's Islamist manifesto, *Milestones*, were smuggled out of his cell and published in 1962. It profoundly influenced a young Osama bin Laden.[31]

Although Nasser pardoned and released him in 1964, Qutb immediately went back to plotting violent revolution with the secret support of Saudi Arabia, whose ruling monarchy feared Nasser's brand of pan Arabism. Six months later Qutb and forty-two conspirators were arrested and put on trial. Qutb received his death sentence gratefully. "I performed jihad for fifteen years until I earned this martyrdom," he declared.[32] Nasser knew that Qutb was more dangerous to him dead than alive.

Nasser dispatched Sadat to visit Qutb in prison and offered him another pardon if he would a write a request for clemency. Qutb refused. He was hung, after prayers, in August 1966. His body was not surrendered to his family for fear his grave would become a shrine. As Wright puts it, "(Qutb's) lonely genius would unsettle Islam, threaten regimes across the Muslim world, and beckon to a generation of rootless Arabs who were looking for meaning and purpose in their lives and would find them in jihad." [33]

Al-Banna and Qutb were the Marx and Vladimir Lenin of the new Islamic fundamentalism that produced the Muslim Brothers, that has spread to every corner of the globe. They have inspired and produced unknown numbers of new leaders of

---

31. Ibid.
32. Ibid.
33. Ibid, 297.

even more violent splinter affiliates: Hamas, the Taliban; Ayman al-Zawahiri's al-Jihad, which conducted the assassination of Anwar Sadat; and Osama bin Laden's al-Qaeda.

Brothers in America, CAIR, and the Smoking Gun

There were 481 officially recognized Mosques in the United States in 1980. By 2009, 1,209 mosques were practicing *Wahhabi* Islam, the virulently anti-Western religion of the Arabian Peninsula. The Saudi Kingdom still has public stonings; a visitor can be imprisoned for the crime of possessing a Bible or wearing a crucifix, and it is against the law to build a Christian church, of course. The Saudi's are playing a double game—pretending to be our ally and a key trading partner while, at the same time, financing and partnering with the Muslim Brotherhood to undermine American institutions and national security. A brief historic timeline of the Brotherhood's development follows:

1960s—The Brothers sent vast numbers of students to American
Universities, mostly in the Midwest.
1973—North American Islamic Trust (NAIT) was formed with massive
Saudi funding. It is an investment vehicle that enabled them to
acquire 300 mosques and schools in the US.
1984—Ahmad Elkadi was made Masul, godfather of the American
Brotherhood.
1985—The Brothers founded International Institute of Islamic Thought
(IIIT).
1987—Hamas, the Palestinian wing of the Brothers, was founded and
largely funded by American Muslims.[34] The stated goal is to destroy
Israel.
1988—Two hundred Brothers were trained in the US for terror
operations here and abroad.
1990—American Muslim Council (AMC) was formed with Abdurrahman
Alamoudi its boss, and the new capo di tutti of the entire syndicate.
1994—Council on American-Islamic Relations (CAIR) was founded. It
is the parent organization that manages and speaks for all the Sunni
Islamist groups in the United States.

The Brotherhood skillfully gained influence in impoverished Egypt by

---

34. Gaubatz and Sperry, *Muslim Mafia*, 67.

constructing hospitals and schools in poor Muslim countries. Yet the Brotherhood grew to become a violent, worldwide, central clearing house for virtually all Sunni terrorists and jihadists that operate inside the US. They have Saudi financed operatives in Mosques all across the country and in plush American offices of CAIR, and its myriad subsidiaries.

Muslim Mafia was a landmark book that implicated the Brotherhood for its ongoing operations in their attempt to compromise the US. It is a compilation of recently declassified FBI documents, agent interviews, transcripts of telephone wiretaps, and thousands of internal documents and memos that were smuggled out of CAIR headquarters. The vast trove of incontrovertible evidence was obtained by Chris Gaubatz, one of the coauthor's sons, who posed as an American convert to Islam. He was hired by CAIR to perform various entry-level tasks, one of which was shredding sensitive documents.[35]

By 2010, the Muslim Brotherhood, with funding primarily from Saudi Arabia, controlled over forty-seven "moderate" Muslim front groups operating openly in the US. With countless other subsidiary shell companies, they form a web of subversion and deception that operates much like a massive organized crime syndicate. As its parent, CAIR provides leadership, political access, funding, manpower, and direction to the syndicate.

Conventional organized crime amasses wealth for wealth's sake. The Brothers amass wealth as a means to fund jihadists who seek to destabilize and bring down Western governments and Muslim regimes that they deem too westernized and not pure enough.

While posing as an Islamic intern, Chris Gaubatz obtained an amazing document, the actual *smoking gun* that outlined the Brothers' ultimate goal to gain control of the US and to impose sharia law. In *Muslim Mafia*, Sperry and Gaubatz published, for the first time, the Brothers' five-phase plan for America:

Phase 1: Establish an elite Muslim Leadership and raise Islamist consciousness in the community.
Phase 2: Create Islamic Institutions that the leadership can control and form autonomous Muslim enclaves.
Phase 3: Infiltrate America's political and social institutions forming a shadow state. Escalate conversions. Manipulate mass media to remove language offensive to Islam.

---

35. Ibid.

Phase 4: Open hostile public confrontation over US policies, riot, and make militant demands for special rights and accommodations.

Phase 5: Wage final conflict and overthrow (jihad).[36]

In 2009, the consensus among counterterrorism officials interviewed for *Muslim Mafia* was that the North American Brotherhood was already in Phase III.

Religious Infiltrators

Many American imams are secretly Muslim Brothers.[37] Posted to major mosques all across the country, they play a pivotal role in implementing the first two phases of the plan, acting as recruiters and organizers. In their internal documents they refer to the US as "Dar al-Arqam," safehouse. FBI wiretaps of secret meetings reveal that the Brotherhood views the US as a pushover.[38]

Like Imam Rauf, who sought to build a huge mosque two blocks from ground zero, many American imams openly espouse insurrection. And they do so with little fear of American law enforcement agencies, knowing that we are a multiculturalist society fixated on tolerance.

Sperry and Gaubatz cite the American Muslim cleric, Zaid Shaker, who was secretly recorded giving a lecture in the San Francisco area. "If we put a nationwide infrastructure in place and marshaled our resources, we'd take over this country in a very short time," he told his fellow Muslim Americans. He then referenced the Brotherhood's plan to overthrow the US. The Brotherhood has made it clear that the US is their big prize. Shaker is a regular speaker at CAIR sponsored events and is considered a prominent Muslim American by the politically correct, easily duped Washington establishment.

With Saudi trained imams as their point men, the Brothers have developed a massive infrastructure inside the US with their own shadow-state and controlled media. A few of these institutions listed in *Muslim Mafia* are:

Islamic Society of North America (ISNA) functions as their own AFL-CIO.

American Muslim Armed Forces and Veterans' Affairs Council functions as their own VFW (Veterans of Foreign Wars).

---

36. Ibid.
37. Ibid.
38. Ibid.

Council on American-Islamic Relations (CAIR) functions as their NAACP
(National Association for the Advancement of Colored People).

World Assembly of Muslim Youth functions as their YMCA. Instead of
holding basketball camps, it holds jihad camps.

Holy Land Foundation, before the FBI shut it down, was its United Way.[39]

US Government Infiltrators

The Brothers have steadily gained access to the highest levels of our government
since the Clinton administration. A few American-based Muslims who were
imprisoned for supporting terror or advocating treason are:

Sami al-Arian

On the morning of 9/11 Sami al-Arian awoke "extremely upbeat."
Finally, all the work he had done in Florida "getting out the Muslim vote"
had paid off. His White House sponsor, Grover Norquist, argued that it
was al-Arian's Muslim voters in Florida who had pushed George W. Bush
over the finish line. In a few hours, he and eight other Muslim leaders
would meet with the President to discuss how Bush would live up to his
campaign pledge to end the use of secret intelligence used to investigate
American Muslims. This would be the culmination of a four-year effort
for the Muslim professor and secret Brotherhood capo.

Unfortunately for al-Arian, the 9/11 attacks preempted their
audience with the President. Instead the "Muslim Nine" along with
White House Muslim Outreach Director, Suhail Khan, met a few blocks
away in Norquist's office to do "damage control." "It was an embarrassing
irony..."[40] On the same day Muslim terrorists staged the worst attack on
the US since Pearl Harbor, our government was negotiating with them to
deny law enforcement the necessary tools to stop the next attack.

Al-Arian was convicted of fraudulently raising money, laundering
it through the Holy Land Foundation, and funneling it to Hamas and
other terrorist organizations conducting suicide operations in Israel.
Al-Arian made many post-9/11 anti-terror pronouncements to American
audiences. He was also recorded telling Muslim gatherings, "We are in
a battle of life and death, in a battle of the fate and future of Western

39. David Gaubatz and Paul Sperry, *Muslim Mafia: Inside the Secret Underworld That's Conspiring to Islamize America* (Los Angeles: WND Books, 2009), 78.

40. Ibid, 301.

hegemony and tyranny. . . . What is needed is the dismantling of the cultural system of the West." [41] Through his fundraising activities, al Arian has been directly linked to the murders of over two-hundred people, including two Americans.

How had the Brotherhood gained such incredible access to the White House? For the answer, one needs to look back to the Clinton years.

Abdurrahman Alamoudi

In 1997, Norquist brokered a meeting with then Governor George W. Bush to develop a plan to bring in a previously untapped voting block. He called it the "Muslim Strategy." The meeting featured Alamoudi (the putative Martin Luther King of American Muslims, an officer in more than a dozen Muslim front groups, and by then, the secret US Brotherhood Boss of Bosses); his lieutenant at the American Muslim Council, Khaled Saffuri; along with Carl Rove; Norquist; and Talar Othman, a Saudi friend of Bush and fellow member of Harken Oil. They met to flesh out the plan to acquire the American Muslim vote which involved a quid pro quo from Bush. If elected, Bush would move to limit the government's use of secret information in the investigation of Muslims. The strategy worked and arguably made the difference in electing Bush.

Born to a Yemeni businessman, Alamoudi had long been the toast of the town in multiculturist Washington. In 1993, he was commissioned to create the first Muslim Chaplin corps for the Pentagon (that has reaped deadly results). The Clinton Administration's state department sent him on numerous missions to Middle East countries. In 1996, he organized the first Ramadan dinner for government officials as well as met with Clinton and Gore in the White House. That same year, he was recorded at the Islamic Association of Palestine's annual convention in Illinois, saying "I think if we are outside the country, we can say, "O Allah, destroy America." But once we are here, our mission in this country is to change it." [42]

Today Alamoudi is a Muslim Gotti, serving a twenty-three-year prison sentence. Busted in 2003 by the British, as he tried to smuggle into

---

41. Ibid, 234.
42. Ibid, 250.

the US $340,000 in sequentially numbered bills from Libya, he eventually pleaded guilty to plotting terrorist attacks on the US with support from Libya. Prosecutors connected him to Hamas and al-Qaeda.

Sheikh Hamza Yusuf

The only Muslim in a group of religious leaders invited to the White House to pray with the President after 9/11, Yusuf is an American born convert to Islam and cultivates his moderate image. But only *two days* prior to 9/11, on September 9, 2001, he spoke to Muslims in Irvine, California, gathered in support of a Muslim imam that had killed a cop, and said, ". . . [this country] stands condemned to suffer a terrible fate. . . . It stands condemned like Europe stood condemned because of what it did. . . . Europe suffered two world wars after conquering the Muslim lands."

Omar Ahmad

Founder of CAIR and an honored guest at the George W. Bush White House, Ahmad was invited to the National Cathedral to mourn the Americans lost on 9/11. In 1998, he was secretly recorded, at an Islamic conference in Fremont, California, saying, "Islam isn't in America to be equal to any other faith but to become dominant. The Qur'an should be the highest authority in America and Islam the only accepted religion." (Translation—someday we will be able to command the American infidel to submit or die.)

Whole American-based Brotherhood front groups have been black-listed by the US Treasury Department or raided and shut down by the FBI. On that list are the big three: Islamic Society of North America (ISNA), Council on American-Islamic Relations (CAIR), and the Holy Land Foundation (HLF). The FBI shut down the largest Muslim charity, HLF, for fraudulently raising money for Hamas and listed CAIR as an unindicted co-conspirator. As Sperry and Gaubatz put it in *Mafia*, "It's no surprise that a group run by ex-Palestinian terrorists would support Palestinian terror. But CAIR supports al-Qaeda, the Taliban and homegrown terrorists. It's a full-service terror support group." [43]

---

43. Ibid, 135.

The Compromised

Nearly ten years after 9/11, many Western leaders and officials were compromised by two interlocking phenomenon. First, their political correctness would not allow them to countenance a belief system that is cloaked in a religious conviction that includes our subjugation. And second, and for good reason, they were driven by fear.

In Northern Virginia, the Muslim Brotherhood targeted a prosecutor, US Attorney Gordon Kromberg, and issued death threats to him and his family for his prosecution of many of their leaders, including CAIR executives.

Robert S. Mueller—FBI Director

The FBI Director appointed by George W. Bush and retained by Obama, allowed his agency to be infiltrated and his agents brainwashed by CAIR/Brotherhood operatives. One of his responses to 9/11 was to sponsor "diversity and sensitivity workshops" conducted by CAIR executives. As Sperry and Gaubatz point out, these quickly turned into nothing less than "dangerous disinformation campaigns designed to desensitize agents from the threat of Islamic terrorism." And they appear to have that effect on Mueller himself, who will not allow the word "Islamic" to be used in reference to terrorism in any public FBI documents.

The FBI's "outreach" to CAIR was temporarily suspended in 2008. One of its agents uncovered a trove of documents in a terror suspect's home just outside DC. The documents named CAIR and numerous other supposedly mainstream Muslim organizations as being involved in the Holy Land Foundation conspiracy, the largest terror financing case in US history. The documents also confirmed that CAIR is plotting the overthrow of the US government.

Incredibly, it was the policy of Mueller's Assistant Director for Public Affairs, John Miller, to keep CAIR and other Muslim groups informed about *FBI plans to raid Islamic targets in counterterrorism investigations.*

Brian Humphrey—Customs and Border Protection

As Customs and Border Protection Executive Director, Humphrey reported to Michael Chertoff, Director of Homeland Security. Brian assured CAIR that his agents would not single out Muslim airline passengers for special screening. Furthermore, his agents must undergo a course in Muslim sensitivity that was put together by Margaret Nydell, an Arabic Studies professor at Georgetown University. Her department is lavishly funded by the Saudis, while she is a leading Muslim apologist and purveyor of misinformation. One border agent described her course as "politically-correct drivel."

Valery Jarret—Presidential Senior Advisor

A longtime associate from Chicago and senior advisor to President Obama, she had the dubious distinction of being the first White

America's First Islamic Congressman
Congressman Ellison's Swearing in
Ceremony with Thomas Jefferson's Qur'an

House official to address a national convention of the Islamic Society of North America (ISNA) by giving the keynote address. ISNA and CAIR are sister organizations with interlocking boards of directors and proven ties to terrorism and murder. Most of their senior members are Brothers. Shockingly, they are also American citizens, professionals, scholars, doctors, many with PhD's, that give them a veneer of respectability. In *Mafia*, Gaubatz and Sperry wrote, "FBI agents who listened in on their private conversations report they talk about murder and killing Jews, like they were ordering pizza."

Keith Ellison—Democrat Congressman from Minnesota

In 2010, through his sources on Capitol Hill, Robert Spencer found out that Ellison, the country's first openly Muslim member of Congress, received $13,350 to fund his hajj (pilgrimage) to Mecca. The money came from the Muslim American Society, a chief operating front group for the Muslim Brotherhood, whose charter states that it is dedicated to "eliminating and destroying Western civilization from within and sabotaging its miserable house by their hands and the hands of the believers so that it is eliminated and God's religion is made victorious over all other religions." [44]

---

44. Robert Spencer, *Muslim Brotherhood Has Its Own Congressman*, (*Human Events Magazine*, September 27, 2010), 17. Mr. Spencer is one of the world's leading authorities on Islam and author of books on Islam; *The Truth About Muhammad*, *The Politically Incorrect Guide to Islam*, and others.

Ellison was predictably a great supporter of Imam Rauf's initiative to build a mosque at ground zero, accusing opponents of bigotry and of "scapegoating" Muslims. Of course, his real motivation for the mosque's construction was that it would signal to the world the ascendancy of Islam over the US. It would celebrate the deaths of three thousand infidels.

Eric Holder—Attorney General

President Obama's Attorney General seemed to be equally compromised by Muslim intimidation and the ideology of the extreme transnational Left. He served as the number two man in the Justice Department during the Clinton years when, as Andrew McCarthy puts it, "nearly as many terrorists were pardoned as were prosecuted." He served during a time when the al-Qaeda attacks on the US occurred every year and escalated in intensity.

His initial desire to close the Guantanamo prison, without a plan for what to do with the two hundred terrorists detained there, along with wanting to try Khalid Sheikh Mohammed (the mastermind of 9/11) in a civilian court, is indicative of a much larger malfeasance in the Obama administration's approach to our war with resurgent militant Islam.

In a 2009 testimony before the house judiciary committee, he made it obvious that he had no idea that his "law enforcement approach" to the war would make the country less safe and our new president look weak and inept. He exhibited an abject ignorance of the fact that a civilian trial for the terrorists would be exactly what our Islamic enemies crave, a new weapon where they would gain intelligence and broadcast propaganda.

During his testimony, Senator Lindsey Graham, of South Carolina, asked Holder if he could cite a case in US history when an enemy combatant caught on the battlefield was tried in civilian court. Holder was only able to stammer, "I don't know. I'd have to look at that." Graham informed him that there had never been one.

By the ten-year anniversary of 9/11, the Islamic Republic of Iran, the world's leading sponsor of terrorism, seemed poised to test its first nuclear weapon. The Islamist networks capable of importing a nuclear device had infiltrated the highest echelons of America's governmental institutions.

The Real Barry Soetoro

"Seventy-two days after his inauguration, at a G-20 summit in London, the forty-fourth President of the United States, Barack Obama, strode purposefully across the floor of Buckingham Palace, under the portraits of Britain's greatest heroes, and, for the leaders of the richest nations and all the world to see, Obama bowed "deeply and reverentially, before King Abdullah, keeper of the two Holy Mosques, the absolute monarch of the Kingdom of Saudi Arabia." [45] Barack Obama must have known that, for the majority of Muslims worldwide, this act of prostration by a US President was proof that Islam was now ascendant over the West. To use bin Laden's phrase, "Islam was the stronger horse."

No president in US history has ever bowed to another head of state. It was as if he wished to send a clear signal to the Muslim world that America would honor its grievances and acquiesce to its demands.

"Obama's first television interview was on an Arabic television network. His first overseas trip was to the Muslim (and the increasingly Islamist) country of Turkey. He then traveled to Saudi Arabia. Then he was off to Egypt to deliver an "address to the Muslim World" in which he saluted their concepts of *freedom* and *scientific advancement* and the contributions of Muslims throughout history to that freedom and advance." [46] His speech surely devastated those American families who lost sons and daughters in Kuwait, Bosnia, Afghanistan, and Iraq, Muslim countries the US has recently freed from tyrannical oppression. He made no mention of their sacrifice on behalf of Muslims. The omission was a gross abdication of his position as Commander-in-Chief.

Later, in his Cairo speech, President Obama absurdly stated that "Islam is not part of the problem in combating violent extremism—it is an important part of promoting peace." [47] The Qur'an is filled with violent verses and its history filled with violent aggression.

His Cairo speech begged the question—was the US to dismiss the Beirut bombing, the original 1993 World Trade Center attack (that if successful would have collapsed one tower against the other and killed 250,000), the Khobar Towers, the Embassies in Africa, and 9/11?

The president's actions and statements during his first few weeks in office were

---

45. Andrew McCarthy, *The Grand Jihad: How Islam and the Left Sabotage America* (New York: Encounter Books, 2010), 2.

46. Bill Bennett and Seth Leibsohn, *The Fight of Our Lives, Knowing the Enemy, Speaking the Truth, & Choosing to Win the War Against Radical Islam* (Tennessee: Thomas Nelson, 2011), 71.

47. McCarthy, *The Grand Jihad*, 25.

absurd and, coming from the leader of Western Civilization, they were dangerous and in violation of several immutables:

The Appeasement Immutable

Appeasement of a ruthless outside power always invites aggression. Bernard Lewis, our greatest living historian of the Middle East, the great professor, agrees and has a phrase for Obama's actions—"anxious propitiation." "Appeasement is the worst thing you can show them if we value our safety and their reticence." he writes.

Hanson's Law

No nation has survived once its citizens ceased to believe its culture worth saving. As one pundit put it, "Obama's prescription was for preemptive cultural surrender."

By late 2010, Pew Research revealed that 18% of the American population believed Obama to actually *be* a Muslim. As Bennett and Leibsohn write, "It was actually odd that the number was so low given not only his name but his very deliberate effort to speak of his 'Muslim roots' as well as his manifold unsolicited attempts to speak on behalf of Islam. Egregiously, while on Muslim soil, he apologized for imprisoning terrorists (another first for a US president). In Egypt he said, "I have known Islam on three continents before coming to the region where it was first revealed." [48]

The actions of the new president, during his first few weeks in office, were aimed at accepting guilt for having gone to war to eliminate the Islamic terrorists who attacked us. He laid down a new marker by saying, "We've never been at war with Islam and will never be." (Translation—I will shut down the war against Islamic terror.) His actions and statements shamed the previous administration, those who supported it, and the military which had done a superlative job defending the country. It opened a grave wound in the American resolve to somehow win the war against resurgent militant Islam, no matter how long it takes, no matter the sacrifice.

His actions and pronouncements did something else, particularly his bow of "national humiliation." It demonstrated that we would revert to the Clinton model and pretend that there was: *no war*, no whole Muslim countries (Iran), no major Islamic terrorist organizations (Hamas, Hezbollah), and no vast numbers of sleeper cells laying in wait and plotting their next attack.

---

48. Bennett, Leibsohn, *The Fight of our Lives*, 105.

By Spring 2011, two and one half years into Obama's presidency and just months before the ten-year anniversary of 9/11, numerous polls recorded that 70% of all Americans thought the country was "headed in the wrong direction." (Translation: 7 out of 10 of us saw the country in decline.) Clearly, the administration had violated the tenth immutable:

IMMUTABLE #10
Declining civilizations will always face superior firepower from ascending civilizations because sovereignty is only temporarily uncontested.

In observing the words and deeds of President Barack Hussein Obama, on his trip to the Middle East, the average jihadist must have believed that the new American president was one of *them* and, *Allah willing*, the new Arab ascendancy was at hand. Consequently, during 2009, the first full year of the Obama presidency, the US suffered its highest number of attacks since 9/11—in terms of failed attempts such as the Times Square bomber and in terms of the most lethal such as the Fort Hood massacre.

Although it did not surface until five months after the inauguration, Barry Soetoro was listed on Obama's 1967 registration card at Indonesia's Fransiskus Assisi School. He was registered there by his Muslim stepfather, Lolo Soetoro, with his religion listed as Muslim.[49]

The forty-fifth president, the person who succeeds Barack Obama, faces a dire situation, similar to 1940, when the country was financially crippled by nearly a decade of massive Keynesian spending, and America's enemies abroad were mobilizing for war with the US. The new president will have an even more dire situation than FDR did because the economy will be too fragile to absorb a major attack. If it is not too late, his task will be nothing short of monumental—if the war has not yet begun he will very likely need to mobilize the American public for preemptive war with the Iranian regime.

---

49. It was July 2009, five months after the inauguration, that a photograph of the registration card surfaced on various Internet sites. It was taken by Tatan Syuflana, an Indonesian AP reporter.

CHAPTER SEVEN

Reigniting American Resolve to Defeat Those Plotting Our Destruction

We will fundamentally transform America.
BARACK HUSSEIN OBAMA
INAUGURAL ADDRESS, JANUARY 20, 2009

Since the mythical era of the demigod Achilles, ascendant civilizations have always produced small cadres of elite warriors. Their prodigious skills and audacity, combined with the element of surprise, have continuously, throughout the history of warfare, produced an astonishing means of martial leverage.

As we saw in the chapter *The Fall of Carthage*, by 207 BC, Rome and its allies of the Italian peninsula had lost approximately one hundred thousand soldiers to the great Hannibal. Moreover, the Carthaginians were in the final stages of securing massive reinforcements from Phillip V of Macedon. That same year the Roman Senate boldly sent a small clandestine group of provocateurs to Northern Greece who started violent insurrections among Phillip's disaffected subject peoples. The Macedonians never sailed.

Generations later, Romans look back at that year as a high-water mark for Roman stoicism. They knew full well that the combined armies of Carthage and Macedon would have brought their destruction.

A Special Forces Presidency

The 9/11 attacks brought about the largest one-day American death toll since Pearl Harbor. It opened a gaping wound in the Pentagon, the symbol of American military might. In response, President George W. Bush, as Commander-in-Chief, correctly sensed that he needed to make a bold statement to the world. He needed to rally the American martial spirit for what he knew would be a long and bloody war against resurgent militant Islam. He saw that the country needed a victory and needed it fast.

Sensing the mood of the country, and correctly ascertaining who had carried out the attacks, President George W. Bush signed an order directing the CIA to destroy bin Laden and al-Qaeda. He ordered George Tenet, CIA Director, to present him with a plan of attack. Tenet delivered his plan in just six days, on September 17. It carried a billion dollar price tag. ". . . half the price of a B-2 stealth bomber. Bush decided to grant all of Tenet's requests including an extra $1 billion. He wanted the paramilitary wing of the CIA to be first on the ground, preparing the way for the military." [1]

The goal was to destroy, with ferocious immediacy, both the Taliban and al-Qaeda and replace them with a regime allied with the US. Bush knew he could not wait the requisite six months needed to mount a conventional invasion of the country. He correctly surmised that the Taliban might have numerous other plots already headed toward the US. Secondly, he did not want to stand by while bin Laden, flushed with his victory, recruited massive numbers of new Jihadists to join his army in the defense of Afghanistan. Finally, the overwhelming desire for retribution amid the nation did not allow him that time.

The plan was to immediately insert the nation's most intrepid Special Forces men into North Afghanistan. Their orders were to link up with the beleaguered Northern Alliance guerillas, a collection of primitive warlike tribes that the CIA supported in exchange for intelligence, who were losing their war with the Taliban.

The mission, like that of their Roman forbearers of the second century BC, would be to befriend, recruit, equip, advise, and lead the Afghan Northern Alliance in their attacks against the Taliban and al-Qaeda. Additionally, they were to provide the necessary on-the-ground GPS/laser technology for precision air strikes. By early October, one of the most audacious and successful episodes in the long history of Special Forces warfare commenced.

An excerpt from Doug Stanton's *Horse Soldiers* is illustrative:

> *"Ahead our horsemen (Northern Alliance) charged the middle of the line, about 600 yards away. The men on foot trotted behind. Grimacing, gripping their rifles and RPG tubes, ducking whenever they heard an explosion or the whine of a passing bullet. Nelson looked up just as the*

---

1.   Ronald Kessler, *The Terrorist Watch: Inside the Desperate Race to Stop the Next Attack* (New York: Crown Forum, Division of Random House, 2007), 36.

Taliban line exploded. The bombs from the jet overhead smashed one of the tanks. . . . As he rode, JJ started passing Taliban fighters who had been hiding in the grass. They jumped up shooting, and JJ spun in his saddle, firing his AK. Spann came upon a Taliban who was running away, when suddenly the soldier turned and took aim. Spann shot him in the head.

Up ahead, Nelson could see the Taliban line breaking in places. Here and there like a sand wall crumbling. And he was amazed when he saw that some of the Taliban were running toward them with their hands held high in surrender. He was equally surprised when they started falling face forward dead in the dirt . . . they had been shot in the back by their commanders still on the line."[2]

Not since the nineteenth century had the American military engaged an enemy in a cavalry charge. By December 7, 2001, the war was practically over when the Taliban abandoned Kandahar. A small number of CIA paramilitary and Special Forces units managed to put together a force of three thousand Afghan fighters to take Kandahar.

Also that December, US and Afghan troops surrounded bin Laden's mountain redoubt at Tora Bora only to let him slip away.

Johnny "Mike" Spann was killed in an uprising of Taliban prisoners where, ironically, an American member of the Taliban, John Walker Lindh, was captured. Spann was the first American killed in the post 9/11 war with militant Islam. Despite the dire predictions issued by leftist members of academia and the media, Afghanistan, the "graveyard of civilizations," succumbed to what will be remembered as an American-assisted paramilitary assault of breathtaking audacity. In the wake of the 9/11 horrific attacks

Johnny Spann

and in a matter of weeks, President George W. Bush provided the wounded American psyche a victory in Afghanistan with the use of our Special Forces and high technology warfare.

It was the Afghan Taliban that America had defeated, not the Afghan people. During the Afghanistan campaign, Abdul Dostum, one of our allied warlords of the Northern Alliance, described the situation on the ground in his troubled land of Islam:

2. Doug Stanton, *Horse Soldiers: The Extraordinary Story of a Band of US Soldiers Who Rode to Victory in Afghanistan* (New York: Scribner, Division of Simon and Schuster, 2009), 166.

> *"The (Afghan) Taliban are like slaves. . . . They are slaves because they are forced to fight. They (foreign Taliban) threaten to kill the soldier's family if he does not fight . . . the Taliban Army which numbered as high as 50,000, were farmers, teachers, shopkeepers conscripted into service. The foreign Taliban, the Pakistanis, the Saudis, the Chechens, even the Chinese, they were fierce men, ferocious fighters. They had infested the country from radical madrassahs in Pakistan. They were often joined by bin Laden's Al-Qaeda army. . . . When we capture the Afghan Taliban . . . they switch sides and start to fight with us . . . As for the Arab Taliban . . . they prefer death. You can't capture them. You must kill them. They never give up."* [3]

The brief Taliban rule over Afghanistan went to the dust bin of fallen civilizations in about the same time it took the allied powers to destroy Nazi Germany, just with far less fanfare. Two decades earlier, the Afghan people had proven indomitable in their war to expel the Soviets. Yet because bin Laden and his foreign Taliban tyrants were seen as hated overlords and foreign tyrants, they could not defend their rule against the American/Afghan allies. The reasons for their failure were many; the biggest being the immutable law proscribed by Herodotus, the father of history, in his account of the Persian War:

IMMUTABLE LAW #2
In battle, free men almost always defeat slaves.
(Herodotus' Law)

The Afghanistan campaign demonstrated that for the US to fight effectively against resurgent militant Islam, it was time to stop the decades-long internal war waged by the American Left against its own intelligence agencies. Instead, it was time to support the intelligence and Special Forces communities because this new war would be asymmetrical, not conventional. America would need to swiftly project Special-Forces power to eradicate terrorist cells that have burrowed into small mountain-based enclaves and which plot WMD attacks. As Richard Miniter points out in *Shadow War*, during the Afghanistan and Iraq wars, American Special Forces quietly killed or captured three thousand al-Qaeda freelance jihadists in 102 countries.

---

3.   Ibid, 118-119.

The First Post-Nationalist President Created a New American Majority

By the time he leaves office, it is inestimable how much damage Barack Obama, America's first post-nationalist president, will have done to the country's fighting resolve. In his inaugural address, he stated that we would "fundamentally transform America." The diminution of the nation's military power and martial spirit, if permanent, would constitute an enormous transformation for the US that had produced the most generous, wealthiest, and finest military of any nation in human history.

Two and a half years into the Obama presidency much of the country had begun to yearn for a new president who would return the country to its nationalist footing. A new American majority was emerging that would reject the transnationalist self-loathing and post nationalism that had so debilitated the country. In the midst of an atmosphere of decline, more and more Americans were craving a leader who had the guts to have a frank conversation with them about the country's survival. They longed for a leader who could rally the nation behind a group of creative initiatives that would reverse the country's economic malaise and keep it on offense against resurgent militant Islam.

With the assassination of bin Laden, Americans were also awakening to the fact that the conflict between resurgent militant Islam could only be effectively waged if the US, forced to act alone, maintains its military supremacy and mounts the most potent intelligence and Special Forces operations ever.

They sensed that to reverse America's decline and preserve it from lethal attack, America needed to renew its support for Israel, for the American military (especially its Special Forces), for female human rights, for energy-independence, and for a new economic freedom.

Welling up was a yearning to take on the daunting tasks necessary to reassert American exceptionalism and leadership in the arenas of science, commerce, and military supremacy. After several years of denial and obfuscation, Americans were beginning to relearn that the enemies of civilization and of their very survival were severe and twofold—fiscal insolvency and lethal attacks (chemical, biological, or nuclear) mounted by resurgent militant Islamists.

They understood what Tony Blankley meant when he wrote, "What is different now is that we have lost most of our margin for error." [4] What they wanted was a leader who would remind them that their ancestors were citizens of great civilizations

---

4. Tony Blankley, *The West's Last Chance, Will We Win the Clash of Civilizations?* (Washington DC: Regnery Publishing, 2005), 197.

and, when faced with imminent mortal peril, rose to the occasion and defeated their enemies, despite the odds against them, so that they, and their children, could live free from bondage.

When referring to enemies, foreign and domestic, Americans sought a new president who would sense that the time for obtuse polite language had passed. By 2011, a new majority of Americans were ready to elect a person who, in his inaugural speech, would echo John F. Kennedy by perhaps saying:

> *Let every nation know whether it wishes us well or ill that we will pay any price, bear any burden, oppose any foe, to come to the aid of those seeking freedom from oppression and protection from cruelty visited upon them simply because they are of another faith or because they chose another faith.*
>
> *As we stood with those who sought freedom from the iron fist of Communism, we will stand with those who simply wish to live without fear of arbitrary punishment. We call on our friends and allies in the Muslim world to renounce harsh punishment for women who seek their own personal ambitions and destinies or for any of your citizens who simply wish to join another faith. And we do this because we believe all men and women are endowed by our creator with certain inalienable rights, among them the right to life, liberty and the pursuit of happiness.*

In this way, the new president would signal to the Left and to militant Muslims, who will join in their relentless determination to destroy him, that he has thrown down the gauntlet that they will run, not the other way around.

Gone are the days when a conservative president will politely absorb endless ad homonym attacks upon his or her character from the Left and from the misunderstood, maltreated Muslims. Using their own idioms as his weapons, the new conservative president will checkmate his enemies while signaling that he is actively going to destabilize their plans and regimes, putting them at war with themselves, not the other way around.

He would reaffirm the Bush Doctrine that was codified by the Pentagon as the National Security Strategy of the United States on September 20, 2002. The doctrine states that the US reserves the right to pursue, interdict, or eradicate any building threats preemptively, before they result in an attack. He will embrace the Patriot Act and add one more principle to it, first enunciated by Pope Benedict—reciprocity.

The new president's call for Muslim reciprocity would include a human rights doctrine. It would make it plain that as long as it is common Muslim practice, in the lands dominated by Islam, to brutalize women, execute gays and apostates, and raid non-Muslim places of worship, the United States would use its influence and power to force the reformation and modernization of Islam. It would do so by calling out Islam's widespread cruelty and draconian double standards. He or she might say,

> *If America is expected to welcome Islam into the brotherhood of man, Americans expect Muslims to respect human rights.*

He would remind the country of the words George W. Bush delivered to a joint session of Congress, some of the most enduring lines that will ever be spoken by a US president, just nine days after 9/11:

> *We have seen their kind before. They're the heirs of all the murderous ideologies of the twentieth century. By sacrificing human life to serve their radical visions, by abandoning every value except the will to power, they follow in the path of fascism, Nazism, and totalitarianism. And they will follow that path all the way to where it ends in history's unmarked grave of discarded lies . . .*
>
> *. . . The advance of human freedom, the great achievement of our time, now depends on us. We will not tire, we will not falter, and we will not fail. . . . The course of this conflict is not known, yet its outcome is certain. Freedom and fear, justice and cruelty, have always been at war, and we know that God is not neutral between them.*

As Norman Podhoretz put it, "Not even Ronald Reagan, the 'Great Communicator' himself, had been so eloquent in expressing the idealistic impetus behind his conception of the American role in the world." [5]

The new president would:

- Name our twin existential enemies—the transnational statists and militant Islam, and call the nation to arms in an equally eloquent manner.
- Outlaw the practice of sharia law on American soil and in the American judicial system. (Islamic legal code of sharia proscribes the

---

5. Norman Podhoretz, *World War IV, The Long Struggle Against Islamofascism* (New York: Doubleday, 2007), 47.

stoning of women for various minor offenses and the execution of apostates who choose to leave the religion.)

- Authorize the closure of any American Mosque that either advocates the overthrow of the US government or threatens the constitutionally guaranteed rights of its own people, American Muslims.

He or she would actively and forcefully confront the American Civil Liberties Union (ACLU), who advocate for outraged Islamists, stating that he is moving to protect the rights of American Muslims because it is moral to do so and he has sworn an oath to defend the constitution.

Economic Freedom and the Laurium Model

During the decade between the infamous battle of Marathon in ancient Greece in 490 BC and the 480 Persian invasions, a huge vein of silver was discovered by the Athenians at Laurium. During the early years of the new Grecian democracy, at the Assembly, the brash young aristocrat and orator, Themistocles, convinced his countrymen that they not disperse the silver among themselves but instead build a navy. Had he not convinced the Athenians to do this, there would have been no battle of Salamis. The Greeks would have been conquered and the progress of Western civilization subsumed, so consequential was his initiative.

Similarly, John F. Kennedy, at the onset of his presidency in 1961, declared it would be the explicit goal of the United States ". . . by the end of this decade, to send a man to the moon and bring him home safely." In this, Kennedy signaled to the Soviets that the space program of the United States would be dedicated to the twin objectives of elevating Americans' love of country and reestablishing military superiority.

In September 2010, then Secretary of State Hillary Clinton, when speaking to the Council on Foreign Relations, stated, "I think that our rising debt level poses a national security threat in two ways: It undermines our capacity to act in our interests and it sends a message of weakness."

Two and half years into the Obama presidency, despite the damage it did to the American economy, including the loss of its AAA credit rating, the US still commanded the world's largest economy. It represented approximately 20% of the world's Gross Domestic Product (GDP). It faced the daunting task of needing to undo nearly everything President Obama had done. Moreover, the country needed to embark on the following three initiatives that would unburden the taxpayers from their massive debt service and quite possibly save the West from destruction:

- Total Energy Independence
- Complete Missile Defense
- A New Transportation Paradigm

Total Energy Independence

The days of vainly trying to turn down the temperature of the planet by crippling our own economy had come to end, making energy exploration and production a national security imperative rather than a liability. By 2011, the country desperately needed to:

- Commit to becoming a net exporter of energy in ten years or less.
- Lift all moratoriums on proven natural gas and oil fields effective immediately.
- Streamline the approval process in every state with the objective of constructing a new nuclear power plant.
- Lower dependence on all foreign energy sources in every way possible.
- Partner with major energy producers to utilize the assets under foot and follow the example of the ancient Athenians.
- Produce indigenously all the energy sufficient to power both its infrastructure and military.
- Convince the electorate that America's readiness to fight a global conflict will make it less likely that it will be forced to do so.

The New Transportation Paradigm

Given that American ingenuity first discovered the means to mass-produce the fossil-fueled combustion engine, it could also discover and produce its replacement technology. As America's new majority looked beyond the Obama presidency, it began to realize that the West would reach a carbonless future far sooner if conventional energy producers and entrepreneurs were empowered with less regulation and handsome tax incentives.

In search for a new transportation paradigm, partnerships between the conventional producers and entrepreneurial companies could be forged, giving birth to the world's foremost new energy producers, whatever that new energy source might be.

The new majority was more than ready for an American president to put the Middle East on notice, stating the US intended to stop financing their double game, just as Kennedy had done with the Soviets.

Complete Missile Defense

The new majority was ready to honor George W. Bush, on whose watch (2001-2008) the US military achieved what the American Left long said was impossible. It proved that America alone had the ability to reliably intercept and destroy a nuclear-armed ballistic missile in flight before it could reach its target. Americans yearned for a new president who would proclaim to the world:

> *Our missile defense system is the realization of Ronald Reagan's vision and a breakthrough of vast significance in the long march of human conflict. With this breakthrough, all humanity can see that someday we may erase the inevitability of mutually assured nuclear annihilation. Our goal over the next decade will be to complete what Presidents Reagan and Bush started so that we can protect not only this nation but our allies around the world from nuclear attack.*

Unfortunately, just as the Carthaginians fatefully elected to decommission a large portion of their fleet at the conclusion of the first Punic War, in 2009, President Barack Obama traded away, to the Russians, some of America's most important and robust missile defense installations located in the Czech Republic and in Poland. They were almost ready to be brought online.

These were traded in exchange for the Russians' duplicitous half-promises regarding Iran, promises they had no intention of keeping. President Obama's head was handed to him diplomatically. He abrogated signed treaties negotiated by the Bush (GW) Administration. This humiliated and deeply angered some of our staunchest allies in the region. In so doing, he let the world know that contracts with the United States were only operative within the term of a single presidency.

Even worse, the cancelled installations were capable of intercepting long range inter-continental ballistic missiles (ICBM). With Iran testing its own ICBM's, Obama left the East Coast of the United States vulnerable to an Iranian attack—when he did not need to do so.

In speaking with James Carafano, a Senior National Security Analyst at the Heritage Foundation, he told me that the US has for some time been underfunding missile defense by 10%-15% a year. "When you turn off the requirement for those European-based two-stage interceptors (as Obama did), a system comprised of proven, cost-effective technology, that would have been in place by 2013, you just can't turn that program back on when all of sudden you decide you need it. You've lost two or three years." [6]

Carafano went on to explain that because the Russians objected to our mutual defense treaties with nations in Eastern Europe, an area they deemed to be their sphere of influence, we folded. Instead, Obama ordered the Pentagon to build a ship-based "phased adaptive" system, **Aegis**. Ominously, this non-proven system is less capable, more expensive, and if deployed will protect only Europe—not the US. And, it was not ready.

This was a colossal blunder, all in an attempt to get Russia to help us isolate Iran and as a prelude to signing the new Strategic Arms Reduction Treaty (START). In exchange for giving away our own defense from nuclear attack, as Carafano puts it, "He got them (the Russians) to sign a treaty that gave them every advantage and us none."

A poll conducted in May 2009 by Opinion Research Corporation found that 88% of US respondents believed that US should field a total missile defense system.

By thinking he could successfully negotiate with former members of the Soviet KGB, Putin, and Dmitry Medvedev, our 44th president violated:

IMMUTABLE #3
Appeasement of a ruthless outside power always invites its aggression. Treaties made with ruthless despots are always fruitless and dangerous.[7]

The majority of Americans had concluded that the complete optimization of our missile defense system as an urgent national priority.

The Supply-Side President
The new majority had come to expect the new president to cut back government spending to 2007 levels, reducing the annual budgets and the payroll of all departments (EPA, Education, Energy, IRS, Health, and Human Services) by 20%, while moving to repeal Obamacare.

The new president will gain support for laying off the newest government hires within an already bloated government. He will encourage sympathetic allies in the alternative media to remind the electorate that the average government employee earns far more than what the corresponding private-sector citizen earns. Allies in the

6.   Special thanks to Mr. Carafano who spoke to me, on the record for this book, September 20, 2010.
7.   While many well-respected American statesmen feel that it was beneficial negotiating arms control treaties with the Soviets and now the Russians, I don't. They have violated almost every treaty they signed, making us less safe not safer.

alternative media can remind the "average" citizen, who pays the government worker's guaranteed-for-life salary and lavish pension, that the taxpayers are the employers of the public servants, not the other way around, and that they have a right to an affordable and accountable government. The American public sector employee has become today's version of the fifth-century Roman bureaucratic elite, who, in Rome's final days, absconded with most of what remained of the Empire's dwindling tax revenues.

The new majority will welcome the new president's initiative to repatriate all offshore divisions of US corporations—allowing them to operate inside the US tax free for one hundred years when their overseas divisions are relocated back to the United States. Savvy Americans will understand that, while these newly repatriated divisions will not pay corporate taxes on earnings, their American workers will earn salaries, pay income taxes, and buy American goods, homes, and services. This will expand the economy and increase tax revenue.

I asked Curtis Dubay, Senior Analyst for Tax Policy at the Heritage Foundation, to comment on whether tax cuts are beneficial to the economy—do they pay for themselves, or are they are detrimental, as the American Left continuously contends?

"It depends somewhat on how high the top tax rate is," Dubay told me. "Back in 1980, when Reagan came into office, the top tax rate was 70%. That was a major disincentive to work. He cut the top rate to 28%, a huge cut and a big incentive to work more and to put more money at risk."

"Wasn't Kennedy the first president to propose tax cuts? How did his policies work out?"

"The top rate when Kennedy was elected in 1960 was 91%. He lowered it and that had an immediate positive effect on revenues." Dubay answered.[8]

"So what about the Bush (GW) tax cuts? Did they cause the economic downturn as Obama and the American Left have incessantly maintained?"

"When we are talking about taking the top rate from 39% to 35% as it did in 2001 (under President George W. Bush), it is not going to have such an immediate effect (as did the Reagan and Kennedy cuts). However, the Congressional Budget Office (CBO) always gets it wrong. It always scores (predicted) tax cuts as causing revenues to decrease by a static amount, yet when those tax receipts come in, they are always higher than the CBO predicted. So in that sense, we can say that tax cuts always *partially* pay for themselves."

---

8.   The Kennedy tax reductions were not enacted until after his assassination, and immediately translated in a continued growth in revenues to the Treasury for seven consecutive years.

Dubay also pointed out that, although the Bush tax cuts reduced tax receipts in the first few years of his administration, the economy and job creation grew tremendously throughout his term. By 2007, tax receipts *increased* to a staggering $2.5 trillion, up from $2 trillion in 2000. They returned to the annual average of 18% of the Gross Domestic Product (GDP). Even more important, the GDP (United States economy) increased from $10 to $14 trillion in the first seven years under Bush, an *increase* roughly the same size as the *entire Chinese economy* (third largest in the world).

Given the lessons inherent in the fall of Rome, the act of a government granting its citizenry the right to keep more of their *own money* can never be trivialized. Its inverse—unfettered taxation—violates the following immutable:

IMMUTABLE #5
*When a free people, through taxation, is deprived of
its ability to acquire wealth and property, collapse is presaged.*

In the fall of Rome, as the middle class was vanquished, the families of merchants and farmers, who had always been counted on to produce good soldiers, disappeared.

The President's Oval Office Address Flushes Out Enemies

If the 45th president needs to invest the nation in a long crusade to eradicate Muslim terrorist threats forming in our midst, we can imagine his first oval office address to the nation.[9] The instant and unremitting attacks that will be leveled against him by his speech will prove a masterful stroke of political subterfuge on the part of the new president, because it will flush out and identify his attackers on the Left who collude with the jihadists from within the Muslim American community and reveal for all the world to see what they are—the enemies within. Imagine the reaction to this speech:

My fellow Americans, I have chosen this occasion to speak with you directly on a difficult topic yet one of dire import. The topic is the likelihood of an attack occurring inside our country that will be far larger than the one we suffered on September 11, 2001. No other nation has extended a more welcoming hand to virtually every creed, ethnicity, and religion then has this country. America faces mortal danger from potential attackers armed with mobile WMDs.

9. This segment is a thought experiment aimed to have the reader consider the troubling notion of whether or not the American Democrat ruling class is allied with the jihadists in our midst.

So I'd like to call on every American to join me in renewing his commitment to extreme vigilance and ask that you report to local law enforcement any suspicious activities you observe. And when you do so, I promise your anonymity will be preserved.

I would also like to ask for help from the Muslim American Community. I'm holding a report that shows three out of four American Mosques, in their sermons and in their literature, preach hatred of our culture and freedoms. They advocate for the eventual dismantling of our American Republic and its replacement by an Islamic state governed by sharia law.[10]

As every American knows, this country protects the rights of all its citizens to practice their religion freely and openly.[11]

Yet, from this point forward, we cannot and will not allow any individual or group to advocate for the violent overthrow of this government. If you do so as a visitor, you will be forced to return to the country of your origin. If you do so as a US citizen, I have instructed my Justice Department that all our laws relative to sedition and treason will pertain to you.

If you are a Muslim visitor or citizen and wish to aid us in uncovering terrorist plots before they are fully formed, to you we offer our debt of gratitude. Just as no American has the right to set foot in any other land without the permission of that sovereign country, no immigrant, or visitor, in America has the right to be governed by a body of laws outside our laws. Furthermore, we believe that tolerance of those who wish to eradicate our culture is not tolerance. It is cowardly submission.[12] You will not hear me or anyone in my administration apologize for our country's unmatched hospitality.

---

10. Undercover agents found the majority of US mosques dispensed literature advocating violence against the infidel. Their Imams espoused takeover of the US and the imposition of sharia law on all Americans.

11. This is a signal to the Muslim world that the new president is going to expect reciprocity. We protect all faiths, including Muslims, whereas attacks go on with impunity for carrying a bible in Saudi Arabia, Iraq, and Egypt.

12. This is a carefully chosen word given that Islam in Arabic means submission. Here the president is putting the Muslim World on notice that Americans will not be intimidated by Muslim taboos and threats of violence.

CHAPTER EIGHT

Empowering Allies
in Our War for Survival

We shall nobly save or meanly lose
the last best hope on earth.
ABRAHAM LINCOLN, DECEMBER 1, 1862
(Shortly before signing the Emancipation Proclamation)[1]

As America's Hegemony Slips Away on a Sea of Red Ink

The national debt was $10 trillion when Obama was elected president. By the end of 2011, it stood at $15.5 trillion, exceeding the entire Gross Domestic Product of the nation.[2] The rising sea of debt prompted Obama's own Secretary of State, Hillary Clinton, to remark, "I think that our rising debt level poses a national security threat in two ways: It undermines our capacity to act in our own interests. . . . And it also sends a message of weakness, internationally." [3]

By March 2011, America's cities and states were also on the brink. This prompted David Patten at *Newsmax* to write, "The end is in sight, just two years down the road. If America's states and big cities fail to get their debt under control, a hundred cities will be pushed to the brink of bankruptcy; huge states like California will see their bonds downgraded to junk status; many firefighters, teachers, and police will lose their jobs." [4]

---

1. Robert C. Etheredge, *The American Challenge* (MiraVista Press, 2011), 277.

2. Grover Norquist, *President of Americans for Tax Reform* (*The Wall Street Journal*, Opinion, August 12, 2011), A15. *Wall Street Journal*'s editorial board also reported that by August 2011, the public debt was $9.924 trillion and the intra-government debt was $4.666 trillion for a total of $14.666 trillion.

3. Council on Foreign Relations (September 8, 2010), http://cfr.org/publication/22896.

4. David Patten, *States Staring at Bankruptcy*, (*Newsmax* Magazine, March 2011), 12.

In April 2011, two bombshells dropped on the Obama economy. First, Standard & Poor's, the international agency that rates sovereign issued bonds, published a warning—they rated American long-term AAA rating as *Negative*.[5] Second, the International Monetary Fund (IMF) published a report predicting the US economy (taking into account the inevitable debasement of our currency) will be eclipsed in real terms by China in 2016. A Dow Jones's subsidiary, *MarketWatch*, labeled the report— *Age of America Nears End*.[6]

Amid the fog of the great Islamic upheaval, America's economic implosion was ominously causing American allies in the Middle East to quietly seek new alliances. In April 2010, details of a secret meeting between our presumed allies, Afghan President Hamid Karzai and Pakistan's Prime Minister Yousuf Raza Gilani, were leaked. The Prime Minister of the only nuclear armed Muslim state and ostensibly a US ally, personally traveled to Afghanistan to tell Karzai that the US had failed both countries. During the meeting, Gilani is said to have repeatedly referred to America's "imperial designs," while adding that "America's economic problems" meant it couldn't be expected to support long-term regional development. "A better partner would be China which the Pakistani's call their *all weather friend*," he said.[7] Pakistani officials, privy to the details of the meeting, told the international press that they no longer have an incentive to follow the American lead. "Pakistan is sole guarantor of its interest," said a senior official. "We're not looking for anyone else to protect us, especially the US. If they're leaving, they're leaving and they should go." [8]

Later in April 2011, there was a massive jailbreak from the Sarapoza prison in Kandahar Province, Afghanistan. Four hundred seventy-five Taliban and al-Qaeda, including some of the most dangerous Taliban commanders, escaped through a tunnel. Felix Kuehn, a Kandahar-based researcher and author of books on the Taliban, wrote, "This escape will have a multiplying effect." [9]

A similar jailbreak was staged in 2008 when nine hundred inmates escaped. Immediately afterwards, assassinations and violence spiked all across Afghanistan. Kandahar's mayor, Haidar Hamid, said of this most recent jailbreak, "There were

---

5.   The negative report was referenced in thousands of newspapers and media outlets across the globe. A visit to the Standard & Poor's website showed that the report had been mysteriously scrubbed. However, the warning was already a shot heard round the world.

6.   *IMF Bombshell:Age of America Nears End* (*MarketWatch*, a subsidiary of Dow Jones and Co., April 25, 2011).

7.   Matthew Rosenberg, *Karzai Told to Dump US* (*The Wall Street Journal*, April 27, 2001), 1.

8.   Ibid.

9.   Maria Abi-Habib and Habib Khan Totakhil, *Taliban Jailbreak Rattles Afghan South* (*The Wall Street Journal*, April 26, 2011), A7.

some corrupt police inside the prison . . . and they likely helped the prisoners to escape."

By late spring 2011, America's fiscal insolvency translated into impotence—a profound lack of ability to influence events that cascaded into chaos and war all across the Muslim world.

In Search of an Islamic Joan of Arc

By 1428, what remained of free France seemed doomed to become another vassal province of England. All French lands north of the Loire River had been lost with Burgundian and Parisian soldiers now fighting on the side of the English.

That year, a seventeen-year-old farm girl, who had received visions of the Archangel Michael, convinced what remained of the French nobility and a skeptical clergy to allow her to lead the dwindling French armies in their desperate war to wrest France from British domination.

In the tradition of the "French Maiden," Islamic heroines living in the US, Europe, and Canada are now in the vanguard of those seeking to expose the Islamists' plans for the destabilization and ultimate domination of the West.

Those who want to preserve Western Civilization must elect a new US President who will begin to destabilize fundamentalist Islam by becoming the Advocate-in-Chief for female human rights and a champion of the heroines of Islamic apostasy. In this effort, he implements a two-pronged attack—turning the jihadists upon their own freedom fighters from the various democracy movements and launching a broader agenda aimed at beginning an Islamic reformation.

He announces that the State Department will apply maximum diplomatic pressure on all Islamic governments to free both men and women apostates who seek asylum in the United States. He orders that their visas be expedited and their cases publicized. (And when necessary, secretly aided by Special Forces to escape their respective countries.) As a recurring feature of his presidency, the new president invites "Islamic women of conscience" to the White House, awards them freedom medals, and extols publicly their heroics. The new president makes sure the world knows the significance of their stories. He recommends the following female Islamic apostates as candidates for the country's highest civilian honor, the Presidential Medal of Freedom, because they are great heroines in the cause of freedom for America and all of Western Civilization.

Ayaan Hirsi Ali

Ayaan Hirsi Ali

In 2005, *Time Magazine* named Hirsi Ali one of the world's one hundred most influential people. Before her escape to the West, she lived in Somalia, Ethiopia, Kenya, and Saudi Arabia. Her story parallels many of today's heroines who have risked their lives to both escape and expose Islam. In her book, *Infidel*, Hirsi Ali describes her circumcision at age six in excruciating detail. "While Grandma held me down, two other women held my legs apart. The man, who was probably an itinerant circumciser, picked up a pair of scissors . . . A piercing pain shot up between my legs, indescribable, and I howled . . . When the sewing was finished, he cut the thread with his teeth."[10] On the same day, the procedure was also performed on her five year old sister, Haweya, who, the author writes, ". . . was never the same afterwards."

Hirsi Ali's grandmother was an Iron Age Somali bush woman. Yet in the aftermath of Somalia's newfound independence, her father, like Obama's father in Kenya, was fortunate enough to be brought to the United States and given a college education. Upon his return he was swept up in the revolutionary ferment that consumed post-colonialist East Africa at the time and was imprisoned for a period.

Although Hirsi Ali received an education in Mogadishu, a pitiless Islamic culture punished her fatherless household. She was a voracious reader and very opinionated. This tormented her mother who regularly beat her into submission. Even her Islamic studies teacher made a special visit to her home, when her mother was away, to beat the precocious youngster.

When the author was sixteen she reunited with her father, who told her that he had arranged for her to be married to a wealthy Somali gentleman. Soon the author was on her way to Canada to become the unwilling bride of a stranger. But while changing planes in Frankfurt, she escaped and fled to Holland. There she became a government translator for Middle Eastern Dutch immigrants, and then eventually a member of the Dutch Parliament.

Ms. Ali, an avid student of the Enlightenment, writes a stunningly perceptive narrative that exposes the endemic cruelty and aggression of Islam and the insipid multiculturalism of her otherwise gracious European hosts:

---

10. Ayaan Hirsi Ali, *Infidel*, (New York: Free Press, Division of Simon and Schuster, 2007), 32. Much of the lurid description is left out.

"This compassion (by the Dutch) for immigrants and their struggles in a new country resulted in attitudes and policies that perpetuated cruelty. Thousands of Muslim women and children in Holland were being systematically abused . . . Little children were excised on kitchen tables. I knew this from the Somalis whom I translated. Girls who chose their own boyfriends and lovers were beaten half to death or even killed.[11]

Before she ran for the Dutch Parliament, she had become a famous spokeswoman in Holland for Islamic female human rights. Although she was a single-issue politician, she won the office easily. Once in office, she found that Dutch crime statistics did not even categorize the murder of women by ethnicity. Due to a bill Ali championed through Parliament, she forced the Dutch government to expose the fact that, in just two Dutch provinces, *eleven* Muslim girls had been murdered by their families during the six-month period between October 2004 and May 2005. The country contained twenty-five provinces. She could no longer be portrayed as a radical by the capitulationist Dutch press.

While in Parliament, Ms. Ali and film maker, Theo van Gogh (related to the famous painter), collaborated on a film, *Submission*, that focused on Islamic cruelty to women. Shortly after its initial screening, van Gogh was murdered by a Moroccan immigrant to Holland. In the presence of fifty witnesses, he plunged a knife, on which was affixed a note decrying van Gogh's crimes against Islam, into Theo's chest. That night thousands massed in central Amsterdam. And over the next few nights, twenty Mosques were burnt down throughout Holland. By Dutch standards, these emotions were unprecedented. In the end their outrage was futile—when a hand grenade was thrown at her security detail, the Dutch Parliament prevailed on Ms. Ali to leave the country.

Today she is a US citizen, working for the Enterprise Institute. Sadly, even in this country, she requires a security detail wherever she goes. Her whereabouts need to be kept secret—all because she stands up against the cruelty visited upon young Muslim girls.

Wafa Sultan

Ms. Sultan, the Syrian born author of *A God Who Hates*, is a practicing psychiatrist in Southern California. She became world famous when she appeared on al Jazeera television and had the unprecedented courage to debate an Imam on the merits of

---

11. Ibid, 246.

Islamic doctrine. Her blasphemous appearance was posted on YouTube and has been viewed more than 680,000 times. In 2006, she was named also one of the world's one hundred most influential people by *Time*.

Her book chronicles her early years living in Syria and deftly provides a psychoanalytical description of the pathology contained within Islamic doctrine and culture. She points out that Islamic theology is the direct result of the harsh desert environment in which the seventh-century Bedouin lived and of his unremitting fear of the unknown. He constantly feared dying of thirst and/or suddenly losing all his possessions in a raid. The Arabia that the Prophet was born into was a land of unremitting harsh scarcity. A Bedouin tribe would, as a matter of course, intentionally foment disputes against a neighboring tribe as a means to justify raiding their camp and stealing their food, water, and women. She writes:

> *"Open any book about the Prophet in Arabic and the first thing you will read about are the Prophet's raiding expeditions . . . Islam tried to justify these raids by regarding them as death in God's cause. Nonetheless, it could not disguise its basic aim, which was, indeed, to gain and booty. The Koran mentions booty more than once. It does not forbid it: On the contrary, it entitles the Prophet to take a fifth of it."* [12]

> *"And know that out of all the booty that ye may acquire, a fifth share is assigned to Allah." (The Koran 8:4)*

In response to his many, many fears, the Bedouin Prophet constructed a new god which contained ninety-nine attributes. Some attributes were moral— "The Merciful," "The Patient." To subdue his myriad enemies, some lurking just over the adjacent sand dune, Allah's other attributes were "The Humiliator," "The Subduer," "The Bringer of Death," and the "Avenger." To this day, Ms. Sultan maintains, most practicing Muslims take pride in Allah's cruelty, that he is an avenger. The amoral attributes serve to sanctify the raid. And it is this raiding mentality which suffuses Islamic thought today.

Ms. Sultan comes to a conclusion of profound significance. She points out that when you teach a child that God is vengeful and a subduer, you have created what will become a vengeful, tyrannical person. Human nature strives for a union with its ideal. "Mohammed Atta did not become a terrorist overnight," she writes.

---

12. Wafa Sultan, *A God Who Hates*, (New York: St. Martin's Press, 2009), 62.
    By assigning to Allah a fifth of the share of the booty you take from your victim, you sanctify the raid. Theft and murder are thereby encouraged in the Islamic ethos.

Additionally, Ms Sultan's experience adds texture to Ayaan Hirsi Ali's. She vividly exposes much pathology that is the direct result of a culture that encourages cruelty toward women and treats them as defects, to be subdued and owned.

In 1977, while in her fourth year as a Syrian medical student, Ms. Sultan worked part-time in a gynecologist's office. There she saw a steady stream of identical family tragedies. A young girl and her mother would arrive completely covered so not to be recognized. They explained that they wanted to ensure that the girl was still a virgin prior to her forthcoming marriage, and that *she had a bad fall when she was younger*:

> *"When the doctor explained after examining the young girl, that she hadn't just lost her virginity but was also pregnant, the two women would weep and beg the doctor to help solve their problem.*
>
> *. . . In most cases, the young woman would confess that, since childhood, she had been sexually abused by her father, her brother, her uncle, or another male relative. One would think that a doctor's attitude to young women in distress would have been one of care and sympathy. The doctor frequently took advantage of the sensitivity of the situation and demanded fantastic sums as payment. The two women would come back the next day with the money which they might have obtained by selling their jewelry. Watching this whole scene play out, I was just as sickened by the doctor's attitude as I was by the abuse—these women were suffering at the hands of their male relatives."* [13]

On her visits to clinics in the poorer rural areas, she ascertained that many of the girls suffered a worse fate. Without the money to perform abortions and do vaginal surgeries to simulate virginity, they simply disappeared—killed by their families and dumped into unmarked graves. In all her years living in the Middle East, Ms. Sultan writes that she never encountered a Muslim man who showed any contrition for his actions. This is because of the ogre who is their god. [14]

She knows that her position and her willingness to expose the brutal truths of Islamic culture puts her life in danger. She considers it her duty to stand up against Islam, which she characterizes as—*A Humanitarian Catastrophe*.

---

13. Ibid, 28.

14. In the beginning of her brilliant book, *A God Who Hates*, Sultan's psychoanalytic description of Islamic culture esposes the fact that a great deal of Islamic fairytales involve a despotic ogre of superhuman powers which preys upon the innocent population. From childhood, Islamic children are taught that their deities are evil predators.

The new president of the United States could proclaim, "We have awakened to the worldwide implications of her crusade and take immediate steps to make the US an easily accessible safe haven for Islamic apostates—especially women of conscience."

Nonie Darwish

Now They Call Me Infidel: Why I Renounced Jihad for America, Israel, and the War on Terror," is the vivid account of Nonie Darwish's journey from the world of Egyptian privilege to an American combatant in the War on Terror. It stands among the growing list of anti-Islamic polemics, filled with incidents and reflections that reveal the pathologies plaguing the Muslim psyche.

Ms. Darwish makes a compelling case that in lands where Islam dominates, like Egypt, underclass inhabitants continue to be brutalized—Coptic Christians, Orthodox Christians, Monophysites, Zoroastrians, Hindus, Buddhists, of course Jews, and especially Islamic women. Her book is a blistering indictment of a misogynistic polygamous world of the supposedly moderate Egyptian society.[15]

In 1955, as a little girl, Ms. Darwish and her family moved from Cairo to Gaza. Her father, a senior intelligence officer in Abdul Nasser's military, had been promoted to secretly head a Palestinian fedayeen movement. It had been tasked with launching overt and covert operations inside Israel aimed to "cause as much death and destruction as possible." As a child attending an Egyptian grammar school in Gaza, Darwish observed that "the hatred of Israel and our obligation to pursue jihad was somehow worked into every subject we discussed in school. . . . Peace was never discussed as an option. . . . With tears running down their cheeks, older girls whom I admired, would stand in front of the class and recite stirring poems pledging jihad . . . declaring their willingness to give up their lives and promising to kill the Jewish enemies of God."

A year after her family moved to Gaza, Darwish's father was killed by the Israelis with a package bomb sent to him in his office. Her four-year-old brother was also hurt when the package detonated. What added to the family's grief was their mother's complete isolation. Since sharia law allows men up to four wives, none of her former friends could risk tempting their husbands with the company of a beautiful, young, needy widow. Her mother's experience points to one of the destructive aspects of the culture of polygamy.

Polygamy also produces vast numbers of jihadists and recruits for suicide missions. The hopeless, seething "Arab Street" is made up of poor men who live in a society of extreme sexual repression, who have no future, and no chance of marrying and

---

15. What follows is an abbreviated excerpt from my review of her book, *Now They Call me Infidel* (*Human Events Magazine*, June 2007).

producing a family. Women of their caste prefer to be the second wife of a wealthier, older man than to be with a poor, potential wife beater.

I spoke with Nonie Darwish the day she returned from speaking at the *Summit on Secular Islam* held in St. Petersburg, Florida. Bret Stevens of the *Wall Street Journal* covered the event and explained that the presenters were either ex-Muslims or reform-minded Muslims. There were no "moderates," a term that Stevens uses to refer to those Muslims who claim to denounce terrorism, and yet deny that their religion has anything to do with it.[16]

Nonie Darwish

A significant number of the presenters were women. Distressingly, a large segment of them live in hiding or have full-time police protection. Wafa Sultan was given an award at the conference. Among her brief remarks she simply said, "I don't believe there is any difference between radical Islam and regular Islam."[17]

I asked Ms. Darwish, as an "American militant" waging psychological warfare against religious zealots of her former faith, about the general progress of the war. And, given the predictions of our demise, whether she believes that the West is winning or losing the war against militant Islam.

Darwish responded, "I think we can win. But so much action is required, and we're still not even united. Our own press criticizes us if we try to save the Muslims of Bosnia or Afghanistan or Iraq. They call us occupiers. If we do nothing but give aid or buy the oil, then we are bad for supporting corrupt Middle Eastern dictators. Americans should all be proud of their country's foreign policy. We have nothing to be ashamed of."

As the crisis with Iran looms ever larger, I asked if she could see how Islamic women worldwide can play a decisive role in defeating jihadism.

"Yes," she said. "The revolt [by Islamic women] is coming. And it's the women inside Islam who really count, because they're the ones who have access to the Arab street."

The Islamic world is increasingly hearing from its own women who are standing up to the Islamic power apparatus and to the imposition of sharia law worldwide.

After Ms. Darwish was interviewed on al Arabiya television, she received hundreds of positive messages on her website from Islamic viewers. Alarmingly, the largest state-owned Egyptian newspaper, *Al Ahram*, followed her interview with a front-page story

---

16. Stevens made the point in subsequent columns that Muslim "deniers," those who deny that their religion has anything to do with terrorism are part of the problem. Muslims who admit that Islam has a lot to do with fomenting terrorism and must be reformed are part of the solution.

17. Secular Islam Summit (Saint Petersburg, Florida, 2007).

that included her picture and the headline "TRAITOR." The editors had to know this story was a threat to her safety.

At the *Summit on Secular Islam*, Manda Ervin, an Iranian expatriate, and Ms. Darwish conducted a session titled "Muslim Women and Children." In this session, they contended that training children to hate the infidel and to glory in jihad is endemic to Islam and is a form of child abuse. Ms. Ervin works with families inside Iran to publicize the plight of their daughters who are imprisoned and awaiting execution. Sadly, she presented a list of eight girls who had recently been killed—publicly hung or stoned to death. She told me that in 2007 the regime in Tehran captured fifty-one girls for the crime of assembling outside the Ministry of Justice. Each week one young girl was executed.

One incident Ms. Darwish describes in her book contains an enormous irony that it could be central to the plot of a modern adaptation of a Greek tragedy. Years after Darwish had moved to the US, her brother returned to Gaza on business. There he suffered a massive stroke and was given a 3 percent chance of survival. Officials at the Egyptian consulate in Gaza voted unanimously to send him to the Hadassah Hospital in Israel where Jewish doctors and nurses performed a miracle in saving his life. The incident proved one startling fact: despite their obsessive hatred of Jews, in times of crisis, Arabs trust Jews. This insight is very hopeful for us Westerners.

Ms. Darwish, now a US citizen, is the founder and director of the website, www. FormerMuslimsUnited.org. It is a vast clearinghouse for the world's most influential Islamic apostates who are waging an enormously high-stakes holy war against resurgent militant Islam. Their holy war pits basic human morality against the intrinsic evil of Islam, a religion that advocates the murder of its own apostates. Two of the Executive Board Members are: Walid Shoebat, a former PLO terrorist, now Christian convert and an outspoken opponent of Islamic dogma; Ibn Warraq, the pen name of the world famous Pakistani author of *Leaving Islam: Apostates Speak Out*. On her website is a *Freedom Pledge* that asks Muslim leaders in the US to renounce the portion of sharia law that mandates death for apostasy. The pledge was mailed to over one hundred leaders of Islamic Institutions based in the United States, including Ibrahim Hooper and Nihad Awad of CAIR and Dahlia Mogahed, Obama's chief advisor for all things Islamic. Only two signed it. Ms. Mogahed, who maintains an office in the White House, was one of the ninety-eight who refused to sign.

Ms. Darwish's website is also a contact point for Muslims seeking help and safe haven as they attempt to escape Islam. I asked her, in the fall 2010, for an estimate of how many women were currently leaving Islam—in actual numbers or percentages.

"That's very difficult to ascertain because Islamic women have no place to go. In Egypt it is against the law to leave Islam. For example, I am currently in touch every day with a very brave Egyptian woman, Nagla Al-Imam, a prominent lawyer and women's rights activist. After she publicly announced her conversion to Christianity, she was lured to a Cairo television studio where, instead of filming an interview, she was turned over to bunch of thugs who beat her," Ms. Darwish told me.

Ms. Darwish went on to explain that she had tried to get the Obama/Clinton State Department to provide Ms. Al-Imam with a visa and enough international exposure to leave Egypt, but to no avail. "I found out recently that the Obama Administration was granting visas to Hamas officials in Gaza. If Ms. Al Imam was in Saudi Arabia, they would immediately execute her in public."

Roya Teimouri

The first time I spoke to Iranian/American Roya Teimouri, she was returning from the 2005 conference, *The Referendum for a Free Iran,* held in Brussels. Iranian expatriates from around the world had gathered to begin the process of forming a new parliament outside Iran. Roya and her family fled Iran when the Shah fell, like her fellow countryman, Amil Imani. Through her network of friends still inside the country, she is a tireless human rights advocate. She has dedicated her life to the overthrow of the current theocratic regime, hoping it will be replaced with a secular democracy. Part of my interview follows:

Roya Teimouri

LK   "Describe how your human rights activities can contribute to the destabilization of the regime."

RT   "I defend women and children's rights in Iran. Through my contacts, I find out about women who are [scheduled] to be stoned to death or executed in public or those who are being tortured, gang raped in prison. I am their voice to the international community. I write letters, put together petitions, and send them to Amnesty International and the UN. And I advocate for their children who are living in prison with their mothers."

LK   "And how does this work to destabilize the regime?"

RT   "Slowly but surely the world is becoming aware of the human rights abuses committed by this regime. This makes other countries less willing to allow Iranian officials to get visas, to travel, and do business outside Iran."

LK   "Iran has one of the two or three worst human rights records on the planet. And so your goal is to shame the rest of the world into isolating the regime?"

RT   "Yes."

LK   "Regarding the women you publicize, what, generally, are their offenses?"

RT   "Some are political prisoners, accused of plotting against the government. Some were taken because their husbands are in prison or are dead, and they are convicted prostitutes, selling their bodies on the street to support themselves and their children."

LK   "How successful have your efforts been?"

RT   "We have saved some lives. But we desperately need more Americans involved in what's happening. We need Americans."

LK   "With respect to the human rights situation in Iran today, how has it changed since the election of President Obama?"

RT   "It's gotten much worse. I just received word that five women were executed yesterday. Now they're killing them in groups."

LK   "Have you received any threats on your life?"

RT   "A year ago, on a day I was away from my business, two men came and told my employee in Farsi that I needed to stop what I was doing because my life was in danger. I never heard from them again."

LK   "Did that experience cause you to do anything differently?"

RT   "No. Once I became a human rights activist, I just trust in God and do what I have to do."[18]

In all likelihood, when the 45th president of the United States assumes office, most of the world's heads-of-state, and their myriad of governmental minions, will still be attempting to appease Iran, while acting as if resurgent militant Islam is not a growing threat to the West. Most Western heads-of-state and their deputies will obediently accept the propaganda that justifies Islamic aggression and grievances as the natural

---

18.   A special thanks to Ms. Teimouri who spoke with me on the record for this book, December 13, 2010.

response to the past crimes of Western colonialism and the ongoing maltreatment of the Palestinians. We can only hope that the new American majority will demand that the new US president provide moral leadership and find common cause with fearless female Islamic apostates. And that he or she will understand that multiculturalism is viewed as weakness by much of the world. Western attempts to curry favor with Islamic supremacists violates:

IMMUTABLE #9
When a civilization accepts the propaganda of its enemy as truth,
it has reached the far side of appeasement and capitulation is nigh.

Operation Free Persia: Regime Change Inside a Nuclear-Armed Iran
(Depicted in a Fictional Account)

Several months prior to the new president's inauguration, the world learned that Iran had successfully tested a nuclear weapon. The international press is filled with news of terrorism and violence. The CIA and the FBI are breaking up plots inside the US every week. The volume of indiscriminate Islamist terrorist attacks around the world has doubled from five to ten a day.[19] The new president has already concluded that World GDP will be crippled if this doubling of violence continues. Hamas and Hezbollah have brazenly resumed their rocket attacks on Israel.

The new president must know the people of Israel are bone weary. He knows that, with Iran's possession of nuclear weapons and Iranian Mullahs holding the threat of annihilation over the Jews, Israel's reason for existence is disappearing. "Again its safety and future does not rest in its hands. Jews by the tens of thousands can now die because someone else determined that they do so."[20] Wealthy Jewish families are leaving the country.

On his breakfast table, next to the stack of newspapers, there is an even taller stack of memoranda and papers that he has requested from the Eisenhower and Kennedy libraries. For several months he has studied papers from their administrations. He hopes to avoid the mistakes that led to the disaster of Kennedy's "Bay of Pigs" invasion.

As he prepares the country's best and bravest to aid the Iranians in

19. The web-base organization, The Religion of Peace computed that, between 9/11/01 and 9/11/10, there were approximately 20,000 Islamic terrorist attacks on a world-wide basis.
20. Daniel Gordis, *The Other Existential Threat* (*Commentary Magazine*, October 2010), 12.

mounting their revolution, he is well aware that the Kennedy Administration, in its first few months, was practically destroyed by the failure of a similar mission. All the men who participated in the invasion of Cuba were captured or killed, and the US was humiliated.

He is also studying how Eisenhower and the allied forces were able to prevent the Nazis and the rest of the world from knowing where and when the Normandy Invasion would take place. Our new president is in the process of gambling his presidency and the prospect of a nuclear conflict on a high-risk operation. It will be the first time any power has ever attempted to conquer a rogue state armed with nuclear weapons. Yet, he judges the prospect of doing nothing as even more dangerous.

In preparation for the launch of *Operation Free Persia*, the new president and a very small group of his closest advisors have been meeting and communicating in total secrecy with; Iranian/American expatriates Amil Imani and Roya Teimouri; recent defectors Farzad Farhangian, Hossein Alizadeh, and Mohammad Reza Heydari, former diplomats from the Iranian Foreign Service. Each member of the president's team of Iranian expatriate advisors is in constant touch with his or her network of resistance leaders poised to begin the fighting inside Iran.

Since the first week of his new administration, the new president has used his relatively unchecked powers as Commander-in-Chief to tear away at the regime's economy. Early in his new administration, the US hosted the first meeting of the *Nations of Liberty Alliance* (NOLA). It is a new international body composed of only nations where open and free elections produce its leaders. He believes the legitimacy of this new body will sink the morally bankrupt United Nations. Using NOLA's first act as a pretext, the condemnation of Iran's nuclear weapons programs, the US Navy has begun to selectively blockade Iranian shipping, by searching ships for prohibited materials destined for Iranian ports.

Through intense diplomatic pressure, the US has greatly slowed the regime's ability to import refined petroleum. All known shipments from North Korea are being interdicted. The US and European allies have seized and shut down nearly all Iranian front groups. Dubai and the Arab Emirates have frozen many of the Mullahs' foreign bank accounts. Most US allies have liquidated their Iranian investments. Iranian diplomats suspected of crimes, including Ahmadinejad, have been banned from travel to Western capitals or have been detained. The Iranian airlines have been banned from operating in the US and Western Europe.

While the world holds its collective breath, few nations, even in the Middle East, have condemned the US and its allies for their actions against the regime. Meanwhile the Iranian economy is collapsing. Over 50 percent of the population is unemployed. Many of the elite Iranian Revolutionary Guard (IRG) are secretly communicating with Iranian resistance groups inside the country and letting their contacts know that when the fighting begins, they will switch sides. Police protection is collapsing. There is widespread looting.

The new president's plan to aid the Iranian revolution is built around the fact that the center of Iran is ringed by disaffected, mostly Sunni, minority provinces: the Kurds in the northwest, the Azeri's in the north, the Arabs in the southwest province of Khuzestan, and the Baluchis in the southeast. For many months, US Intelligence and Special Forces, based in Afghanistan to the east, in Iraq to the west, and even from Turkmenistan to the north, have been supplying revolutionary commando brigades with ultra secure satellite phones, weapons, ammunition, money, and rations. In turn they are mounting incessant attacks on government targets and escaping back across the border.

Iranian Kurds entering from the northwest have launched the most attacks. But in the lawless southeast province of Baluchistan, the attacks have been the most lethal and dramatic. They even attacked Iranian President Ahmadinejad's motorcade, killing one of his bodyguards, and waged an all-out gun battle with Iranian security forces in the center of the Baluchi capital city of Zahedan. Twenty-three-year-old Abdol Maleck Rigi has emerged as the commander of the Baluchi revolutionaries. The CIA arranged for him to be interviewed by Voice of America that was transmitted into Iran in Persian. The program introduced him as the "leader of the Iranian resistance movement."

One morning, when the new president arrives at the Oval office to meet with his national security advisors, he is handed a report with alarming news from his CIA Director. The Iranian missiles, photographed by satellite as they were loaded onto huge trailers and moved south by military truck transport toward the southern Iranian port of Bandar-e-Abbas, *are now missing*. Although the new president has greatly improved intelligence gathering operations inside Iran, the administration is still only guessing if the missiles, seen in transit, are nuclear armed and if they will be assembled as part of an impending EMP attack. At the end of meeting the new President tells his advisors to launch *Operation Free Persia* the next night.

The plan is to send in units comprised of US armed Iranian commandos who have formed camps inside Turkmenistan, Afghanistan, and Iraq. They will lead fellow Farsi-speaking expatriates, from Europe and US, and join with Special Forces and CIA paramilitary officers disguised as Iranian revolutionaries. The Americans have been ordered not to be taken prisoner under any circumstances—this is a do or die mission.

As the first units cross into the country from the north, east, and west, a signal is sent via secure satellite phones to other teams of commandos and civilian revolutionaries inside Tehran and other key Iranian cities. It is time to attack government installations, fire smuggled rockets into weapons depots, and blow up bridges and key roads leading away from military installations to disrupt troop movements. Additionally, they send out the call to encourage every citizen to join in the revolution and come out into the streets to fight the Basiji (the regime's thug force) with rocks, bottles, and any other homemade weapons they can fashion. Their call-to-arms is to create chaos, set fires on military and government buildings, disrupt military movements, and overwhelm the regime.

Under the cover of darkness, the first units coming in from the outside, wearing Chinese-made night vision goggles, will attack weapons depots and other military storage facilities where Iranian Revolutionary Guard (IRG) units are billeted in border towns. Before engaging in combat they will attempt to make contact in Farsi and convince the Iranian soldiers to surrender and switch sides. Once those border installations have been taken or neutralized, mobilized units of armored hummers will cross and begin moving a second wave of reinforcements, men and material, inland.

The plan contains numerous layers of contingency plans. The president knows that the Mullahs, seeing the regime in its death throws, may elect to launch their nuclear missiles at Europe, Israel, or even at the East Coast of the United States. For missile defense, the Navy has strategically stationed every available Aegis (ship-based) interceptor vessel in the US arsenal. Roughly half the Aegis ships are in the Eastern Mediterranean to defend Israel and Europe with the balance arrayed in the Atlantic to defend the Eastern Seaboard of the US. In the Persian Gulf, a carrier group is ready to engage the Iranians should the regime begin to turn its airpower upon its own citizens. Massive American air and naval powers stand ready to launch several hundred aircraft and cruise missiles at military targets. Bombers with tactical "bunker buster" nuclear weapons are poised to take out hardened underground nuclear weapons centers. In both Iraq and Afghanistan, vast numbers of Army and Navy paratroopers are poised and ready to be dropped into the country, if needed.

The President's plan provides the means for the Iranians to conduct the overthrow of their own county in a manner that allows the world to see it as legitimately *their* revolution. The plan is conceived to prevent the conflict from escalating to include Russia or China, Pakistan, or India. In his final consultations with Pentagon officials regarding the US missile defense systems, he repeatedly asks, "Is the system fail safe?" To which he receives the answer, "We hope so."

Four days later, having slept very little, the bleary-eyed new president stands before the television monitors inside the war room in the basement of the White House. Tech-savvy Iranians have posted to YouTube scenes of unimaginable jubilation in the streets of Tehran. While he watches, he is handed a note from his CIA Director letting him know that Ahmadinejad is alive and in the custody of revolutionaries. He looks up to see choppy footage shot by Iranian hand-helds of just released prisoners streaming out of the notorious Evin prison into the arms of their tearful families.

Next, there is footage of the first NATO troops arriving to aid in securing the military installations. Iranian women are singing and dancing in the streets and there is not a head covering to be seen anywhere in the crowds.

The new President's thoughts turn to President Kennedy on that Sunday morning October 28, 1962, the day Khrushchev agreed to remove the Soviet missiles from Cuba. As Bruce Herschensohn wrote in his epic novel of the Cold War, *Passport*, "Millions of people returned to the life they feared would not be lived." [21]

On the following day, hundreds of thousands of Iranians return to the streets of Tehran. Singing ancient Persian nationalist hymns, they march solemnly toward the city's central mosque and watch as it is consumed in flames. Fourteen centuries of Arab/Islamic rule over Persia has come to an end.

The New American Crusade

Western Civilization was almost extinguished by Islam on at least two occasions. Had Charles Martel, the first king of united France, or the Polish King, Jan Sobieski, not prevailed, the ascendancy of Western Civilization would have been subsumed by Islam. As it was for Miltiades and Themistocles, the great Greek generals of antiquity, the leadership of one man on those momentous days led our European ancestors away from the precipice of defeat and slavery. Yet it must be noted that those leaders were

21. Bruce Herschensohn, *Passport*, (New York: Simon & Schuster, 2003), 138.

only successful due to the character, skill, and virility of those that they led. As Tony Blankley so aptly puts it in his book, *The West's Last Chance*:

> "*. . . one must be careful to avoid literalism with historic analogies. History is a guide to human potentialities; it is not necessarily a blueprint or predictor of particular strategies or tactics. The Ottoman Turks rode forth on horseback with curved swords in hand. The energy of Islam today insinuates itself through the forces of globalization and the Internet.*"[22]

And as did Thucydides, Blankley develops companion constructs:

> *Stability is an illusion.*
> *We have lost our margin for error.*

With the prospect of Iran, the leading sponsor of Islamic terrorism, soon to possess nuclear weapons, Blankley believes that Western Civilization is very likely inching closer to the precipice once again. Yet, it seems self-efident that the way back from that fall is at least partially bound up in the Bush Doctrine and in his memorable phrasing:

> *America has always been less secure when freedom is in retreat*
> *. . . more secure when freedom is on the march.*[23]

With the military conquest of Afghanistan and Iraq, and the liberation of seventy-five million people from tyrannical rule, the US has established important alliances (American Special Forces Command would say—assets) within the Muslim world. The native-language speakers will prove vital in a Special Forces-led war. We will need every set of "ears and eyes on the ground" we can muster. The West needs the 45th president to fully understand the importance of bringing into our intelligence services large numbers of newly liberated native speakers to aid in the effort to uncover a potentially lethal attack before it is fully formed.

Yet, in a report issued June 2005 by the Senate Foreign Relations Committee, eighty experts from around the world concluded that there is a 70 percent chance we will suffer a WMD attack, somewhere in the West, over the next decade. The

---

22. Blankley, *The West's Last Chance*, 24.

23. From speech delivered by President George W. Bush at the Air Force Academy, June 2, 2004.

Committee chairman, Richard Lugar, concluded, "Even if we succeed spectacularly at building democracy around the world . . . we will not be secure from the actions of small, disaffected groups that acquire weapons of mass destruction. Everything is at risk if we fail in this one area." [24]

Given that the West can't possibly democratize every Muslim country, what are the options? Initially, allied Intelligence services should aggressively recruit from and penetrate all the Islamic freedom movements fighting to overthrow tyrannical rule. With the old order of Islamic autocrats on their way to prison, American intelligence agencies must know who will emerge as our allies and who are our Islamist enemies. Additionally, America should retool the State Department so that it can be an efficient conduit, providing a safe haven for those seeking freedom from Islam *itself*. The West will need vast numbers of native speakers if it is to understand the new Islamic world that is still emerging.

Who can doubt that, for the West and Islam to avoid a cataclysmic clash of civilizations, Islam must either undergo a reformation or go the way of paganism? Both Roya Teimouri and Amil Imani are Iranian/American advocates for the liberation of Iran and believe that, when the Iranian "theocracy" falls, it will create a tsunami of apostasy within the Islamic world. Although most in Western "ruling class" circles view this as mere wishful thinking, Teimouri and Imani know that the majority of Iranians now see Islam as an alien Arab culture that was brutally imposed by the sword. Most Iranians understand that they are heirs to a rich Persian heritage that predates Islam by thousands of years. And as such, the fall of Iran provides a template for other blocks of people to reject Islam. As Imani puts it, "Because the regime is so hated, Iranians are ready to dump it into the dust bin of history. Almost everyone in Iran has lost a family member or close friend to the murder by the Islamist regime." With a zealous optimism, he adds, "After it falls, the world will see that Iran will renounce Islam. And like dominoes, Muslims from Indonesia to the Atlantic will do the same."

The new president of the free world needs to become a beacon for the Islamic world, welcoming it to share in the heritage of the West, its antiquity, reformation, enlightenment, industrial, and information revolutions. News of America's altruistic liberations of Bosnia, Kuwait, Iraq, and Afghanistan needs to reach the rational minds of the Islamic world, even though today's Muslims can go to a thousand jihadist sites and self-radicalize. What if the 45th president uses the internet so effectively that ordinary Muslims, from Jakarta to Tangiers, want to emulate the

24. *High Risk of WMD Attack in Decade*, CNN, June 25, 2005. The report went on to determine the type of weapon that would most likely be used would be a radioactive dirty bomb, followed by a biological or chemical attack.

West in terms of its respect for women, its freedom of expression, technological inquiry, and worship?

As Nonie Darwish writes:

> "The 21st century has brought major change to the Muslim world. This is perhaps the first time in the history of Islam that Muslims finally have access to the truth about their own religion, thanks to the Internet and satellite dishes (invented by infidels). There are daily news reports of heart-broken Muslims who say they cannot believe what is written in Muslim scriptures and say that Muslims have been living under the greatest lie in human history, others simply deny the undeniable saying that it can't be. While Saudi Arabia is spending billions to Islamize the West, many Muslim prisoners of Islamic law are dying or leaving the religion quietly."[25]

Will the fall of Iran precipitate the reformation of Islam? This is not knowable. But it must be remembered that the immolation of one Tunisian fruit vendor set off revolutions all across the Middle East.

25   Nonie Darwish, "Apostasy from Islam," *Former Muslims United* (blog) http://formermuslimsunited.org/?page_id=2142

Epilogue

> By a continuing process of inflation,
> government can confiscate, secretly and unobserved,
> an important part of the wealth of their citizens.
> JOHN MAYNARD KEYNES

The Destruction of the Middle Classes

Most fallen civilizations, on the way to their demise, preside over the destruction of their own middle classes. Examples of this phenomenon covered in this book are the fall of the Romans (in Western Europe) and the Ottomans. One could certainly add pre-revolutionary France, Imperial Japan, and the Soviet Union to what would be a long list of civilizations that destroyed their middle classes by violating:

IMMUTABLE #5
When a free people, through taxation, is deprived of its ability to acquire wealth and property, collapse is presaged.

Edward Gibbon, and numerous fifth-century sources who wrote accounts of Rome's final days, tell us of corrupt officials who simply stole the dwindling taxes paid into the desperate regime by a beleaguered and destitute Roman citizenry. By the middle of the fifth century, the once mighty Roman Empire could no longer afford to field its armies. The small farmer and independent merchant had no more gold to pay in. What little gold did arrive, was stolen. Similarly, once the Ottomans lost their ability to win wars and conquer new lands, they lacked the industry to support a middle class. The vast majority of the Ottoman realm reverted back to lawless tribalism and poverty.

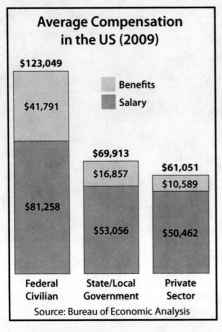

Average Compensation in the US (2009)

$123,049

$41,791

Benefits

Salary

$69,913

$16,857

$61,051

$10,589

$81,258

$53,056

$50,462

Federal Civilian

State/Local Government

Private Sector

Source: Bureau of Economic Analysis

By 2011, the wealth and buying power of the American middle class was being besieged on all fronts by its own government. Throughout the previous decade, the US government ravaged the underlying fundamentals of American real estate values by massively intervening in the market. It propped up quasi governmental agencies, such as Fannie Mae and Freddie Mac, in a scheme that guaranteed $2 trillion worth of sub-prime mortgages to low-income "disadvantaged" borrowers who could not have qualified for them otherwise. This intervention was a thinly disguised transfer of wealth mechanism aimed at buying Democrat votes. While it made some chosen insiders very rich, it ultimately created the great liquidity crisis of 2008. The housing bubble burst. Despite trillions of fiat deficit spending, three years into the Obama administration, American middle class homeowners saw large portions of their wealth vanish. The value of their homes, their single largest asset, continued to sink below the value of their mortgages. In response, large numbers walked away and left their homes to be repossessed by the lenders.

Meanwhile, America's new bureaucratic ruling elite in Washington DC grew in number and continued looting the treasury. In 2007, Freddie Mac paid its CEO, Richard Syron, $19.8 million. Even after the crash, when it was clear that agency directors had a great culpability in the debacle, taxpayers paid the new CEO, Charles Haldeman, $6 million in 2009. In 2011, the DC based agency, which arguably should have been shut down, still employed 7,000 people. Virginia's 11th district, the upscale Washington DC suburb where most of Freddie's employees lived, grew by 200,000 people since 1991 and did not participate in the housing price crash. Homes there were the equivalent of the country villas owned by the Roman ruling elite during the final days of the crumbling empire. On average, the value of DC suburban homes was 75% higher than it had been in 2000. The neo-Roman "kleptocrats" paid themselves handsomely throughout the Obama recession. Despite the fact, as Iain Murray put it, "Not one of the top ten employers in the county is a wealth-generating industry; they all live off the taxpayer."[1]

---

1.   Iain Murray, *Stealing You Blind: How Government Fat Cats Are Getting Rich Off of You*

Debt Man Walking

The liquidity crisis of 2008 tipped the presidential election in favor of Barack Hussein Obama. When he assumed office in 2009, the cost of US federal government was $2.9825 trillion. By fiscal year 2011, federal spending had grown to $3.708 trillion, a 24.3% increase. Whereas, President Bush's last years deficit was $641.8 billion, Obama's unsustainable deficit by 2011 was $1.48 trillion—a 230.6% increase.[2] This was accomplished solely through the President and his Democrat allies who controlled both houses of Congress the first two years of the Obama administration. What made the unprecedented spending so reckless was that it was institutionalized spending that expressed itself in *annual recurring deficits* of $1.5 trillion indefinitely into the future. By 2011, for every dollar collected and spent by the US government, an additional 40 cents needed to be borrowed. In just three years of Obama's presidency, the deficit climbed to 100 percent of GDP, from $10 to $15.5 trillion.[3]

The Impending Bankruptcy of the Western Welfare State

"Alas, cruel history," Daniel Henninger wrote, "Three years into their presidency, they find themselves trapped in the twilight years of the welfare state."[4] Just as the Obama administration was imposing a fourth entitlement, Obamacare, on the US taxpayer, many of the European welfare states, that had long renounced the need to provide for their own defense, were struggling to forestall bankruptcy. At the prospect that their transfer payments might be decreased, Europeans rioted in response to their governments' desperate efforts to remain solvent.

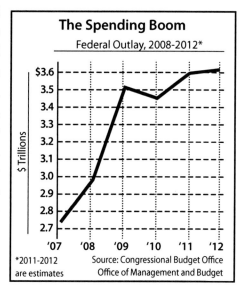

The Spending Boom
Federal Outlay, 2008-2012*

*2011-2012 are estimates
Source: Congressional Budget Office
Office of Management and Budget

(Washington DC: Regnery Publishing, 2011), 5-6.

2. The 2008 numbers are from *The Budget and Economic Outlook: Fiscal Years 2011-2021* (Congressional Budget Office, January 2011), 151.

3. A special thanks to Romina Boccia, Patrick Tyrell, and Rhoda Irene of the Heritage Foundation who aided in collecting these figures from various sources; Congressional Budget Office, White House, and others.

4. Daniel Henninger, *Obama's Deal With the Debt Devil*, (*The Wall Street Journal*, Opinion, August 4, 2011), A15.

At the precise moment when Europe's welfare state spending was threatening to bankrupt the European Union, run away neo-welfare state spending in the US was institutionalized. The vast numbers of new regulations imposed the need for additional armies of regulators to be installed as permanent enforcers at a host of agencies including the EPA, and the Health and Human Services Department. The effects were evident for all to see. In August 2011, Congressman Tom McClintock put it to me, "We could shut down the entire Federal Government, send the military home, fire every federal employee, close every department, shutter the White House, and it would still not be enough to balance the federal budget. Just the mandatory spending: Social Security, Medicare, Medicaid, unemployment, other welfare programs, and interest on the debt is consuming more than the entire revenues of the Federal Government." [5]

Congressman McClintock, who sat on the US House of Representatives Budget Committee, told me that experts who regularly testified before his committee estimated that the US had between two and four years before it would experience a "debt crisis." When I asked him what that meant, he replied that it referred to the moment when the US would run out of sources from which to borrow. In essence, it would mean a systemic breakdown of an unprecedented magnitude.

The Middle Class Bait and Switch

Another effect of three years of runaway government spending was to put the United States on a financial trajectory where all but the country's favored elite would face impoverishment. Grover Norquist, President of Americans for Tax Reform, publishes a column every year called "Tax Freedom Day." This is the day when Americans in the aggregate stop working to cover the cost of government, and begin working for themselves. In 2011, tax freedom day was August 12, an increase of 27 days from when Obama took office.[6] In disbelief, Americans discovered that their government added nearly a month's worth of bondage to its working citizens, precisely at a time when real unemployment had reached near depression levels of 16.2%.

Throughout the American debt-ceiling negotiations of July 2011, President Obama offered his class-warfare rhetoric, advocating for higher taxes on the rich, the "millionaires and billionaires." Yet the President's falling poll numbers signaled that

---

5.   From an interview with California Congressman Tom McClintock of the 4th Congressional District, United States Congress, August 7, 2011.

6.   Grover Norquist, *Happy Cost of Government Day! You Worked for It* (*The Wall Street Journal*, Opinion, August 12, 2011), A15. To come up with a total cost of government, the Tax Foundation adds total federal, state, and local taxes, deficit spending, and a conservative estimate of regulatory burdens. This figure is then divided by total national income to arrive at tax freedom day.

more and more Americans were becoming aware that a $3.8 trillion dollar federal government could not be financed by raising marginal tax rates on the top one or two percent of taxpayers. According to the IRS data for fiscal year 2011, the top 2% of American earners made $299,307 or more, and already paid a whopping *53% of all federal income taxes.*[7]

The new American majority instinctively knew that the real tax burden always falls on the middle class in a capitalist society because that is where the vast majority of country's taxable income is generated. It understood that taxing the rich and the promise of free health care for all was simply part of a familiar con. Most Americans awakened to the fact that individuals making $200,000 a year were hardly rich, nor were there enough of them to feed Obama's welfare state leviathan.

The middle class was his target. The president's real plan was to extract the money from the middle class in a myriad of ways—fees, hidden taxes, higher Medicare deductibles, penalties and fines, carbon taxes, special assessments to cover failing hospitals and school districts, crony-capitalist value-added taxes, and the biggest hidden tax of all—inflation. Despite a floundering economy constrained by a fear of what the mountains of Obama's new regulations would mean, US food and fuel prices rapidly climbed while the buying power of the middle class fell. In one year, from August 2010 to August 2011, the value of the American dollar fell 32% against the Swiss Franc. The new American welfare state was destroying the small investor's capital at an alarming rate and violating:

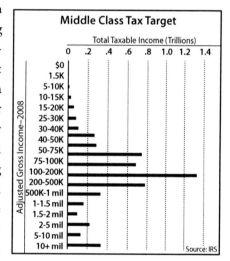

IMMUTABLE #8
*Debasing the currency always
destabilizes the governing authority*

7.   Guinevere Nell, "The Truth About the 2001-2003 Tax Cuts," *The Foundary* (blog), August 4, 2010, http://blog.heritage.org/2010/08/04/the-truth-about-the-2001-2003-tax-cuts/.

Britain's Double Game and Its Cultural Suicide

During the so-called Arab Spring, Britain, a member of the nearly defenseless western European nations in NATO (North Atlantic Treaty Organization), continued to play its double game with its indigenous Islamists, a game of appeasement that it will ultimately lose. London had become the world's capital for *known* Islamic terrorists, the world's capital for men who are wanted in their own native Muslim countries for sedition and insurrection. Britain granted asylum to thousands of wanted jihadists, such as Saad al-Faqih; a Saudi-born medical doctor, a leading proponent of the overthrow of the Saudi monarchy, an open supporter of al-Qaeda and the late bin Laden, and wanted by the Saudi government. In 2011, in an overt act of cultural suicide, the Brits refused to extradite him and continued to house thousands of his ilk, subsidizing their ongoing jihadist activities, while showering them with welfare benefits. And while al-Faqih waited for the Saudi monarchy to fall, he and his Islamic conspirators continued to radicalize more and more Muslim Brits.

Peter Neuman, a terrorism analyst in London told Erick Stakelbeck, "The government quite cynically thought that whatever happened in other countries was of no concern to the British government. . . . If you allowed them (the Muslim terrorists) to do whatever they wanted, they would not be attacking Britain."[8] As Stakelbeck put it—Great Britain made a deal with the devil who isn't known for keeping up his end of the bargain. London suffered attacks on its mass transit system which killed 52 in '05. A year later, in 2006, the city was the staging ground for the al-Qaeda plot to blow up ten transatlantic airliners bound from Britain to the US. By 2008, Britain's Home Secretary declared to the press that British intelligence services were monitoring 2,000 potential terrorists, 200 radical Islamic networks and thirty active plots.[9]

In Britain, the Muslim population has exploded. They have self-segregated into enclaves, both in the countryside and in the cities. These are now "no-go zones" for police and where sharia courts constitute the legal code not British Common Law. Some small towns, such as Luton, thirty miles north of London, have become war zones where radicalized Pakistani's roam in gangs and beat up non Muslims. There are 400,000 Britains of Pakistani origin that travel annually to their homeland. Once in country, many divert from the roads leading to the homes of their relatives in Peshawar or Lahore and travel to the country's tribal regions where they train with jihadists so that when they return home to jolly old England, they are fully-formed terrorists in waiting.

---

8. Erick Stakelbeck, *The Terrorist Next Door: How the Government is Deceiving You About the Islamist Threat* (Washington DC: Regnery Publishing, 2011), 140.

9. "Britain Monitoring 30 Terror Plots," *The Australian*, April 13, 2008
    http://theaustralian.com.au/news/britain-monitoring-30-terror-plots/story-e6frg6to-1111116047789.

During the Arab Spring of 2011, Britain continued to slide into Islamic domination. One shocking poll found that one-third of Muslim students *at British Universities* believed that killing in the name of Islam is justified.[10] Britain's Prime Minister, David Cameron, in July of 2010, while in Turkey blamed Turkey's exclusion from the European Union on "anti-Muslim bigotry" and went on to condemn Israel for its treatment of Hamas and "turning Gaza into a prison camp." [11] As Stakelbeck put it—despite his woeful record of groveling to the Islamic world, Cameron made headlines in early 2011 for proclaiming British multiculturalism a failure. The overture was too little too late and will have no effect because, as the author observed, for the British, with their declining birth rate and their lack of love for country, there is not enough energy left to push back against the tide of Islamic cultural aggression. In Stakelbeck's discussions with Brits, most concede that by the middle of this century Britain will be an Islamic realm. While many in the Western Europe hoped to believe that 2011 would bring about an "Arab Spring," for the purposeless Brits, those who inherited England from T.E. Lawrence, Winston Churchill, and the boys who defeated Rommel at El Alamein, it began to look like the *British twilight*.

Britain—A Society in Free Fall

Of all the formerly great western powers, tragically Britain has gone the farthest down the road toward Islamic subjugation. "Declining civilizations composed of big government swamps eventually destroy their human capital as well," was how author Mark Steyn characterized the shocking riots that broke out in numerous British cities during the summer 2011.[12] Once the flower of Western civility, the riots revealed that an appallingly large number of young Britons had been reduced to opportunistic drunken mobs who smashed shop windows and stole not food but electronic toys and designer tennis shoes. British commentator Theodore Dalrymple wrote, "The fault of the riots were the distorting effects of the welfare state and a degenerate British popular culture." For Dalrymple, the looting mobs were composed of unemployable punks, the inevitable product of parents who had been long schooled by leftist academics and Britain's political class to believe that they were the new "entitled" class. Any perceived slight was an injustice that gave the rioting looters the right to revert to a sort of tribalism with the creed—whatever is mine is mine, and whatever is yours, I have the right steal.

10. "A Third of Muslim Students Back Killings," July 27, 2008, http://richarddawkins.net/articles/2906 (Reposted from: http://.timesonline.co.uk/tol/news/uk/article4407115.ece). By Abul Taher *TimesOnline*.
11. A transcript of a speech given by Prime Minister David Cameron in Ankara, Turkey, July 27, 2010. "PM's Speech in Turkey," http://number10.gov.uk/news/pms-speech-in-turkey/.
12. Taken from an interview by Mark Steyn broadcast on KSFO Radio, San Francisco, August 7, 2011.

Residents of London protest a visit to the House of Lords by Geert Wilders of the Netherlands who lives in hiding due his critical remarks of Islam.

Britain's 2011 riots were a further testament to the bankruptcy of the western welfare state signaling that dependency was both unaffordable and a curse, that breeds resentment instead of gratitude. Moreover, the rioters, though they were citizens of Britain, were actually the enemies within. They were dependents who could be counted on to attack, and not defend, their own culture, proof that much of British society was in decline and in violation of:

IMMUTABLE #1
No nation has survived once its citizenry ceased to believe its culture worth saving. (Hanson's Law)

Gutting National Security

President Obama's unremitting quest to impose a takeover of the health care industry was part of a grand strategy that began in the 1930s during the administration of Franklin Roosevelt. With Obamacare, Obama's true goal was the same as FDR's. It would create enough new dependent voters to establish the Democrat party in America as the permanent majority, the permanent Marxist majority. But by the summer 2011, Obama's grand plan was breaking apart. It became evident that the new law would not "bend the medical cost curve down," as the President had so often promised before its passage. Not even his most trusted spokespeople would perpetuate the lie any longer. When the contents of the law finally became apparent, after its passage, an emerging American majority saw that Obamacare was simply a new unaffordable entitlement. It would make the country less able to maintain its position as the world's preeminent military power.

Part of the debt ceiling agreement of 2011 involved an automatic plan to reduce defense spending over the next decade by $500 to $600 billion if $1.5 trillion in other budget cuts were not agreed to by both political parties. As a result, these new defense cuts would follow Obama's $400 billion cuts to the American military already made during his first two years in office. He was poised to go down in history as a president who cut his country's military defenses by more than a trillion dollars while increasing spending on all other departments. Extremely alarmed by these developments, General Martin Dempsey, Obama's own Joint Chiefs Chairman, made the pithy statement, "There's a very high risk, following this path." [13]

The West Hurtled Towards Insolvency, While al-Qaeda, Iran, and China Plotted

In August 2011, former Ambassador to the UN, John Bolton reported, "President Obama is rapidly scaling down US missile defense programs."[14] During that same month, after three years of attempting to appease the Iranian regime, the Obama Treasury Department quietly reversed course, released documents, and gave interviews admitting that al-Qaeda had been working with Iran since 9/11.[15] Treasury officials announced they had frozen the assets of six al-Qaeda operatives who were "shipping men and money from the Persian Gulf to senior al-Qaeda leaders in Afghanistan and Pakistan."[16] The story was released quietly because it signaled an embarrassing reversal by the Obama administration, the Democrat party, and their media allies. They had spent almost three years and untold political capital convincing the world that there was no such thing as a war on terror.

Additionally, the *Wall Street Journal* reported that files recovered from bin Laden's safe house in Pakistan where he was assassinated in a brilliant raid by US special forces, revealed that Treasury officials had frozen assets and movements of Atiya Abd al-Rahman. The documents showed that bin Laden had appointed Rahman to serve as al-Qaeda's emissary in Iran and was allowed to move freely to and from Iran. He was planning attacks to coincide with the ten-year anniversary of 9/11. The type and scale of the planned attacks remained classified. For the first time, the Obama administration

---

13. Gary Schmitt and Tom Donnelly, *Defining Defense Down* (*The Weekly Standard*, August 15, 2011), 8.

14. John R. Bolton and Paula A. Desutter, *A Cold War Missile Treaty That's Doing Us Harm* (*The Wall Street Journal*, Opinion, August 15, 2011), A 14.

15. This admission came as a result of the Treasury Department's move to freeze the financial assets under its jurisdiction of al-Qaeda operatives supported by Iran. It was a vindication of Ken Timmerman's account that appeared in *Countdown to Crisis* published in 2005.

16. Stephen F. Hayes, and Thomas Joscelyn, *The Hidden Hand: The Obama administration finally highlights Iran's key role in supporting al-Qaeda* (*The Weekly Standard*, August 15, 2011), 21-24.

admitted that bin Laden, his son Saad, and al-Qaeda's most senior members had been sometimes harbored and financially aided for ten years by the Iranian theocracy.[17]

Iran, the world's leading sponsor of terrorism, supported al-Qaeda, the most dangerous terrorist organization on the planet, while it worked relentlessly on producing long range missiles and nuclear weapons. Questions vital to the security of the western world abounded for the Obama administration. If it had suppressed the truth about Iran's complicity with al-Qaeda's for so long, what other existential security threats were they hiding from the American public and our allies? Even more importantly—how many American's would Iran kill before the US would retaliate militarily?

Moreover, it became clear that Iran and China were conspiring to bring down the US. Rebiya Kadeer is the slight, elderly female leader of China's Uighers who are a beleagured peoples seeking self-determination from Communist rule. Despite being imprisoned for many years by Beijing, she is a fearless author and spokesperson for Uighers' cause. From inside China, she wrote, "China after all, has consistently supported radical, anti-western currents in the Middle East. It is a stalwart ally of Iran's murderous regime and has opposed international measures to curb Syria's rulers. Within days of 9/11, China's official Xinhua news agency was lauding the attacks as a "humbling blow" against America, a theme that continued this anniversary year."[18]

Scipio Africanus, the Bush Legacy, and Iraq

On the ten-year anniversary of the 9/11 attacks, the American public and even many in the begrudging pundit class acknowledged the accomplishments of President George W. Bush. While campaigning, candidate Obama ran against most of Bush's anti-terror policies. Yet three years into the Obama presidency, Bush's Patriot Act was still operative, Guantanamo Bay still open, and the drone attacks had been dramatically increased. He had changed practically nothing. The ten-year 9/11 ceremonies reminded Americans that it was Bush that kept the American mainland safe for a decade.[19]

In his article, *What We Got Right in the War on Terror*, Abe Greenwald wrote, "The prosecution of the war in Iraq was central to the to the efforts against al-Qaeda."[20]

---

17. Ibid.

18. Rebiya Kadeer, *China's Double Game on Terrorism* (*The Wall Street Journal*, Opinion, September 23, 2001), A13.

19. Depending on the source, it has been reported that our intelligence services have thwarted at least 25 major al-Qaeda attacks aimed at the US since 2001.

20. Abe Greenwald, *What We Got Right in the War on Terror, The Surprising Lessons and Truths of a Nightmarish Decade* (Commentary, September 2011), 24.

Greenwald's position is one that I have held since before the invasion of Iraq. Bush's decision to open a second theater of war in Iraq was very much a kin to that of Scipio, the young general who convinced the Roman Senate to give him an army and allow him to launch an invasion of Carthage. It was Scipio's brilliant initiative that rid the Italian peninsula of Rome's most lethal enemy, Hannibal, and it allowed the Romans to move the Carthaginian armies away from Roman population centers and onto a battlefield of their choosing. In military parlance, it is a time-honored strategy, often called "seizing the initiative."

In the Fall of Carthage, Scipio's strategy ultimately allowed him to annihilate Hannibal's army on the sands of today's Tunisia. Similarly, George W. Bush created a zone inside modern Mesopotamia that was too hard for the resurgent militant Islamists to resist and which ultimately became a killing zone for al-Qaeda. The initial invasion of Iraq that began on March 20, 2003, achieved its initial mission of toppling Saddam Hussein in a stunning three weeks. And yet by December 2006, due to the huge influx of foreign jihadists and the support from Iran and Syria, 90 soldiers, Americans and Iraqis, were being killed everyday. Against the advice of many of his own advisors, Bush decided to send in an additional 30,000 troops, a decision referred to as the surge. As Greenwald writes, "Then Senator Barack Obama (stated) I am not persuaded that the 20,000 additional troops in Iraq are going to solve the sectarian violence there. In fact, I think it will do the reverse."

The Surge resulted in the "Sunni Awakening." Sunni tribal elders in Anbar Province, fed up with the killing of Iraqis by the foreign jihadists, switched sides to join the Americans and the new Iraqi government. Thousands of jihadists and al-Qaeda members were killed and captured with mountains of intelligence gained necessary to protect the lives of Americans in New York City, in DC and throughout the homeland.

What George W. Bush demonstrated was that Western Civilization was not finished but still preeminent. As Greenwald puts it, "The United States came face-to-face with the very worst al-Qaeda could muster and, against all odds, prevailed.... The war that was supposed to break America's back broke al-Qaeda's instead. "[21]

IMMUTABLE # 10
Declining civilizations will always face superior firepower from ascending civilizations because sovereignty is only temporarily uncontested

21. Ibid, 26.

The second great Bush (GW) achievement, Greenwald adds, was the establishment of the first Arab Muslim democracy. Iraq's first successful nationwide election took place in January 2009. Eighteen months later, Tunisian rebels began the revolutions that would convulse the Arab world.

Hope Springs Exceptional In America

Despite the fact the country spent three years doing severe damage to its economy, having elected a president and congress bent upon taking the country down the road to serfdom; there was a palpable feeling by many Americas that this destination could be changed. By the summer 2011, President Obama's approval numbers fell below 40%. A new grass-roots movement continued to rise up demanding that the US government face harsh realities, put the country's finances back on a path toward solvency, reorder its priorities, and take control of its own destiny,

Although they had elected a president who said he was not sure he believed in American exceptionalism, Americans were clearly demonstrating exceptionalism. Americans were the only people of the major western democracies who demonstrated in the streets and marched on their capital to demand that their government stop spending. It was the only country fielding large armies of peaceful protestors who wanted less from their government not more, who simply wanted their government to get out of their way. This was exceptionalism.

The U turn in the road to serfdom began a year earlier. Obama had been elected to the presidency with Democrat majorities in both houses yet, "The Republicans in November 2010 pocketed one of the most breathtaking off-year wins in the past century. They won the House of Representatives, the governorships in the key swing states of Ohio, Wisconsin, Pennsylvania and Michigan. . . . Independent voters, who made up about a third of any presidential vote, went overwhelmingly for GOP candidates."[22]

Ronald Reagan warned that freedom is never more than a generation away from extinction. We don't pass it on to our children in the bloodstream. It must be fought for and protected and handed on for them to do the same. And it is almost impossible to find examples where a governing elite, having gained vast powers over its subjects, voluntarily relinquished that power back to them. Nevertheless, grass-roots America will need to show exactly how that can be done.

The alternative is the relentless decline and eventual fall of Western Civilization birthed over one hundred generations ago on the plain of Marathon.

22. Daniel Henninger, *America's Dog Days* (*The Wall Street Journal*, Opinion, August 18, 2011), A13.

Action Items

*For Americans who wish to
take back the control of your government!*

In conducting a California-based survey of white- and blue-collar book buyers regarding the impending publication of *Lessons from Fallen Civilizations*, we learned some startling facts:

- One hundred percent of those surveyed said they believed the country was in decline.
- Sixty-eight percent wanted to read a book that provided concrete solutions to strengthening the country and making it safer.

Learn and Understand

- Research and gain a rudimentary knowledge why great civilizations fail.
- Study the history and mores of Islam and realize that it has attempted to conquer the West for most of its 14-century existence.
- Doubt and corroborate everything your read in the main stream media
- Understand that in the age of portable WMD's, a small group of Muslim terrorists poses an existential threat to America.
- Realize that, as our country becomes financially weaker and ultimately insolvent, the threat of a mortal attack grows exponentially.

Act AS IF You Know Your Nation is at War

- In the 2012 elections, find out which of your congressional candidates advocates lifting *all* bans on energy exploration. Order a lawn sign early, write him with encouragement, send letters to your hometown newspaper, and let everyone you know that it is not just about jobs but that our national survival may depend on our being energy independent.
- Call all the presidential campaigns and tell them that you will not vote for them unless they publicly commit to taking federal spending back to the '07

level ($2.2 trillion). Tell them, "Bankruptcy is not an option, the country ran just fine at that spending level and no one can demonize it because it was *Democrat* budget."

- Be very selective in patronizing the Hollywood movie industry. With few exceptions, it coarsens our culture and teaches young people to distrust American institutions. It also reinforces Muslim hatred of the West.
- Be extremely vigilant of young Middle Eastern men who mysteriously appear in your communities with no visible means of income. Don't hesitate to report any suspicious behaviors.
- Let your children's teachers and the school board know that you see what they are doing. Expose them when you can clearly see they are indoctrinating your children to believe in socialism, multiculturalism, and anti Americanism.
- Advocate for Islamic reciprocity in America. Because we accept complete religious freedom, then Islam should not enjoy Americans welcome and respect unless it lifts the ban on non-Muslims entering Mecca and Medina, until it allows its adherents to leave Islam, and until it respects female human rights.
- Campaign and vote against any politician who wants to expand the American collectivist welfare state. Europe is now bankrupt and defenseless due to the very same policies they advocate.

Appoint Yourself the Chairman of Your Populist Movement

In our system, understand that you still have considerable power. Pick one issue below and appoint yourself its grass-roots regional or even national chairman. First find out which member of congress is the most ardent supporter of your initiative (this can be done with just a few phone calls because most good staffers can tell which congressman is the point person for key initiatives), make contact with his or her office, find out if there is any related legislation pending or in the writing process as well as any other pertinent fact related to a bill's potential passage. Gather a group of friends and hold meetings to discuss the strategy needed to convince your existing member of congress or his *challenger* to take up your cause.

You will want to do fundraising, write op-eds in your hometown newspaper and send letters to, make phone calls and generate face-to-face meetings with your congressional representative advocating for your objective. Your preparation, knowledge of the topic, and passion will point the way to many other tactics and to your ultimate success because your cause is just, and your country needs you.

- **Close the Energy Department:** It was founded to make us energy independent. Since its founding, we're less energy independent and the department generates no energy, only vast amounts of regulations and red tape.
- **Close the Education Department**—It was founded by Jimmy Carter in the 70s to win teacher union votes. American test scores and student competitiveness have declined ever since. Our teachers do not need three layers of bureaucracy, local, state, and federal.
- **Close the National Labor Relations Board (NLRB):** It tried to prevent Boeing, one of the nation's premier companies, from relocating a plant from Washington to North Carolina. The country can live without a thuggish agency that conspires against the private workforce that is forced to pay the agencies salaries.
- **Close the Environmental Protection Agency:** The country's *real* unemployment rate is approximately twenty percent because the regulatory overreach over the past three years is unprecedented. The cost of regulatory compliance on US industry is $1.75 trillion, larger than the entire GDP of Canada. In 2011, 71,000 pages of new regulations were added to the federal registry. And the unelected officials at the EPA are the worst offenders. It is a rogue agency that is attempting to install the crushing cap and trade mandates by stealth now that the majority of Americans have rejected their climate change ruse.
- **Demand that the Government Build Out Missile Defense:** During the Bush years, the US once again proved to world that we could do what the experts in the international left said couldn't be done—hit a speeding bullet with a bullet. Obama has not killed the program but has not given it the priority it needs to be fully built out so that we can protect not just our homeland but those of allies from nuclear annihilation. It is a program with biblical implications.
- **Repatriate the Country's Off-Shore Workers and Assets:** Convince your local congress person (or presidential candidate) to initiate a bill in congress to repatriate our *off-shore assets*. If the next president were to sign an executive order making the repatriation of all US corporations' off-shore workforce a 50-year tax-free event, industrial patriotism would reign and America would again become the undisputed world leader:
    1. Trillions of dollars of revenue would flow into the US Treasury from the income, sales, and property taxes paid by the repatriated workers.

2. The US economy would again boom.
3. Vital industries necessary for the defense of the homeland would be domiciled back inside the country.
4. The event would expose and serve to nullify the entire massive tax code which strangles our corporations and destroys jobs and entire industries. It would be the catalyst to scrap the thousands of pages of laws that threaten to ruin American prosperity and national security.

- **Repeal the Dodd–Frank Wall Street Reform and Consumer Protection Act:** This 2,000 page bill was written by Democrats to protect Democrats and their donors. Written to ostensibly protect us from the next great banking crisis, it leaves Fannie Mae and Freddie Mac, the agencies that turbocharged the meltdown, completely untouched. Get rid of Dodd-Frank and find the means to send some senior governmental officials to jail.
- **Repeal the Patient Protection and Affordable Care Act (Obamacare):** The *Wall Street Journal* editorial board dubbed the bill "the worst by any congress, ever." It doesn't protect patients nor does it make medicine more affordable. By offloading the cost of healthcare to the government, it will make the US government permanently unaffordable. When Medicare was passed in the late 60s, its projected cost in 1990 was estimated to be about $10 billion annually. The cost by that year was $100 billion— its promoters were off by a factor of ten! The new law will provide for 16,000 new IRS agents, 11 new agencies, and baker's dozen of new taxes. Not only will Obamacare's implementation ensure America's economic perpetual downward spiral, it will make Obama's proclamation—"We will fundamentally transform America," a reality. It will fundamentally transform the relationship between the governed and the state.
- **Demand that the Progressive Tax Code be Deemed Unconstitutional:** Find and support a congressperson who will bring forward legislation aimed at scraping the entire progressive tax code and replace it with a flat tax. The 14th Amendment guarantees that justice not be administered selectively. Our constitution guarantees that every American is equal before the law regardless of race or economic status. Any tax policy that punishes one group of citizens and privileges another violates the equal protection statues of our founding documents.

Photographs and Illustrations

GREECE

p40   Map by Rik Rice.

p46   I, Johnny Shumate, the copyright holder of this work, release this work into the public domain. This applies worldwide.

p57   Deutsches Museum, Munich, Germany.
This file is licensed under the Creative Commons Attribution-Share Alike 3.0 Unported license.

p70   Photograph of an original painting by Leo von Klenze (1784–1864).
This image is in the public domain because its copyright has expired.
This applies to Australia, the European Union and all countries where the copyright has a duration of 70 years after his death.

p75   © Marie-Lan Nguyen/Wikimedia Commons.

p82   Stock footage provided by alperium/Pond5.com.

p83   Source/Photographer, Yair Haklai (Own work).

p91   Source/Photographer, Marie-Lan Nguyen (2011).

CARTHAGE

p94   © 2011 Jupiterimages Corporation.

p95   Map by Rik Rice.

p99   Map by Rik Rice.

p107   Source/Photographer, Jastrow (2006).
I, the copyright holder of this work, release this work into the public domain.
This applies worldwide.

p108   This work has been released into the public domain by its author, Vissarion. This applies worldwide.

p109   © 2011 Jupiterimages Corporation.

p117   Time & Life Pictures/Photographer: H. Motte.

p118   Time & Life Pictures/Photographer: Time & Life Pictures.

p123   © Jozef Sedmak | Dreamstime.com.

p125   Map by Rik Rice.

p127   As a work of the US Federal Government, the image is in the public domain.

ROME

p135   Map by Rik Rice.

p136   Photograph of an original painting by Lionel Noel Royer (1852–1926).
This image is in the public domain because its copyright has expired.
This applies to Australia, the European Union and all countries where the copyright has a duration of 70 years after his death.

p145   Stock footage provided by fotola/Pond5.com.

p151   Photographer Rasiel Suarez/Wikipedia.org.

p155   Map by Rik Rice.

p159   Photograph of an original painting by Paul Jamin (1853–1903).
This image is in the public domain because its copyright has expired.
This applies to Australia, the European Union and those countries with a copyright term of life of the author plus 70 years.

p165 Map by Rik Rice.
p171 Stock footage provided by snem/Pond5.com.
p179 US Army photo by Spc. Daniel Herrera.
p185 This work has been released into the public domain by its author, Victor Hugo King. This applies worldwide.

CHRISTIAN MIDDLE EAST
p187 Photographic reproduction of an original two-dimensional work of art.
This image is in the public domain because its copyright has expired.
This applies to Australia, the European Union and those countries with a copyright term of life of the author plus 70 years.
p206 Ann Ronan Picture Library / Heritage Images
p210 Photographic reproduction of painting by Carl von Steuben (1788–1856).
This work is in the public domain in the United States, and those countries with a copyright term of life of the author plus 100 years or fewer.
p219 Drawing by Rik Rice.
p221 Painting by Jean-Joseph Benjamin-Constant (1845–1902).

OTTOMANS
p239 Map by Rik Rice
p244 Photograph of an original painting by Jerzy Siemiginowski-Eleuter (1660–1711).
p248 Drawing by Gentile Bellini (1429–1507).
This image is in the public domain because its copyright has expired.
This applies to Australia, the European Union and those countries with a copyright term of life of the author plus 70 years.

MODERN THREAT
p280 Photo credit: Michaela McNichol, Library of Congress.
Source [http://www.flickr.com/photos/9904636@N02/1478868154/ Congressman Ellison's Swearing In Ceremony with Thomas Jefferson's Qur'an]

REIGNITE RESOLVE
p287 As a work of the US Federal Government, the image is in the public domain.

EMPOWER ALLIES
p302 This file is in the public domain.
p307 Nonie Darwish/Wikipedia.
p309 Photograph courtesy of Roya Teimouri.

EPILOGUE
p320 Chart created for hire.
p321 Chart created for hire.
p323 Chart created for hire.
p324 © Tal Cohen.

Acknowledgements

Ever since I was an English literature college student, the completion of this book has been a never ending, yet elusive goal. I want to thank and recognize those who provided me with the inspiration, support, and guidance so essential to the realization of this dream come true.

To Larry Townsend, my college roommate, lifelong friend, and author of the excellent, *Secrets of the Wholly Grill*, thanks for leading the way.

To Robert Bluey, my editor at *Human Events Magazine*, you gave me my start in political commentary. I will never forget.

To Chris Field my editor at *Townhall Magazine* and now at the Blaze.com., thanks for your trust in me and for selecting my articles for two of your magazine's covers. And to Elizabeth Meinecke, my current editor at *Townhall*, I can't even express my gratitude enough.

To the brilliant American scholars and historians who informed this work . . .

- The late great Tony Blankley, author of *The West's Last Chance*
- James Pierson, author of *Camelot and the Cultural Revolution*
- Lee Harris, author of *Civilization and Its Enemies*
- Barry Strauss, author of *The Battle of Salamis*
- Bernard Lewis, America's Professor Emeritus of Middle Eastern Studies
- Roger Crowley, author of *1453*
- Robin Waterfield, author of *Athens: A History*
- Victor Davis Hanson, the greatest military historian of our age

I stand on your shoulders.

To the unflinching observers of the threat presented by resurgent militant Islam . . .

- Frank Gafney, President of the Center for Security Policy
- Clifford May, President of the Foundation for the Defence of Democracies
- Ken Timmerman, author of *Countdown to Crisis*
- Jerome Corsi, author of *Atomic Iran*
- Eric Stakelbeck, author of the *Terrorist Next Door*
- Catherine Herridge, author of *The Next Wave*

I thank you for your brilliant research. Your work has caused me to know that my observations and conclusions, though daunting are accurate. I hope to join your club—the modern Paul Revere's.

To Robert Spencer, your body of work on the nature and scope of the Islamic threat facing our country makes you one of the most courageous writers alive today. My book is only made possible by your towering leadership.

To Jack Cashill, your level of investigative reporting provides me with the literary standard for which I will continue to strive.

To my good friend, Sue Farley, thank you for introducing me to my publisher, to Patricia Ross and George Gluchowski at Hugo House. They have become the patient mentors and fellow travelers I'm certain that I would not have found without you.

To Pete Charles, my favorite musician and cowboy bard, thanks for the *Larry Kelley Compilation*. It proved a great collaboration.

To Renée Robinson, my agent, publicist, and advisor, your tireless work on this project has given it a balance and a female perspective that it would not have had without you. What you bring to publishing a book transcends craft. You are an artist.

To my father, Dr. Warren J. Kelley, while you are permanently off somewhere, often no doubt, hitting it straight and long, I chose to believe you've made some time to be my secret editor. I wish you could have lived to see this day.

To my mother, Kathryn, I lovingly remember what a terrific tutor you were when I got behind in my sixth-grade sentence diagramming lessons. I never faltered again as a literature student. You and Dad made my brother, James, and I secure in the knowledge that you loved us more than you loved yourselves.

To my sons, Brendan and Austin, I urge that you trust in our God who works in mysterious ways. Please try to learn how He can be your guide.

To Debbie, my loving wife and most severe critic, I can't count the ways you helped me get this book finished. I love you for your tireless trust.

To my reader, I thank for reading this book. I'd like to second Catherine Herridge's request to her reader. Please, the next time you see man or women in uniform, approach and thank them for their selfless service in keeping America free.

Index

CPSIA information can be obtained at www.ICGtesting.com
Printed in the USA
LVOW090434260412

279199LV00003B/1/P